HUSBANDS AND WIVES

Associated with

Early Alexandria, Virginia

(And the Surrounding Area)

3rd Edition
Expanded and Revised

Wesley E. Pippenger

HERITAGE BOOKS
2014

HERITAGE BOOKS

AN IMPRINT OF HERITAGE BOOKS, INC.

Books, CDs, and more—Worldwide

For our listing of thousands of titles see our website
at
www.HeritageBooks.com

Published 2014 by
HERITAGE BOOKS, INC.
Publishing Division
5810 Ruatan Street
Berwyn Heights, Md. 20740

International Standard Book Numbers
Paperbound: 978-1-58549-192-6
Clothbound: 978-0-7884-6014-2

CONTENTS

PREFACE TO THE THIRD EDITION

Since "Husbands and Wives" was first published nearly a decade ago, additional data has been collected which documents marital relationships in the Alexandria, Virginia area. Also, researchers can now find clues on the Internet—clues that must, of course, be verified. This edition reflects husbands and wives contained in over three dozen publications by this compiler, as well as numerous sources which are identified and are readily available to researchers.

In many cases, multiple sources are used for a composite entry for a marital relationship. Dates and spellings often differ among sources. When discrepancies occur, researchers should consult each of the cited sources and consider the merit of each source.

Newspapers, minister returns, and marriage bonds were used up through 1830. There are several instances where information is presented after this period—primarily in cases where the information is not easily found by researchers.

Additions and corrections welcome.

Wesley E. Pippenger
Arlington, Virginia
Spring 2001

INTRODUCTION

With the general absence of early marriage records in the form of court or parish register, genealogists are greatly handicapped in the pursuit to prove family relationships of persons associated with Alexandria, Virginia. As an example of this great loss, we know a large number of Alexandria residents were married in Christ Episcopal Church—unfortunately no 18th century parish register of marriages exists though the church was formed in 1773. Also, St. Mary's Catholic church protects its early marriage register which is virtually inaccessible to researchers.

This work primarily contains records of marriages for persons who were at some time associated with Alexandria, Virginia, and in most cases, early residents there. Many are implied marriages. In the case of records extracted from probate records or deeds, e.g. of the Hustings Court, Circuit Court and Corporation Court, it generally is not possible to determine either the date or place of marriage. Since the scope of the work is to include married couples who had a connection to Alexandria, it sometimes may be known a couple was *not* married in Alexandria. When this is known to be true, the place of marriage is noted.

Dates given are *marriage dates* with the following exceptions: (1) if a date is preceded by a hyphen, e.g. "-17 MAY 1788," it means that this is the date of the earliest record found for which a marital relationship is revealed (hence, the couple was married *previous to this date*); and (2) if circa is used, e.g. "**c.**24 DEC 1800," the source is not specific (such as a newspaper announcement, marriage license or marriage bond), and the date given is an approximation. Additional information may be found in an endnote, a list of which precedes the index.

Most of the early Presbyterian Church (now known as the Old Presbyterian Meeting House) marriages were performed by Reverend Doctor James Muir in and around Alexandria. The handwriting of Dr. Muir in an original register was nearly illegible, and a transcript of the ledger was made after Muir's death by Mr. Auld. Unfortunately, the location of the original record is not known, and we have been left with what might be considered a secondary source. Be this as it may, we are also confronted with discrepancies between the transcript, original marriage bonds and minister returns, and newspaper notices. The transcript which was restored by a chapter of the Daughters of the American Revolution in 1953, is entitled: <u>Register of Baptisms, Marriages, and Funerals During the Ministry of the Rev[d] Doct[r] James Muir in the Presbyterian Church of Alexandria, D.C.</u> The original transcript, kept by the church at 316 S. Royal St., has been carefully examined. I am extremely grateful for the time taken by Frances Kilpatrick of the meeting house for standing by me when questions surfaced in interpreting the register. A photostat of the register was made in July 1929 and is catalogued as accession number 20078 in the Archives Division of the Virginia State Library in Richmond. Muir's original minister returns, amongst the collections of the Library of Virginia, show his small and nearly illegible lettering.

The compiler consulted minister returns and marriage bonds for the period 1801-1830. In many cases spelling differed between documents, and it is the spelling from the signature of the prospective groom, or parent giving consent, that is given first consideration.

Because little distinction was made between eastern Fairfax County and the City of Alexandria, occasional records have been included which were found for Fairfax County citizens who had siblings or issue found in the Alexandria area.

Most marriages referenced in this work occurred before 1831, and references generally do not extend further. Early Quaker marriages which took place before 1841 have been extracted from the Alexandria Monthly Meeting records, as found in William Wade Hinshaw's Encyclopedia of American Quaker Genealogy, Volume VI, pp. 725-794.

If an Alexandria owner or occupier was found with the same name in the 1791 Alexandria City Directory, the record is noted by "1791:[page]," to indicate where the information can be found in Marjorie D. Tallichet's Alexandria City Directory, 1791 (Bowie: Heritage Books, Inc., 1986).

Several early town censuses were taken, primarily for the benefit of determining taxes. Among these the compiler used those for 1799 and 1800. The 1799 census of ward two is inscribed: *A Census of the Inhabitants of the Second Ward of the Town of Alexandria, being that part which lies to the south of King street, & from the River Potowmak to its Western limits.* The original is catalogued as accession number 24665c, volume 276, at the Library of Virginia in Richmond. Page references in this work correspond to pencil markings made to the original.

The original of the 1800 census for the fourth ward is cataloged as accession number 24665c, volume 277, at the Library of Virginia in Richmond. It was published in the January-March 1960 issue of the Virginia Genealogist, at pages 51-59. It is described as being an enumeration for the area of the city south of Duke Street. Heads of households with the same name as one included in these census works have been noted with the year, then page, i.e. "1800:37." Page references in this work correspond to page numbers in the published version.

Cemetery records have been used to document a marital relationship and/or location of the grave site. In some instances, a record of lot ownership may be found, but a gravestone has not been located. Persons extracted from cemetery records generally were born before 1800 or soon thereafter.

I am grateful for the assistance of many, but specifically the following persons who gave their time and assistance in support of this project: Yvonne Carignan and Sandy O'Keefe, formerly of the Alexandria Library; Joyce McMullin, Alexandria Library; Frances Kilpatrick, Old Presbyterian Meeting House; Beth Mitchell, McLean, Virginia; the late Constance Ring, former Archivist of Fairfax County Circuit Court; and Edith Sprouse, Alexandria, Virginia.

Wesley E. Pippenger
Arlington, Virginia
Spring 2001

REFERENCE ABBREVIATIONS

Following is a list of abbreviations used for the "Reference" column of this volume. The years following a newspaper or other serial indicate those reviewed for use, and do not necessarily indicate the total period during which the source was published.

–   before the date given

A   Alexandrian, November 1820 to March 1821

AA   The Times and Alexandria Advertiser (est. 10 APR 1797, disc. 16 APR 1799); includes The Times; and District of Columbia Daily Advertiser (est. 17 APR 1797, disc. 1800), date:page

ABC   Sigismunda Mary Frances Chapman, A History of Chapman and Alexander Families (Richmond: Dietz Printing Company, 1946)

ACFF   Arlington County Chancery Final File. As of this update, the Arlington Circuit Court is flat-folding old chancery files, assigning unique numbers, and entering date for posting on a Library of Virginia Web page.

ACM   Marriages of Alleghany County, Maryland

AD   Arlington County Deeds, book:page

AG   Alexandria Gazette (commonly known as), had multiple names during its early evolution: The Columbian Mirror and Alexandria Gazette (est. 10 APR 1792); The Virginia Journal and Alexandria Advertiser (est. 5 FEB 1782, disc. 4 JUL 1789); The Virginia Gazette and Alexandria Advertiser (est. 30 JUL 1789, disc. NOV 1793); Alexandria Advertiser and Commercial Intelligencer (to SEP 1803); Alexandria Daily Advertiser (to 11 JUL 1808), Alexandria Daily Gazette, Alexandria Gazette & Daily Advertiser, and Phenix (Alexandria) Gazette (through 1830). Cited as AG:year (DD/MM/YY):page

AH   Alexandria Herald, 1815-1822

AHy   Alexandria History, Vol. 5 (1983), p. 11

AHM   Arlington Historical Magazine, volume:page

AM   T. Michael Miller, Artisans and Merchants (Bowie: Heritage Books, Inc., 1991), 2 volumes, volume:page

ANSC   Adams-Nelson-Sewall-Waters Cemetery, Potomac Hills, Chesterbrook, Fairfax County

AW   Wesley E. Pippenger, Alexandria, Virginia Wills, Administrations and Guardianships, 1786-1800 (Westminster, Md.: Willow Bend Books, 1994)

B   Margie G. Brown, Genealogical Abstracts, Revolutionary War Veterans, Scrip Act, 1852 (Decorah: Anundsen Publishing Co., 1990)

BA   Baltimore American, 1799-1801, 1804-1816

BFG   Baltimore Federal Gazette, 1796-1816

BFR   Baltimore Federal Republican and Commercial Advertiser, 1808-1812

BM   Robert W. Barnes, Maryland Marriages, 1634-1777 (Baltimore: Genealogical Publishing Co., Inc., 1987)

BPEA   Baltimore Patriot and Evening Advertiser, 1813-1815

BR   F.L. Brockett, The Lodge of Washington, A History of the Alexandria Washington Lodge, No. 22, A.F. and A.M. of Alexandria, Va. (Alexandria: George E. French, Publisher, 1876)

br/o	Brother of
BT	Baltimore Telegraphe, 1796-1806, 1815
BUR	Louis A. Burgess, Virginia Soldiers of 1776 (Richmond: Richmond Press, Inc., 1927), 3 volumes
BWM	Baltimore Weekly Museum, 1797
B1	Carson Family Bible (Philadelphia: M. Carey, 1816), Alexandria Library
B2	Leven Powell Bible (1803), Alexandria Library
B3	Benjamin Brookes and John Smith Brookes Bible (London: Thomas Baskett, 1759), Alexandria Library
B4	Doway Bible, undated, p. 790, Alexandria Library
B5	Bible of William Alexander of "Effingham," Prince William County, Virginia (1759), Alexandria Library, as published in Wesley E. Pippenger's, John Alexander - A Northern Neck Proprietor (Baltimore: Gateway Press, Inc., 1990), pp. 357-360
B6	Bible of Hampton C. Williams, in possession of Jean (Williams) Auldridge of Alexandria, Virginia
B7	John Hunter Bible, as published in Daughters of the American Revolution's D.C. G.R.C., Volume 10, 1932-1934, pp. 3-8.
B8	John Lloyd Bible, Alexandria Library
B9	John McKnight Bible, Old Presbyterian Meeting House, Alexandria
B10	William Devaughn Bible (1813), Library of Virginia, Bible Records Collection, #823
c.	Circa
(C)	Colored or Negro (also see "M" for Mulatto)
CBL	William Randolph Sengel, Can These Bones Live?, Pastoral Reflections on the Old Presbyterian Meeting House of Alexandria, Virginia Through its First Two Hundred Years (Kingsport Press, 1973)
CC	Christ Church records, as published in F. Edward Wright and Wesley E. Pippenger, Early Church Records of Alexandria City and Fairfax County, Virginia (Westminster, Md.: Willow Bend Books, 1996), page.
CCC	Christ Church Episcopal Cemetery (1808), Wilkes Street; a lot owner and/or location is noted in parenthesis
CCG	Christ Church Episcopal Church Graveyard (c.1772); or Lenora DeRossi, Christ Churchyard Gravestones and Burial History (Alexandria, Office of Historic Alexandria, 1985), copy at Alexandria Library. References include Tables 1 and 2, and Appendices 1 through 4
CCGB	Christ Church Graveyard burial permits, date
CCR	Christ Church register of baptisms, marriages and funerals, 1828-1847
CFF	See Fairfax County Circuit Court Chancery (FC)
CL	The Centinel of Liberty and George-Town Advertiser, 27 MAY 1796-4 APR 1800
CLB	Chapman Land Book, copy on file at the Alexandria Library: will of George Chapman (p. 25); will of Pearson Chapman (p. 28); will of Simon Pearson (p. 34)
CMG	Cecil County, Maryland, Marriage Licenses, 1777-1840 (Baltimore: Genealogical Publishing Co., Inc, 1976)
ColC	Columbian Chronicle (Washington)
CRA	Complete Records "A", 1786-1800, original at the Library of Virginia. Abstracts found in Wesley E. Pippenger, Alexandria, Virginia Wills, Administrations and Guardianships, 1786-1800 (Westminster, Md.: Willow Bend Books, 1994)
CT	Columbian Telescope and Literary Compiler, 1819-1820
CWA	Carrie White Avery, Genealogical Records (Gathered from Graveyards, Public Monuments and Family Papers, in Virginia, Maryland and the District of Columbia), 1922, 4 volumes, unpublished manuscript in the Library of Congress,

	Manuscript Division, file #2522
d/o	Daughter of
DAR	Daughters of the American Revolution
DB	Alexandria City and County Deeds, book:page
DCM	Wesley E. Pippenger, Marriage Licenses of Washington, D.C., Register 1, 1811-1858 (Westminster, Md.: Willow Bend Books, 1994)
E	Enquirer (Richmond), 1810
ES	Edith Moore Sprouse, Colchester: Colonial Port on the Potomac (Fairfax: Office of Comprehensive Planning, 1975)
FB	Fairfax County Marriage Bonds; see also Constance K. Ring, comp., "Fairfax County Marriages Prior to 1853," The Historical Society of Fairfax County, Virginia, Inc., Vol. 16 (1980), pp. 52-74
FC	Fairfax County Circuit Court Chancery, file number (often begins with CFF#)
FCOB	Fairfax County Court Orders, book beginning year:page
FD	Fairfax County Deeds, book:page
FF	Melvin Lee Steadman, Jr., Falls Church by Fence and Fireside (Falls Church, 1964)
FGRC	Fairfax County Genealogical Records Committee, (year), volume:page, at Daughters of the American Revolution Library, Washington DC
FLC	Fairfax County Land Causes, (book year):page
FM	Fairfax County Minutes, (book year):page
FMI	Fairfax County Archives, card index to marriages; most entries containing additional references
FO	Fairfax County Order Book, (book year):page
FPC	Register of Baptisms, Marriages, and Funerals During the Ministry of the Revd Doct^r James Muir in the [First] Presbyterian Church of Alexandria, D.C.; marriages performed during the ministry of Rev. James Muir, 1757-1820; the church is now known as the Old Presbyterian Meeting House; see Introduction for locations. This register data were published by F. Edward Wright and Wesley E. Pippenger, Early Church Records of Alexandria City and Fairfax County, Virginia (Westminster, Md.: Willow Bend Books, 1996).
FPCC	First Presbyterian Church Cemetery (1809), Hamilton Lane off Wilkes Street, (section:lot) when known, followed by "ns" if no tombstone is present
FPCG	First Presbyterian Church Graveyard (1773), now known as the Old Presbyterian Meeting House, South Fairfax Street
FqMin	Fauquier County Minute Book, (book year):page
FRD	Fairfax County Register of Deaths, 1853-1869, page
FRM	John Vogt and T. William Kethley, Jr., Frederick County [VA] Marriages, 1738-1850 (Athens: Iberian Publishing Co., 1984)
FRSD	Frederick County Superior Court Deeds, book:page
FS	The Fireside Sentinel, Newsletter of the Alexandria Library, Lloyd House, date:page
FSH	Frank Snowden Hopkins, The Powell and Lloyd Families of Alexandria, Virginia (c.1989), Alexandria Library
FW	Fairfax County Wills, book:page
FX	Fairfax County Archives, drawer X
GA	Graveyards of Arlington County, Virginia (Arlington: National Genealogical Society, 1985)
GL	District of Columbia Library, Georgetown Branch, Peabody Room; file name
GT	Georgetown Times and Patowmack Packet (Washington)
H	William Wade Hinshaw, Encyclopedia of American Quaker Genealogy, Vol. VI

(Baltimore: Genealogical Publishing Co., Inc., 1973): meeting house locations: Alexandria Monthly Meeting (Alexandria, Va. and Washington, D.C., 1802); Crooked Run Monthly Meeting (south of Winchester, Warren Co., Va., 1760); Fairfax Monthly Meeting (Loudoun County, Va., 1733); Goose Creek Monthly Meeting (west of present Lincoln, Loudoun Co., Va., 1745); Hopewell Monthly Meeting (Frederick Co., Va., 1734); South River Meeting House (Campbell Co., Va.); and Indian Spring Monthly Meeting (on Patuxent River in Anne Arundel Co., Md.); special permission for use granted by publisher. This data is also published in F. Edward Wright and Wesley E. Pippenger, Early Church Records of Alexandria City and Fairfax County, Virginia (Westminster, Md.: Willow Bend Books, 1996), page.

HC Alexandria Hustings Court Deeds, 1783-1801, book:page. Book A, 1783-1785; Book B, 1785-1787; Book C, 1787-1789; Book D, 1789-1793; Book E, 1793-1794; Book F, 1793-1796; Book G, 1795-1796; Book H, 1795-1797; Book I, 1796-1797; Book K, 1796-1798; Book L, 1798-1799; Book M, 1798-1800; Book N, 1799-1800; and Book O, 1799-1801. Also used are transcripts as found in James D. Munson's Alexandria, Virginia Alexandria Hustings Court Deeds, 1783-1797 (Bowie: Heritage Press, Inc., 1990), and Alexandria, Virginia Alexandria Hustings Court Deeds, 1797-1801 (Bowie: Heritage Press, Inc., 1991)

HCMin Alexandria Hustings Court Minutes, date (DD/MM/YY)

HCOrd Alexandria Hustings Court Orders, date (DD/MM/YY)

HV Elizabeth Hambleton and Marian Van Landingham, A Composite History of Alexandria, Vol. 1 (Alexandria Bicentennial Commission, 1975)

IGI International Genealogical Index, created and maintained by the Church of Jesus Christ of Latter-day Saints, a version of which can be found on the Internet at <http://www.familysearch.com>. Submitting sources vary.

IHC Virginia Irene Sullivan Bruch, Beneath the Oaks of Ivy Hill (Alexandria: Jennie's Book Nook, 1982)

J   Jane Farrell Burgess, Genealogy of the Janney Family in America (Rockville: By the Author, 1990)

JW Chart by John A. Washington, Chevy Chase, Maryland

KGM King George County, Virginia Marriages, book:page

LCC Lebanon Union Church Cemetery, 100 North Breckinridge Place

LD Loudoun County, Virginia Deeds, book:page

LHFC Alexandria Library, Queen Street (formerly Lloyd House), filing case, family name

LP   Legislative Petition from Alexandria (number), at the Library of Virginia

LPC Lewinsville Presbyterian Church Cemetery, Chain Bridge Road, Fairfax County

LW Loudoun County, Virginia Wills, book:page

LV Edmund Jennings Lee, Lee of Virginia (Philadelphia, 1895)

LVA1 Arlington County Exhibit Materials, 1776-1915, Library of Virginia, Accession #24121, folder

M   Beth Mitchell, Beginning at a White Oak (1977)

(M) Mulatto

MB Marriage Bonds, 1801 [Reel 31], 1802-1807 [Reel 32], 1807-1815 [Reel 33], 1815-1820 [Reel 34], 1820-1825 [Reel 35], and 1825-1830 [Reel 36]. As a large number of bonds are in the handwriting of G. Deneale, who is known to be more literate than others, his spelling is given first priority over other less reliable records. No bonds are on film for the year 1819. Records before 1801 are for Fairfax County, and are found at the Fairfax County Circuit Court Archives.

MD Montgomery County, Maryland Deeds, book:page

MG Maryland Gazette, date:page

MGB	Maryland Genealogical Society Bulletin, "Register of West River Meeting of the Religious Society of Friends (Quaker) on the Western Shore of Maryland,¹" Vol. 14, Nos. 2-4, and Vol. 15/1 (1973), page
Miller1	T. Michael Miller, Alexandria Library, filing case: cemeteries, notes from a tombstone found in the back yard of residence at 311 South St. Asaph Street, Alexandria (24 SEP 1988)
MPC	Methodist Protestant Cemetery (c.1833), Wilkes Street and Hamilton Lane (section:lot)
MR	Minister's Returns, 1801-1852 [LVA Reel 31], originals at the Library of Virginia
ni/o	Niece of
NE	New England Historical and Genealogical Register, Vol. C (January 1946), page
NH	Norfolk Herald, 1799-1803
NI	National Intelligencer (Washington DC), 1800-1820
OH	Oak Hill Cemetery, Georgetown, D.C.
OT	Our Town: 1749-1865 (Alexandria: Alexandria Association, 1956)
P	Wesley E. Pippenger, John Alexander, A Northern Neck Proprietor - His Family, Friends and Kin (Baltimore: Gateway Press, 1990)
Page	Richard Channing Moore Page, Genealogy of the Page Family in Virginia, reprint ed., (Harrisonburg: C.J. Carrier Company, 1983)
PC	Pohick Church Cemetery (Truro Parish), Fairfax County
PF	Silas Emmett Lucas, Jr., The Powell Families of Virginia and the South (Vidalia: Georgia Genealogical Reprints, 1969)
PGM	Brown, Marriage Licenses of Prince George's County, Maryland
PM	Penny Morrill, Who Built Alexandria? (Architects in Alexandria, 1750-1900) (Northern Virginia Regional Park Authority, 1979)
PS	The Peytons of Virginia (Peyton Society of Virginia, 1976)
PW	Patrick G. Wardell, War of 1812: Virginia Bounty Land & Pension Applicants (Bowie: Heritage Books, Inc., 1987)
PWD	Prince William County Deeds, book:page
PWW	Prince William County Wills, book:page
QC	Quaker Cemetery, Queen Street
QM	Alexandria Monthly Meeting (Quaker) membership records, as published in F. Edward Wright and Wesley E. Pippenger, Early Church Records of Alexandria City and Fairfax County, Virginia (Westminster, Md.: Willow Bend Books, 1996), page.
R	Patrick G. Wardell, Virginia/West Virginia Genealogical Data From Revolutionary War Pension and Bounty Land Warrant Records, Volume 1-Aaron through Cyrus (Bowie: Heritage Books, Inc., 1988), and Volume 2-Dabbs through Hyslop (Bowie: Heritage Books, Inc., 1990); volume:page
RMSD	Diary of Richard Marshall Scott, 3 volumes, Volume 1 (1811-1820); Volume 2 (1821-1825); and Volume 3 (1825-1830), from abstracts made and shared by Edith M. Sprouse of Alexandria, Virginia
RWP	Revolutionary War Pensions, National Archives, file
s/o	Son of
si/o	Sister of
S	Elizabeth Jane Stark, Recollections of Old Alexandria and Other Memories of Mary Louisa Slacum Benham (Starkville, 1978)
SC	Summers Family Cemetery (c.1790), Off Deming Avenue and Lincolnia Road
SD	Stafford County Deeds, book:page
SM	Records of St. Mary's Catholic Church
SMC	St. Mary's Catholic Church Cemetery (c.1798), Church Street off South

	Washington Street
SP	Records of St. Paul's Episcopal Church, published by historian Ruth Lincoln Kay in the *National Genealogical Society Quarterly*.
SPC	St. Paul's Episcopal Church Cemetery (1809), Hamilton Lane off Wilkes Street (lot:section)
SS	William Francis Smith and T. Michael Miller, A Seaport Saga (Norfolk: The Donning Company, 1989)
SV	Gay Montague Moore, Seaport in Virginia (Richmond: Garrett and Massie, 1949)
SW	Stafford County Wills, book:page
T	Tyler' Quarterly Historical and Genealogical Magazine, volume:page
TA	Timothy Alden, A Collection of American Epitaphs and Inscriptions with Occasional Notes, Volumes IV and V (New York: Arno Press, 1977)
TMCC	Trinity United Methodist Church Cemetery, Wilkes Street, (row:section)
T0	Marjorie E. Tallichet, Alexandria, Virginia City and County 1850 Census (Bowie: Heritage Books, Inc., 1986), family number
UC	Union Cemetery (1860), now known as Washington Street United Methodist Church Cemetery, Hamilton Lane off Wilkes Street (section:lot)
UT	United States' Telegraph (Washington), 1826-1828. For the issue between November 21, 1826, and March 6, 1827, the title changes to United States' Telegraph and Commercial Herald, and contains fewer notices on marriages and deaths. The Telegraph absorbed the Alexandria Herald; date (DD/MM/YY):page
VC	Virginia Centinel (Winchester), 1793, date (DD/MM/YY):page
VG	Virginia Gazette and Alexandria Advertiser, (Alexandria), date (DD/MM/YY):page
VH	Virginia Herald (Fredericksburg), date:page
w/o	Wife of
wid/o	Widow of
W	John W. Wayland, Washingtons and Their Homes (Berryville: Virginia Book Company, 1944)
WB	Alexandria City and County Wills, book:page
WG	*Washington Gazette*, year (DD/MM/YY):page
W(1)	William and Mary College Historical Magazine, first series, volume:W(1)page
X	Ethelyn Cox, Historic Alexandria, Virginia Street by Street, 1976
1787	Nettie Schreiner-Yantis and Florene Love, The Personal Property Tax Lists for the Year 1787 for Alexandria Town, Virginia (Springfield: Genealogical Books in Print, 1987). Generally, only the head of household was taxed, and therefore this record will not reveal a spouse, but is used to associate property owners with Alexandria. The tax list enumerates for each person chargeable: the number of white male tithables above the age of 21 years; blacks above 16 years; blacks under 16 years; horses, mares, colts and mules; and cattle
1791	Marjorie E. Tallichet, Alexandria City Directory, 1791 (Bowie: Heritage Books, Inc., 1986), page
1799	The 1799 census of the second ward of Alexandria, page (pagination of original at the Library of Virginia in Richmond). Also published in the Virginia Genealogist, Volume 4.
1800	The 1800 census of the fourth ward of Alexandria, page (pagination as published in the Virginia Genealogist (January-March 1960), pp. 51-59)
5GM	Pamela C. Copeland and Richard K. MacMaster, The Five George Masons, Patriots and Planters of Virginia and Maryland (Charlottesville: University Press of Virginia, 1975)

MINISTER ABBREVIATIONS

(A)	Rev. Mr. [Ethan] Allen	(JF)	Rev. Joseph William Fairclough, St. Mary's Catholic Church
(AB)	Rev. Alexander Balmain, d. 1820		
(AC)	Rev. Archbishop John Carroll of Baltimore MD, d. 1815	(JG)	Rev. John Glendy, Second Presbyterian Church, Baltimore MD
(AG)	Rev. Alfred Griffith		
(AH)	Rev. Andrew Hemphill	(JJ)	Rev. John Johnston
(AS)	Rev. Asa Shinn	(JL)	Rev. John Lindsay
(B)	Rev. Balch[2]	(JM)	Reverend Dr. James Muir, of the First Presbyterian Church (now known as the Old Presbyterian Meeting House), d. 1820
(BN)	Rev. Seely Bunn, Trinity Methodist Church		
(BW)	Rev. Beverly Waugh, d. 1853		
(By)	Rev. Byng	(JMH)	Rev. John M. Hanson
(C)	Rev. Jeremiah Cosden, Cecil County MD; Trinity Methodist Church	(JMc)	Rev. James McConchie
		(JR)	Rev. James Reed
		(JT)	Rev. James Thompson
(CO)	Rev. Charles O'Neal	(JW)	Rev. John E. Weems
(D)	Rev. Duke	(JeW)	Rev. Jesse E. Weems
(DB)	Rev. Dr. Bowers	(K)	Rev. Kemp
(E)	Rev. Eaton	(L)	Rev. Mr. George Lemmon
(ED)	Rev. Mr. Eden	(LA)	Rev. Jacob Larkin
(EH)	Rev. Elias Harrison, 1st Presbyterian Church	(LM)	Rev. Lee Massey, d. 1814
		(LO)	Rev. Lowe
(EM)	Rev. Edward C. McGuire	(LR)	Rev. Lewis Richards
(F)	Rev. Mr. Fenwick	(M)	Rev. William Meade, Christ Church
(FB)	Rev. Francis Barclay, Christ Church		
		(MB)	Rev. M. Breckenridge, d. 1838
(FN)	Father Francis Ignatius Neale, Holy Trinity Parish, Georgetown DC; St. Mary's Catholic Church	(Mc)	Rev. Thomas McCormick
		(McW)	Rev. William McCormick
		(MI)	Rev. Mines
(G)	Rev. William Lewis Gibson, Christ Church; 1809, St. Paul's Episcopal	(MN)	Rev. Munn
		(MO)	Rev. Moore
		(OB)	Rev. Obadiah B. Brown, Chaplain to Congress
(GM)	Rev. George L. Mackenheimer		
(GR)	Rev. Dr. George Roberts	(ON)	Rev. Oliver Norris, Rector of Christ Church
(Gu)	Rev. Job Guest		
(H)	Rev. William Hill	(P)	Rev. Mr. Paradise
(HA)	Rev. Mr. Elias Harrison	(PA)	Rev. Patrick Allison
(HJ)	Rev. Hamilton Jefferson	(PS)	Rev. Philip Slaughter
(I)	Rev. Inglis	(R)	Rev. Dr. Rogers
(IR)	Rev. Isaac Robbins	(RA)	Rev. George Ralph
(JC)	Rev. John Childs	(RD)	Rev. Riland / Wm. Ryland
(JD)	Rev. John Dunn	(RE)	Rev. Caleb Reynolds
(Jda)	Rev. John Davis	(RH)	Rev. Ralph Higginbotham
(JE)	Rev. John Eversfield	(RK)	Rev. Reuel Keith

(RO)	Rev. Joseph Rowen	(Wal)	Rev. William C. Walton
(Rz)	Rev. Stephen G. Roszell	(WDA)	Rev. Walter D. Addison, d. 1866
(S)	Rev. Simpson	(WE)	Rev. Joshua Wells, Trinity Methodist Church
(SA)	Rev. Samuel Adams		
(SC)	Rev. Spencer H. Cone of NY, First Baptist Church	(WG)	Rev. William Gilmore
		(WH)	Rev. William Hawley, St. John's Church, Washington DC
(Sco)	Rev. Samuel Cornelius		
(SG)	Rev. Spence Grayson	(WJ)	Rev. William Jackson, Rector of St. Paul's Church
(SH)	Rev. Shay		
(Ski)	Rev. Skinner	(WM)	Reverend William Maffitt, d. 1828
(SN)	Rev. Samuel Knox	(WHW)	Rev. William Holland Wilmer, D.D., Christ Church; St. Paul's Episcopal, 1812-1826; after 1816, pastor of St. John's Church of Washington DC
(SP)	Rev. Mr. Spiller		
(SR)	Rev. S. Reid (also see "JR")		
(ST)	Rev. Steele		
(SY)	Rev. Sayre(s)		
(TC)	Bishop Thomas John Claggett, d. 1816	(MLW)	Rev. Mason Locke Weems
		(WW)	Rev. William Watters, Methodist Episcopal Church of Georgetown and Washington DC; Trinity Methodist Church
(TD)	Rev. Thomas Davis, Christ Church		
(TM)	Rev. Thomas Matthews		
(W)	Rev. Walter	(Y)	Rev. [Noble] Young
(WA)	Rev. Wells Andrews, 2nd Presbyterian Church		

HUSBANDS AND WIVES

Husband	Wife	Event or Marriage	Reference(s)
A			
ABERCROMBIE, Robert Place: Prince George's Co. MD	SMALLWOOD, Martha	5 AUG 1787	DBQ:222; 1799:8; 1800:59; TMCC(R:5); IGI; Note[3]
ABERCROMBIE, Robert	WOOD, Susan	25 JAN 1820	FWN:202; MB; AG:29/1/20:3(WE)
ADAM, James	_____, Elizabeth	-22 FEB 1787	HCOrd:23/2/87
ADAM, John	HAYES, Mary	28 JUL 1803	AG:29/7/03:3(WM)[4]; FPCC(41:13); MB
ADAM, John	DUNLAP, Mary	22 FEB 1816	AG:22/2/16:3(JM); MR(JM); MB
ADAM, Robert	_____, Ann(a)	-27 JUL 1786	HCC:194; FPCC; DBD:256; FDQ:266; FWE:315; 1791:3
ADAM, Robert	_____, Emily	-14 OCT 1807	DBU:231
ADAMS, _____	HOWARD, _____	c.JUL 1796	WG:20/7/96:43
ADAMS, Abednigo Place: Charles Co. MD	PEAKE, Mary d/o William Peake	17 DEC 1746	FDU:80; FWB:247; IGI
ADAMS, Abednigo	_____, Clarissa	-25 APR 1816	1800:55; AG:30/4/16:3
ADAMS, Abijah	WHERRY, Margaretta H. d/o Jesse Wherry	12 JUN 1821	NI:15/6/21(HA); MR(EH); MB; AG:14/6/21:3(EH)
ADAMS, Edward	WEST, Jemima d/o Hugh West	-16 SEP 1786	FWE:235; FC#115
ADAMS, Francis	NEWTON, Mary R. d/o William Newton	20 DEC 1814	FPC:2(JM); MB; AG:22/12/14:3(JM)
ADAMS, James	_____, Elizabeth	-2 AUG 1785	FDQ:53
ADAMS, James	BRUNER, Catharine	25 FEB 1802	MR(JM); MB
ADAMS, James	SIMPSON, Sarah "Sally"	3 MAR 1802	MR(JM); DBS:263
ADAMS, James	WILLIAMS, Sally d/o George and Rachel Williams	-31 JUN 1841	FDG3:289; FWU:261
ADAMS, Jeremiah	_____, Susannah	-28 JUL 1808	WBC:167
ADAMS, Leonard	DAVIS, Ann "Nancy"	4 MAR 1802	MR(JM); MB; TMCC(H:4)
ADAMS, Leonard	_____, Sally	-7 NOV 1811	FPCC(41:17)
ADAMS, Leonard Place: Washington DC	SPUNAGLE, Catharine	28 JUN 1812	AG:30/6/12:3; MB
ADAMS, Rev. Samuel	WREN, Hannah d/o James Wren	-20 DEC 1806	DBS:263; FF:224; 1799:34; ANSC
ADAMS, Simon	WREN, Catherine	-20 DEC 1806	DBS:263; FF:224
ADAMS, Rev. Wesley	HUGHES, Elizabeth	-20 DEC 1806	DBS:263; FF:224
ADDISON, Henry	CLAGETT, Martha E.	4 JAN 1821	AG:11/1/21:2

Husband	Wife	Event or Marriage	Reference(s)
ADDISON, Thomas A. Place: Georgetown DC	ELIASON, Eliza	12 MAY 1818	AG:14/5/18:2(B); DCM
ADGATE, Andrew Place: Baltimore MD	DORSEY, Elizabeth O. d/o Owen Dorsey	15 OCT 1822	AG:24/10/22:3
ADIEU, Peter	ESTAFV, Kitty	5 AUG 1797	BT:11/8/97
ALABY, James	WEBB, Verlinda	c.4 SEP 1827	MB
ALDRIDGE, W. Joseph	REYNOLDS, Mrs. Dorothy	11 MAY 1799	NH:14/5/99
ALEXANDER, Amos Place: *Cameron*, seat of John Ricketts	RICKETTS, Ann, d/o John	12 OCT 1797	AA:13/10/97:3; FPC:2(JM); HCM:430; 1799:36; AG:17/1/04:3
ALEXANDER, Amos[5]	WROE, Eliza(beth) d/o Absalom Wroe	10 JAN 1805	DBS:113; FPC:2(JM) AG:11/1/05:3(JM); MB
ALEXANDER, Austin	SHERWOOD, Eleanor	24 DEC 1816	MR(JM); MB; P:270
ALEXANDER, Charles, Jr. Place: *Shuter's Hill*	ARMISTEAD, Mary Bowles	10 MAR 1800	AG:13/3/00:3; P:196
ALEXANDER, Charles, Sr.	BROWN, Frances	c.1769	WBB:278; P:140
ALEXANDER, Edmund B. Place: Detroit	CRAIG, Elizabeth	21 MAR 1826	UT:14/4/26:3
ALEXANDER, Gerard	_____, Mary	-9 AUG 1760	FWB:327
ALEXANDER, Gustavus B. Place: *Chestnut Hill*, King George Co.	STUART, Sarah B.	18 OCT 1824	AG:26/10/24:3
ALEXANDER, John	_____, Frances	-AUG 1753	FDC:635
ALEXANDER, Lawrence G.	McLEAN, Eliza eldest d/o Daniel McLean	17 JUN 1824	AG:19/6/24:3(WHW); SP; MB
ALEXANDER, Mark Place: Cecil Co. MD	GILPIN, Elizabeth d/o Joseph Gilpin	12 APR 1798	DBE:56; WBA:88; 1800:56; CMG:18(C)
ALEXANDER, Philip	HOOE, Sarah	11 NOV 1726	B5
ALEXANDER, Philip	_____, Catharine	-11 MAR 1767	FDG:231
ALEXANDER, Robert, Jr.	TRIPLETT, Elizabeth d/o Thomas Triplett	c.1792	FM(1835):59; CLB:112; NI:27/3/44:3
ALEXANDER, Robert, Sr.	STODDERT, Mariamne Truman	-15 DEC 1766	DBF:85; OH; HCG:105
ALEXANDER, Walter S.	DADE, Catharine F. d/o Baldwin Dade	5 FEB 1804	AG:6/2/04:3; MB; DBQ:240; P:285
ALEXANDER, William	MASSEY, Sigismunda Mary	18 APR 1765	B5
ALEXANDER, William B. Place: Prince William Co.	BROWN, Susan Pearson	17 SEP 1818	AG:26/9/18:3(ST); P:216
ALEXANDER, William T.	TALIAFERRO, Lucy	7 DEC 1788	KGM1:1
ALLEN, Andrew	RUDD, Mary	8 OCT 1822	SP; AG:10/10/22:3
ALLEN, Rev. Ethan Place St. Peters Church, Baltimore MD	GRIFFITH, Elizabeth	11 DEC 1821	AG:20/12/21:3
ALLEN, Capt. Ignatius	_____, Eliza	-7 OCT 1813	SPC(60:2)
ALLEN, Ignatius	POSEY, Eliza	22 JAN 1823	MR(ON); MB
ALLEN, James	MURRAY, Mrs. Lucretia	2 JAN 1828	MR(WJ); MB; SP; AG:7/1/28:3(WJ)
ALLEN, John	DEARY, Mrs. Bridget	26 JAN 1797	WG:28/1/97:247
ALLEN, John Place: Washington DC	DEARY, Mrs. Bridget	11 JUN 1816	AG:17/6/16:3
ALLEN, Hon. Robert Place: Washington DC	Van HORNE, Alethia d/o Archibald Van Horne	3 MAR 1825	AG:8/3/25:3

Husband	Wife	Event or Marriage	Reference(s)
ALLEN, Salathiel/Nathaniel	WESTON, Mary	6 DEC 1798	FPC:2(JM); 1800:57
ALLEN, Samuel	DONAL(D)SON, Ann	20 MAR 1803	MR(SA)
ALLEN, Thomas	BARRET, Peggy	c.JAN 1797	WG:28/1/97
ALLEN, William	DONALDSON, Anna	c.11 MAR 1803	MB
ALLISON, Amos	GEIGER, Ann	30 MAR 1803	MR(JM); MB
ALLISON, Bryan	BARR, Mary Ann	8 APR 1801	MR(JM); MB
ALLISON, Daniel	STEWART, Mary	c.31 DEC 1821	MB
ALLISON, Elias	KENT, Nancy d/o John Kent	17 FEB 1803	MR(JM); MB
ALLISON, Henry Place: Petersburg	SWIFT, Mary S.	9 AUG 1826	UT:17/8/26
ALLISON, James	CHILDS, Elizabeth d/o Rev. John Childs	8 DEC 1814	AG:13/12/14(WW); MB
ALLISON, John	McCREA, Rebecca	24 APR 1788	R1:13; FB
ALLISON, John	_____, Elizabeth	- SEP 1813	DBY:508; 1791:3
ALLISON, John	DARNES, Nancy	26 DEC 1815	MR(IR); MB
ALLISON, Patrick	_____, Mary	-21 NOV 1795	HCE:196; 1791:3
ALLISON, Robert	RAMSAY, Ann d/o William Ramsay	-1 MAY 1784	HCA:60; 1787:70; 1791:3; FPCG; HCB:413
ALLISON, William	GREEN, Sarah	15 MAR 1798	FPC:2(JM)
ALLISON, William Place: Montgomery Co. MD	WATERS, Ann d/o Benjamin Waters	30 SEP 1819	AG:13/10/19:3
ALLISTON, Thompson	LANE, Jane d/o Richard Lane	-16 MAR 1815	FWL:173
ALTERFREH, Peter	BARTLETT, Margaret	26 SEP 1805	MR(IR); MB
ALVERSON, James	_____, Sabitha	c.1781	R1:14
AMAST, Feline	BROWN, Martha	12 NOV 1815	MR(WHW)
AMORY, Bullard	SHARPE, Frances d/o Peter Sharpe	23 JUL 1811	AG:30/7/11:3(JL)
ANDERSON, George Place: Washington DC	SULLIVAN, Elizabeth	6 MAR 1817	AG:7/3/1817:3
ANDERSON, James	WEYLEY, Eleanor "Nelly"	2 SEP 1802	DBQ:222; FPCG; MB; TMCC(J:3); MR(JM)
ANDERSON, James W.	MINOR, Mary d/o Col. George Minor, of Fairfax Co.	16 MAY 1830	AG:26/5/30:3(EH)
ANDERSON, John	DUNLAVEY, Eleanor	c.15 DEC 1810	MB
ANDERSON, Nimrod	DAVY, Mrs. Elizabeth (Cockrell) d/o Sampson and Anne Cockrell	17 DEC 1808	FC#42n; MR; DBT:411; MR(IR)
ANDERSON, Ninian	_____, Margaret	-8 FEB 1791	HCD:255; 1787:73; CRA:73
ANDERSON, William	_____, Elizabeth	-22 MAY 1783	HCC:74; 1787:70; 1791:3; HCOrd:22/5/83
ANDERSON, William	COMPTON, Susannah	5 FEB 1815	AG:9/2/15:3(ON)
ANDOLL, Bernard	STONE, Eleanor	27 AUG 1801	FPC:2(JM); MR(JM); MB
ANDREW(S), Benjamin	DAVIES, Eliza	DEC 1795	FPC:2(JM)
ANDREWS, Elijah	WHEATLEY, Ann	c.1 MAR 1821	MR(JF); MB
ANDREW(S), Jacob	BAXTER, Polly	7 APR 1810	FPC:2(JM); MR(JM); MB
ANDREWS, Joshua	POTTS, Harriot	4 JUL 1822	MR(EH); MB
ANDREWS, Richard	_____, Margaret	-23 AUG 1798	HCN:54

Husband	Wife	Event or Marriage	Reference(s)
ANDREWS, Rev. Wells	HARPER, Nancy	14 SEP 1819	MR(JM); AG:17/9/19:3(JM)
ANNIN, Daniel	ROBERDEAU, Jane	-1 DEC 1809	DBS:162
	d/o Daniel Roberdeau		
ANSART, Felix	BROWN, Martha L.	12 NOV 1816	MR(WHW); MB
ANTRIM, Parnell	MANLEY, Sarah	28 JUN 1802	MR(JM); MB
APPLEMAN, Conrad	_____, Ann	-23 DEC 1786	HCOrd:23/12/86
APPLEMAN, Conrad	_____, Elizabeth	-27 FEB 1787	HCOrd:27/2/87
ARCHDEACON, Richard	LENNOX, Margaret	20 DEC 1791	FPC:2(JM)
ARELL, David	CAVERLY, Mrs. Phoebe	c.12 MAY 1785	AG:12/05/85:3;
	div/from Joseph Caverly[6]		1787:70; 1791:3
ARELL, Richard	_____, Eleanor	-24 SEP 1771	DBB:31; FPCG; 1787:70; 1791:3; FDJ:315; LVA1:1
ARELL, Samuel	CAVERLY, Dorothy "Dolly"	-26 MAY 1790	HCD:201; 1791:3; AHM:6/1:10; FWG:130
ARMAT, Thomas	_____, Sarah	-30 APR 1775	FDM:159
ARMSTRONG, James L.	SMITH, Mary Jane	10 MAR 1829	MB; AG:12/3/29:3(Gu)
	eldest d/o Sam Smith		
ARMSTRONG, John	CAYWOOD, Susan	28 JUL 1807	FPC:2(JM); MB
ARMSTRONG, John T.	TENNISON, Catherine	23 DEC 1823	MR(Sco); MB
	d/o Samuel Tennison		
ARNOLD, Alexander	FUGITT, Mary Ann	6 SEP 1837	MR:47; MPC:E76
ARNOLD, Garrett	CHISAM, Elizabeth	25 DEC 1803	MR(WW); MB[7]
	d/o William Chisam		
ARNOLD, James	LINDSAY, Sarah	c.17 SEP 1827	MB
ARNOLD, William	STEPHENSON, Ann	4 SEP 1816	MR(IR); MB
ARTHUR, Samuel	TRESCOTT, Catharine	3 DEC 1817	MR(AG); MB
ARUNDALL, John	DAVIS, Jemima	10 SEP 1793	R1:28
ARUNDELL, John	BOYD, Catherine	23 JUL 1818	MR(WHW); MB
ASHFORD, George	COMPTON, Susanna	25 DEC 1806	FPC:2(JM); MB
ASHFORD, John	BROWN, Sarah	c.30 DEC 1826	MB
ASHMORE, Maj. William	LEGGE, Mrs. Sarah M.	8 DEC 1829	AG:31/12/29:3(JeW)
Place: *Vermont*, Prince William Co.			
ASHTON, Charles	CHAPIN, Margaret		B:233
	d/o Benjamin Chapin		
ASHTON, Charles Henry B.	ANDERSON, Sarah	23 DEC 1819	AG:5/1/20:3(AB)
Place: Winchester	d/o Nathan Anderson		
ASHTON, Henry W.	ROSE, Ann A.	25 MAR 1822	AG:28/3/22:3
ASHTON, John	WEST, Hannah	-27 MAR 1776	FWD:25;
	d/o Col. John West		NI:17/5/27
ASHTON, Richard Watts	CHAPIN, Elizabeth	c.16 NOV 1786	B:233; 1787:70; 1791:3; NE:74; AG:16/11/86:2
	d/o Benjamin Chapin		
ASTOR, William B.	ARMSTRONG, Margaret	20 MAY 1818	AG:30/5/18:2
s/o John Jacob Astor	d/o Gen. Armstrong		
ATCHESON, Gustavus	COBY, Elizabeth	c.13 JAN 1810	MB
ATKINS, Nathaniel	HOSKINS, Sarah	17 OCT 1797	FPC:2(JM)
ATKINSON, Archibald	CHILTON, Elizabeth	24 APR 1829	AG:29/4/29:3
Place: Middleburg	second d/o William Chilton		

Husband	Wife	Event or Marriage	Reference(s)
ATKINSON, Guy	BIRCH, Albina d/o Joseph[8] Birch	7 APR 1803	DBV:153; MR(JM); CCC(75); FPC:2(JM); MB; AG:8/4/03:3(JM)
ATKINSON, James	BOGGESS, Verlinda	c.1786	CCC(91); IGI
ATKINSON, Samuel C. Place: Trenton NJ	MULLEN, Marian R. d/o Samuel Mullen	4 FEB 1826	UT:23/2/26:2
ATWELL, Joseph	DAVIS, Nancy	c.11 APR 1822	MB
ATWELL, Richard	MEADS, Elizabeth	30 MAY 1811	MR(IR); MB
ATWELL, Samuel	ADAMS, Harriet S. d/o Leonard Adams	c.1 JAN 1829	AG:3/1/29; MB
ATWELL, William	DORSEY, Julia Ann	14 JUL 1828	MB; AG:19/7/28:3(Sco)
ATWELL, William	ROTCH, Mrs. Susan	24 NOV 1829	MB;AG:28/11/29:3(Sco)
AUBINOE, Sommerset	CLIFORD, Jane d/o Ann Randall	c.3 SEP 1829	MB
AUDLEY, Thomas	JAVINS, Catharine s/o William Javins	16 MAR 1816	MR(IR); MB
AUSTIN, John	PERRY, Mary Ann	22 NOV 1798	FPC:1-2(JM)
AUSTIN, William	KIDWELL, Prescilla	15 JUL 1813	MB(BN)[9]
AVERY, John, Sr.	_____, Ann	-20 JUN 1830	MPC:E186
AVERY, Philip	SLATFORD, Sarah	7 DEC 1809	MR(IR); MB

Husband	Wife	Event or Marriage	Reference(s)
B			
BACON, Capt. Eben	_____, Sarah		SPC
BACON, Capt. Ebenezer	GREENLEAF, Mrs. Susan	24 JAN 1828	UC:E166;
Place: Washington DC			AG:26/1/28:3(Ski)
BADDEN, Sainttobin	BALL, Mary Ann	16 JAN 1804	MR(WM); MB
BADEN, Benjamin	_____, Elizabeth	-21 SEP 1807	DBQ:200; 1799:18
BADEN, John	NOBLE, Margaret	c.1805	IGI
BADEN, John B.	_____, Peggy	-24 FEB 1797	CRA
BAGGETT, Alexander	CHATHAM, Ann	c.12 MAY 1803	MB; DBR:484;
	d/o James Chatham		SMC
BAGGETT, Charles	BAGGETT, Elizabeth	24 MAR 1803	MR(JM); MB
BAGGETT, Ignatius	BAGGETT, Julia	20 APR 1819	AG:22/4/19:2(Mc);
Place: Washington DC			DCM
BAGGETT, James	KIDWELL, Mary	31 DEC 1829	AG:8/1/30:3(JR)
BAGGETT, John	MADDOCKS, Mary	13 MAY 1804	AG:14/5/04:3(E); MB
b/o Alexander Baggott			
BAGGETT, Robert	DYER, Sarah	14 JUL 1808	FPC:4(JM)
BAGGETT, Samuel	KEATING, Elizabeth	c.22 SEP 1813	MB
BAGGETT, Townsend, Sr.	_____, Ann		MPC:W189
BAGGETT, William	BROWN, Elizabeth	28 JUL 1825	MR(Sco); MB
BAGNET, William	ROBINSON, Nancy	JUL 1794	FPC:4(JM)
BAILISS, Robert	PORTER, Peggy	12 FEB 1801	MR(JM)
BAILESS, Thomas	HUNTINGTON, Mary	13 JAN 1825	AG:18/1/25:3(JR)
BAILEY, Carr, Jr.	HUNTER, Catharine A.	19 APR 1807	MB; DBT:320;
			FPC:4(JM)
BAILEY, Elisha Thomas	_____, Jane	-3 SEP 1799	HCM:296
BAILEY, George W.P.	SISSON, Sarah "Sally"	JAN 1795	FPC:4(JM); DBQ:417
BAILEY, William L.	MOLDEN, Jane Eliza	21 DEC 1830	AG:28/12/30:3(Rz)
Place: Washington DC			
BAILISS, Thomas	COOK, Ellen	27 NOV 1828	AG:11/12/28:3; MB
	d/o David Cook		
BAINBRIDGE, Rev. Absalom	BEATTY, Betsey	18 APR 1790	GT:12/5/90
Place: Frederick MD	d/o James Beatty		
BAKER, Albert J.K.	LANPHIER, Eliza S.	18 NOV 1827	AG:21/11/27:3(RD)
Place: Washington DC			
BAKER, Carroll	CHILES, Mary	27 FEB 1817	MR(WHW); MB
BAKER, Daniel	GOODRICK, Sarah	c.7 FEB 1804	MB
	d/o Benjamin Goodrick		
BAKER, James	VALIENT, Mary	30 JUN 1796	FPC:4(JM)
BAKER, John	JONES, Elizabeth	c.JAN 1825	AG:18/1/25
BAKER, Capt. Michael	DIXON, Jane	7 FEB 1826	AG:11/2/26:3(WHW);
			MB
BAKER, Samuel	GLADDEN, Susan	30 MAY 1815	FPC:5(JM); MB
BAKER, Zachariah	GREEN, Elizabeth	c.30 JUL 1805	MB
BALANGER (also see "Ballenger")			
BALANGER, Thomas	_____, Sally	-4 AUG 1849	TMCC(L:5)
BALCH, Lewis P.W.	WEVER, Eliza E.	14 MAR 1811	NI:1811
	d/o Adam Wever of Jefferson Co.		
BALCH, Rev. Stephen B.	PARROTT, Mrs. Jane	9 NOV 1830	AG:22/11/30:3
Place: Easton, Talbot Co. MD			
BALCH, Rev. Thos. B.	CARTER, Susan	22 AUG 1820	NI:1820(WM)
Place: *Solona*			

Husband	Wife	Event or Marriage	Reference(s)
BALDWIN, George	HAYES, Jane	24 JUL 1801	MR(WM); MB
BALDWIN, William	GOLDSMITH, Elizabeth	9 MAR 1826	UT:10/3/26:3(Mc)
BALE, Richard	NELSON, Sally	26 MAY 1810	MR(IR)
BALFOUR, James	_____,	- 1800	FPCG; 1787:70
BALFOUR, James	BANKS, Ann	c.1 JUN 1802	MB
BALL, Allan	WILEY, Anne	31 DEC 1801	MR(JM); MB
BALL, Erasmus	WEYLIE, Sarah d/o John Weylie	c.24 OCT 1805	MB
BALL, Horatio	MARCEY, Catherine	c.10 OCT 1815	DCM
BALL, John	THRIFT, Mary Ann	12 DEC 1773	GA:60; AHM:6/1:14
BALL, John	PARKINS, Susannah (Brown) wid/o Joseph Parkins d/o David and Sarah Brown	c.28 OCT 1797	H:467; DBZ:497
BALL, John	BOWLING, Marian (Plummer)	-9 JUL 1805	DBL:100; FC#63w; AHM:6/1:14
BALL, John W. Place: Montgomery Co. MD	MEDLEY, Delila	9 FEB 1828	MPC:E42; WB7:366; IGI
BALL, Robert	THRIFT, Ann	c.9 JUN 1803	MB
BALL, Spencer	LUKE, Eliza	25 FEB 1814	MR(ON); MB
BALL, Spencer M. Place: Fairfax Co.	DULANY, Mary d/o Daniel F. Dulany	7 MAY 1833	FRD:6; IGI
BALL, Thomas	MACKLEROY, Jane	23 DEC 1815	MR(ON); MB
BALL, William	CASSIDY, Sarah d/o Solomon Cassidy	-2 SEP 1840	DBN:232
BALLARD, Richard	HUDSON, Sarah	c.6 MAR 1804	MB
BALLARD, Severon	BALLARD, Liven	26 JUN 1808	FPC:4(JM)
BALLENGER (also see "Balanger")			
BALLENGER, James	STEPHENSON, Ann	14 NOV 1816	MR(JMH); MB
BAL(L)ENGER, Valentine	FARR, Frances	c.3 JUN 1809	MB
BALLINGER, Andrew	MORGAN, Elizabeth	MAR 1794	FPC:4(JM)
BALLINGER, John	FREEMAN, Sarah	14 DEC 1806	FPC:4(JM)
BALMAIN, Rev. Alexander	TAYLOR, Lucy d/o Erasmus Taylor	c.23 NOV 1786	AG:23/11/86:2
BANK, Hugh	HOLLOWOOD, Rhoda	7 JAN 1817	MR(JM); MB
BARBER, Peter	KENNEDY, Patty	12 AUG 1811	MR(IR); MB
BARCLAY, David	GRETTER, Ann	30 JUN 1810	DBU:129; E:13/7/10
BARCLAY, Rev. Francis Place: Chestnut Hill	BROWN, Helen Bailey Clarke d/o Dr. William Brown	28 JUN 1810	DBU:523; FPC:4(JM); AG:30/6/10(JM)
BARCLAY, Rev. Francis	SWAIN, Eliza	JAN 1811	AG:23/4/11:3(AS)
BARCLAY, Thomas	_____, Ann	-2 APR 1795	DBM:239; 1787:90
BARCROFT, Titus	PIERCY, Maria	6 JUN 1820	AG:8/6/20:3(JM); MR(JM); MB
BARKER, James of Caswell Co. NC	SIMPSON, Maria L.G. d/o Edward Simpson	18 MAR 1830	AG:26/3/30:3(Sco)
BARKER, John	JONES, Elizabeth	11 JAN 1825	AG:18/1/25:3(JR)
BARKER, Presley Place: Washington DC	CONNOR, Charlotte	8 APR 1823	SP; AG:12/4/23:3
BARKER, Quinton	KEENE, Lucretia	29 DEC 1829	AG:8/1/30:3(JR)
BARKER, Reason	MORRIS, Julia	20 JUL 1816	MR(JMH); MB
BARKLEY, Samuel	JAMIESON, Teresia C.	30 JUL 1817	NI; DCM
BARKMAN, Peter	NEVITT, Rosanna	c.1 MAY 1815	MB
BARNES, _____	_____, Mrs. Victory	-3 MAY 1816	SPC

7

Husband	Wife	Event or Marriage	Reference(s)
BARNES, Abraham	McCARTY, Sarah (Ball)	-19 JUN 1758	FM(1756):268; FWB:32
BARNES, Henry	POWELL, Margaret	c.26 NOV 1822	MB
BARNES, Jesse	GREEN, Susannah	9 JAN 1803	MR(JM); MB
BARNES, Thomas B.	TAYLOR, Kemer T.	3 FEB 1825	AG:10/2/25:3(JR)
BARNES, William H.	McMURRAY, Mrs. Margaret	28 MAR 1826	UT:1/4/26:3(Mc)
BARNET, John	_____, Harriet	-24 FEB 1816	AG:28/2/16:3
BARNETT, George	CRANSTON, Mary Ann	15 MAR 1810	FPC:4(JM); MB
BARNETT, William	PARSONS, Elizabeth	c.9 MAY 1829	MB
BARNEWALL, William	RUTGERS, Clementina	23 JUL 1818	AH:29/7/18; AG:28/7/18:2
Place: St. Mark's of New York City NY, d/o N.G. Rutgers			
BARON, James	DAVIS, Mrs. Sarah	4 NOV 1821	MR(WA); MB
BARRETT, Isaac	BURGESS, Lucy	4 AUG 1803	FPC:4(JM); MR(JM); MB
BARRON, Henry A.	LATIMER, Rebecca A.	23 FEB 1825	AG:3/3/25:3
Place: Georgetown DC			
BARRON, Capt. James	DAVIES, Ann	14 MAR 1811	NI:19/3/11(JM); AG:16/3/11:3(JM)[10]
BARRON, Comm. James	WILSON, Mary Ann	12 NOV 1829	AG:19/11/29:3
Place: Norfolk	eldest d/o John Wilson, of Portsmouth		
BARRON, William H.	MASON, Leeanah	11 MAY 1817	NI:1817(Mc)
Place: Analostan Island			
BARRY, Daniel	ADAM, Mary	16 OCT 1793	HCF:379; FDX:533; CM:19/10/93
	d/o Robert Adam, of Four Mile Run		
BARRY, Edward	_____, Mary	-8 AUG 1730	CC:102
BARRY, James C.	WEDGE, Matilda	c.DEC 1823	AG:30/12/23
BARRY, Robert	O'RILEY, Eliza H.	c.29 DEC 1823	MB
	d/o Elizabeth O'Riley		
BARRY, Robert	RAMSAY, Amelia	21 OCT 1824	AG:23/10/24:3(WA); NI:23/10/24(WA); MR(WA); MB
	d/o Col. Dennis Ramsay		
BARRY, Thomas	ADAM, Mrs. Ann	-19 NOV 1795	FDZ:446
	wid/o Robert Adam		
BARRY, William	COOK, Mrs. Mary	20 MAY 1803	MR(JM); MB
	wid/o William Cook		
BARTLE, Andrew	_____, Mary	-24 AUG 1812	DBW:233
BARTLE, Samuel	RHODES, Susan	24 MAR 1814	FPC:5(JM); MB
	d/o Anthony Rhodes		
BARTLEMAN, William	DOUGLASS, Margaret	12 APR 1800	FPC:4(JM); BT:19/4/00; AG:15/4/00:3; FPCC(41:31)
BARTLETT, Peter O.	EMERSON, Sebina	c.NOV 1830	AG:23/11/30
BARTON, Richard C.	BURDIT, Delilah	8 JUN 1824	BR:176; MPC:E12
BASFORD, Jacob	PATTERSON, Mrs. Sarah	21 MAR 1822	MB; AG:23/3/22:3
BASS, Samuel	RHOE [Wroe], Sarah	JUL 1792	FPC:4(JM)
BASSETT, Capt. William H.	O'NEILLE, Eleanora	22 JAN 1822	MR(JF);MB; NI:2/3/22[11] AG:25/1/22:3(JF)
BATCHELLER, Josiah	JOHNSON, Mary Ann Thomas	15 NOV 1821	UC:W179; IGI
Place: Waynesboro			
BAUGH, Lewis K.	BEEDLE, Eliza Ann	c.30 OCT 1817	MR(SC); MB
BAVERS, Thomas	DAVIS, Delila	21 NOV 1815	FPC:5(JM); MB
BAYLISS, Robert	POWER, Peggy	12 FEB 1801	FPC:4(JM)

Husband	Wife	Event or Marriage	Reference(s)
BAYLISS, Thomas	_____, Sarah		LCC
BAYLISS, William	JOHNSTON, Susanna	17 MAY 1796	FPC:4(JM)
BAYNE, Henry	_____, Sarah	-12 JUN 1809	DBR:235
BAYNE, John	PELTY, Sally	c.10 JUL 1823	MB
BEACH (also see "Beech")			
BEACH, James	HARRISON, Theodocia	c.16 DEC 1830	MB
BEACH, John	REEVES, Sarah	25 DEC 1820	AG:12/1/21:3
BEACH, Rezin	TILLETT, Levina	19 MAR 1829	AG:25/3/29:3(JR)
BEACH, Silas	GARNER, Theodotia	3 JAN 1822	AG:10/1/22:3(JR)
BEAKLEY, John	WHITNEY, Sophia	7 MAY 1828	MR(SC)
BEALE, John	McKEIVOR, Mary	24 MAY 1815	FPC:5(JM)
BEALE, John S.H.H.E.	ALEXANDER, Elmira E.E.	26 FEB 1829	AG:6/3/29:3(Mc)
BEALE, Richard	NELSON, Sally	c.26 MAY 1810	MB
BEALL, Benjamin Lloyd	TAYLOR, Elizabeth	13 JUN 1825	NI:25/1/25; MB;
	d/o George Taylor		AG:27/1/25:3(ON)
BEALL, Gideon	WESTON, Ann Farrell	10 MAY 1825	MB; AG:14/5/25:3(RD)
	d/o Capt. Wm. Weston		
BEALL, John	HARPER, Elizabeth	-6 JUN 1804	DBI:341
	d/o John Harper		
BEALL, John	McKERVEN, Mary	c.23 MAY 1812	MB
BEALLE, Thomas K.	HARPER, Elizabeth	-20 MAR 1816	DBBB:241
	d/o John Harper		BUR:1417; CCC(52)
BEAN, Benjamin	HUGHUELY, Matilda Lee	18 AUG 1823	MR(IR); MB
BEARCROFT, Domini	WATSON, Sarah (C)	20 DEC 1811	WB3:361; MR(IR); MB
BEARD, George	HUNTER, Elizabeth	20 OCT 1796	AG:22/10/96:3
BEARD, George	BERRY, Elizabeth	13 SEP 1818	MR(ON); MB
	s/o Bayne S. Berry		
BEARD, George	DISNEY, Jane	17 DEC 1829	AG:8/1/30:3(JR)
BEARD, Capt. W.C.	JOHNS, Matilda H.	9 AUG 1821	AG:13/8/21:3
Place: Wood Lawn, Prince George's Co. MD, d/o Aquila Johns			
BEATTY, Dr. R.H.	OTT, Mary C.	7 MAR 1826	UT:10/3/26:3(B)
Place: Georgetown DC	d/o Dr. John Ott		
BEATTY, Capt. Thomas	HARRISON, Anne	c.FEB 1792	GT:4/2/92
BECK, William	KEENE, Margaret	14 FEB 1824	PW:28(F);
			AG:14/2/24:3(JR)
BECKLEY, Archibald	BURNS, Lavinia	c.11 JUL 1826	MB
BECKLEY, John	WHITING, Sophia	7 MAY 1828	MR(Sco); MB
BECKLEY, William	WATSON, Ann	8 NOV 1827	MR(Sco); MB
BECKWITH, Marmaduke	ELLZEY, Sybill	-27 DEC 1788	FWF:70; FWE:227
	d/o Lewis Ellzey		
BEDINGER, Jacob	PEPPER, Eliza	8 DEC 1799	FPC:4(JM)
BEECH (also see "Beach")			
BEECH, James	HUTSON, Elizabeth	c.8 JUN 1825	MB
BEECH, John	GLASGOW, Mary	6/7 JAN 1801	FPC:4(JM); MR(JM)
BEECH, Thomas	RILEY, Margaret	7 DEC 1790	FPC:4(JM)
BEECH, Thomas	SMITH, Cordelia	1/2 OCT 1812	FPC:5(JM); MR(JM); MB
BEECH, William	HARRISON, Sally	8 DEC 1796	FPC:4(JM)
BEEDLE, John Wesley	DOGAN, Harriet W.	9 DEC 1813	DBX:404;
			AG:14/12/13:3(S)
BEELER, Christian Louis	EAKIN, Mrs. Frederica Augusta	19 JAN 1809	AG:21/1/09:3(G);
	wid/o Matthew Eakin		FMI; LP#A525
BEELER, Christopher	_____, Henrietta Wilhelmina	-17 JAN 1772	HCE:409; FDK:65

Husband	Wife	Event or Marriage	Reference(s)
BEELER, Lewis Place: Washington DC	KNELLER, Mrs. Mary	11 OCT 1825	SP; AG:15/10/25:3
BEHIER, Peter	LAVAZON, Elizabeth	2 NOV 1797	FPC:4(JM)
BEHIER, Peter	KING, Ann	15 APR 1806	MR(JM); MB
BEIDEMAN, Henry	_____, Charlotte	-7 JUL 1784	FDP:35
BELFOUR (see "Balfour")			
BELL, Alexander	EVANS, Susanna	23 DEC 1830	MR(LA);[12] MB
BELL, George (C)	WAUGH, Sally (C)	17 AUG 1820	MR(WHW); MB
BELL, James	WOOLLS, _____	c.18 NOV 1802	MB
BELL, Nicholas	CREASE, Jane d/o Anthony Crease, Sr.	-18 SEP 1819	WB2:383; FWM:281
BELL, Robert	HARLE, Brittania	c.11 NOV 1802	MB
BELL, Thomas D.	MOSS, Mary	25 MAR 1827	AG:31/3/27:3(JR)
BELLMIRE, Thomas	BRUFFIELD, Sarah	JUL 1795	FPC:4(JM); 1799:30; 1800:52
BENHAM, Joseph S.	SLACUM, Mary Louisa d/o George Slacum si/o W.A. Slacum	17 JUN 1829	CCR; NI:24/6/29; MB; AG:23/6/29:3
BENNET, Francis	STEWART, Elizabeth	c.28 FEB 1818	MB
BENNET, Richard	_____, Sarah		1800:52
BENNETT, James H.	HOOFF, Mary Amelia	4 SEP 1823	NI:10/9/23(WHW); MB;AG:6/9/23:3(WHW)
BENNETT, John	PERRY, Anne	30 AUG 1804	FPC:4(JM); MB
BENNETT, Joseph Turner	MANN, Elizabeth Brown	c.22 DEC 1802	WBA:176; MB
BENNETT, Mordecai	McCARTY, Milly	16 SEP 1817	MR(JMH); MB
BENNETT, Walter	FURGUSSON, Mary ward of William Evans	c.9 AUG 1827	MB
BENNETT, Washington	DENNISON, Maria	c.4 DEC 1830	MB
BENSON, James	DORSEY, Elizabeth	24 JAN 1828	MR(Sco); MB
BENSON, Robert	MOON, Elizabeth	17 FEB 1791	FPC:4(JM)
BENSON, William C.	YOUNG, Eleanor	29 NOV 1814	AG:8/12/14:3
BENT, Lemuel	LEWIS, Elizabeth	13 SEP 1792	FPC:3; HCE:50; IGI
BENTER, Wesley	BONTZ, Ann	12 DEC 1816	MR(IR); MB
BENTER, William, Sr.	AVORY, Elizabeth	14 FEB 1826	TMCC(P:4); DCM; UT:21/2/26:2
BENTLEY, Caleb s/o Joseph Bentley Place: Sandy Spring Meeting House	BROOKE, Sarah d/o Roger Brooke	28 APR 1791	H:474[13]; MGB:14/2:2
BENTLEY, Robert	LONGDEN, Catherine "Kitty" d/o John Longden	9 OCT 1817	AG:13/10/17:3(WHW) WB3:366; MR(WHW); MB
BENTON, James M.	LEDDY, Virginia C. d/o Owen Leddy	-11 AUG 1816	SMC; FDK3:82
BENTON, James M.	HARRISON, Margaret A. d/o John D. Harrison	-4 APR 1837	FDV3:247
BENTON, Samuel	VOWELL, Elizabeth	8 JUL 1805	MR(IR); MB
BERKLEY, Burgess	ELLZEY, Stacy	-1 OCT 1786	FWE:223
BERKLEY, Robert	CARTER, Julia d/o Robert Carter	-18 JAN 1802	FLC1812:127
BERNARD, John	DOVE, Sarah d/o Zachariah Dove	30 MAY 1807	MR(IR); MB
BERRY, George	COLE, Elizabeth d/o Mary Cole	c.8 MAR 1820	MB

Husband	Wife	Event or Marriage	Reference(s)
BERRY, James	DAVIES, Ann	14 MAR 1811	MR(JM)
BERRY, John C.	WEDGE, Malinda	22 DEC 1823	AG:30/12/23:3
Place: Baltimore MD	s/o Simon Wedge		
BERRY, Dr. John E.	HARPER, Rachel Wells	5 SEP 1811	AG:7/9/11:3(R);
	d/o Capt. Samuel Harper		MB
BERRY, Thomas	_____, Elizabeth	-22 DEC 1813	AG:25/12/13:3
BERRY, Thomas	SILMON, Elizabeth	c.18 SEP 1827	MB
BERRY, William	FOX, Lucinda (C)	c.15 JUL 1830	MB
BEVERAGE, John	PAYNE, Keziah	-13 NOV 1799	HCM:408; DBA:323
	d/o Josiah Payne		
BIERS, Wm. K.	PENINGTON, Sarah	5 FEB 1822	AG:8/2/22:3(EH)
Place: *Cameron*			
BIGGS, James	TALBUTT, Rebecca	28 DEC 1801	MR(JM); MB
BIGGS, James	TALBUTT, Nancy	4 FEB 1804	MR(WM); MB
BILLEY, Peter	SIMPSON, Mary Ann	7 JAN 1796	FPC:4(JM); 1799:40;
			1800:56
BINES, David	CANNON, Margaret M.	23 OCT 1817	MR(JMH); MB
BINNS, Charles Wm. D.	ALEXANDER, Mariamne T.S.	27 JAN 1825	AG:1/2/25:3; MB
	d/o Walter S. Alexander		
BIRCH (also see "Burch")			
BIRCH, Caleb	BOWLING, Mary	c.4 SEP 1806	MB
BIRCH, Isaac	WALKER, Elizabeth	8 SEP 1815	FPC:5(JM); MB
BIRCH, James	GREEN, Priscilla	5 JAN 1799	DBD2:340; FPC:4(JM);
			AHM:6/2:21
BIRCH, James	BUCHANAN, Mrs. Aletha	c.4 FEB 1823	MB
s/o James Birch, Sr.			
BIRCH, Joseph, Sr.	ROBERTSON, Janet Bowmaker	c.1774	DBS:479;
			AG:21/9/11:3;
			P:59, 68;
			ADT:471
BIRCH, Joseph	POSEY, Sinah	22 JAN 1818	MR(IR); MB
BIRCH, Samuel	RICHARDS, Carey	c.9 MAR 1815	MB
BIRCH, Col. Samuel	CLEVELAND, Ann	27 SEP 1821	PW:34; PB
BIRCKHEAD, Dr. Lenox	HOFFMAN, Mary Eliza	-5 DEC 1836	WB6:233
BIRD, John	CLEARPOLE, Rebecca	c.20 AUG 1811	WB2:345; MB
BIRD, Thomas	KING, Mary	c.8 JUL 1824	MB
BIRD, William	DALTON, Catharine	-13 DEC 1790	HCE:63; 1791:4;
	d/o John Dalton		FWD:38; FDZ:296;
			FDU:416
BIRD, William	SULLIVAN, Margaret Virginia	22 NOV 1829	AG:28/11/29:3
Place: Washington DC			
BISHOP, John S.	HORWELL, Amanda Maria	23 APR 1829	MR(LA); MB
	d/o Richard Horwell		
BLACK, Alexander	_____, Sarah	-1 APR 1813	DBX:102
BLACK, Capt. David	_____, Eliza	-25 APR 1799	FPC:3; DBU:250;
			1800:57;
			FPCC(41:11)
BLACK, James	TALBOT, Helen	3 AUG 1831	MR(WJ)
BLACKBURN, Col. Thomas	SCOTT, Christian	-4 JUL 1785	FWE:232;
			AG:19/1/15:3
BLACKBURN, Thomas	JENKINS, Mary	22 DEC 1790	FPC:4(JM)
BLACKBURN, Thomas, Jr.	SINCLAIR, Elizabeth	18 DEC 1806	AG:24/12/06(H)
BLACKFORD, Henry	PARSONS, Sarah	27 MAR 1815	FPC:5(JM); MB

Husband	Wife	Event or Marriage	Reference(s)
BLACKLOCK, Nicholas F.	RAMSAY, Eliza J.	9 DEC 1813	AG:11/12/13:3(JM); FPCC(42:72); MB
BLACKLOCK, Robert S.	RAMSAY, Ann M. d/o F.A. Ramsay	16 APR 1816	AH:19/4/16(JM); FPCC(42:72); MB; AG:19/4/16:3(JM)
BLADEN, John B.	MAUSSEE, Millie	16 DEC 1811	PW:35
BLADEN, Kinnellum	BURR, Nancy	1788	FB
BLADEN, Thomas, Jr.	CAROLIN, Ann	4 SEP 1811	AG:7/9/11(IR); MB; MR(IR)
BLADEN, William L.	DANIEL, Catharine	c.27 OCT 1810	MB
BLAGDEN, George	DAVIES, Ann	29 DEC 1799	FPC:4(JM)
BLAKENEY, Abel	[WROE], Mary	-8 SEP 1808	DBQ:323; 1799:12
BLANCHARD, Jason	JENKINS, Ann J. d/o M. Jenkins	c.12 JAN 1822	MB
BLAKENEY, John	SPRIGGS, Jane	24 DEC 1803	MR(WW); MB
BLONDELY, Michael Simon	_____, Jane	-3 JUL 1788	HCD:111
BLOXHAM, James	_____, Mary	-20 JUL 1795	FDY:14
BLOXHAM, James	DUNINGTON, Catharine	c.17 MAR 1803	MB
BLUE, John J.	EVANS, Catharine	27 MAR 1806	MR(JM); MPC:E83; FPC:4(JM); MB
BLUME, Joseph H.	LYLES, Elizabeth	c.15 SEP 1823	MB
BLUNT, Washer Place: Montgomery Co. MD	JACKSON, Sarah	29 JAN 1778	DBQ:386; 1787:70; 1791:3; 1799:34; 1800:52; FPCG; IGI
BOBEST, George	_____, Maria	-30 JAN 1800	HCN:14
BODINE, James Place: Fairfax Co.	BUTLER, Catherine	27 JAN 1815	PW:39
BOGAN, Benjamin L. Place: Woodstock	OLT, Sara	3 JUN 1819	AH:18/6/19
BOGAN, John Place: Frederick Co.	LEWIS, Catharine	12 JUN 1788	AG:9/4/06:3; IGI
BOGGESS, Henry	LINDSAY, Mary Ann d/o Robert Lindsay	-11 SEP 1784	FWE:29; LDO:174; FDF3:289
BOGUE, Francis S.	BOYD, Elizabeth	4 MAR 1830	MR(IR); MB
BOGUE, John	_____, Judith	-19 APR 1797	DBE:214; FPCG; HCI:9; FPC:3
BOGUE, John	_____, Frances	-12 MAY 1803	DBE:214
BOHRER, Peter	_____, Magdalena	-6 MAR 1797	HCK:15; 1787:70
BOHIER, Elias	MILLER, Elizabeth	c.24 MAY 1810	MB
BOISSEAU, Joseph	JENKINS, Mary Ann	19 FEB 1819	AG:20/2/19:2; MR(JF)
BOLLING, Joseph	MOXLEY, Nancy	14 MAY 1796	FPC:4(JM)
BOLLING, Samuel	PLUMMER, Miriam d/o Joseph Plummer	20 FEB 1787	FC#63w; FDE2:229
BOND, Joseph Place: Fairfax Meeting House, d/o Thomas Moore	MOORE, Elizabeth	31 DEC 1794	H:472
BOND, Joseph Place: Fairfax Meeting House, d/o John S. Littler	LITTLER, Rachel B.	4 JUN 1817	H:472
BOND, Joseph	STABLER, Elizabeth	2 OCT 1828	H:731
BOND, Richard	GRAHAM, Polly d/o John Graham	c.20 SEP 1787	AG:20/09/87:2; 1791:4
BOND, William	TAYLOR, Nancy	3 OCT 1807	FPC:4(JM); MB
BONTEMPT, Francis	PATERSON, Catharine	c.MAY 1794	FPC:4(JM)
BONTZ, George	BENTER, Mary	25 JUN 1818	MR(IR); MB

12

Husband	Wife	Event or Marriage	Reference(s)
BONTZ, Jacob	CARLIN, Sarah	11 MAR 1818	MR(AG); MB; AG:14/3/18:3
BONTZ, John	HOUSE, Elizabeth	c.28 MAR 1816	MB
BONTZ, Valentine	_____, Mary	-5 JAN 1820	WB2:347
BOONE, Arnold	SHOEMAKER, Elizabeth	28 SEP 1808	H:732
Place: Sandy Spring Meeting House MD			
BOONE, Arnold	_____, Hannah	-20 NOV 1817	H:732
BOOTHE, Jeremiah	_____, Ann	-20 OCT 1821	SPC
BOOTHE, William	CRYS, Ann	c.25 OCT 1828	MB
ward of James Nowel			
BOSS, Abraham	HICKEY, Ann D.	15 OCT 1816	MR(WHW); MB
BOSTICK, George	WILSON, Eleanor	c.13 AUG 1812	MB
BOSTON, Joshua	THRIFT, Ann	c.14 MAR 1805	MB
d/o Pricilla Thrift			
BOSTON, Samuel E. [or C.]	LOVE, Julia Ann	28 FEB 1828	MR(IR); MB
BOSWELL, Lemuel	TROTTER, Jane	19 MAY 1796	WG:15/6/96
BOSWELL, Lemuel	COLLARD, _____	19 JUN 1796	WG:15/6/96:3
BOUIS, Joseph C.	HUBBALL, Eletia	22 SEP 1830	MB; AG:30/9/30:3(Sco)
BOURNE, Daniel	BURK, Rebecca	c.10 OCT 1805	MB
BOUSMAN, William	JACOBS, Rebecca	2 MAY 1807	BFG:6/5/07(B)
BOWEN, James	_____, Rachel	-1815	ACFF, John W. Bowen
BOWEN, John	NEWMAN, Jeanette J.	25 OCT 1836	PW:45
Place: Fairfax Co.			
BOWIE, Davis	_____, Wineford	-19 OCT 1808	DBQ:373
BOWIE, James P.	_____, Dorothy	-15 JUL 1807	DBR:191; CCC(57)
BOWIE, Rubin S.	YOUNG, Eliza	22 OCT 1816	BA:23/10/16(JG)
BOWIE, Theophilus	FLEMING, Catharine	-18 OCT 1808	DBQ:417; WB1:340
BOWIE, Walter	BROOKES, Mary	16 NOV 1771	B3
BOWIE, William	GOLDSMITH, Mary	-5 APR 1796	FPC:3
BOWLER, John L.	LEARY, Frances	10 FEB 1822	SP; MR(ON); MB; AG:12/2/22:3(ON)
d/o Andrew Leary			
BOWLES, Richard	PIPER, Betsey (M)	c.27 FEB 1822	MB
BOWLES, Thomas (C)	SALES, Susan (C)	9 JUN 1813	MR(IR); MB
BOWLES, William (M)	HENRY, Ann, alias Phillis (M)	c.26 MAY 1823	MB
BOWLING, Ambrose G.	JAMES, Margaret	29 JUL 1808	MR(IR); MB
BOWLING, George	STAPLES, Sarah	18 MAR 1801	MR(JM)
BOWLING, George	VEITCH, Elizabeth	24 FEB 1805	FPC:4(JM); MB
BOWLING, John	COCKRELL, Elizabeth	-5 NOV 1805	WBB:202; 1799:20; FC#42n
BOWLING, John	GRIFFIN, Frankey	11 FEB 1818	MR(IR); MB
BOWLING, Robert	NEILLE, Jane Christie	28 NOV 1816	MR(JMH); MB; AG:30/11/16:3
BOWNE, Matthew Franklin	QUINBY, Elizabeth	20 DEC 1775	H:473; HCG:157
Place: Westchester Meeting House, d/o Aaron Quinby			
BOYD, Dr. John	_____, Ann	-17 JUL 1778	FDD4:218
BOYD, John	MacMANNIN, Elizabeth	NOV 1792	FPC:4(JM)
BOYD, John	WATKINS, Jane	c.5 JUL 1809	MB
BOYD, John	KIRK, Mary	30 JUN 1810	MR(IR); MB
BOYD, Robert	BAYLEY, Betsy	20 NOV 1810	MR(IR); MB
BOYDSTONE, Presley	ROBERTSON, Elizabeth	-17 MAR 1777	DBA:135; FDM:287
d/o James Robertson, Jr.			

Husband	Wife	Event or Marriage	Reference(s)
BOYER, Elias	BRUCE, Ann	16 AUG 1803	FPC:4(JM); MR(JM); AG:17/8/03:3(JM); MB
BOYER, John	REYNOLDS, Martha Ann	9 NOV 1812	MR(IR); MB
BOYLE, John	HUDSON, Julia Ann	25 FEB 1830	MR(LA); MB
BOZMAN, Thomas	_____, Mary	-9 DEC 1753	FWB:55
BRADFORD, Capt. Charles	_____, Catharine	-12 OCT 1827	AG:15/10/27:3
BRADLEY, Abraham	HALL, Mary G. d/o William I. Hall	-OCT 1830	AG:12/10/30
BRADLEY, Gabriel	TAYLOR, Eliza	c.1 AUG 1822	MB
BRAD(L)EY, Harrison	HUGUELY, Elishaba Harris	23 APR 1816	TMCC(Q:5); MR(IR); MB
BRADLEY, James	DAVIS, Eliza	4 JAN 1827	AG:13/1/27:3(JR)
BRADLEY, Robert	SHARPE, Sally d/o Peter Sharpe	23 JUL 1811	AG:30/7/11:3(JL)
BRADLY, John A.	ARRUNDLE, Mary Ann	19 JAN 1826	AG:25/1/26:2(JR)
BRADY, Benjamin	_____, Susanna	-26 JUL 1808	DBR:181; DBX:326
BRADY, John S.	BROWN, Susan	22 JAN 1828	MR(IR); MB
BRADY, Thomas	McCROCKLIN, Sally	c.1 DEC 1802	MB
BRAMEL, William W.	JONES, Mary H.	20 SEP 1827	MR(Sco); MB
BRAMMELL, Isaac	HENNIKEN, Ann	DEC 1793	FPC:4(JM)
BRANDT, Capt. Richard B.	_____, Catharine	-11 JAN 1815	AG:14/1/15:3
BRANDT, Richard Henley	SMOOT, Ann Caroline youngest d/o Rev. Charles Smoot	8 JAN 1828	SP; MR(WJ); MB; AG:11/1/28:3(WJ); P:157
BRANSON, Vincent	COLE, Lydia	OCT 1795	FPC:4(JM)
BRANTHWAITE, William	CURRY, Elizabeth	15 AUG 1802	MR(JM); MB
BRAWNER, Henry	McREA, Kitty d/o Kitty McRea	9 JUN 1815	MR(JM); MB
BRAWNER, Henry s/o John Brawner	ANNESS, Elizabeth	25 JUN 1815	MR(WHW); DBE2:55; MB
BRAWNER, Thornton	PARSONS, Lucretia	13 JUN 1826	UT:16/6/26
BRAY, John Place: Washington DC	HUNT, Sophia	22 SEP 1808	AG:26/9/08:3
BRAY, Richard	NEIL, Rosanna	NOV 1794	FPC:4(JM)
BREAST (also see "Brest")			
BREAST, James A.	TALBOTT, Eliza	30 NOV 1826	AG:2/12/26:3(Sco); MR(Sco); MB
BRENT, George	LANHAM, Susannah	7 DEC 1819	AG:13/12/19:3; SP
BRENT, Henry	EVANS, Elizabeth [Blue]	27 DEC 1818	AG:29/12/18:3(WHW); SP; MR(WHW); MB
BRENT, Robert Y. Place: Baltimore MD	CARRERE, Eliza L.	c.8 JAN 1814	AG:8/1/14:3(AC)
BREST (also see "Breast")			
BREST, Clement	FLOOD, Margaret	c.12 FEB 1827	MB
BRIANT, John	NOLEN, Harriet A.B.	2 SEP 1830	AG:4/9/30:3(Sco)
BRICK, Samuel	CLEAVELAND, Ann	c.30 SEP 1822	MB
BRICKLES, George	GREENE, Elizabeth	22 MAY 1797	FPC:4(JM)
BRIDWELL, Timothy	HOLMES, Sythia C.	1 FEB 1822	AG:12/2/22:3(JR)
BRIGHT, John	WILLIAMS, Sybil	NOV 1795	FPC(JM); 1787:70; 1791:4:4
BRIGHT, John	WRIGHT, Nancy	6 DEC 1812	AG:8/12/12:3(SP)
BRIGHT, John	DEETON, Frances "Fanny"	12 MAR 1818	AH:16/3/18(JH); MB; AG:14/3/18:3(JH)

Husband	Wife	Event or Marriage	Reference(s)
BRIGHT, John	YOUNG, Ann "Nancy"	23 DEC 1823	AG:30/12/23:3; MB; MR(WA)
BRIGHTMAN, Joseph	SHEARMAN, Mary	c.23 JUL 1805	MB
BRISCOE, Dr. Warner W.	SLACUM, Jane Harriet d/o George and Jane H. Slacum	16 NOV 1825	NI:11/19/25; SP; MR(WHW); MB; AG:19/11/25:3(WHW)
BRISON, John	McKINNEY, Mary	16 APR 1818	MR(ON); MB
BRITTINGHAM, Dixon	HYNEMAN, Ann	-16 NOV 1797	HCI:471
BRITTINGHAM, Dixon	HOAKS, Ann d/o George Hoaks	-19 JAN 1798	DBR:83; 1800:55; DBAA:230; 1799:36
BRITTINGHAM, James	BROWN, Polly	3 JUL 1803	MR(JM); MB
BRITTINGHAM, James	HOAKS, Mary	-8 MAY 1814	DBAA:230
BROAD, Michael	MARTIN, Jane d/o Edward Martin, Sr.	14 JAN 1804	MR(WM); MB
BROAD, Thomas	MAY, Mary	28 DEC 1820	MR(EH); MB
BROADWATER, Chas. Guy Place: Fairfax Co.	GUNNELL, Catherine	18 DEC 1808	FF:276
BROADWATER, William E.	DARNE, Margaret	22 NOV 1816	MR(IR); MB
BROCCHUS, Thomas	ASHTON, Rachel	5 NOV 1801	MR(JM); DBQ:343; CCC(55); FPC:4(JM); MB
BROCKETT, Robert	BURNETT, Annabella d/o John Burnett	c.1781	HCM:216; DBA:407; 1787:70; 1791:4; FPCC(41:9); BR:195
BROCKETT, Robert, Jr.	LONGDEN, Elizabeth "Betsey" d/o Ralph Longden	14 DEC 1815	BR:195; FPC:5(JM); AG:16/12/15(JM); MB
BROCKETT, Walter Burn.	BYRNE, Elizabeth d/o Patrick Byrne	18 NOV 1815	BR:195; FPC:5(JM); MB
BRODERS, James	CURTAIN, Elizabeth	29 JAN 1814	MR(IR); MB
BRODERS, John H.	COMPTON, Elizabeth	26 DEC 1822	AG:31/12/22:3(IR)
BRODERS, Joseph	STOOPS, Eliza	16 SEP 1824	NI:23/9/24(ON); MB
BROGDON, George (C)	SOLOMON, Sarah (C)	24 AUG 1809	MR(JM); MB
BROMLEY, Joseph	SMITH, Mary	5 MAR 1801	MR(JM)
BRONAUGH, Carey	JACOB, Ann G.	27 JAN 1814	MR(ON); MB
BRONAUGH, Jeremiah	FIELD, Simpha Rosa Ann	c.1731	FWB:315; IGI
BRONAUGH, John	BECKWITH, Peggy d/o Marmaduke Beckwith	-20 FEB 1802	FD1803:296
BRONAUGH, Dr. John Place: Prince William Co.	GRAHAM, Fanny d/o Robert Graham	30 MAY 1811	AG:8/6/11:3(LM)
BRONAUGH, William L., Jr.	MITCHELL, Mary C.	7 JAN 1816	AG:13/1/17:3(B)
BROOK, Benjamin M. Place: Lexington KY	SATTERWHITE, Paulina Ann	26 SEP 1812	AG:18/8/12:3
BROOKE, Lt. Edmund Place: Prince George's Co. MD, d/o Benjamin Young	YOUNG, Ellen M.	4 FEB 1817	AG:8/2/17:3
BROOKE, Ignatius	ROLLINS, Martha	24 DEC 1799	FPC:4(JM)
BROOKE, James Place: Fairfax Meeting House, d/o Amos Janney	JANNEY, Hannah	13 OCT 1759	H:474
BROOKE, John Henry	NASH, Jane Ann	15 SEP 1829	MB; AG:17/9/29:3(Wal)
BROOKE, Roger	MATTHEWS, Mary	c.25 MAR 1758	H:474
BROOKE, Thomas	COFFIN, Sarah	5 SEP 1809	FPC:4(JM); MB
BROOKE, Walter D.	TRIPLETT, Lucy d/o William Triplett	c.OCT 1799	DBS:155; FWI:183; IGI
BROOK(E), William	TROUT, Margaret	10 AUG 1790	FPC:4(JM)

Husband	Wife	Event or Marriage	Reference(s)
BROOKES, Benjamin Place: near Croom MD	TOWNLEY, Elizabeth	6 JUN 1745	B3(JE)
BROOKES, Benjamin	HALKERSON, Mrs. Elizabeth	13 FEB 1799	CL:12/3/99
BROOKES, George	BOSWELL, Sarah	19 FEB 1797	FPC:4(JM)
BROOKES, John Smith	BOWIE, Ann Blizard d/o Allen Bowie	7 DEC 1781	B3(TC)
BROOKES, John Smith	HARWOOD, Eleanor eldest d/o Benjamin Harwood	4 JUN 1786	B3(TC)
BROOKS, David	JONES, Mary	13 SEP 1829	SP; MR(WJ); MB
BROOKS, George	KERBY, Elizabeth	c.13 SEP 1821	MB
BROOKS, Hanson	FUGGIT, Peggy	4 DEC 1819	MR(JM)
BROOKES, James	JOHNSTON, Sarah	27 AUG 1817	MR(AG); MB
BROOKS, Capt. John	DAINGERFIELD, Sarah T. d/o Capt. [Bathurst] Daingerfield	12 JAN 1830	SP; MR(WJ); MB; AG:16/1/30:3(WJ)
BROOKS, William (C)	_____, Mary (C)		1800:54
BROUGH, Heppel	LUNT, Betsey d/o Ezra Lunt	4 FEB 1804	MR(WW); MB
BROWERS, John	MAHANNY, Maria	9 MAR 1820	MR(JF); MB
BROWN, Benjamin	_____, Anne	-25 FEB 1813	DBX:28
BROWN, Charles	WHEELER, Charlotte	c.8 JUN 1809	MB
BROWN, David	MOXLEY, Mary	11 SEP 1798	FPC:4(JM)
BROWN, Edmund L.	BAYNE, Catharine B.	14 JUL 1825	AG:19/7/25:3; MB
BROWN, Henry (C)	PIPER, Sarah Ann (C)	25 JUN 1813	MR(ON); MB
BROWN, James	MASTIN, Susan	15 NOV 1817	MR(WHW); MB
BROWN, James b. Newport, R.I.	WHITING, Lucy	c.2 OCT 1829	MB
BROWN, James	STEUART, Catharine	8 APR 1796	FPC:4(JM); 1799:2
BROWN, John Place: Fairfax Meeting House	BALL, Martha	10 APR 1776	H:476
BROWN, John	COATES, Margaret	2 AUG 1812	FPC:5(JM); MB
BROWN, John	BOWLIN, Martha	3 JUN 1816	MR(JM); MB
BROWN, John	LEATHRUM, Maria	25 AUG 1823	MR(JF); MB
BROWN, John Douglas	GRETTER, Mary Goulding	22 OCT 1811	FPC:4(JM); OT:54; SPC(65:2); MR(JM); MB
BROWN, Nicholas	JUDGE, Margaret	21 SEP 1827	H:759; AG:25/9/27:3
BROWN, Richard Place: Fairfax Meeting House, d/o Joseph Cox	COX, Sarah	11 JAN 1786	H:477
BROWN, Samuel Montgy.	_____, Mary	-10 MAY 1784	DBF:391; 1797:70; FDO:304
BROWN, Samuel	ROBERTS, Susannah	c.14 MAR 1811	MB
BROWN, Thomas	DAVIS, Catherine	-13 FEB 1786	R2:90(SG)
BROWN, William	VENABLE, Ann	17 DEC 1827	AG:21/12/29:3(OB)
BROWN, Dr. William	SCOTT, Catharine d/o James Scott	-24 NOV 1791	CRA:59; FDP:54
BROWN, William Hunt Place: Hopewell Meeting House	NEILL, Sarah	17 DEC 1801	H:769
BROWN, William Hunt Place: Jefferson Co.	WILSON, Martha d/o Thomas Wilson	3 OCT 1810	H:734(20); DBW:61; FDU2:407; AG:12/10/10:3
BROWNE, Archibald	BEALL, Eleanor	FEB 1795	FPC:4(JM)
BROWNING, James	BROOK, Sarah Ann	10 NOV 1799	FPC:4(JM)
BROWNING, Richard	ROBINSON, Elizabeth	1788	FB

Husband	Wife	Event or Marriage	Reference(s)
BROWNLY, Thomas	WEYLIE, Elizabeth	-16 FEB 1773	Miller:1
BRUCE, Aaron	SMITH, Nancy	2 SEP 1815	FPC:5(JM); MB
BRUFFIELD, Samuel	FARRELL, Sarah	19 NOV 1790	FPC:4(JM)
BRUMLEY, Joseph	SMITH, Mary	5 MAR 1801	FPC:4(JM)
BRUNDIGE, Timothy Place: Dumfries	LINTON, Mrs. Mary	2 JUN 1811	AG:6/6/11:3(CO)
BRUNER, Andrew	_____, Phoebe/Phillipine	-11 NOV 1807	DBQ:11
BRUSH, John C.	DOYNE, Mrs. Mary	27 MAR 1813	AG:12/4/13:3
BRYAN, Bernard	_____, Mary Ann	-12 MAR 1799	HCM:425; DBB:158
BRYAN, Hanson	FLUDD, Eleanor	11 NOV 1796	FPC:4(JM)
BRYAN, John J.	NOLAND, Harriet A.B.	c.1 SEP 1830	MPC:W62; AG:4/9/30; MB
BRYAN, Samuel	SKINNER, E.	28 OCT 1808	AG:29/10/08:3
BRYANT, Daniel	PEARSON, Nancy	28 DEC 1822	AG:7/1/23:3(JR)
BRYANT, Rev. John Place: Centreville, Fairfax Co.	NORRIS, Lucinda I.	26 NOV 1823	AG:29/11/23:3
BRYCE, John	_____, Hannah	-19 NOV 1784	HCB:392; 1791:5; FDQ:124
BUCKINGHAM, Isaac	BROWN, Mary Worth	15 JUL 1821	MR(ON); UC:W31; WB8:194; MB
BUCKLAND, William	LYNN, Ann "Nancy" d/o Adam Lynn	c.24 NOV 1795	FPC:4(JM); DBA:205 HCM:91; PGM
BUCKLER, James	GILLBREATH, Mary	27 AUG 1812	MR(IR); MB
BUCKLEY, James	GOULD, Julia	29 JAN 1826	AG:9/2/26:3(JR)
BUCKLEY, John D.	LEGG, Margaret d/o Eli Legg	25 AUG 1817	MR(AG); MB
BUCKLEY, Nimrod	SMOOT, Eliza third d/o George Smoot	NOV 1820	SP; AG:12/1/21:3
BUCKLEY, Samuel G. Place: Fairfax Co.	REEVES, Nancy	10 SEP 1815	PW:61
BUCKNER, Richard	_____, Catherine	-2 OCT 1798	DBQ:511
BUDD, _____	_____, Amy	-11 DEC 1793	AG:18/12/93:3
BULL, Rev. George S.	JOURDAN, Rebecca A. of St. Mary's Co. MD	25 MAY 1815	BA:1/6/15(BW); MB
BUNUFF, John	KEACH, Elizabeth	14 SEP 1815	MR(IR); MB
BURCH (also see "Birch")			
BURCH, Joseph N. Place: Montgomery Co. MD, eldest d/o Dr. Wm. Brewer	BREWER, Ellen	13 JAN 1825	AG:22/1/25:3
BURCHELL, Edward	BATES, Ann	20 FEB 1821	MR(IR); MB
BURFORD, Henry	_____, Rositter		1799:34; 1800:58
BURFORD, John A.	DYSON, Hannah	23 FEB 1804	FPC:4(JM); MB
BURFORD, John Atkins	SMITH, Mary	c.9 OCT 1802	MB
BURGESS, William	THOMSON, Nelly	3 DEC 1799	FPC:4(JM)
BURKE, James	POWER, Ann	SEP 1793	FPC:4(JM)
BURKE, Levi	COFFER, Jane Catharine	31 DEC 1829	AG:8/1/30:3(JR); FWZ:368
BURKE, Richard	_____, Margaret	-24 JUN 1785	HCOrd:24/6/85
BURKE, Richard	_____, Frances	-24 NOV 1785	HCOrd:24/11/85
BURKE, Richard S.	McDENNICK, Mary Ann	18 FEB 1830	MR(EH); MB; AG:24/2/30:3(EH)
BURNET, Francis	STEWART, Elizabeth	1 MAR 1818	MR(WHW)
BURNS, James Place: Washington DC	WATKINS, Catherine	29 APR 1823	AG:1/5/23:3

Husband	Wife	Event or Marriage	Reference(s)
BURROWS, John	PAYNE, Jane	c.27 APR 1824	MB
BURROWS, Capt. Robert	BROWN, Sophia	17 OCT 1830	MB; AG:21/10/30:3
BURSON, Stephen T.	MYERS, Rebecca	17 JAN 1822	MR(ON); MB
BURTON, Thomas W.	BUCKEY, Caroline M.	c.23 DEC 1828	MB
BUSHBY, James	BOYER, Margaret E.	11 JUN 1838	MR:61; UC:W58
BUSHBY, William	_____, Mary	-14 JUN 1788	HCD:440; 1787:70; 1791:5; FDR:265
BUSHBY, William	HITE, Mary d/o Jacob Hite	c.26 AUG 1794	FRSD2:210; AG:21/2/17:3
BUSSELL, William	CLARK, Rhody	c.15 APR 1809	FPC:34(JM); MR(JM); MB
BUTCHER, John Place: Pennsylvania	EVANS, Ann	30 OCT 1770	HCF:405; 1787:70; 1791:5; 1799:26; 1800:57; FMI
BUTCHER, Jonathan	ROSS, Phoebe d/o David Ross	4 SEP 1806	H:735; DBW:339
BUTLER, _____	PRICE, Elizabeth d/o David Price	-23 FEB 1785	FWE:62
BUTLER, Abraham	DULANY, Mary G.	c.6 SEP 1821	MB
BUTLER, David	HARRIS, Selia	c.2 DEC 1823	MB
BUTLER, Edward	WATKINS, Elizabeth	c.26 NOV 1810	MB
BUTLER, Edward G.W. Place: *Woodlawn*, Fairfax Co., d/o Maj. Lawrence Lewis of *Woodlawn*	LEWIS, Frances Parke	4 APR 1826	AG:12/4/26:3; SP; UT:11/4/27:3
BUTLER, Eliab C.	TURLEY, Susan	22 DEC 1827	AG:30/1/28:3(JR)
BUTLER, Harry	HOYE, Nelly d/o Francis Hoye	c.1 MAR 1827	MB
BUTLER, Horatio	FORRESTER, Lucy	c.24 DEC 1807	MB
BUTLER, John Place: Fairfax Co.	TAYLOR, Catharine	7 APR 1815	PW:67; DCM
BUTLER, Silas Place: New York City NY	WALDRON, Phebe	c.8 JAN 1814	AG:8/1/14:3
BUTLER, William	SMOOT, Mary eldest d/o George Smoot	25 DEC 1820	SP; AG:12/1/21:3
BUTLER, William H. Place: Fairfax Co.	JENKINS, Frances d/o Elisha Jenkins	DEC 1822	PW:67; FDX3:188
BUTTS, Adam	HESS, _____ si/o Jacob Hess	-23 FEB 1788	FWE:251; 1787:70; 1791:5, 11; CCG:A4
BUTTS, Augustus	TATTERSON, Catharine	c.5 JUL 1817	MB
BUTTS, Capt. Mark	WINTERBURY, Elizabeth d/o John Winterbury	1 MAR 1798	FPC:4(JM); 1799:24; AA:2/3/98:3; CCC(29)
BYRD, Thomas	ELLZEY, Patience d/o Lewis Ellzey	-1 OCT 1785	FWE:223; FLC1788:80
BYRD, Thompson C. Place: Fairfax Co.	ROSE, Lavinia	26 SEP 1822	PW:68; AG:5/10/22:2(JR)
BYRNE, Patrick	_____, Margaret	-27 SEP 1796	HCH:475; HCI:392

Husband	Wife	Event or Marriage	Reference(s)

C

CABLE, George	STOTT, Polly	16 JUN 1810	MR(IR); MB
CADDIS, David	HENDERSON, Sarah	5 JUL 1820	MR(ON); MB
CADDIS, Henry	HEATH, Adeline	c.2 DEC 1828	MB
CADEN, James	WHITE, Eleanor M.	18 MAY 1820	MR(JF); MB; AG:20/5/20:3(JF)
CAIN, John	_____, Eloisa	-19 JAN 1787	HCOrd:19/1/87
CAIN, John	HAMILTON, Lucy	15 NOV 1817	MR(WHW); MB
CAIRNS, William Douglass of Gloucester Co.	DENEALE, Mary Catharine d/o George Deneale	3 MAY 1826	MB; AG:4/5/26:3(RK)
CAITHER, Samuel	MEARSHEIMER, Mary	1 JUN 1797	FPC:7(JM)
CALDWELL, James H. Place: Fredericksburg	WORMELEY, Mrs. Maria Carter	25 NOV 1819	AG:29/11/19:3
CALDWELL, Josiah F.	MAGRUDER, Maria H.	27 NOV 1815	AG:29/11/15:3(JM); MR(JM); MB
CALLAHAN, James	WALLHOUSE, Rebecca	11 AUG 1790	FPC:7(JM)
CALLEHAN, Patrick	SUMERILLE, Jane	-11 FEB 1799	FDB2:194
CALLENDER, Bartholomew	LATHAM, Ellinder	c.13 NOV 1806	MB
CALLIT, Joseph	DAY, Ann	c.4 JUN 1816	MB
CALVERT, Henry	WILLIS, Ellenor	6 JUL 1821	MR(IR); MB
CAMPBELL, Hugh Place: Baltimore MD	DEATH, Mariah T.	MAY 1815	AG:11/5/15:3(I)
CAMPBELL, James	_____, Leah	-11 OCT 1803	CCG:A1
CAMPBELL, Capt. James	CAHILL, Catharine "Kitty"	25 JUL 1805	WB3:1; 1791:5; MB; AG:26/7/05; MB
CAMPBELL, James	WILSON, Malvina Allen youngest d/o James Wilson	25 NOV 1828	AG:27/11/28:3(EH); NI:29/11/28; MB
CAMPBELL, John	LOCKHART, Marian	-24 DEC 1782	HCA:26; 1787:71
CAMPBELL, Loudon	_____, Ann	-30 NOV 1825	TMCC(N:4)
CAMPBELL, Loudon	_____, Hetty	-8 JAN 1834	TMCC(N:4)
CAMPBELL, Robert Place: Winchester	M'MUNN, Fanny d/o George M'Munn	12 DEC 1810	AG:28/12/10:3
CAMPBELL, Robert Place: Bellmont, Loudoun Co.,	LEE, Mary Ann d/o Ludwell Lee	12 JUN 1815	AG:16/6/15:3(ON)
CAMPBELL, William	SMEDLEY, Elizabeth	27 JUL 1818	MR(IR); MB
CANBY, Samuel Place: Loudoun Co.	HOUGH, Elizabeth	25 FEB 1770	QM:44; IGI
CANBY, William	JANNEY, Sarah d/o Abel Janney	2 NOV 1820	H:735
CANNELL, Isaac	_____, Sarah	-AUG 1824	AG:/26/8/24
CANNON, John Newton	WATTLES, Ann	5 JUN 1802	MR(JM); MB
CANNON, Joseph	BROWN, Amie	c.18 DEC 1817	MB
CANNON, Granderson	SINCOX, Mary		TMCC(G:3)
CANNON, Nathaniel	HALL, Elizabeth	15 DEC 1796	FPC:7(JM)
CANNON, Washington	SIMMES, Ann	c.28 MAY 1822	MB
CARBERY, Capt. Thomas Place: Washington DC	MANNING, Mary H.	2 NOV 1826	UT:4/11/26:3
CARD, John	ALLEN, Mrs. Mary Jane	18 JUL 1799	FPC:7(JM); AA:20/7/99:3
CAREW, Capt. Thomas	KORN, Margaret	2 OCT 1806	AG:3/10/06:2(TD); MB
CAREY, Benjamin	LUTZ, Catherine	17 JUN 1796	FPC:7(JM)

Husband	Wife	Event or Marriage	Reference(s)
CAREY, John Ellicott	IRWIN, Anna Head d/o Thomas Irwin	2 MAR 1820	H:735; QM:48; AG:4/3/20:3
CAREY, Patrick	REED, Jane	OCT 1793	FPC:7(JM)
CARLENDER, Bartholomew	LATHAM, Ellender d/o William Latham	c.13 NOV 1806	MB
CARLIN, George W.	HARRIS, Elizabeth	20 APR 1810	MR(IR); TMCC(L:3); MB
CARLIN, James	SKYDMORE, Letitia	22 NOV 1821	AG:26/11/21:3; MB
CARLIN, Westley	RICHARDS, Catharine	c.5 JUL 1811	MB
CARLIN, William	_____, Sarah	-22 MAR 1779	HCH:303; FDP:290
CARLIN, William	_____, Elizabeth	-22 NOV 1813	DBX:220; WB2:378
CARLISLE, Christopher	MANDEVILLE, Ann	c.22 MAY 1811	MB
CARLISLE, Daniel	DOUGLASS, Martha	11 MAY 1789	FPC:7(JM)
CARLL, James	_____, Ann		1800:54
CARLOS, Francis	DeWARREN, Mary	c.10 APR 1805	MB
CARLYLE, Maj. John	FAIRFAX, Sarah d/o William Fairfax	-22 JAN 1761	TA:85; FPCG; FWD:203
CARMICHAEL, Dr. Edward	TAYLOR, Sarah L.	c.1819	SPC(146:4); IGI
CARLYLE, John	WEST, Sybil d/o Hugh West	22 OCT 1761	DBN:395; AHM:6/1:21
CARNE, Joseph	DAVIS, Rebecca	17 AUG 1808	FPC:7(JM)
CARNE, Richard Libby	SHAKES, Cecelia Cath. Latruite d/o John Shakes	3 JUL 1821	MR(JF); MB; AG:6/7/21:3(JF)
CARNES, Wm. D.	DANEAL, Catherine	1826	MR(RK)
CAROLIN, Hugh	LATIMER, Mercy Hawkins	-24 OCT 1808	DBQ:257; TMCC(N:6)
CAROLIN, Westley	RICHARDS, Catharine	c.5 JUL 1811	MB
CARPENTER, Randall	WILLIAMS, Sophia	28 MAY 1816	MR(JMH); MB
CARR (also see "Kerr")			
CARR, Caldwell Place: Washington DC	REYNOLDS, Cornelia d/o Enoch Reynolds	13 JAN 1829	AG:17/1/29:3
CARR, David	GALLAHAN, Eleanor	c.18 NOV 1815	MB
CARRINGTON, Eli	KELL, Alesanna	31 AUG 1815	MR(IR); MB
CARROLL, James	HUTSON, Mary Ann	c.9 AUG 1824	MB
CARROLL, Sinclair	JOHNSTON, Agnes	9 MAY 1802	MR(JM)
CARROLL, Sinclair	ALEXANDER, Ann	c.12 MAY 1802	MB
CARSON, Dr. James	BROWN, Ursula	-4 MAY 1808	B1; CCC(5)
CARSON, John	JEROME, Elizabeth	21 MAY 1809	TMCC(F:5); FPR:7(JM); MR(JM); MB
CARSON, Nehemiah Place: Baltimore MD	BULL, Rachel	18 SEP 1806	BA:25/9/06(LR)
CARSON, Dr. Samuel	HAMILTON, Jane	28 NOV 1806	CCC(5); FPC:7(JM); AG:29/11/06(JM); MB; AG:19/1/28:3
CARTER, A.G. Place: *Salona*	CARTER, Elizabeth L. d/o Mrs. Ann B. Maffitt, of Fairfax Co.	21 DEC 1830	AG:24/12/30:3
CARTER, Bernard Moore Place: *Sully*	LEE, Lucy Grymes d/o Gen. Henry Lee	30 NOV 1802	AG:4/12/02:3
CARTER, Ellzey	HOWARD, Elizabeth	c.16 JAN 1828	MB
CARTER, James	BRADDOCK, Nancy d/o Robert Braddock	-27 AUG 1812	WB1:206
CARTER, James	EARLE, Lucinda d/o Esaias Earle	-23 AUG 1826	WB3:292

Husband	Wife	Event or Marriage	Reference(s)
CARTER, James B. Place: Fairfax Co.	DULIN, Maria d/o Edward Dulin	2 NOV 1816	AG:4/11/13:3(WW)
CARTER, John	JOHNSON, Reb.	5 JUN 1796	WG:15/6/96:3
CARTER, Libren	HOWARD, Nancy	c.26 JUN 1826	MB
CARTHINGTON, John	_____, Prisiler		1800:58
CARTWRIGHT, Seth	LEVERING, Mary	SEP 1792	FPC:7(JM); WB1:31; 1799:24; 1800:59; CCC(7); ACFF[14]
CARUSI, Nathaniel	HOLLEYWOOD, [Mary] Jane	16 NOV 1830	AG:19/11/30:3[15]; MR(EH); MB
CARVEL, Peter	LOWE, Catherine	23 JUN 1790	FPC:7(JM); 1787:71
CARVER, William	_____, Mary Ann		1800:56
CARY, Joseph	_____, Mary Elenor	-28 FEB 1800	WBA:167; 1799:30; 1800:53
CARY, Nicholas	ARMSTRONG, Isabella	14 DEC 1808	MR(IR)
CARY, Wilson Jefferson	RANDOLPH, Virginia d/o Thomas Mann Randolph	-2 MAY 1852	SPC(145:4)
CASH, Craven Place: St. Francisville LA	DAVIS, Evelina W.	22 MAR 1825	AG:30/4/25:3
CASH, Joseph	JAVINS, Sinah	c.2 JAN 1804	MB
CASH, William, Jr.	_____, Mary	-3 NOV 1796	HCH:353
CASSETTE, Solomon (Cassidy)	BATES, Jane	c.27 DEC 1788	FB; DBZ:283; WB2:121
CASSIDY, William B. Place: Georgetown DC	CASH, Eliza V. d/o Joseph Cash	25 JAN 1816	DBC2:226; FMI; AG:27/1/16(B); DCM
CASSO, John Joseph	HEATH, Margaret	2 MAY 1799	FPC:7(JM)
CATLET, Joseph	DAY, Ann	c.4 JUN 1816	MB
CATLET, Peter	MEEKS, Susannah	c.1770	1800:59; IGI
CATLETT, Charles Jeff. Place: *Woodville*	FAIRFAX, Ann d/o Bryan, Lord Fairfax	1 MAY 1806	AG:2/5/06:3(JM); FPC:7(JM)
CATLETT, George W.	MURRAY, Mrs. Margarett	c.8 JUL 1823	MB
CATON, John R.	GRIGSBY, Eliza d/o Enoch Grigsby	11 APR 1822	AH:19/4/22; AG:16/4/22:3
CATON, William G.	BUCKLY, Artimesi	24 JAN 1826	AG:27/1/26:3(JR)
CATTERTON, Thomas Ward	FINNIX, Linney	23 FEB 1804	MR(WM); MB
CATTS, Samuel Walker	LEGG, Elizabeth Hughes d/o Eli Legg	27 DEC 1815	MR(JMH); MB
CAVERLY, Joseph	_____, Ann	-21 SEP 1786	1787:71; HCOrd:21/9/86
CAWOOD, Benjamin	FERGUSON, Anna	12 NOV 1814	FPC:7(JM); MB
CAWOOD, Benjamin H.	MAGEE, Mary Ann	9 JUL 1829	MR(LA); MB; AG:13/7/29:3(LA)
CAWOOD, Daniel	M'AFEE, Mary	16 MAR 1816	AG:19/3/16:3(WHW); TMCC(K:3);MR(WHW); MB
CAWOOD, Grafton	MADDEN, Sally R.	24 FEB 1824	AG:26/2/24:3(WA); MR(WA); MB
CAWOOD, Moses O.B.	ROBINSON, Delilah[16]	13 JAN 1818	TMCC(D:4); MR(AG); MB; AG:17/1/18:3
CAZENOVE, Anth. Chas.	HOGAN, Anne	29 JUN 1797	DBD:15; 1799:16; FS:7/90:73; FPCC(43:107)

Husband	Wife	Event or Marriage	Reference(s)
CAZENOVE, Charles I. Place: Boston MA	GREENLEAF, Sarah E. d/o Samuel Greenleaf	19 SEP 1826	AG:26/9/26:3; NI:27/9/26; UT:27/9/26:3
CHAMBERLAIN, Lincoln	HARRIS, Mary d/o Joseph Harris	3 NOV 1822	MR(EH); MB; AG:5/11/22:3(EH)
CHAMBERLAIN, Luther	ADAM, Jane S. d/o John Adam	18 JAN 1825	MR(WA); MB; AG:22/1/25:3(WA)
CHANCE, John	PAGET, Mrs. Mary	14 MAR 1814	MR(WHW); MB
CHANDLEE, George	BROOKE, Deborah	27 AUG 1783	H:474
Place: Fairfax Meeting House, d/o James Brooke			
CHANDLER, Lemuel Place: Windham CN	FOWLER, Mary d/o Samuel Gardner Fowler	2 APR 1807	AG:19/2/11; IGI
CHANDLER, Walter Story Place: Anne Arundel Co. MD	ROGERS, Margaret	19 SEP 1799	DBH:326; IGI
CHAPIN, Charles	WISE, Mary Ann Martha d/o George Wise	4 DEC 1827	MB; OT:48; CCC(12); AG:8/12/27:3
CHAPIN, Gurden s/o Dr. Benjamin	REEDER, Margaret "Peggy" d/o Thomas Reeder	31 JAN 1793	FPC:7(JM); WB1; 1787:70; 1791:6; 1799:16; WB4:374; CCC(12); NE:74; AG:2/2/93:3
CHAPMAN, Thomas	EWELL, Susanna	-10 JUL 1830	WB4:142
CHAPMAN, Charles Thomas	GADSBY, Margaret Sarah	15 OCT 1807	AG:16/10/08:3(SY); MB
CHAPMAN, George	ALEXANDER, Susan Pearson	3 JAN 1799	1791:6; DBA:170; WB7:157; 1799:18
CHAPMAN, George	MACRAE, Amelia	c.9 JUN 1774	DBD:438; 1791:6; DBZ:355; HCM:5; WB1:333; PC
CHAPMAN, John Grant	CHAPMAN, Susan P.A.	3 JAN 1821	CLB:25; P:188
CHAPMAN, John Seabury Place: *Thoroughfare*	CHAPMAN, Matilda L. Alexander eldest d/o George Chapman	9 MAR 1826	CLB:25; FPCC(44:142); AG:15/3/26:3; NI:18/3/26; P:164
CHAPMAN, Nathaniel	PEARSON, Constantia	31 AUG 1732	PC; FWG:359; FWF:1; P:376[17]; FWB:339
CHAPMAN, Pearson	ALEXANDER, Sigismunda Mary	-13 FEB 1827	P:165
CHAPPELL, John	YAYMAN, Mary	c.1782	R1:191
CHARLES, Duncan	STONE, Margaret	3 NOV 1796	FPC:7(JM); 1799:32
CHASE, Peter	SMALLWOOD, Eleanor	c.9 APR 1803	MB
CHISSON, Lewis	FREEMAN, Ann	4 OCT 1801	FPC:7(JM); MR(JM)
CHATHAM, Henry	_____, Fanny	c.DEC 1830	AG:10/12/30
CHATHAM, James	_____, Dianer		1799:30; 1800:53
CHAUNCEY, John	_____, Elizabeth		MPC:W175
CHEW, Joseph	_____, Mercy	-1 SEP 1753	FDC:635
CHEW, Roger			1787:71
CHESHEUR, Archibald	SHANKS, Rosanna	11 MAY 1813	AG:18/5/13:3
CHICHESTER, Richard	McCARTY, Sarah d/o Daniel McCarty	-23 JUL 1786	DBA:239; FWG:194
CHICK, Charles	GOODING, Eleanor	SEP 1795	FPC:7(JM)
CHICK, William M.	SMITH, Ann Eliza d/o Joseph Smith	9 APR 1816	AG:13/4/16:3(JH); MR(JMH); MB
CHILDS, David	MITTCHUM, Mary	22 JAN 1806	MR(IR); MB

Husband	Wife	Event or Marriage	Reference(s)
CHILDS, John	ADAMS, Margaret d/o William Adams	-14 JUL 1801	DBA:135; FDY2:411; WB3:319
CHILDS, Thomas	CORYTON, Ann Eliza ni/o Gen. Adam Lynn	5 JAN 1819	AG:7/1/19:2(WHW); SPC(32:1); SP
CHILDS, William	ALLISON, Rebecca d/o James Allison	c.7 MAR 1815	MB
CHING, Thomas Place: Devon, Eng.	SHEPHERD, Grace d/o John & Elizabeth Shepherd	31 MAR 1803	TMCC(J:5); WB4:179; IGI
CHISHOLM, John	GRIGSBY, Mary Ann	5 JAN 1801	MR(JM)
CHISSOM, Lewis	FREEMAN, Ann	c.3 OCT 1801	MB
CHRISTIE, John	JACKSON, Jane	29 NOV 1808	FPC:7(JM)
CHRISTMAN, John	BARR, Elizabeth	25 NOV 1804	AG:26/11/04:3(JM); MB
CHRISTOPHE, Christian	COX, Harriet	15/16 APR 1811	FPC:7(JM); MB; AG:22/4/11:3(JM)
CHURCH, Gilbert	HAYES, Sarah	12 MAR 1807	FPC:7(JM); MB
CHURCH, Henry	McCALLESTER, Margaret	7 MAY 1802	MR(JM); MB
CHURCH, Samuel Place: Washington DC	STEVENSON, Amelia	15 MAY 1827	AG:18/5/27:3(JDa)
CHURCH, Thomas	TURLEY, Jane d/o Paul Turley	-23 MAR 1772	FWC:221; FPCC
CHURCHMAN, Frederick	_____, Mary	-28 JAN 1821	WB2:419; 1799:22
CHURCHMAN, John	_____, Ann		SPC
CHURCHMAN, John	_____, Elizabeth	-10 DEC 1844	UC:E192
CLAGETT, Benjamin D. Place: Georgetown DC	BENNETT, Mary d/o Dozier Bennett of Fairfax Co.	8 JUN 1819	AH:14/6/19(TD); AG:12/6/19:2
CLAGETT, Darius	THOMPSON, Ann Louisa d/o Jonah Thompson	18 JAN 1818	CCC(46); MR(ON); AG:24/11/19:3; MB; AG:18/1/18(ON)
CLAGETT, Horatio[18]	BARNES, Catharine "Kitty"	-12 NOV 1813	OT:61; CCC(105)
CLAGETT, Richard H.	RAMSAY, Sarah	11 NOV 1823	MR(WA); MB
CLAGETT, Thomas	DULANY, Julia d/o Benjamin Dulany	12 APR 1798	AG:13/4/98:3(TD)
CLAGETT, Thomas	COURTS, Eliza	c.31 AUG 1824	MB
CLAGETT, William H.	PAGE, Ann "Nancy" d/o Charles & Ann Page	15 JUN 1815	AH:19/6/15; SPC(4:1); AG:17/6/15:3(WHW); MR(WHW); MB
CLAPDORE, John Michael	VERNON, Ann	c.6 APR 1802	MB
CLARE, James	SMEDLEY, Ruth d/o David Smedley	28 DEC 1819	AG:31/12/19:3(WE)
CLARE, John M. Place: Washington DC	EMMERSON, Alitha	11 JUN 1829	AG:22/6/29:3
CLARKE, Elias	MITCHELL, Catherine	6 JAN 1825	MR(WHW); MB
CLARK, Hezekiah	CLARK, Margaret	27 NOV 1790	FPC:7(JM)
CLARK(E), Isaac	SMITH, Mary d/o John F. Smith	10 OCT 1815	BPEA:13/10/15; MB; AH:13/10/15(JM); AG:13/10/15:3(JM)
CLARK, John	LUCKETT, Cloughley	30 DEC 1799	FPC:7(JM)
CLARK, John M.	KING, Nancy	2 NOV 1815	MR(WHW); MB
CLARKE, Horatio D.	WILLIAMS, Nancy d/o Bazil Williams	26 AUG 1821	MR(ON); MB
CLARKE, Michael	_____, Elizabeth	-2 AUG 1784	FDP:91
CLARKE, Richard	_____, Sarah	-25 SEP 1783	FDO:135

Husband	Wife	Event or Marriage	Reference(s)
CLARK, Robert	MONTGOMERY, Nancy	14 NOV 1795	FPC:7(JM)
CLARKE, Samuel	TATSAPAUGH, Mary	12 OCT 1830	AG:27/10/30:3
Place: *Castle Calhoun*			
CLARK, Thomas	FORD, Jane	28 JAN 1788	R1:206
CLARK, Thomas	JONES, Elizabeth	26 SEP 1799	AG:28/09/99:3
Place: Maryland			
CLARKE, Thompson	ESSEX, Billezid	c.2 FEB 1816	MB
CLARK, William	WHEELER, Ann	3 APR 1828	AG:8/4/28:3(JR)
CLARK, William	DEAGEN, Catharine	-12 FEB 1832	TMCC(K:6)
	d/o George & Fanny Deagen		
CLARKSON, Edward	GREEN, Elizabeth H.	28 NOV 1827	SP; MR(WJ); MB;
	ward of William Call		AG:5/1/28:3(WJ)
CLEARY, Michael	_____, Mary	-3 MAY 1815	SMC
CLEMENTS, Henry	JONES, Elizabeth	16 AUG 1817	MR(AG); MB
CLEMENTS, Capt. Robert H.	_____, Lucretia	c.DEC 1822	AG:2/1/23
CLEMENTS, Capt. Robert H.	RAMSAY, Alice L.	19 JUL 1825	MR(Sco); MB;
			AG:21/7/25:3(Sco)
CLEMENTS, Samuel	GARRETT, Eleanor	OCT 1792	FPC:7(JM)
CLEMENTS, William	BOOTH, Sarah	2 JUN 1802	MR(JM); DBR:315;
			FPC:7(JM); MB
CLEMENTSON, George	SANFORD, Jane	c.16 SEP 1790	AG:16/09/90:2;
	d/o Capt. Robert Sanford		1799:26; 1800:58
CLEVELAND, James	JOHNSON, Frances	-1 MAY 1769	FWC:177
	d/o Samuel Johnson		
CLIFFORD, Nehemiah	FERGUSSON, Jenny	1 AUG 1797	FPC:7(JM); 1787:71;
			1791:6
CLIFFORD, Nehemiah	NELSON, Nancy	21 AUG 1805	MR(IR); MB
CLIFFORD, Obedier	_____, Betsey		1800:54
CLINE, William H.	WINDSOR, Rosanna N.	13 DEC 1830	AG:17/12/30:3
Place: Rockville MD			
CLINTON, Samuel	LINDSAY, Susanna	JUN 1792	FPC:7(JM)
CLOUD, James	ALEXANDER, Ann	23 SEP 1819	AH:27/9/19(RO)
COAD, John	_____, Drady	-18 JUN 1818	WB2:240
COAD, John	DAW, Mary Ann	c.1 JAN 1820	DCM
COAKE, William	BOWIE, July Ann	28 SEP 1823	AG:30/9/23:3
Place: Georgetown DC			
COALE, Lewis	HOUGH, Amelia	1 DEC 1825	H:750
	d/o Mahlon Hough		
COATES, Samuel	SAUNDERS, Lydia	12 MAR 1775	FWF:251; IGI;
Place: Philadelphia PA	d/o Joseph Saunders of Philadelphia		FDP:290
COBURN, Priemier	MOODY, Jane	9 FEB 1797	FPC:7(JM)
COCHRAN, William	_____, Deborah	-20 AUG 1811	DBV:300
COCHRELL, William	DAVIES, Jane	24 FEB 1829	AG:27/2/29:3(JW)
Place: Dumfries			
COCKBURN, Martin	BRONAUGH, Ann	c.1756	5GM:88; IGI
	d/o Jeremiah Bronaugh		
COCKERELL, Richard H.	COLEMAN, Ann	8 DEC 1823	AG:17/1/24:3
COCKERELL, Thomas	LUCAS, Million	-13 FEB 1786	R2:90(SG)
COCKERILL, Benjamin D.	THOMAS, Ann	23 APR 1829	AG:29/4/29:3(JR)
COCKRILL, Jeremiah	TILLETT, Winny	25 MAY 1828	AG:3/6/28:3(JR)
COCKRILL, Martin	STONEMETZ, Mary	1 JAN 1805	MR(IR); MB
	d/o Casper Stonemetz		
COCKSON, Charles	GULATT, Mary	c.29 AUG 1822	MB

Husband	Wife	Event or Marriage	Reference(s)
COFFER, George	POSEY, Sarah ward of Ignatius Allen	c.17 FEB 1825	MB
COFFIN, Daniel	FINDLEY, Sarah	17 DEC 1801	FR(JM); MB(JM)
COFFIN, John	BENNETT, Elizabeth	5 JUN 1802	MR(JM); MB
COGAN, Anthony	ROOE, Maria	c.7 APR 1823	MB
COHAGEN, John	WRIGHT, Anne	20 OCT 1799	FPC:7(JM); 1800:52
COHAGEN, John	BOWIE, Elizabeth	24 MAY 1812	FPC:7(JM); DBE2:66; SPC(76:2); MR(JM); AG:27/5/12:3; MB
COHAGEN, John F.	GUEST, Sarah E. d/o Robert Guest	12 JUL 1829	AG:17/7/29:3
COHEN, William	CARY, Catharine	30 APR 1801	MR(JM); FPC:7(JM); DBW:366; SPC(54:2); MB
COLBERT, Thomas	EARP, Jane	14 AUG 1800	FPC:7(JM)
COLE (also see "Coles")			
COLE, James	PARSONS, Elizabeth	14 NOV 1822	MR(ON); MB
COLE, James (C)	BOYLE, Lucy (C)	c.4 DEC 1826	MB; MR(RK)
COLE, James (C)	MORGAN, Elizabeth (C)	c.4 APR 1811	MB
COLE, Lewis	HOUGH, Amelia	c.22 DEC 1825	QM:31
COLE, Sollomen (C)	_____, Nancey (C)		1800:55
COLE, Capt. Thomas	HAND, Tryphosa N. d/o John Hand	6 NOV 1806	FPC:7(JM); MB; AG:7/11/06:3(JM)
COLE, William	_____, Fillis		1799:24; 1800:58
COLEGATE, Edward	LAWS, Ann E. d/o Elizabeth Laws	14 AUG 1823	MB; AG:16/8/23:3(WHW)
COLEMAN, Capt. George	MARSTELLER, Elizabeth	25 SEP 1806	AG:26/9/06:3(TD); DBZ:459; SPC(33:1); MB
COLEMAN, James	BARKER, Eliza	14 DEC 1826	AG:20/12/26:3(JR)
COLEMAN, James Prater	CAROLIN, Caroline d/o Hugh Carolin	c.14 MAY 1832	MR:68; OT:51; TMCC(M:6)
COLEMAN, Joseph, Sr.	_____, Alice	-19 JAN 1810	WBC:344
COLES (also see "Cole")			
COLES, Hezekiah	JONES, Hellen	c.25 DEC 1823	MB
COLLARD, George Place: Fauquier Co.	JOHNSON, Elizabeth	30 APR 1792	DBF:450; IGI
COLLARD, Samuel	DARRELL, Mrs. Rachel wid/o William Darrell	18 JUL 1799	FPC:7(JM); FC#99a
COLLARD, Samuel	BURKE, Margaret	-10 JAN 1838	FDD3:570
COLLEN, Samuel	_____, Elizabeth		1800:54
COLLINSWORTH, A.D.	TENNISON, Mary Ann d/o James Carter	14 SEP 1827	MR(Sco); MB; AG:15/9/27:3(Sco)
COLLINS, Thomas	LINDSAY, Ellen	c.10 MAY 1830	MB
COLLINS, William A.	SLATFORD, Sarah	13 JUN 1802	MR(JM); MB
COLONE, Vincent	DONALDSON, Catharine	17 MAR 1810	MR(IR); MB
COLSTON, Joseph	ANDERSON, Nancy	c.3 MAY 1806	MB[19]
COLTART, William Place: Kirkcudright, Scot.	KIRKPATRICK, Katharine	9 JAN 1762	HCD:398;FDZ1:352;IGI
COLUMBUS, Charles	RIXTER, Eliza	2 NOV 1820	MR(JF); MB
COLVERT (see "Calvert")			
COLVILL, Thomas	_____, Francina "Frances"	-8 OCT 1766	FWB:424
COMPTON, Cyrus	TALBOT, Elizabeth M.	27 OCT 1819	AG:3/11/19:3(SC)

Husband	Wife	Event or Marriage	Reference(s)
COMPTON, Henry T.	SWANN, Ann	17 NOV 1797	WB3:210; AG:6/12/21; PGM
CONDON, Richard	_____, Mary	-20 AUG 1793	HCE:377
CONN, Gerrard Trammell	DONALDSON, Mildred	-1756	FWB:275; FWE:10
	d/o William Donaldson and Sybil Reagan		
CONN, Gerrard Trammel	GIBSON, Amelia Thame	-11 FEB 1794	HCE:245; FWE:19
	d/o Sybill Gibson		
CONN, Philip	_____, Catherine	-7 OCT 1785	DBH:227; HCI:344; 1787:71; 1791:6
CONN, Philip	SMITH, Ann	c.13 JUL 1809	MB
CONN, Thomas	LAKE, Cassina	7 FEB 1791	FPC:7(JM); 1787:70;
	d/o Richard Lake		FDX:31
CONNER, John	McATEE, Catharine L. Wales	-13 FEB 1786	R2:90(SG)
CONNER, Francis	APPLEBY, Elizabeth	19 DEC 1796	FPC:7(JM)
CONNEY, Dennis	COCKRILL, Susanna	OCT 1792	FPC:7(JM)
CONRAD, Dr. Edward	ROBERDEAU, Harriet	16 FEB 1809	DBZ:141;
Place: Winchester			AG:2/3/09:3
CONSOLOE, Capt. Samuel	BYRNE, Mary	14 FEB 1811	AG:22/2/11:3
	d/o Patrick Byrne		
CONWAY, John Spann	CHAPLINE, Susannah	c.1765	HCA:101; IGI; HCOrd:19/5/85
CONWAY, Joseph	_____, Lucy	-19 MAR 1787	HCC:7
CONWAY, Richard	WEST, Mary	-27 MAR 1776	HCA:10; 1787:71;
	d/o John West		1791:6
			WBB:370; FWD1:25
CONWAY, Richard	ASHTON, Margaret	c.8 NOV 1806	MB
CONWAY, Robert	_____, Mary	-19 MAY 1785	HCOrd:19/5/85
CONWAY, Robert	SWEET, Margaret	22 MAY 1809	FPC:7(JM); MB
CONWAY, Robert	JAMIESON, Margaret	-23 FEB 1814	DBY:498; WB4:60; FPCC(44:131)
(Cook and Cooke)			
COOK, George	SPICKETT, Polly	1 DEC 1796	FPC:7(JM)
COOKE, George	DALL, Eleanor Addison	-16 JUN 1815	DBZ:450, 515
COOKE, George Mason	EUSTACE, Eliza	25 MAR 1817	AG:28/3/17:3
Place: Stafford Co.	d/o Hancocke Eustace		
COOK, Rev. James	CHAMBERS, Rebecca	22 SEP 1808	AG:1/10/08:3
COOK, John	HARRISON, Matilda	25 MAY 1828	AG:3/6/28:3(JR)
COOKE, John R.	PENDLETON, Maria	30 NOV 1813	AG:2/12/13:3
Place: Martinsburg	d/o Philip Pendleton		
COOKE, Joseph	GILBRETH, Jane	19 DEC 1810	MR(IR); MB
COOK, Joseph	BAGGOTT, Anna	10 JUL 1827	MR(Sco); MB
COOK, Leonard	_____, Rebecca H.	-9 MAY 1804	DBH:214
COOKE, Leonard	SUTER, Elizabeth	29 MAY 1825	AG:31/5/25:3(ON); MB
COOKE, Lewis	_____, Elizabeth	-30 APR 1795	HCG:86
COOK, Lewis	BAYLEY, Lydia	30 NOV 1809	MR(IR); MB
	d/o Elizabeth Bayley		
COOKE, Dr. Stephen	ESTEN, Catharine	12 JUL 1782	FPC:6; HCD:449;
Place: Bermuda			1799:16; IGI
COOKE, Thomas	KING, Susanna	JUL 1792	FPC:7(JM)
COOK, Thomas	OFFUTT, Serena Malvina	12 MAY 1803	DBH:214; IGI
Place: Montgomery Co. MD			
COOK, Thomas	_____, Christiana	-10 OCT 1812	DBW:353
COOK, Whiting	POTTER, Sarah	1795	FB; FO1855:6

Husband	Wife	Event or Marriage	Reference(s)
COOK, William	KING, Mary	c.16 NOV 1809	MB
COOK, William Place: Georgetown DC	WEAVER, Elizabeth	3 FEB 1825	AG:8/2/25:3(RD)
COOK, William B.	FUGETT, Catharine	31 OCT 1819	AG:3/11/19:3(JR)
COOLEY, Azariah	TAYLOR, Susan	6 APR 1828	MR(Sco); MB
COONES (see "Koones")			
COOPER, Joel	_____, Elizabeth	-6 MAR 1786	DBE2:19; 1791:7
COOPER, Joseph	MORRIS, Ann	7 APR 1821	MR(WHW); MB
COOPER, Samuel	MASON, Sarah Maria	c.4 APR 1827	CCC(101); DCM
COOPER, Wm. (C)	DOVE, Sally (C)	9 DEC 1830	MR(LA); MB
COOPER, William, Jr.	BELL, Harriet	4 MAY 1826	UT:5/5/26:3(Mc)
COPEN, _____	YOUNG, Charlotte	-30 MAR 1810	DBS:352
COPPER, Cyrus	ARELL, Elizabeth d/o Richard Arell	-16 MAY 1774	DBA:465; HCL:319; DBK:374; FDA2:503; CRA:143; FDL:314; HCOrd:24/6/86
COPPER, Thomas	FOSTER, Sarah	12 SEP 1797	FPC:7(JM); 1787:70; 1791:7
COPPER, Thomas	COCKRILL, Nancy	2 APR 1799	FPC:7(JM)
CORDERY, Henry	GREEN, Elizabeth	7 DEC 1813	MR(ON); MB
CORE, Daniel	LAMBERT, Mary	5 AUG 1815	MR(IR); MB
CORNELADY, Peter	WEDGEWORTH, Kitty	22 OCT 1798	FPC:7(JM)
CORNWELL, Harrison	KING, Mary	20 FEB 1827	AG:5/3/27:3(JR)
CORNWELL, John B.	STEVENSON, Mary	22 APR 1824	AG:29/4/24:3(JR)
CORSE, John	TALBOTT, Julia Grenville	11 NOV 1813	SPC(43:1); MR(WHW); AG:13/11/13:3(WHW); MB
CORWIN, Stephen	HOPEWELL, Julia	26 JUN 1806	MR(IR); MB
CORYELL, George	_____, Ann	-23 MAR 1795	DBQ:249; 1787:71; 1791:7; 1799:30; 1800:52
CORYTON, Josiah	LYNN, Catherine "Kitty" d/o Adam Lynn	12 OCT 1795	DBL:17; 1799:10; AG:29/10/97:3
COULTER, Henry	McCUTCHEN, Martha d/o Jacobina McCutchen	4 JUN 1806	AG:5/6/06:3; MB
COURTNEY, Capt. Malachi Place: Westmoreland Co.	BROWN, Mary	17 AUG 1826	AG:2/9/26:3
COURTS, Daniel	PEARSON, Margaret	14 APR 1798	FPC:7(JM)
COVERT, John	DORCEY, Elizabeth	23 AUG 1807	FPC:7(JM); MB
COWAN, John	DOWNS, Sarah	17 MAR 1790	FPC:7(JM)
COWING, Robert	BIGGS, Sophia Ann	26 JUN 1829	MR(LA); MB
COWLING, John	_____, Elizabeth		MPC:W53
COWLING, Thomas	_____, Mary C.		SC
COWMAN, John P.	EDMONSON, Mary Ann	29 APR 1817	MB(ON); AG:1/5/17:3(ON)
COX, J.I.	WILKERSON, Ann d/o Walter Wilkerson	10 FEB 1814	AG:22/2/14:3(W)
COX, Jesse	HARRIS, Nancy "Ann"	9 MAR 1799	FPC:7(JM); 1800:56; LVA1:2
COX, Presley	MINOR, Mrs. Elizabeth wid/o John Minor	-21 MAY 1799	FD1798:390
COX, William	WEBSTER, Joanna Catharine	c.1 JUL 1790	AG:1/7/90:3; 1799:40

Husband	Wife	Event or Marriage	Reference(s)
COX, William	CURTIS, Mary si/o Hannah Spears	8 MAY 1811	AG:10/5/11:3(IR); MR(IR); MB
COXEN, Charles	GULLATT, Mary	29 AUG 1822	AG:3/9/22:3(IR)
COXEN, Nathaniel	GULLATT, Catharine d/o William Gullatt	18 OCT 1821	MR(IR); MB
COZEEN, John	AVEREY, Anne	9 JUL 1799	FPC:7(JM)
CRABB, John N.	GRAY, Jane	18 MAY 1806	AG:19/5/06:3(TD); MB
CRABB, Lt. Thomas	CRAVEN, Jane Louisa	19 APR 1827	AG:23/4/27:3(A)
CRABTREE, Eleazer	BELCHER, Elizabeth	5 AUG 1816	MR(JM); MB
CRAIG, Robert	_____, Mary Ann	-22 SEP 1786	HCOrd:22/9/86
CRAIG, Samuel	_____, Joanna	-12 MAY 1806	WBC:32; 1799:8; FPCG
CRAIGER, Michael	RANTHINE, Rebecca	1788	FB
CRAIK, Adam	HARRISON, Sarah d/o Robert Hanson Harrison	-3 NOV 1795	HCI:411; HCK:27; FDY:237
CRAIK, George Wash.	TUCKER, Maria Dorcas d/o Capt. John Tucker	c.3 OCT 1805	MB; B:378; WBC:175
CRAIK, Rev. Dr. James	EWELL, Marianne d/o Charles Ewell	c.1760	SV:186; WB2:56; 1787:71; BR:112; 1791:7; 1799:30; 1800:52; FPCG; AG:11/4/15:3
CRAIK, William	HALL, Hannah	9 NOV 1796	ACM
CRAIK, William	FITZHUGH, Ann Randolph d/o William Fitzhugh	29 OCT 1800	AG:1/11/00:3 WBC:308
CRAM(M), Samuel	HICKMAN, Mary	1 JAN 1812	FPC:7(JM); MB
CRAMOND, William	_____, Sarah	-17 JUN 1808	DBS:420
CRANCH, William Place: New Bedford MA	GREENLEAF, Anna "Nancy"	6 APR 1795	DBD2:480; IGI
CRANDELL, Joseph	TALBOTT, Jane d/o McKenzie Talbott	30 NOV 1806	FPC:7(JM); WB1:253; FPCG
CRANDELL, Lemuel	_____, Polly	-12 OCT 1815	DBBB:234
CRANDELL, Thomas	_____, Mary	-16 JAN 1800	FPCG
CRANDLE, James	HARCUM, Priscilla	12 APR 1821	MR(WA); MB
CRANDLE, Thomas	STRAIT, Sarah	21 JAN 1802	MR(JM); MB
CRANDLE, Thomas	MOXLEY, Maria d/o Ann Bowling	c.10 JAN 1810	MB
CRANFORD, James	ATHA, Susanna(h)	22 JUN 1826	NI:24/6/26; UT:24/6/26:3(RD)
CRANSON, John	_____, Eleanor	-29 MAR 1812	DBV:380
CRANSTON, _____	COOPER, Mary Barnett	-4 MAR 1817	DBE2:19
CRANSTON, John	COOPER, Nancy	2 AUG 1789	FPC:7(JM)
CRANSTON, Samuel	VARNELL, Mrs. Sarah	1 OCT 1822	AG:5/10/22:2(WA) MB; MR(WA)
CRAVEN, Tunis Place: Washington DC	TINGEY, Hannah d/o Capt. Thomas Tingey	25 SEP 1803	AG:29/9/03:3(Mc)
CRAWFORD, Nathaniel	BLACKBURN, Sarah Brown d/o Thomas Blackburn	-1785	WB1:337; LDP:327
CRAWFORD, John	DELAWHAN, Martha	15 DEC 1796	FPC:7(JM); 1799:2
CRAWFORD, William	HIGDON, Elizabeth	12 NOV 1822	MR(JF); MB

Husband	Wife	Event or Marriage	Reference(s)
CREASE, John Hipsley	NEWTON, Jane P.	20 OCT 1813	AG:21/10/13:3(JM); FPC:7(JM); MR(JM); MB
CREDIT, Harry (C)	COLE, Ann (C)	27 APR 1820	MR(ON); MB
CREIGHTON, Dr. Robert	_____,	-18 NOV 1801	FPCG
CREIGHTON, Robert Place: Baltimore MD	CRUSE, Eliza d/o Thomas Cruse	20 DEC 1823	NI:25/12/23
CREMITT, Ebenezer	STEWART, Mary Ann	28 JUL 1801	MR(WM); MB
CRISPIN, John	POTTER, Kitty	15 OCT 1796	FPC:7(JM)
CRISWOLD, Rev. George	COOMBE, Eliza d/o Griffith Coombe	27 MAY 1828	NI:29/5/28
CROAK, Richard	BLACKBURN, Elizabeth	21 SEP 1790	FPC:7(JM)
CROGGEN, Charles S.	HILLYARD, Mary	c.28 MAY 1830	MB(LA); MB
CRONMILLER, Samuel	MARTIN, Elizabeth	c.20 MAY 1830	MB
CROOK, Bernard	_____, Ann	-13 JAN 1807	DBQ:277; TMCC(D:1)
CROOK, Charles	MONEY, Nancy d/o Nicholas Money	c.4 JAN 1791	R1:266; FWG:434
CROOK, Jeremiah	WILLIAMS, Jane	c.1783	RWP
CROOK, Joseph	GIBBONS, Emeline Jane	c.SEP 1830	AG:28/9/30
CROOK, Thomas	PHILIPS, Polly	10 JUN 1818	MR(IR); MB
CROOK(C), William	KING, Mary	16 NOV 1809	MR(IR); MB
CROSBY, Lewis	RUSSELL, Sarah Ann	17 MAY 1809	FPC:7(JM); MB
CROSS, Reid	_____, Mary	-24 OCT 1820	TMCC(Q:1)
CROSS, Reid Place: Georgetown DC	BASSFORD, Sarah	25 JAN 1821	AG:27/1/21:3(B); DCM
CROSS, Samuel	JONES, Milly Ann	c.18 JAN 1806	MB
CROSS, Walter	NASH, Mrs. Jane	28 JUL 1821	MB; AG:3/76/21:3(EH)
CROSS, William	JOHNSTON, Sarah	24 MAR 1799	FPC:7(JM)
CROWE, Lanty	_____, Mary	-24 JUN 1794	CCG:A1; 1787:74; 1791:7
CROWE, Lanty	_____, Elizabeth	-15 MAY 1810	DBS:349
CROWLEY, Timothy	_____, Mary		1799:32; 1800:51
CROWLEY, Timothy	MAHONY, Nancy	7 FEB 1826	UT:15/2/26:2
CROZEN, Esquire	BECKLEY, Susanna	29 MAR 1825	AG:5/4/25:3(JR)
CRUMP, Daniel	SKIDMORE, Elizabeth d/o Edward Skidmore	c.23 NOV 1811	MB
CRUMP, George Place: Fairfax Co.	POWELL, Jane	11 JUL 1816	PW:106
CRUMP, Thornton	BUTLER, Teresa	c.22 SEP 1826	MB
CRUMP, Townshend	TURNER, Molly	6 OCT 1825	RMS:2
CRUSE, Thomas	_____, Anne	-2 APR 1800	FPC:6
CRYSS, Frederick	_____, Delila	-1819	SPC
CULBERT, James	DIXON, Grace	c.1 OCT 1810	MB
CULLINS, James	CARTER, Nancy	c.13 NOV 1822	MB
CUMINGS, George M.	TURNER, Elizabeth Jane	c.16 APR 1824	MB(ON)
CUMMINGS, William	McALLISTER, Fanny	22 JUN 1793	AG:26/6/93:3
CUMMINS, James	THOMAS, Mary Ann	16 MAR 1828	NI:21/3/28
CUNNINGHAM, John Scott	BROCKETT, Elizabeth d/o Robert Brockett, Sr.	-25 JAN 1848	ACFF, Wm. Gregory
CUNNINGHAM, William	FITZGERALD, Ann	13 MAY 1812	MR(IR); MB
CURBY, Thomas	BEST, Susan	10 AUG 1820	MR(IR); MB
CURRIE, James	INGLIS, Ann	-15 APR 1794	HCG:39

Husband	Wife	Event or Marriage	Reference(s)
CURRY, Anthony	MIT(T)CHELL, Nelly	c.13 AUG 1804	MB[20]
CURRY, Thomas	BARNETT, Mrs. Mary Ann	2 OCT 1817	AG:4/10/17:3(ON); MB
CURSINE, Bartholomew	CARLIN, Peggy	c.18 JUL 1807	MB
CURTAIN, Daniel	_____, Susanna	-23 DEC 1799	CRA:313
CURTIS, Isham	SMITH, Nancy	c. 1 MAR 1816	MB
CURTIS, Capt. Jacob	_____, Elizabeth	-10 AUG 1813	DBY:178; CCC(25)
CURTIS, Joseph	CHISHOLM, Elizabeth	SEP 1795	FPC:7(JM)
CUSTIS, George W.P.	FITZHUGH, Mary Lee d/o William Fitzhugh	c.7 JUL 1804	MB; WBC:308; BFG:14/7/04(TD)
CUSTIS, John Parke Place: *Mt. Airy*, Prince George's Co. MD	CALVERT, Eleanor	3 FEB 1774	P:295
CUTLAR, Roger	KIRKPATRICK, Elizabeth	-12 JAN 1785	HCD:398; FDZ:352; FWE:36
CUTTING, John B.	CARTER, Mrs. Sarah	27 DEC 1806	AG:29/12/06:3

Husband	Wife	Event or Marriage	Reference(s)

D

Husband	Wife	Event or Marriage	Reference(s)
DABNEY, John Bass Place: Dedham MA	LEWIS, Roxa	c.22 NOV 1792	HCE:50; AG:22/11/92:3
DADE, Baldwin	WEST, Catherine d/o John West, Jr.	c.1781	FWE:235; 16:T:171; FDR1:65; HCOrd:22/5/83
DADE, Capt. Chas. Stuart	ADAM, Jane d/o Robert Adam	23 MAY 1809	FPC:9(JM); B:18; WB1:182; FPCC; AG:25/5/09:3(JM); MB
DADE, Dr. Francis	SHEPHERD, Harriet s/o William Shepherd	12 DEC 1811	FPC:9(JM); MB
DADE, Langhorn(e)	SCOTT, Eliza C.	18 JUL 1816	AG:20/7/16:3(WHW); SP; MR(WHW); MB
DADE, Robert Townshend	SIMMONS, Ruth	27 DEC 1808	P:117
DADE, Rev. Townshend	SIMMONS, Mary	31 AUG 1784	P:116
DAFFEN, Joseph Green	COOK, Eliza "Betsy"	7 NOV 1799	FPC:9(JM); AG:9/11/99:3
DAILEY, Hugh	O'BRIAN, Eleanor	-7 DEC 1769	R2:2(F)
DAILEY, Richard B.	BEANE, Ann Elizabeth	c.16 AUG 1826	MB
DAILY, Edward	_____, Rebecca	-10 MAR 1810	DBS:345
DAINGERFIELD, Bathurst Place: Liverpool, Eng.	KAY, Eliza	c.1795	AM1:93; CCC(39); DBC:360; WB3:275
DAINGERFIELD, Edward	VOWELL, Margaret B.	20 OCT 1831	MR(WJ)
DAINGERFIELD, Henry	SEWALL, Susan L.B. d/o Robert Sewall	21 OCT 1823	AG:25/10/23:3; SP; NI:23/10/23
DAINGERFIELD, Henry P.	ROZIER, Harriet	-25 SEP 1810	DBT:313; CCC(39)
DAINGERFIELD, Wm. A.	ROZIER, Maria H.H. wid/o Francis Hall Rozier	c.20 NOV 1807	DBQ:168; X:70; DBA:61
DALL, James Place: Baltimore MD	LAMMING, Eleanor	18 FEB 1803	DBZ:450; IGI
DALRYMPLE, John	LEE, Lucinda	-10 FEB 1797	DBT:541
DALTON, Daniel	EMMIT, Margaret d/o D. Emmit	11 JUN 1801	MR(JM); MB
DALTON, John	SHAW, Jemima d/o Thomas Shaw	DEC 1749	Note[21]
DALZIEL, John	LYLE, Jane	-9 MAY 1812	DBW:81; DBBB:140
DANIEL, Chisley Place: Raleigh NC	WEIGHTMAN, Mary P.	9 MAY 1811	AG:14/5/11:3
DANIEL, James	WRIGHT, Sarah	31 DEC 1789	FPC:9(JM)
DANIEL, Thomas	BERRY, Catharine S. d/o Thomas Berry	c.30 JUN 1810	MB
DANIEL, William	BERRY, Julianna	c.13 NOV 1815	MB
DANIELL, Stephen of *Air Hill*, Fairfax Co.	_____, Ann W.	20 NOV 1826	AG:25/11/26:3
DARLEY, Michael Place: Baltimore MD	MILLER, Caroline	16 SEP 1788	WBB:198; 1799:14; IGI
DARLEY, Thomas	KIDWELL, Chloe	19 FEB 1807	MR(IR); DBU:322; MB
DARLING, George	ISLER, Mazey	9 MAR 1797	FPC:9(JM); FPCG; 1787:72; AG:14/3/97:3

Husband	Wife	Event or Marriage	Reference(s)
DARNE, James W.	KITCHEN, Amelia Ward d/o Daniel Kitchen	1 FEB 1786	FGRC(1977)1:109
DARNALL, Henry	GRA(Y)SON, Letty	17 MAY 1815	MR(IR); MB
DARNALL, John	TAYLOR, Rhodey	16 AUG 1810	FPC:9(JM); MB
DARRELL, George	STANHOPE, Mrs. Kitty wid/o William Stanhope	- 1812	FWR:300
DARRELL, Philip	_____, Sarah	-7 JUN 1811	DBU:364
DARRELL, William	BROOKE, Rachel	-18 JUL 1799	FPC:7(JM); FC#99a; FWG:394
DARREN, Henry	HOOFF, Elizabeth d/o Lawrence Hooff	-22 OCT 1793	WB1:130
DASHIELL, Thomas B.	McCOBB, Mary M. d/o Capt. John McCobb	29 MAR 1825	NI:4/1/25; MB
DAVENPORT, James	BROWN, Mary, of Ireland si/o Winsor Brown	-7 OCT 1799	DBB:225; 1799:16 HCM:54
DAVEY (also see "Davy") DAVEY, Davey	KEITH, Mary	25 JUL 1789	FPC:9(JM); 1791:7; FPCC; AG:31/1/06:3
DAVEY, David	BOWLING, Elizabeth "Betsy"	21 AUG 1806	MR(JM); FPC:9(JM); DBT:411; MB; WBB:403; FPCG
DAVEY, Thomas	GLANVILLE, Mary	1 NOV 1820	TMCC(C:6); MR(WA)
DAVIDSON, Capt. Bazil H.	HUNTER, Eliza d/o John Hunter	9 JUL 1807	AG:10/7/07:3(JM); FPC:9(JM); MB
DAVIDSON, Francis K.	WELLBORNE, Jane	24 MAR 1831	MR(WJ)
DAVIDSON, Capt. James	_____, Margaret	-18 AUG 1797	FPC:8; DBF:234
DAVIDSON, James	KIRBY, Nancy	c.29 SEP 1804	MB
DAVIDSON, John	_____, Maria	-7 FEB 1810	WBC:346
DAVIDSON, Lt. William B.	HUNTER, Elizabeth Chapman	5 JUL 1821	NI:9/7/21(WHW)
DAVIES, William	VIOLET, Jane E. youngest d/o John Violet	21 SEP 1830	AG:30/9/30:3(Wal)
DAVIS, Allen	_____, Ann		1800:55
DAVIS, Benjamin	_____, Ann	-26 JUL 1808	WBC:500; CCC(16); WB2:4
DAVIS, Benjamin	TURNER, Mary	24 SEP 1812	MR(WHW); MB
DAVIS, Cadwallader	WRIGHT, Mrs. Eliz. "Betsey"	16 MAR 1817	MB; AG:19/3/17:3(ON)
DAVIS, Charles	NEWTON, Mary	c.JAN 1797	WG:7/1/97:223
DAVIS, Cornelius	STANTON, Maria	30 DEC 1813	MR(IR); MB
DAVIS, Cornelius	BOLLING, Polly	12 APR 1821	MR(IR); MB
DAVIS, Daniel	GRIMES, Nancy	14 MAY 1802	MR(JM); MB
DAVIS, Daniel	CARTER, Louisa d/o Ann Carter	c.13 DEC 1830	MB
DAVIS, Edward	DAVIS, Frances	c.12 OCT 1826	MB
DAVIS, Edward	GIBSON, Mary Ann d/o William Gibson	c.18 JUN 1829	MB
DAVIS, Elias	CREBLE, Mary	c.19 NOV 1810	MB
DAVIS, Elijah	BRITTINGHAM, Elizabeth	27 APR 1800	FPC:9(JM)
DAVIS, George	HICKEY, Sarah E.	1 APR 1819	PW:113
DAVIS, Gideon	DAVIS, Nancy (Hughes)	2 FEB 1803	H:748; QM:45; IGI
DAVIS, Gideon	RHODES, Maria W. d/o William Rhodes	20 FEB 1821	NI:21/4/21(RO); MB

Husband	Wife	Event or Marriage	Reference(s)
DAVIS, Hanson	DARNE, Penelope "Penny"	-2 OCT 1799	HCM:60; DBG:25; FDJ2:263
DAVIS, Rev. Henry J.	WINTER, Jane B. d/o Walter & Jane Winter	- APR 1838	SPC(39:1)
DAVIS, Hughes	LONG, Mrs. Sarah	2 JUN 1814	BA:19/8/14(JG)
DAVIS, John	TAYLOR, Sarah "Sally"	18 JUN 1803	MR(WW); MB
DAVIS, John	SMITH, Eleanor	1788	FB; 1799:20
DAVIS, John Place: Fairfax Co.	BIDDLE, Margaret	17 JAN 1792	R2:17; 1799:16
DAVIS, John	CRANDELL, Sarah	1 AUG 1801	MR(WM); MB
DAVIS, John	WRIGHT, Sally	21 MAR 1816	MR(WHW); MB
DAVIS, John	KITELY, Matilda	20 JUN 1818	MR(ON); MB
DAVIS, John	THROOP, Elizabeth	11 JUL 1820	MR(IR); MB
DAVIS, John W.	LYNN, Nancy	5 JAN 1830	AG:8/1/30:3(JR)
DAVIS, Josiah Hewes Place: Baltimore MD	LONG, Sarah M. (Harper) wid/o Capt. Seth Long, and d/o Edward Harper	2 JUL 1814	DBC2:161; IGI; BR:104; FPCC(43:114)
DAVIS, Luke Place: Fairfax Co.	GRIMES, Ann	16 DEC 1819	CT:18/12/19(B); DCM; AG:17/12/19:3(B)
DAVIS, Moses	HENSON, Elizabeth	30 AUG 1827	MR(Sco); MB
DAVIS, Noah	YOUNG, Mary	10 JUL 1823	NI:24/7/23; MR(WA); MB
DAVIS, Peter	WILLIAMS, Jane	c.1 JUL 1824	MB
DAVIS, Presley of Nelson Co. KY	DAVIS, Mrs. Sarah Ann (Dade)	12 OCT 1814	AG:15/10/14:3(OB); FC#23v; DCM
DAVIS, Rodney	SHOEMAKER, Elizabeth		QM:51
DAVIS, Samuel	_____, Mary	-1 SEP 1795	DBA:385; 1791:7; CRA:268
DAVIS, Samuel H. Place: Grove, Fauquier Co.,	BROWNE, Mary E.B. d/o William Browne	25 OCT 1819	AH:29/10/19
DAVIS, Thomas	MARKELL, Sarah Ann Charl.	c.11 SEP 1828	MB
DAVIS, Rev. Thomas	_____, Elizabeth	-9 MAY 1800	CCG:T2; DBB:517; 1799:22
DAVIS, Thomas H. Place: Fairfax Co.	HAWLEY, Mary	20 OCT 1816	PW:115
DAVIS, Thomas M.	DADE, Sarah d/o Baldwin Dade	14 FEB 1808	AG:15/2/08:3(G)
DAVIS, Washington (C)	PIPSICO, Lucinda (C) d/o John Pipsico	13 SEP 1821	MR(ON); MB
DAVIS, William	DAVIS, Nancy	c.15 MAR 1825	MB
DAVIS, William	MILSTEAD, Sophia	5 JAN 1826	AG:11/1/26:3(JR)
DAVIS, William	MERCHANT, Martena Ann	29 AUG 1826	AG:1/9/26:3(RD);
DAVIS, William	VIOLETT, Jane E.	c.28 SEP 1828	MB
DAVIS, William	COXE, Catharine	1 JUN 1830	MR(LA); MB
DAVY (also see "Davey")			UT:1/9/26:3
DAVY, Thomas	GLANVILLE, Mary	1 NOV 1820	MR(WA)
DAWE, P.D.	PICKET, Patty W.	21 DEC 1824	AG:25/1/25:3
DAWES, Rufus	CRANCH, Elizabeth Eliot d/o Hon. William Cranch	18 APR 1829	AG:21/5/29:3
DAWSON, Philemon	ORD, Nancy	12 MAY 1818	MR(ON); MB
DAWSON, Capt. Samuel Place: Hollin Hall	MASON, Ann E. d/o Gen. Thomas Mason	2 MAR 1819	AH:5/3/19(ON)

Husband	Wife	Event or Marriage	Reference(s)
DAWSON, William	_____, Elizabeth		1800:53; 1799:30
DAY, Baldwin	GUTHRIE, Lucretia	20 JAN 1828	NI:24/1/28; SP;
	d/o Capt. John Guthrie		MR(WJ); MB;
			AG:25/1/28:3(WJ)
DAY, Dr. Benjamin	COOKE, Elizabeth Mary	11 SEP 1821	MB;
	d/o Leonard Cooke		AG:14/9/21:3(ON)
DAY, Hanson	TARLETON, Peggy	17 OCT 1822	MR(JF)[22]; MB
DAY, Horatio	DUNINGTON, Martha	18 MAY 1815	FPC:9(JM); MB
DAY, Horatio	ANDERSON, Mrs. Elizabeth	6 JAN 1822	SPC(54:2); SP;
Place: Washington DC			AG:14/1/22:3(RD)
DAY, John	PADGETT, Mary	4 JUN 1822	AH:12/6/22
DEAKINS, William	MILBURN, Jane	-9 MAY 1808	FPC:8; WB3:30;
	d/o Joseph Milburn		FPCC(42:62)
DEAN, Joseph	_____, Hannah	-16 MAY 1803	DBQ:18; 1799:12
			WB2:232; FPCC(42:75)
DEAN, Samuel	KOONES, Catherine	23 AUG 1819	AH:25/8/19; SPC(28:1);
Place: Georgetown DC			DCM; AG:25/8/19
DEARBORN, Capt. Charles	MARKLEY, Elizabeth	22 APR 1830	NI:28/4/30; MR(EH);
	d/o Capt. Markley		MB; AG:26/4/30:3(EH)
DEAVERS, William	OGDEN, Cloe	13 AUG 1820	AG:15/8/20:2(JR)
DEBUTTS, John H.	FORREST, Sophia	c.13 AUG 1818	NI:13/8/18; DCM
	d/o Joseph F. Forrest		
DEBUTTS, Richard	DULANY, Louisa F.	25 APR 1812	FPC:9(JM);
s/o Samuel DeButts	d/o Benjamin Dulany		BFR:29/4/12;
Place: Shuter's Hill, Fairfax Co.			AG:27/4/12(JM);
			NI:30/4/12
DEBUTTS, Dr. Samuel	WELBY, Mary	-16 JAN 1826	WB3:304
DeCOURCY, Wm. Henry	ROZIER, Eliza Bond	3 OCT 1815	DBC2:194;
	d/o Notley Hall Rozier		AH:6/10/15; MB;
			AG:6/10/15:3
DEEBLE, Edward	M'CLEISH, Margaret	11 JUN 1816	AG:13/6/16:3(JM);
			MR(JM); MB
DEETON, Christopher	LAMBERT, Isabell	-22 JUL 1827	TMCC(L:3)
DEGGE, Robert	EVANS, Rebecca	c.19 JUL 1814	MB
DEIZ (see Dietz)			
DeJEAN, Peter	M'PHERSON, Henrietta	8 APR 1817	AG:30/4/17:3
DeKRAFFT, F.C.	SCOTT, Harriet	13 FEB 1812	FPC:9(JM); MB
DeLaMARCH, Baron	MURRAY, Mary	c.12 OCT 1789	AG:12/10/86:3
	d/o Patrick Murray		
DELLEWAY, John W.	BARNETT, Nancy	c.28 JAN 1818	MB
DELOZIER, Daniel	ELDER, Ann	c.1772	DBX:336; IGI;
DELPHY, Bartholomew	CRAVALL, Mary	2 SEP 1817	MR(JMH); MB;
			AG:6/9/17:3
DEMAINE, Job	_____, Jane		MPC:E72
DEMENT, Richard	SHANNON, Violetta	17 NOV 1814	MR(WHW); MB
DEMPSEY, Thomas	FLEMING, Nancy	30 APR 1799	DBB:316; FDZ:486;
	d/o Thomas Fleming		AA:2/5/99:3
DENEALE (also see "Oduneal")			
DENEALE, George	PATTEN, Mary	3 JUL 1796	FPC:9(JM); WB2:241;
			VG:25/4:298;
			1787:71; 1791:8;
			1799:26; 1800:58;
			CCC(22)

Husband	Wife	Event or Marriage	Reference(s)
DENEALE, George, Jr.	SMITH, Elizabeth Doniphan	28 MAY 1806	FqMin1851:397
DENEALE, James, Sr.	CONYERS, Theodosia d/o Henry Conyers	-26 OCT 1789	FDZ:1
DENEALE, James C.	YOUNG, Ann	24 JAN 1811	AG:28/1/11:3(MB)
DENEALE, James C.	_____, Ann Jackson	-30 AUG 1815	DBZ:497
DENEALE, John C.	EARLE, Matilda d/o Esaias Earle	-23 AUG 1826	WB3:292
DENEALE, William	WEST, Sybil d/o Hugh West	-16 SEP 1786	FWE; FC#115 FDA2:233
DENNY, John P.	CRANDELL, Lucinda Const. only d/o Jane Crandell	1 JUL 1830	AG:2/7/30; NI:3/7/30; MB
DENTY, Samuel	BAILESS, Nancy	6 NOV 1830	MR(IR)
DERMOTT, James R.	JAMES, Alice	c.JAN 1797	WG:7/1/97
DESHIELDS, Joseph	MONROE, Sarah A.E.G. d/o Joseph Jones Monroe	24 MAR 1825	MR(WA); MB; AG:26/3/25:3(WA)
DETERLY, Michael	COONES, Mary	1 APR 1804	FPC:9(JM); MB[23]
DEVANN, Jonathan	IAMS, Becca	JAN 1792	FPC:9(JM)
DEVAUGHN, John	_____, Ruth	-14 AUG 1774	B10
DEVAUGHN, John	CADY, Nancy d/o Mary Cady	21 MAR 1816	MR(WHW); MPC:W49; MB
DEVAUGHN, John	WORKMAN, Catherine	8 MAY 1816	SPC(79:2); MR(JMH); MB
DEVAUGHN, Samuel	GLASGOW, Anna	AUG 1794	FPC:9(JM)
DEVAUGHN, Thomas	HARPER, Nancy	c.13 NOV 1823	MB
DEVAUGHN, William	CHURCHMAN, Mary	29 JUN 1815	MR(WHW); MPC:W24; MB[24]; B10
DEVAUGHN, William	_____, Elecia	-6 NOV 1816	DBD2:108
DEVILBISS, Christian	_____, Mary	-8 AUG 1785	DBB:94
DEWITT, Aaron	MARK, Eliza	11 JUL 1814	FPC:9(JM)
DICK, Archibald B. Place: *Clifton*, Fairfax Co.	HAMMERSLEY, Sarah S.	21 SEP 1820	AG:25/9/20:2(F); FDX2:133
DICK, David	_____, Elizabeth	-3 JAN 1799	FPC:8; FPCC(42:70)
DICK, David	POSEY, Sarah Ann	18 SEP 1810	FPC:9(JM); MB
DICK, David	ATWELL, Mary d/o John and Charity Attwil [sic]	23 FEB 1823	AG:1/3/23:3; MB
DICK, Elisha Cullen Place: Chester Co. PA	HARMON, Hannah d/o Jacob Harmon	-1 AUG 1795	HCF:196; SV:163; 1791:8; 1799:4; QC; BR:128
DICK, Joseph (C)	PIPSICO, Catharine (C)	3 JUL 1817	WB4:315; IGI; MR(WHW); MB
DIER, Thomas	_____, Susaner		1800:58
DIE(T)Z, Adam	FREDERICKSON, Eve Cath.	13 APR 1820	SP; MR(WHW)[25]; MB; AG:18/4/20:3(WHW)
DIFFENDAFFER, John	WILKES, Barbary	7 JAN 1816	MR(JMH); MB
DISNEY, John	ATHA, Catharine	22 JUN 1826	NI:24/6/26; UT:24/6/26:3(RD)
DIXON, James	_____, Elinor/Eleanor	-7 FEB 1800	CRA:314
DIXON, John	_____, Frances	-1 MAR 1798	WBB:294; CCC(47)
DIXON, John	JERRA, Mary	14 APR 1805	FPC:9(JM); MB
DIXON, John	DAVIS, Jane	c.2 JAN 1806	MB
DIXON, John	GRAY, Nelly	c.20 MAR 1806	MB
DIXON, John	WHITE, Sarah	c.17 JUN 1806	MB
DIXON, Patrick	MORAN, Henrietta	-6 OCT 1833	WB4:78

Husband	Wife	Event or Marriage	Reference(s)
DIXON, Samuel	_____, Jane		1799:28; 1800:55
DOBBIN, Archibald	_____, Mary	-9 JAN 1796	HCH:80; 1787:73
DOBER, Samuel	_____, Eliza	-23 SEP 1809	DBS:194
DOBIE, William	JEFFERSON, Nancy "Ann" d/o Jeremiah Jefferson	25 JUN 1817	MR(AG); MB
DOE, Josiah H.	BUTLER, Mary R.	13 MAY 1818	SP; MR(WHW); MB; AG:15/5/18:2(WHW)
DOERR, Conrad	REYNOLDS, Elizabeth d/o William Reynolds	18 JUN 1814	MR(IR); MB
DOGAN, Anthony s/o Philip Dogan	ROOE, Maria	7 APR 1823	MR(WA); MB[26]
DOGAN, John	FULLER, Jane	c.3 NOV 1818	MB
DOGAN, John D.	BATES, Anna Maria L.	c.NOV 1830	AG:23/11/30
DOLPHIN, Swann	CARNE, Rebecca	3 APR 1790	FPC:9(JM)
DONALDSON, Andrew	_____, Elizabeth	-9 MAR 1815	WB2:82
DONALDSON, Robert	MUIR, Elizabeth si/o John Muir	-18 APR 1796	HCG:93; HCG:93 1787:71; 1791:8
DONALDSON, Robert	BIRCH, Elizabeth	c.4 JAN 1815	MB
DONALDSON, Thomas	GREGORY, Matilda	2 NOV 1819	MR(WA); AG:4/11/19:3(WA)
DONALDSON, William	DONALDSON, Hannah	c.1 JAN 1817	MB
DONELSON, Gen. Daniel S. Place: Washington DC	BRANCH, Margaret d/o Hon. John Branch	18 OCT 1830	AG:21/10/30:3
DORAN, James	VAUGHAN, Jane	JAN 1793	FPC:9(JM); FDU:454
DORCEY, Biscoe S.	GOODS, Eliza	c.11 JUN 1811	MB
DORSET, Fielder	M'REA, Ann Allison d/o Kitty M'Rea	19 JUN 1817	MR(WHW); MB
DORSEY, Edward	_____, Mary	-20 JAN 1817	DBD2:328
DORSEY, Edward I.	ROSS, Ann	7 OCT 1823	AG:9/10/23:3(RD); MB
DORSEY, George	ROOS, Nancy	23 NOV 1819	AG:26/11/19:3(SC)
DORSEY, Miles	MOLAN, Sina	OCT 1792	FPC:9(JM)
DORSEY, Rev. Thos. J.	ROBBINS, Jane Prince d/o Rev. Isaac Robbins	24 DEC 1829	TMCC(L:2); MR(JL); MB
DOUGAN, Philip	BOTTS, Kitty	c.20 FEB 1823	MB
DOUGHERTY, Arthur	SMITH, Rebecca	27 JUN 1801	MR(JM); MB
DOUGHERTY, Daniel	SUMMERS, Jane M. s/o William Summers	14 DEC 1818	MR(JF); MB; AG:19/12/18:2(JF)[27]
DOUGHERTY, James (Douglas and Douglass)	ST. GEORGE, Nelly	JAN 1793	FPC:9(JM)
DOUGLAS, _____	HELLRIGEL, Elizabeth	-8 AUG 1807	WBC:326
DOUGLAS, Dr. Charles	_____, Susanna	-26 JAN 1797	LDX:328
DOUGLASS, Daniel	ORME, Charlotte	28 AUG 1795	FPC:8-9(JM); 1799:30; 1800:52; FPCG
DOUGLASS, Heathy A. Place: Belvoir	HENDERSON, Amey E.	12 MAR 1822	AG:20/3/22:3(WHW)
DOUGLASS, Jacob D.	GUTHRIE, Mary Ann	19 DEC 1816	MR(WHW); MB; AG:21/12/16:3(WHW)
DOUGLASS, James	_____, Mary	-26 SEP 1806	AG:26/9/06; 1791:8
DOUGLASS, James	_____, Sarah	- OCT 1810	AM:112; FPCG
DOUGLASS, James	KINCAID, Eliza	17 NOV 1812	FPC:9(JM); MB; AG:19/11/12:3(JM)

Husband	Wife	Event or Marriage	Reference(s)
DOUGLASS, James	BLUE, Jane Selina d/o John J. Blue	6 SEP 1827	AG:10/9/27:3(Gu); MB
DOUGLASS, James, Jr.	FLEMING, Margaret	25 OCT 1825	MR(WA); MB
DOUGLASS, John Orme	VOWELL, Eliza C. Keith d/o John C. Vowell	17 MAR 1819	AG:18/3/19(WA); FPCC(44:135)
DOUGLAS, John Wallace	MOXLEY, Mary	3 APR 1791	FPC:9(JM); FPCG
DOUGLASS, Richard L.	BLACKLOCK, Maria	31 DEC 1816	MR(WHW); MB; AG:2/1/17:3(WHW)
DOULYLIES, John Lane	CAMERSON, Anne	SEP 1794	FPC:9(JM)
DOVE, Jilson Place: Baltimore MD	DUGAN, Mary	1 NOV 1810	Note[28]
DOVE, John	GRANT, Nancy	7 JUL 1795	FPC:9(JM)
DOVE, Joseph	HALE, Lucinda	c.23 JUN 1810	MB
DOVER, Samuel	MOORE, Sarah	c.3 JUN 1824	MB
DOWDALL, Colin	STOKELY, Margaret	23 APR 1804	FPC:9(JM); MB
DOWELL, Jeremiah	VIOLETT, Ellen d/o Ann Violett	c.14 DEC 1815	MB
DOWNEY, _____	CARD, Elizabeth wid/o John Ramsay	-7 DEC 1802	DBF:215; FDR:242
DOWNING, _____	MILLER, Elizabeth si/o Mordecai Miller	-4 MAR 1832	WB4:44
DOWNS, Ignatius	CHRISE, Eliza	19 SEP 1818	MR(IR); MB
DOYLE, Conrad	HOOFF, Mary d/o Lawrence Hooff	-22 OCT 1793	WB1:130; 1787:71
DOYLE, Ganet	DENICK, Martha	24 NOV 1796	FPC:9(JM)
DRAKE, Edward	CAZENOVE, Juliana	11 FEB 1800	FPC:9(JM)
DRANE, Washington Place: Washington DC	DADE, Ann M.S. d/o Baldwin Dade	23 JUN 1816	AG:25/6/16:3(OB); FDY2:168; DCM
DREES, Nicholas	WARD, Hersey d/o Josiah Ward	c.16 DEC 1814	MB
DREW, Charles	HUBBALL, Mrs. Mary "Polly" wid/o John Hubball	9 DEC 1804	FPC:9(JM); MR(JM); WBA:293; MB
DRINKER, George	MILLER, Ruth d/o Warwick Miller	9 JUL 1795	H:738; HCM:133; 1799:14; QC
DRINKER, Joseph	_____, Hannah	-5 DEC 1766	QM:45
DRINNEN, Thomas	TAYLOR, Mary	10 FEB 1808	FPC:9(JM)
DRISCOLL, James W.	GOODWIN, Elizabeth		MPC:E117
DROWN, John	HIGDON, Sally	30 DEC 1805	MR(IR); MB
DROWN, Thomas	GOODS, Abey "Ebby"	29 NOV 1806	MR(IR); MB
DRYDELL, Frederick	_____, Hannah	-5 AUG 1802	DBC:508
DUCKWORTH, Charles, Jr.	KING, Elizabeth d/o Benjamin King	28 MAR 1826	UT:29/3/26:3
DUDLEY, John	WARD, Elizabeth	15 FEB 1821	MR(IR); MB
DUDLEY, John	GREENWOOD, Rebecca	c.25 DEC 1823	MB
DUDLEY, Joseph	SIMMES, Mary D.	7 FEB 1828	AG:12/2/28:3(Sco); MB; MR(Sco)
DUDLEY, William (M)	CREDIT, Mrs. Nancy (M)	c.6 NOV 1826	MR(RK); MB
DUDLEY, William	BOWLING, Sarah	c.13 AUG 1817	MB
DUFF, John Place: Baltimore MD	GREEN, Sarah	10 SEP 1791	DBB:268; 1787:71; WBB:526; IGI
DUFFEY, John	DEEBLE, Mary	5 FEB 1796	FPC:9(JM); 1791:8; 1799:4

Husband	Wife	Event or Marriage	Reference(s)
DUFFEY, John	TINSELL, Mary	14 SEP 1808	FPC:9(JM); AG:15/9/08:3(JM)
DUFFEY, John H.	NEVITT, Mrs. Susan Georgiana	21 NOV 1826	UT:24/11/26:3(Mc)
DUFFY, George Hurd	FORTNEY, Mrs. Rosina	9 MAY 1819	AH:12/5/19(ON)
DUGAN, Phillip (C)	_____, Florrer (C)		1800:52
DUGAN, William (C)	MARVEL, Betsey (C)	c.30 JUL 1829	MB
DUGLASS, Charles	_____, Susannah		1800:58
DULANEY (see "Dulany")			
DULANY, Benjamin, Jr.	ROZIER, Eliza	c.20 FEB 1796	AM1:117; 1799:22; AG:20/2/96:2
DULANY, BenjaminT., Sr.	FRENCH, Elizabeth d/o Daniel French	c.FEB 1773	X:28; DBP:475; 1787:71; FDK1:330; DBR:358
DULANY, Bladen	CARTER, Mary W. ward of Thomas Turner	c.17 JUN 1823	MB
DULANY, Daniel F.	TINGEY, Sarah Ann d/o Thomas Tingey	4 APR 1811	CWA:479; CWA:481; AG:8/4/11:3(Mc)
DULANEY, Henry R. Place: Fredericksburg	CARTER, Frances A. d/o Landon Carter of *Sabine Hall*	3 APR 1827	AG:6/4/27:3(EM); UT:5/4/27:3
DULANY, John Peyton Place: *Mt. Welby*	DEBUTTS, Mary Ann	18 MAY 1812	WB3:304, 371; PGM; AG:21/5/12:3(RA)
DULANY, Walter	FARRELL, Anne	1 JUN 1790	FPC:9(JM)
DULANY, William	SIMMS, Ann	23 MAR 1798	FPC:9(JM)
DULANY, William	TOWERS, Mary G.	c.4 JUN 1810	MB
DULANY, Zachariah Place: *Mt. Pleasant*	BRADEN, Mary d/o Robert Braden	7 MAR 1816	AG:12/3/16:3(MI)
DULIN, Edward	HURST, Sarah d/o John Hurst	c.1756	FWE:348; FWD:298; IGI
DUNBAR, Jesse	GRIFFIN, Elizabeth	7 JUL 1796	FPC:9(JM)
DUNBAR, Jesse	STRICKLEN, Sarah	3 AUG 1797	FPC:9(JM)
DUNBAR, Peter	CRACROFT, Anne Rose	27 JUN 1816	AG:29/6/16:3(ON); MR(ON); MB
DUNCAN, Andrew	BELLONA, Anne	9 SEP 1797	FPC:9(JM)
DUNCAN, Charles (C)	SNOWDEN, Allevy (C)	2 JUN 1808	MR(IR)
DUNCAN, George	_____, Elizabeth	-28 MAR 1781	FDD4:290
DUNCAN, Robert	BENNETT, Hannah	17 DEC 1801	MR(JM); MB
DUNCAN, Samuel J.	COATS, Ann Jane	8 SEP 1829	MB; AG:9/9/29:3(Sco)
DUNDAS, John	HEPBURN, Agnes "Nancy" d/o William Hepburn	c.7 APR 1785	WB1:239; X:33; AG:7/4/85:3; WB2:365; FPC:8; FPCG; 1787:72
DUNDAS, William H. Place: Baltimore MD	HESSELIUS, Mary	9 MAY 1824	SP; AG:13/5/24:3
DUNLAP, James	_____, Nancy	-6 JUN 1809	DBR:259
DUNLAP, John	HANNA, Elizabeth	14 NOV 1795	FPC:9(JM); 1787:71; 1799:30; 1800:53; FPCG
DUNLAP, Samuel Place: Fredericksburg	CAMPBELL, Maria Ann	c.SEP 1810	AG:6/9/10:3
DUNLAP, William	GREER, Ann (Crawford)	-11 MAR 1811	FPCC(41:23); BR:194
DUNN, James	CAYTON, Penelope	21 OCT 1810	FPC:9(JM); MB
DUNN, William	_____, Elizabeth	-22 DEC 1795	HCF:441(JM); 1787:71; HCH:292

Husband	Wife	Event or Marriage	Reference(s)
DUNNINGTON, William P. Place: Prince William Co.	WYATT, Malenda	29 SEP 1808	AG:1/10/08:3
DURKEE, Nathaniel	LYLES, Mrs. Catharine	-18 JUL 1806	DBBB:203
DUVALL, John P.	TEBBS, Ann F.	20 DEC 1815	MB[29]
DUVALL, William	POPE, Ann "Nancy" eldest d/o Nathaniel Pope	25 JUN 1772	HCE:17; 1787:71; 1791:8; 9W(1)240
DYE, Reuben	TURNER, Elizabeth d/o Walker Turner	17 JUL 1804	WB2:92; CWA:481; DBW:146; FPC:9(JM); MB
DYE, Vincent	_____, Sarah	-6 JAN 1796	PWWH:166
DYER, Anthony	_____, Sarah	-18 MAR 1811	DBT:391
DYER, Francis	HUNTER, Margaret d/o John Hunter	18 MAR 1813	FPC:9(JM); MR(WHW); AG:22/3/13:3(JM); MB
DYER, Gideon	BARWELL, Mary	NOV 1793	FPC:9(JM)
DYER, John	ROLLINS, Elizabeth	c.22 APR 1824	MB
DYER, Capt. John R.	BOONE, Jane Maria d/o Ignatius Boone	23 MAY 1826	UT:25/5/26:3
DYER, Walter	DYER, Deborah	21 JUN 1815	MR(JMH); MB
DYKES, Andrew	LUTZ, Ann	31 OCT 1816	MR(ON); MB
DYKES, Mungo	LONGDON, Ann	1788	FB; 1791:8 AG:2/11/90; 1787:71
DYKES, Mungo	WADE, Anne	22 DEC 1791	FPC:8-9(JM); 1791:8
DYMEM, Philip	WALKER, Fanny	3 MAY 1797	FPC:9(JM)
DYSON, Joseph	_____, Hannah	-16 MAY 1796	HCH:86; 1799:2

Husband	Wife	Event or Marriage	Reference(s)

E

Husband	Wife	Event or Marriage	Reference(s)
EARHART, Rev. Jacob Place: Washington DC	DEVAUGHN, Polly	22 AUG 1825	AG:27/8/25:3(B)
EARLE, Esaias	_____, Sally	-23 AUG 1826	WB3:292
EARLE, Henry Stanton	_____, Phoebe	-8 DEC 1810	DBT:329; 1799:16
EARLE, Samuel	WAY, Margaret	4 JAN 1813	MR(IR); MB
EARP, Jesse	ROBERTSON, Ann	- MAY 1813	DBX:246
EARP, Simon	SCOTT, Milly	2 NOV 1803	MR(WW); MB
EASTON, David	BOND, Sarah d/o Dr. Thomas Bond	c.24 JUL 1793	FDY1:395; CM:24/7/93
EASTON, David	CRAIK, Sarah (Harrison) d/o Robert Harrison and wid/o Adam Craik	18 OCT 1796	FPC:9b(JM); B:85; HCK:27, 43; AG:22/10/96:3
ECKLE, Charles E.	PERRY, Charlotte d/o Alexander Perry	19 MAY 1818	MR(WA); MB; AG:22/5/18:2
EDELEN, Edward	MOORE, Sarah	6 JAN 1802	MR(JM); MB
EDELEN, Samuel	HAMILTON, Sally C. d/o Mary Hamilton	c.21 JUL 1817	MB
EDMONDS, Edmund	_____, Sarah		1787:71; 1799:34; 1800:57; FPCC(42:71)
EDMONDS, Elias	HITE, Courtney Ann (Briscoe)	-26 APR 1827	WB4:210
EDSON, Silas Dunbar	SAUNDERS, Sarah Pancoast	18 DEC 1834	H:775
EHLERS, John C.[30]	_____, Catherine	-27 SEP 1819	WB3:272; WB2:415
EICHENBRADE, William	_____, Magdalina	-9 JUL 1790	HCD:145
EISSERMANN, Jacob	SHOEMAKER, Anna	c.22 SEP 1807	MB
ELDRIDGE, Levi	PETTIT, Valinda	31 OCT 1807	FPC:9b(JM)
ELIASON, Ebenezer	_____, Ann	-9 MAR 1814	DBY:518
ELLICORN, George	MASON, Eleanor	27 MAR 1790	FPC:9b(JM)
ELLICOTT, John, Jr. Place: Baltimore MD	MITCHELL, Mary d/o John Mitchell	16 APR 1817	H:739
ELLIOTT, John	MILLS, Amelia	20 DEC 1812	MR(JM); MB
ELLIOTT, Rezin	CONN, Catharine d/o Hugh Conn	-1 APR 1817	DBD2:449 FDZ2:324
ELLIOTT, Silas	BRADLEY, Ann	2 SEP 1812	MR(IR); MB
ELLIS, John W.	CHING, Sarah S. eldest d/o Thomas Ching	2 APR 1829	MB; NI:7/4/29; AG:6/4/29:3(Gu)
ELLIS, Joel	ARELL, Dorothea (Caverly) wid/o Samuel Arell	-25 OCT 1805	DBK:374 AHM:6/1:10
ELLIS, Joseph	EMERSON, Sarah	18 MAY 1812	MR(IR); MB
ELLISTON, Cuthbert	CONWAY, Mary d/o Thomas Conway	-19 MAY 1785	HCH:270; FDQ:226; HCOrd:19/5/85
ELLZEY, Lewis	GRIFFIN, Mrs. Mary wid/o Walter Griffin	-3 MAY 1734	CC:102; FDA2:424
ELTON, John	SHAW, Isabella d/o William Shaw	-20 MAY 1785	HCI:347; DBC:93; FWC:223
ELTON, William	_____, Sarah	-27 MAY 1797	HCI:347
ELVANS, John Place: Georgetown DC	WRIGHT, Mary d/o John Wright	28 MAY 1829	AG:6/6/29:3(B)
EMBERSON, Richard D.	WILLIAMS, Catherine	14 NOV 1815	MR(IR); MB
EMBREE, Daniel	_____, Sarah		QM:45

Husband	Wife	Event or Marriage	Reference(s)
EMERSON, Aquila	ELLIS, Phillippe	19 MAY 1808	FPC:9b(JM); SPC(38:1)
EMERSON, Aquila	COAD, Mrs. Drady	26 NOV 1818	MR(ON); MB; AG:28/11/18:3(JM)
EMERSON, Harrison	WATSON, Jane	6 JAN 1820	MR(EH); MB[31]; AG:14/1/20:3(EH)
EMERSON, John	BALL, Ann Catharine d/o John Ball	24 MAY 1822	SP; MR(EH); MB
EMERSON, John S.	COADE, Sarah Ann	24 DEC 1818	SPC; MR(ON); MB
EMERSON, William D.	DOWELL, Ellen	21 JUN 1825	MR(Sco); MB
EMMETT, Josiah	_____, Catharine		1799:26; 1800:56
EMMONS, William	_____, Hannah		1799:8; 1800:57
ENDICOTT, Samuel	CALL, Polly	1 OCT 1805	FPC:9b(JM); MB
ENGLISH, David	SLADE, Mary C.	8 DEC 1816	MB; AG:7/12/16:3(WW)
ENGLISH, James	RICHARDS, Ann	8 JUN 1820	MR(WHW)
ENGLISH, William B.	VIOLETT, Juliet G. d/o John Violett	7 FEB 1828	MB; AG:11/2/28:3(Gu)
ENTWISLE, Isaac	RYAN, Mrs. Ann	13 JAN 1806	FPC:9b(JM); MB; DBY:72; SPC(12:1); AG:14/1/06:3(JM)
ENTWISLE, Isaac	_____, Parthenia H.	-1814	SPC
ENTWISLE, James	MASON, Mary Ann	c.6 JUL 1815	DCM
ENTWISLE, James of Bolton, Eng.	ZIMMERMAN, Eliza d/o John Zimmerman	6 JUN 1822	AH:10/6/22; SP; FDO3:113; FC#201; AG:11/6/22:3(WHW)
EOLFF, John Valentine	HITCHMANN, Mary	8 APR 1796	FPC:9b(JM)
EPPES, John Wayles	JEFFERSON, Maria d/o Thomas Jefferson	13 OCT 1797	AA:13/10/97:3
ERVINE, David	LANHAM, Sarah	6 AUG 1806	MR(JM); MB
ERWIN, William	_____, Mary	-20 JUN 1801	DBA:128
ESHON, George	BLAKENEY [Blakeley], Liddia	1 AUG 1801	MR(WM); MB
ESKRIDGE, William	CRANSTON, Nancy d/o John Cranston	23 DEC 1819	AH:29/12/19(IR)
ESTEY, John	CAWOOD, Elizabeth Ann	10 FEB 1825	AG:12/2/25:3(ON); MB
EUSTACE, John	CHICHESTER, Sinah	18 OCT 1785	R2:90(SG)
EVANS, Daniel	_____, Rosanna	-30 NOV 1824	AG:30/11/24
EVANS, Ephraim	_____, Catharine	-6 MAY 1790	AG:6/5/90:3; 1787:71
EVANS, Ephraim	_____, Sarah	-5 NOV 1817	DBD2:488; 1799:16
EVANS, Ephraim, Jr.	WADSWORTH, Jane L.	6 JUN 1823	AG:28/6/23:3(WA); MR(WA); MB[32]
EVANS, John	ROBERTSON, Jane	JUL 1794	FPC:9b(JM); 1799:20
EVANS, John	_____, Sarah	-17 MAY 1802	DBD:37; 1799:34
EVANS, John	DIMENT, Elizabeth	c.28 MAR 1809	MB
EVANS, John	_____, Elizabeth Eleanor	- 1834	SPC(186:4)
EVANS, John T. Place: Georgetown DC	BOWIE, Lucinda	28 SEP 1823	SP; AG:30/9/23:3
EVANS, John R. Place: *Frankham*, Charles Co. MD	BRAWNER, Catharine	15 MAR 1821	AG:23/3/21:3(Y)
EVANS, Robert	RANDELL, Harriet	c.19 APR 1811	MB
EVANS, Robert	SEARS, Jane d/o Eliza Sears	c.28 NOV 1818	MB
EVANS, Robert, Jr.	_____, Ann	-14 AUG 1811	DBU:354; 1791:9

Husband	Wife	Event or Marriage	Reference(s)
EVANS, Robert, Sr.	_____, Lucilla [Drucilla]	-1 MAR 1794	DBU:354; 1787:71; 1791:9; 1799:6; DBH:1
EVANS, Thomas	SLIMMER, Catherine	SEP 1793	FPC:9b(JM); 1799:20
EVANS, Thomas	HUMPHREY, Mary	c.18 MAY 1812	MB
EVANS, William	THOMPSON, Betsey	c.15 OCT 1807	MB
EVANS, William Place: *Buckland*	SUMMERS, Penelope	9 JAN 1823	AG:14/1/23:3
EVELETH, Capt. Ebenezer	SANDFORD, Sally	27 AUG 1795	AG:29/8/95:3
EVELETH, Ebenezer	BUTTS, Mary W.	27 APR 1832	SP; MR(WJ); Note[33]
EVELETH, John	CAROLIN, Julia	23 JUN 1831	TMCC:N6; MB
EWART, Horatio	DUDLEY, Cloanna	11 JUL 1803	MR(JM); MB
EWELL, Charles	BORROWDALE, Bridget	19 FEB 1812	AG:20/2/12:3(JM); MB
EWELL, Maj. Charles	CRAIK, Mrs. Maria Dorcas, wid/o George Washington Craik, d/o John Tucker	1 OCT 1818	AG:6/10/18:2(ON); FWO:138; MR(ON); MB

Husband	Wife	Event or Marriage	Reference(s)

F

FAGAN, Joseph	_____, Mary	-18 SEP 1802	DBD:243
FAGAN, John	WILEY, Elizabeth	c.23 JUN 1829	MB
	d/o George Wiley		
FAIRALL (also see "Fareall")			
FAIRALL, Grafton	GREEN, Sarah	8 MAY 1823	SP; MB; AG:10/5/23:3(WHW)
FAIRBROTHERS, John	ENDS, Elizabeth	30 MAY 1805	FPC:11(JM); MB
FAIRFAX, Ferdinando	CARY, Eliza Blair	18 JAN 1796	OT:20; IHC:143; AG:3/3/96:3
Place: Celey's, near Hampton, d/o Wilson Miles Cary			
FAIRFAX, George William	_____, Sarah	-23 SEP 1772	FDK:124
FAIRFAX, Henry	SCOTT, Sophia	3 DEC 1818	AH:7/12/18
Place: Dumfries	d/o Jesse Scott		
FAIRFAX, Henry	HERBERT, Ann Caroline	9 OCT 1827	AG:15/10/27:3
Place: *Walnut Grove*	d/o Hon. John C. Herbert		
FAIRFAX, John H.	DAVIS, Mary	24 JUL 1823	AG:31/7/23:3(JR)
FAIRFAX, Dr. Orlando	CARY, Mary Randolph	21 MAY 1829	AG:1/6/29:3
Place: *Carysbrooke*, Fluvanna Co., d/o Wilson Jefferson Cary			
FAIRFAX, Thomas	HERBERT, Margaret	JAN 1800	FS(1987):51
FAIRFIELD, Reuben	BEALL, Ann	20 NOV 1791	FPC:11(JM)
FALCONER, Abraham	HALL, Sarah	-16 JAN 1793	HCE:356; DBF:51; FDS:19
	d/o Jonathan Hall		
FANT, John	SHREVE, Elizabeth	c.25 OCT 1815	MB
FARDY, Patrick	WHEATON, Catharine	16 APR 1822	MR(JF); MB
FAREALL (also see "Fairall")			
FAREALL, Jason	CROWE, Nancy	c.15 JAN 1811	MB; AG:17/1/11:3(RO)
FARISH, Hazelwood	_____, Fanny	-6 AUG 1813	DBAA:29
FARQUHAR, Charles	BROOKE, Sarah	23 MAY 1833	H:740
FARRALL (see "Fairall")			
FARRELL, Robert	INSLEY, Peggy	JUN 1794	FPC:11(JM)
FARRELL, Thomas	WESTON, Ann	JAN 1794	FPC:10-11(JM); 1799:26
FARROW, Nimrod	_____, Dolly	-27 APR 1810	DBS:431
FAULKNER, James	ROBERTSON, Mrs. Elizabeth	- MAY 1813	DBX:246
FAUNTLEROY, Robert	_____, Sarah	-11 APR 1812	DBW:147
FAW, Abraham	_____, Mary Ann	-16 AUG 1797	HCK:22; DBE:199; TMCC(F:3); FPCG; HCG:271
FAW, Abraham	MOODY, Sarah	20 APR 1806	FPC:11(JM); MB; DBR:187; 1799:12; TMCC(F:3); AG:22/4/06:3(JM)
FAWCETT, John	MITCHELL, Janet	9 SEP 1799	FPC:11(JM); 1791:9
FAWCETT, Thomas	ROBERTSON, Sarah	- MAY 1813	DBX:246
FAWCETT, Willis	STABLER, Susan	c.4 APR 1837	MR:83; QC; H:741; AG:22/1/52:2
	d/o Edward Stabler		
FEAGANS, Joseph	LESTER, Mary	23 OCT 1790	FPC:11(JM)
FEARSON, Samuel S.	ALLSTAN, Maria	-3 NOV 1819	CCC(96)
	d/o Thomas Allstan		
FELL, Christopher	SMALLRIDGE, Gurtrude	27 AUG 1818	MR(RO); MB; OT:57; P:316; WB5:181
FENDALL, Benjamin T.	DADE, Elizabeth		
	d/o Townshend Dade		

Husband	Wife	Event or Marriage	Reference(s)
FENDALL, Philip Richard	LEE, Sarah Lettice	30 SEP 1759	MG:4/10/59; LV:574; 1787:72; 1791:9
FENDALL, Philip Richard	LEE, Mary "Molly" d/o Henry Lee	c.17 NOV 1791	WBB:344; WBB:137; 1791:9; NI:13/11/27; AG:17/11/91:3
FENDALL, Philip Richard	YOUNG, Elizabeth Mary d/o Gen. Robert and Elizabeth Young	31 MAR 1827	MB; AG:2/4/27:3(EH) UT:3/4/27:3
FERGUSON, Cumberland	_____, Mary		1787:72; 1799:32; 1800:51
FERGUSON, Joseph	SUMMERS, Sarah d/o John Summers	-28 JAN 1788	FWE:238; IGI
FERGUSON, Josiah	FORD, Priscilla d/o Thomas Ford	-29 AUG 1774	FWC:257
FERGUSON, Zaccheus	WALLACE, Susanna	NOV 1794	FPC:11(JM)
FERNEAU, Philip	_____	-1799	1799:22[34]
FERNEAU, Philip	RYE, Nelly	c.31 JUL 1803	MB; DBQ:352
FEUGIT (see "Fugett")			
FIELD, [Horace] Horatio	BOYER, Elizabeth d/o Margaret Myers	4 NOV 1804	FPC:11(JM); DBS:13; CCC(33); MB
FIELD, John Place: Philadelphia PA	WILLIAMS, Deborah	16 NOV 1786	HCL:260; IGI
FIELD, Oliver	DIXON, Jane	10 AUG 1826	MB; AG:15/8/26:3(AH)
FIELDS, Stephen	WHITINGTON, Mary Ann	14 JUN 1821	MR(IR); MB; AG:19/6/21:3(IR)
FIELD, Stephen	HOWARD, Catharine L.	c.11 JUL 1828	MB
FIELDON, William	DEREA, Catherine	28 NOV 1789	FPC:11(JM)
FILBERT, Peter	GREEN, Mrs. Hannah	8 NOV 1805	BA:11/11/05
FINDLAY, James	DEVAUGHN, Ruth	c.2 JUN 1825	MB
FINLAY, Henry	CARROLL, Polly	4 MAR 1796	FPC:11(JM)
FINLEY, Hugh	HURST, Susanna d/o John Hurst	-20 JUN 1785	HCA:74; FWE:348
FISHER, Michael	HIRSH, Catherine	25 FEB 1831	SP; MR(WJ)
FISHER, Robert	_____, Ann		MPC:W43
FISSOUR, John M.	_____, Adele	-19 JAN 1814	DBY:261
FITZGERALD, John	_____, Jane	-15 MAR 1784	DBE:351
FITZGERALD, John	DIGGES, Jane d/o Dr. Digges of *Warburton Manor*	2 JAN 1799	HCB:399; 1787:71; 1791:9; SM; DBA:107; X:62
FITZGERALD, William	FRANCES, Mary	12 JUN 1826	UT:16/6/26:3(Mc)
FITZGERALDS, Thomas	EVANS, Henny Ann d/o James Evans	c.17 DEC 1827	MB
FITZHUGH, Alexander Place: *Woodlawn*, Frederick Co.	CLARE, Eliza L.G.	15 FEB 1816	AG:23/2/16:3(M)
FITZHUGH, Edmund	ROBERTS, Eliza A. eldest d/o John Roberts	30 MAY 1818	AH:15/6/18(B); DCM; AG:6/5/`8:2(B)
FITZHUGH, George W. of Brentsville	HENRY, Sarah S.B. of Stafford Co.	17 APR 1828	AG:22/4/28:3(JW)
FITZHUGH, Harrison	LANE, Ann Carr d/o William Lane, Sr. and wid/o Andrew Lane	-11 FEB 1808	DBE2:447; FDS2:291; FWJ:110
FITZHUGH, Henry Place: Fairfax Co.	FITZHUGH, Henrietta S. d/o Hon. Nicholas Fitzhugh	14 NOV 1811	NI:19/11/11(WM); AG:21/11/11:3

Husband	Wife	Event or Marriage	Reference(s)
FITZHUGH, John Thornton of King George Co.	McCOBB, Rachael D. youngest d/o Capt. John McCobb	5 FEB 1828	AG:7/2/28(WJ); SP; NI:7/2/28; MR(WJ); MB
FITZHUGH, Nicholas	ASHTON, Sarah d/o Burdett Ashton	-12 AUG 1813	WB1:329
FITZHUGH, Norman R.	VOWELL, Mary Ann d/o Thomas Vowell	8 APR 1823	NI:12/4/23(WA); SP; MR(WA); MB; AG:12/4/23:3(WA)
FITZHUGH, Philip	[THORNTON], Charlotte d/o Col. Presley Thornton	-18 FEB 1802	DBC:239; 4W(1)200
FITZHUGH, William Henry	GOLDSBOROUGH, Anna Maria	10 JAN 1814	OT:28
FITZHUGH, William W.	HALLEY, Jane	9 NOV 1815	AG:10/11/15:3(WHW); MR(WHW); MB
FITZPATRICK, Thomas	WILKINSON, Ann	MAR 1795	FPC:11(JM); 1787:71; 1791:9
FLANNERY, Michael	TURNER, Mrs. Rebecca	26 APR 1806	DBV:282; MB[35]; AG:28/4/06:3(TD)
FLATFORD, Thomas	WILEY, Sarah	2 MAR 1791	FPC:11(JM)
FLATFORD, William Thomas Place: *Summerfield*, Prince William Co.	ALLEN, Chloe	5 AUG 1830	AG:28/8/30:3
FLEET, Charles	KENT, Malinda	24 DEC 1801	MR(JM)
FLEMING, Andrew	STEELE, Catherine	25 APR 1793	FPC:10-11(JM); FPCG
FLEMING, Thomas	_____, Betty	-16 DEC 1783	DBB:316; 1787:72; 1791:9
FLEMING, Thornton	COHAGAN, Sally	8 JAN 1806	MR(IR); MB
FLETCHER, Aaron (C)	_____, Nancy (C)		1800:52
FLETCHER, Charles Place: Charles Co. MD	BRISCOE, Sarah M.	5 SEP 1820	AG:11/9/20:2
FLETCHER, Charles	TAYLOR, Marie	21 AUG 1828	MR(IR); MB
FLETCHER, Capt. George Place: Washington DC	BRISCOE, Lucinda M. d/o Richard S. Briscoe	19 SEP 1822	SPC(74:2); DCM; NI:24/9/22; AG:26/9/22:3(WH)
FLETCHER, James	_____, Mary	-1787	1787:72; 1799:8; 1800:56
FLETCHER, John Walter	_____, Mary	-25 JUL 1794	HCE:354
FLETCHER, William	WRIGHT, Catherine	21 APR 1796	FPC:11(JM); 1799:8
FLETCHER, Wm. Walter	_____, Mary	-25 JUL 1794	HCE:254
FLEURY, John Rudolph	KINCAID, Sarah Elizabeth	c.21 JUL 1825	MB
FLINTON, Richard	_____, Jane	-1 DEC 1799	HCM:322
FLOWER, Samuel	LOWDEN, Mary	27 JUL 1798	FPC:11(JM)
FOLEY, Dennis	DUNN, Elizabeth wid/o William Dunn	27 JUL 1790	FPC:11(JM); HCH:292; 1799:18
FOLLIN, William	_____, Mary	-5 JUN 1800	DBE:136; HCO:109
FOOTE, Alexander	DANIEL, Julia Ann	1 MAR 1825	AG:8/3/25:3(EH)
FOOTE, Frederick	RAMSAY, Catharine R. d/o John Ramsay	20 OCT 1825	FPCC(41:8); MB; MR(WA); AG:22/10/25:3(WA)
FOOTE, William Hayward Place: *Bush Hill*	SCOTT, Mary Marshall only d/o David Wilson Scott	31 MAY 1830	BR:131; FX; AG:31/7/27:3; AG:8/6/30:3
FORCE, Peter	EVANS, Hannah	c.31 DEC 1817	MR(SC); MB
FORD, Andrew	MULEY, Jane	5 SEP 1796	FPC:11(JM)

Husband	Wife	Event or Marriage	Reference(s)
FORD, West	BELL, Priscilla	c.14 AUG 1812	FPC; MR(JM); MB
FORD, William	ARRINGTON, Eunice	30 SEP 1818	MR(ON); MB
FORDHAM, William	KITELEY, Mary Ann	c.12 MAR 1823	MB
FOREMAN, David	HOKES, Elizabeth	3 OCT 1822	MR(EH); MB; AG:10/10/22:3(EH)
FORREST, David M. Place: *Shuter's Hill*, Fairfax Co.	CLAGETT, Mary E.	1 FEB 1820	CT:5/2/20; MR(ON); AG:4/2/20:2(ON); MB
FORREST, Joseph	DULANY, Elizabeth d/o Benjamin Dulany	17 MAR 1793	HCI:62; AG:20/3/93:3
FORSTER, John	GILPIN, Ann	JAN 1792	FPC:11(JM)
FORTNEY, George	_____, Susan	-12 MAR 1817	WB2:207
FORTNEY, Henry	WHITE, Susannah	2 APR 1818	AH:4/2/18(Mc); DCM; AG:7/4/18:2(McW)
FORTNEY, Jacob, Jr. Place: Fairfax Co.	LOTZ, Rosanna	13 JUL 1815	WB2:273; 1787:72; 1791:9; AH:17/7/15; AG:17/7/15:3(ON)
FORTNEY, Jacob, Sr. Place: Georgetown DC	HICKEY, Priscilla	23 MAY 1816	DBD2:510; 1791:9; AG:28/5/16:3(B); FPCC(42:67)
FORTNEY, Richard	PHILIPS, Elizabeth	31 JUL 1823	MB(ON)
FORTUNE, James	SANE, Mary	8 JUL 1830	MB; AG:13/7/30:3(JF)
FOSET, John	ROBERTSON, Sarah	-27 JAN 1810	DBS:479
FOSTER, James Place: Prospect-Hill	FAIRFAX, Elizabeth d/o Capt. Henry Fairfax	29 AUG 1822	AG:5/9/22:3
FOSTER, John	_____, Jane	-22 OCT 1798	HCL:452; DBD:442; 1799:4; AG:7/10/03:3
FOSTER, John S.	FRANCIS, Mary	c.23 MAY 1816	MB
FOULKE, Anthony	_____, Eleanor		QM:45
FOWLE, William	TAYLOR, Hetty D.	c.30 APR 1807	MB
FOWLER, Daniel	RAWLINGS, Julia Ann	3 JUN 1830	MR(IR); MB
FOWLER, William	_____, Margaret	-22 APG 1784	HCOrd:22/4/84
FOX, James b/o William Fox	PIPER, Catharine	28 APR 1815	MR(ON); DBD2:446; MB(JM)
FOX, James	MILLAN, Ann	6 NOV 1828	AG:14/11/28:3(JR)
FOX, John	BARKER, Matilda Ann	19 MAY 1829	AG:30/5/29:3(JR)
FOX, Joseph	CARTER, Mary Ann	11 AUG 1829	SP; MR(CJ); MB
FOX, Robert W.	KITCHEN, Nancy	16 MAR 1826	AG:21/3/26:3(JR)
FOX, William	SUMMERS, Eleanor d/o Isabel (Shaw) Summers	c.25 JUN 1805	MB; DBU:147; DBX:64
FOXTON, William	RICKS, Hannah	28 JUN 1799	FPC:11(JM)
FOXWOOD, Daniel	HILL, Sarah	25 JUL 1811	FPC:11(JM); MB
FOYSER, Adam	_____, Catherine	-9 APR 1801	DBA:34
FRANCE, Edward	BROCKETT, Anabella d/o Robert Brockett, Sr.		ACFF, Wm. Gregory
FRANCE, Philip	_____, Catherine	-6 JUL 1802	WBA:67
FRANCIS, Edward	_____, Hannah		MPC:W47; WB5:303
FRANCIS, John G.	HAYS, Jane	10 MAY 1807	FPC:11(JM); MB
FRANCIS, Matthew	DURRINGTON, Ann	10 JUN 1804	FPC:11(JM); MB
FRANCIS, Matthew	IRWIN, Mrs. Sarah	c.9 MAR 1811	DBU:259; MB
FRANCIS, Thomas	SMITH, Margaret	5 NOV 1797	FPC:11(JM)
FRANKLIN, Thomas	HORWELL, Nancy E.	6 FEB 1825	AG:10/2/25:3(WHW); MR(WHW); SP

Husband	Wife	Event or Marriage	Reference(s)
FRAZER, Anthony Reintzel	LEE, Presha	23 OCT 1823	NI:30/10/23; Note[36]
Place: Montgomery Co. MD	d/o Daniel Lee of Montgomery Co. MD		
FRAZER, George	DAVIS, Sarah	17 APR 1814	MR(WHW); MB
FRAZER, William Alex.	REINTZEL, Mary (Magdalena)	c.1782	HCD:166; 1799:10; IGI
FRAZER, William A., Jr.	HIPKINS, Sarah	3 APR 1817	Note[37]
FRAZIER, Jeremiah	KINSEY, Lucy	c.16 JUL 1807	MB
FRAZIER, Joseph	_____, Letty		MPC:S23
FREDERICK, Henry	MacMANNIN, Sarah	6 SEP 1790	FPC:11(JM)
FREEMAN, Bennett	GUZMAN, Peggy	JUN 1792	FPC:11(JM)
FREEMAN, Richard	_____, Cecelia	-8 NOV 1814	DBZ:47
FREEMAN, Samuel	McDONALD, Nelly	28 OCT 1795	FPC:11(JM)
FREMAN, William	BOWZER, Elizabeth	6 NOV 1814	MR(WHW); MB
FRENCH, Charles	MURDOCK, Marianne Craik	c.12 DEC 1809	PGM
FRENCH, Daniel	MANLEY, Penelope	-20 MAY 1771	FWC:134
FRENCH, George	_____, Ann Brayne	-7 AUG 1809	DBQ:487
FRENEAU (see "Ferneau")			
FRENNELL, Isaac	JENSON, Caroline	c.15 OCT 1815	MB
FRIGNETT, John	HANEY, Elizabeth	9 AUG 1815	MR(IR); MB
FRIZZEL, William	FOLLIN, Jane	1788	FB
FROBEL, John Jacob	MARSHALL, Mary S.	26 JAN 1809	AG:28/1/09:3(G);
Place: *Bush Hill*, res. of Richard M. Scott			FVW:161
FRY, Leonard	ALLAN, Mary	17 JUN 1797	FPC:11(JM)
FRYE, Rev. Christopher	MOSS, Mrs. Margaret (Harper)	16 AUG 1819	WB4:364; BR:105;
	wid/o Robert Moss, and		TMCC(P:2)
	d/o John Harper		AH:20/8/19;
			AG:19/8/19:2
FUGATE, William	THOMAS, Mary	c.2 AUG 1822	MB
FUGETT, James	JAVINS, Susan	c.15 MAY 1821	MR(IR); MB
	si/o Dennis Javins		
FUGITT, Gustavus	WARD, Catharine	c.17 APR 1817	TMCC(D:1); DCM
FULFORD, Joseph	SPICOTT, Polly	MAY 1792	FPC:11(JM)
FULFORD, Robert	_____, Mary	-10 NOV1794	CRA:144
FULLERTON, Peter	SAVERY, Rose	30 OCT 1820	MR(JF); MB
FULLMORE, Joseph	_____, Nancy	-19 OCT 1786	HCOrd:19/10/86
FULMORE, John	GARLIC, Mary Ann	2 JUL 1809	FPC:11(JM); MB
FULTON, Joseph	CURTIS, Jane W.	1 JUL 1819	AH:7/7/19(SC);
			AG:5/7/19:3(SC)
FULTON, Robert	_____, Mary Ann	-6 MAY 1795	HCG:366; 1791:10;
			CRA:235
FULTON, Robert	O'BRIEN, Ann Maria	27 NOV 1817	AG:2/12/17:3
FURNEAU, Philip	_____, Barbara	-24 JUL 1797	HCI:253
FURNESS, William	_____, Nancy	- 1820	R2:153

Husband	Wife	Event or Marriage	Reference(s)

G

GADSBY, John Place: Georgetown DC	M'LAUGHLIN, Margaret	3 NOV 1805	DBT:344; AG:13/2/12:3; AG:5/11/05:3(SY)
GADSBY, John	NORRIS, Providence	-31 DEC 1813	DBX:344; GT
GADSBY, John Place: Baltimore MD	LANGWORTHY, Provy	12 JAN 1813	Note[38]; IGI
GA(I)THER, John	CAREW, Margaret	3 MAR 1811	AG:4/3/11:3; MR(FB); MB; MR(FB)
GAITHER, John	DULANY, Rebecca d/o Benjamin Dulany	7 MAR 1811	AG:8/3/11:3(G)
GALLAGHER, James C.	LYLES, Julia Ann Maria	c.12 JAN 1825	MB
GALLOWAY, Jeremiah	STEWART, Mary "Polly"	20 SEP 1798	FPC:13(JM); 1800:53
GALT, Alfred Place: Washington PA	HALLAM, Rebecca	c.OCT 1830	AG:26/11/30:3
GALT, James	RESLER, Eve	28 APR 1804	MR(WM); MB
GALT, James	VEITCH, Eliza	23 JUL 1818	AH:27/7/18:(JF); DCM
GANES, Griffin	PARSONS, Elizabeth	27 JUL 1827	SP; MR(WJ); MB
GANT(T), Charles	PRESTON, Margaret	20 DEC 1821	MR(IR); MB
GANTZ, Adam	_____, Mary	-26 APR 1782	FDO:131
GARDNER, Henry	_____, Rachel	-4 JAN 1787	1787:72; AG:4/1/87:2
GARDNER, William C.	CAZENOVE, Eliza F. d/o Anthony C. Cazenove	16 MAY 1816	AG:20/5/16:3(JM); MR(JM); MB
GARDNER, Zachariah	_____, Betsey		1799:26; 1800:58
GARFORD (see "Gofford")			
GARNER, Thomas	GREEN, Elizabeth	2 JUN 1797	FPC:13(JM)
GARNER, Tristram H.	PIPSICO, Priscilla d/o John Pipsico	-19 NOV 1839	WB4:315
GARNER, William	SIMMS, Mrs. Margaret	12 SEP 1809	AG:13/9/09:3(JM); MB; FPCG; FPCC(42:84); FPC:13(JM); MR(JM)
GARRELL, James	FRANKS, Lucinda d/o Mary Frank [sic]	c.25 MAR 1824	MB
GARRELL, James	COWING, Elizabeth	c.15 DEC 1830	MB
GARRET, Joseph	POTTER, Hathey	15 APR 1813	AG:19/4/13:3
GARRISON, James	KILHAM, Elizabeth	22 MAY 1817	MR(JMH); MB
GARROW, John	DAVIS, Susanna	16 MAR 1790	FPC:13(JM)
GARVEY, Lucas	CHEW, Ann Ruth d/o Mercy (Jackson) Chew	-16 MAY 1774	DBB:105; FWC:243
GASCH, Frederick	CATHERBY, Molly	7 OCT 1804	FPC:13(JM); MB
GASTON, Hon. William Place: Georgetown DC	WORTHINGTON, Eliza	3 SEP 1816	AG:10/9/16:3
GATES, Horatio Place: Washington Co. MD	VALANCE, Mary	7 AUG 1786	AG:10/8/86:3
GATES, Samuel	WILEY, Martha	JAN 1794	FPC:13(JM)
GATES, Thomas	RISINGER, Sally	15 JUL 1816	MR(JMH); MB
GATES, William	THOMAS, Jemima	26 DEC 1797	FPC:13(JM)
GATHER (see "Gaither")			
GAY, James	_____, Elizabeth		1800:55

Husband	Wife	Event or Marriage	Reference(s)
GEE, Thomas R. Place: Washington DC	BRENT, Lucretia	16 SEP 1818	AG:18/9/18:3; DCM
GEIER, Moses Place: Snow Hill MD	HAILS, Margaret	9 FEB 1826	UT:7/3/26:3
GEIGER, Jacob	_____, Elizabeth	-28 MAR 1804	DBH:121
GEMENY, John	FIGG, Matilda	c.24 JUN 1816	MB
GENERES, John Const.	De POINCY, Zephorine	c.2 JUN 1804	DBAA:32; PGM
GEORGE, Marcus Place: Warrenton NC	CAMPBELL, Mrs. Mary F.	c.4 MAY 1807	AG:7/5/07:3
GEORGE, Martin	KLINE, Catharine d/o Gabriel Kline	12 MAY 1807	AG:13/5/07:3; FPC:13(JM); MB
GETTINGS, Thos. Freeman	WEDDINGS, Maria d/o Mashac Weddings	10 JUN 1819	AG:18/6/19:3(JW)
GIBBARD, John	_____, Margaret	-24 JUL 1785	HCOrd:24/7/85
GIBORIE, John	GARAT, Jeanie	FEB 1794	FPC:13(JM)
GIBBS, James (C)	_____, Ustley (C)		1800:57
GIBBS, John H.	WILLIAMS, Sarah S.	5 NOV 1817	MR(IR); MB
GIBBS, John H.	TATSAPAUGH, Mary Ann	24 JAN 1826	SP; MB; AG:27/1/26:3(WHW)
GIBBS, Theodore	WILLIAMS, Jane d/o Alexander Williams	25 SEP 1816	MR(IR); AG:2/10/16:3(IR)
GIBBS, Thomas D.	SKINNER, Winifred	30 NOV 1815	PW:167(F)
GIBBS, Walter	CURTIS, Charlotte	26 DEC 1816	MR(ON); MB; AG:30/12/16:3(ON)
GIBSON, Gustavous	_____, Basheba	-14 DEC 1834	MPC:S31
GIBSON, Isaac	FOUSHEE, Susanna Garner	30 DEC 1798	FPC:13(JM); DBV:419; 1799:12
GIBSON, Theodore	WILLIAMS, Jane	25 SEP 1816	MR(IR); MB
GIBSON, William	FLEMMING, Ann	c.25 DEC 1821	MB
GILBERT, John	CARY, Eliza	10 APR 1813	MR(IR); MB
GILBERT, Capt. Joseph R.	HEBB, Sarah T.	31 JUL 1816	AG:2/8/16:3(WHW); MR(WHW); MB
GILDART, Francis Place: Frederick Co.	MARTIN, Ann	c.24 NOV 1785	AG:24/11/85:3
GILDEN, John	GILLWITH, Joanna	25 NOV 1817	MR(JMH); MB
GILES, Mathew	COLVILL, Esther si/o Thomas Colvill	- MAY 1719	FWB:424
GILL, James	VAUGHAN, Nancy	c.JUL 1795	ColC:17/7/95
GILL, James	SMALL, Elizabeth	13 MAY 1799	FPC:13(JM)
GILL, John	LOWREY, Esther	17 FEB 1791	FPC:13(JM)
GILLAN, Benjamin	RAKES, Eleanor	c.FEB 1797	WB:22/2/97
GILLICK (see "Gulick")			
GILLIES, Dr. James	_____, Frances	-13 MAR 1802	DBB:383; FPCG
GILLINGHAM, William	_____, Jane		QM:46
GILMAN, Ephraim	CRAWFORD, Ann	18 JUN 1805	FPC:13(JM); MR(IR); AG:21/6/05(IR); DBD2:38; MB
GILPIN, George	PETERS, Katherine	-16 JUN 1777	FDM:299; Note[39]
GILPIN, George Place: Anne Arundel Co. MD	PETERS, Jane	19 FEB 1780	HCC:225; 1791:10 1799:14; WB1:280; CCC(76); IGI; FDO:104
GILPIN, Capt. George Place: Baltimore MD	SMULL, Mrs. Margaret	15 MAY 1820	AG:6/8/20:3

Husband	Wife	Event or Marriage	Reference(s)
GILPIN, John	_____, Jane	-16 JUL 1810	DBY:191
GILPIN, Joshua	_____, Mary	-11 MAY 1811	DBU:459
GIRD, Christopher	_____, Hannah	-20 NOV 1797	WB2:305
GIRD, Henry	_____, Mary	-2 FEB 1805	WBB:472
GIRD, John	KENNEDY, Sarah d/o James Kennedy, Sr.	25 SEP 1810	DBV:476; MB; WB3:315;FPCC(42:78); AG:27/9/10:3(G)
GIRD, Joseph C. Place: Washington DC	DORSEY, Eudocia d/o Richard Dorsey	22 JUL 1815	DBE2:144; SPC(30:1); WB3:65; WB2:336; AH:24/7/15; DCM
GIVEN, George	MITCHELL, Elizabeth	23 JUL 1826	UT:25/7/26:3
GLADMAN, Thomas	COLLINS, Susan	18 MAY 1826	UT:20/5/26:3
GLANDERS, John	MYERS, Fanny	29 MAR 1815	FPC:13(JM); MB
GLANDES, Anthony	ARMSTRONG, Tabitha	OCT 1792	FPC:13(JM)
GLASSCOCK, Robert	ROBEY, Ann	28 MAR 1829	AG:12/5/29:3(JR)
GLAS(S)GOW, George W.	JACOBS, Mrs. Hannah Ann	4 NOV 1830	AG:10/10/30:3; SP; MR(WJ); MB
GLISSART, Thomas J.	LUCKETT, Ann	9 SEP 1817	MR(WHW)
GLENN, Robert	JOURDOUN, Elizabeth	c.5 JUL 1817	MB
GLENN, Robert	HOLTON, Elizabeth	c.15 FEB 1823	MB
GLOVER, Thomas	_____, Mary (Mariah)	-23 SEP 1786	1787:72; 1799:40; 1800:51; HCOrd:23/9/86
GLOVER, Thomas R.	STEWARD, Elizabeth	20 DEC 1789	FPC:13(JM)
GLOVER, William	MARTIN, Nancy	12 APR 1814	MR(JM); MB
GLOVERMAN, Martin	WASSER, Elizabeth	8 OCT 1803	MR(JM); MB
GODDARD, William (C)	_____, Elender (C)		1800:58
GODDARD, William	VIOLETT, Eleanor	c.5 MAY 1809	MB(ON)
GOFFORD, James	KELLY, Mary Ann	10 DEC 1816	MR(ON); MB
GOING, Robert	ROWE, Mary		Note[40]
GOING, Robert	BIGGS, Sophia	24 JUN 1829	AG:30/6/29:3(LA)
GOINGS, Calvert	DUFF, Jane	c.28 OCT 1830	MB
GOING(S), John	DUFF, Susan d/o James Duff	c.8 OCT 1828	MB
GONSOLVE, Samuel[41]	BYRNE, Mary	7 FEB 1811	FPC:13(JM); MB; AG:22/2/11
GOODING, John	ANGELY, Margaret	9 SEP 1800	FPC:13(JM)
GOODING, John	SIMPSON, Elizabeth (Gretter) d/o Michael Gretter and wid/o William Simpson	-21 AUG 1810	DBU:129; FWN:148; FDA3:377
GOODRICH, William	ROBERTSON, Jane	-27 JAN 1810	DBS:479
GOODS, James Cottingham Place: Washington DC	SIMPSON, Elizabeth	25 OCT 1825	MPC:W4; DCM
GOODS, Samuel	COTTINGHAM, Ebbe	1788	MB; 1791:10
GO(O)DWIN, Peter F.	GOTARE, Dorcus	23 AUG 1813	MB; MR(ON)
GOODWIN, William	CARTER, Nancy	7 FEB 1821	AG:15/2/21:3(JR)
GOODWIN, William	CHICK, Mary	5 APR 1827	AG:23/4/27:3(JR)
GOOSE (see Gantz)			
GORDON, Alexander	_____, Mary	-9 JUN 1797	DBQ:90; 1791:10; CCC(73)
GORDON, Lt. Alexander G.	TAYLOR, Amanda Wentworth d/o George Taylor	6 SEP 1827	AG:10/9/27:3
GORDON, George Fredk.	CHARD, Hannah	c.27 FEB 1822	MB

Husband	Wife	Event or Marriage	Reference(s)
GORDON, John	_____, Susannah	-18 OCT 1798	DBD:336; 1799:12
GORDON, Samuel	_____, Susan F.	-23 DEC 1813	DBAA:180
GORMAN, John B.	MEADE, Jane F.M.B.A.	22 JUN 1820	AG:24/6/20:3(JF)
Place: Washington DC			
GORRAM, Thomas	BEACH, Catharine	17 MAY 1829	AG:30/5/29:3(JR)
GORRELL (see "Garrell")			
GOSS, Andrew	PEARSON, Sarah	5 JUN 1804	FPC:13(JM); MR(JM); MB
GOSSUM, Alexander W.	BATES, Matilda	24 DEC 1818	AG:7/1/19:2(JR)
GOTIER, Matthew	_____, Dorcas	-30 JUL 1801	DBA:385; 1799:20
GOULD, John	RUMNEY, Eliza	c.14 FEB 1824	MB
GOVER, Anthony Poultney	JANNEY, Sarah	8 NOV 1815	H:744; QC; QM:46;
s/o Samuel Gover	d/o Elisha Janney		AG:5/5/69:2;
Place: Fairfax Co.	of *Hillsborough*, Loudoun Co.		AG:14/11/15:3;
			AH:13/11/15
GOWEN, Joseph	SHERRON, Mary	17 JUL 1803	MR(JM); MB
GOWEN, Johnson	RUSSELL, Sarah	6 MAR 1798	AA:14/3/98:3
GRACE, John	_____, Celia	-27 DEC 1799	CRA:321
	of Co. Galway, Ire.		
GRACE, John	_____, Sarah	-21 JAN 1804	WBB:56
GRADY, Grigsby	BAGGETT, Mary	24 FEB 1801	MR(JM)
GRAEFF, John	BROOK(S), Ann	29 SEP 1818	AH:2/10/18(ON); MB
GRAFF, Wedell	BRIGHT, Ann Elizabeth	-1 DEC 1784	FWE:38
	d/o Wendall Bright		
GRAFFORT, Benjamin	WILLIAMS, Sarah	-27 MAR 1786	FWG:299
	d/o John Williams		
GRAFFORT, Thomas	FULFORD, Mary	28 JUN 1796	FPC:13(JM)
GRAHAM, Alexander	CLEMENTSON, Sarah	24 DEC 1815	AG:12/1/16:3(OB)
GRAHAM, David	_____, Mary		1799:32; 1800:52; BT:14/10/03; FPCG
GRAHAM, George	WATSON, Jane	-8 AUG 1830	NI:9/8/30
	d/o James Watson		
GRAHAM, John	_____, Margaret	-8 AUG 1773	CCG:A1
GRAHAM, John	FREEMAN, Cecilia	c.1 JAN 1818	MB[42]
GRAHAM, John, Jr.	HATTERSLEY, Sarah	21 MAY 1814	MB; MPC:E3
GRAHAME, George	HARRIS, Mary	1 MAR 1813	BFG:4/3/13(GR)
Place: probably Baltimore MD			
GRAMMER, G.C.	DOYNE, Eliza	11 APR 1813	AG:12/4/13:3
GRANT, John W. (C)	BOWLES, Susan (C)	3 FEB 1820	MR(WHW); MB
GRANT, Joseph	GRIFFIN, Ann	9 FEB 1826	UT:16/2/26:2
GRAY, Edward	DARLY, Mary	20 APR 1795	FPC:13(JM); 1799:38
GRAY, James	WEEDEN, Priscilla	12 SEP 1801	FPC:13(JM); MR(JM); MB
	s/o Henry Weeden		
GRAY, John	HELMBOLD, Ann Maria	18 APR 1804	AG:19/4/04:3(B)
Place: Georgetown DC			
GRAY, John W.	GLADDEN, Diana	c.10 JAN 1826	MB
GRAY, Levi	OSBURN, Anne	22 FEB 1814	FPC:13(JM); MB
GRAY, Robert	NELSON, Polly Killam	9 OCT 1800	FPC:13(JM); DBV:239
GRAY, Robert	NICHOLAS, Mildred Ann	c.27 NOV 1828	MB
GRAY, Spencer	_____, Virgin	-20 NOV 1822	WB3:77
GRAY, William A.	BUSBY, Ann	19 AUG 1809	MR(IR); MB

Husband	Wife	Event or Marriage	Reference(s)
GRAY, William F. Place: Fredericksburg	STONE, Mildred d/o William S. Stone	25 SEP 1817	AG:1/10/17:3
GRAYSON, Benjamin	BERKLEY, Stacy (Ellzey) d/o Lewis Ellzey	-1 OCT 1786	FWE:223
GRAYSON, Capt. Spence	BLUNT, Sarah	31 OCT 1811	AG:2/11/11:3(JM); MR(JM); MB
GRAYSON, William	WAGENER, Mary Elizabeth d/o Peter Wagener	-21 APR 1793	FWG:404
GRAYSON, Dr. William Place: Georgetown DC (Green and Greene)	THRELKELD, Mary d/o John Threlkeld	1 MAR 1810	AG:27/3/10:3(WDA)
GREEN, Capt. Caleb	ROBINSON, Hannah	30 OCT 1796	FPC:13(JM); AG:1/11/96:3
GREEN, Charles Place: Washington DC	HAISLIP, Elizabeth Jane	2 SEP 1830	AG:10/9/30:3
GREEN, Edward	CARSON, Ann	c.20 DEC 1827	MB
GREEN, Frederick	CHEVERILL, Catherine	5 FEB 1812	FPC:13(JM); MB
GREEN, George	PATTERSON, Catherine	8 MAR 1802	MR(JM); MB[43]
GREEN, James	HUCORN, Esther H.	16 OCT 1815	FPC:13(JM); MB
GREEN, James	MUIR, Jane d/o John Muir	22 NOV 1825	SP; MB; AG:26/11/25:3
GREEN, Jesse	_____, Elizabeth	-4 NOV 1797	HCK:293; DBW:153
GREEN, Job	_____, Lydia	-10 AUG 1791	HCD:287
GREEN, John	_____, Mary	-1804	DBQ:425; SPC(52:2)
GREEN, John	_____, Hannah	-24 APR 1811	DBU:201
GREEN, Thomas	LANHAM, Susannah	8 SEP 1804	FPC:13(JM); MR(JM); MB
GREENE, Thomas B.	HICKEY, Rebecca	24 APR 1809	MR(IR); MB
GREEN, Waddell	_____, Mary		UC:W130
GREEN, William	_____, Mary	-21 SEP 1818	SPC(31:1)
GREEN, William	COLEMAN, Susan J.	4 SEP 1821	AG:7/9/21:3(ON)
GREEN, William P.	TARLTON, Hopewell Ginther	27 APR 1828	MB; AG:29/4/28:3(Wal)
GREENFIELD, Thomas	ALEXANDER, Marianne T. wid/o Robert Alexander d/o John Stoddert	- 1798	DBF:85; DBI:371; MDBS9:153; FX
GREENLEAF, Thomas	BAYNE, Susan	31 MAY 1821	WB3:237; DCM
GREENOLDS, John	ALLEN, Mary	c.27 APR 1807	MB
GREENWAY, Capt. Jos.	HARPER, Rebecca d/o Capt. John Harper	-9 MAR 1785	HCC:160; X:51; 1787:72; 1791:10; FPCG; FSH:A-9
GREENWELL, Cornelius	SOUTHARD, Eliza G.	c.9 APR 1830	MB
GREENWOOD, Benjamin	MYERS, Catharine	4 DEC 1817	SP; MR(WHW); MB; AG:6/12/17:2(WHW)
GREENWOOD, John	BELTZ, Elizabeth	NOV 1793	FPC:13(JM); 1799:24
GREENWOOD, William	YOUNG, Mary Ann	-1834	CFF#36I
GREER, William	COLEMAN, Susan	4 SEP 1821	MR(ON); MB
GREGORY, William	BARTLEMAN, Margaret Douglass eldest d/o William Bartleman	3 DEC 1822	MR(WA); MB; AG:5/12/22:2(WA)
GREGORY, William	HARPER, Sally	- 1824	FS:1/90:1
GRETTER, Elias Thomas	GRETTER, Mary	JUN 1793	FPC:13(JM)
GRETTER, John	GOULDING, Margaret	-13 JUL 1782	HCE:258; FWD:267; 1787:72; 1791:10; IGI

Husband	Wife	Event or Marriage	Reference(s)
GRETTER, Michael	_____, Elizabeth	-4 JUL 1774	HCD:311; 1787:72; 1791:10; FDM:12; HCOrd:22/6/87
GRETTER, Michael, Jr. Place: Henrico Co.	HEWITT, Johanna	21 DEC 1808	DBC2:178; IGI
GREW, John	FOWLE, Rebecca H.	27 MAY 1835	SP
GRIFFITH, David	COLVILL, Hannah	c.1767	HCB:238; IGI HCC:47
GRIFFITH, David	WILLIAMS, Mary	28 JAN 1804	MR(WM); MB
GRIFFITH, Kinsey Place: Washington DC	M'LEOD, Elizabeth d/o Daniel M'Leod	4 SEP 1817	AG:6/9/17:3(Mc)
GRIFFITH, Samuel Gold. Place: Baltimore MD	LAYFIELD, Mary	2 JUN 1807	DBQ:328; IGI
GRIFFITH, Thomas Place: Washington DC	PATTON, Catharine d/o James Patton	29 OCT 1829	AG:2/11/29:3
GRIFFIN, William	LANNUM, Letitia s/o John Lannum	c.3 APR 1804	MB
GRIGG, Joseph	SOLOMON, Caroline	c.5 MAR 1828	MB
GRIGSBY, James	FREEMAN, Nancy	8 DEC 1814	MR(WHW); MB
GRIMES (also see "Grymes")			
GRIMES, George	_____, Elizabeth	-12 SEP 1782	HCOrd:12/9/82
GRIMES, James	_____, Elizabeth	-8 JUN 1798	DBC:85; 1787:72; 1799:34
GRIMES, John	BEDINGER, Hannah	8 MAY 1790	FPC:13(JM)
GRIMES, John	HANNAH, Jane	DEC 1795	FPC:13(JM); 1799:20
GRIMES, Joseph	BARNES, Mrs. Margaret	30 SEP 1830	MB; AG:2/10/30:3(Sco)
GRIMES, Nicholas	PAYNE, Mrs. Mary w/o George Payne	c.13 JAN 1803	MB
GRIMES, Thomas (C)	HEPBURN, Latitia (C)	28 AUG 1821	MR(ON); MB
GRIMES, William	PURKIS, Rhode d/o Thomas Purkis	10 JUL 1811	MR(IR); MB
GRIMSHAW, Thomas	RADDEN, Onnar	c.7 JUL 1804	MB; DBU:220
GRISWOLD, Rev. George Place: Washington DC	COOMBE, Eliza d/o Griffith Coombe	27 MAY 1828	AG:30/5/28:3(By)
GRISWOLD, Lyman	TAYLOR, Ann	24 JUN 1830	MR(LA); MB
GROVES, Caleb	DAVIS, Nancy	28 MAY 1811	AG:1/6/11:3(IR); MR(IR); MB
GRUB, Curtis	TOMLINSON, Sarah	24 SEP 1801	AG:25/9/01:3
GRUBB, John	KILTON, Eliza Mary	19 SEP 1816	WB2:209; LVA1:3; AG:21/9/16(WHW); MR(WHW); MB
GRUBB, Samuel	WILSON, Eleanor A.S.	28 MAR 1826	AG:31/3/26:3
GRUVER, John	TYLER, Elizabeth Maria	11 MAY 1825	TMCC(G:5); MR:93; MB
GRYMES (also see "Grimes")			
GRYMES, Edward	SINCLAIR, Nancy	c.29 MAR 1802	MB
GRYMES, Robert	GRAY, Precilla	24 NOV 1803	MR(JM); MB
GRYMES, William	LANHAM, Letty	3 APR 1804	FPC:13(JM)
GUEST, Joshua	REINTZELL, Catherine	29 FEB 1790	FPC:13(JM)
GUIONNET, _____	EWELL, Susanna si/o Thomas W. Ewell	-10 JUL 1830	WB4:142
GUIREY, Rev. William	PHILIPS, _____	15 JAN 1807	AG:27/1/07:3

Husband	Wife	Event or Marriage	Reference(s)
GULLAT, William	TAYLOR, Elizabeth "Betsey"	18 DEC 1800	FPC:13(JM); AG:24/4/12:3
GULLATT, James	COOPER, Elizabeth "Betsy" d/o Joel Cooper	4 MAR 1797	FPC:13(JM); HCK:413 FPCG
GUNN, Obediah	WHITE, Ann	3 FEB 1799	FPC:13(JM); 1800:55
GUNNELL, George West Place: Fairfax Co.	RATCLIFFE, Lotion youngest d/o Richard Ratcliffe	5 OCT 1819	AG:13/10/19:3(SR)
GUNNELL, George West Place: Fairfax Co.	YOUNG, Emmaline	3 OCT 1839	PW:184
GUNNELL, Hugh W. Place: Fairfax Co.	TRAMMELL, Elizabeth	5 NOV 1839	PW:184
GUNNELL, Ira	VERMILLION, Margaret	c.24 DEC 1812	DCM
GUNNELL, James	DENEALE, Ann "Nancy"	1783	Note[44]
GUNNELL, Dr. James S.	MACKALL, Hellen M.	c.12 OCT 1825	DCM
GUNNELL, John	HALL, Letty	7 SEP 1798	FPC:13(JM)
GUNNELL, John	SPENCER, Sarah Ann	c.22 FEB 1825	DCM
GUNNELL, Presley	HUNTER, Ann d/o John Hunter	-24 FEB 1806	DBE2:292; WBB:339; FDD4:216
GUNNELL, William	_____, Martha	-3 MAR 1714	Note[45]
GUNNELL, William	NEALE, Jemima si/o Shapleigh Neale	-8 JUN 1777	FWD:36
GUNNELL, Hon. William	COLEMAN, Sarah	28 OCT 1779	
GUNNELL, William Place: Fairfax Co.	LANHAM, Elizabeth	5 JAN 1809	PW:184
GUNNELL, William Hunter	LANHAM, Elizabeth	5 JAN 1809	PW:184
GUTHRIDGE, John	SHANNON, Elizabeth	c.23 OCT 1805	MB
GUTHRIE, John	_____, Mary		1799:40; 1800:55
GUTHRIE, John Pollard	HUTCHENSON, Elizabeth	c.21 AUG 1799	R2:227; 1800:52
GUTHRIE, William	COUCHMAN, Eliza d/o Letitia Couchman	29 JUL 1814	MR(IR); MB
GUY, John	BUSTLE, Winefred	29 DEC 1815	MR(IR); MB
GWYNN, Caleb Dorsey	HAWKINS, Adelaide Eleanor d/o John Hawkins	12 APR 1815	AG:18/4/15:3(RE); BR:106

Husband	Wife	Event or Marriage	Reference(s)

H

Husband	Wife	Event or Marriage	Reference(s)
HADEN, Garret	WOOD, Eleanor	17 APR 1803	MR(JM); MB
HADEN, Stephen	HARDEN, Elizabeth	10 JUL 1808	FPC:15(JM)
HAINES, Daniel	GRUBB, Beulah	13 JUN 1804	H:744
HAINES, Daniel	HENDERSON, Frances	8 OCT 1822	SP;
Place: *Bellevoir*			AG:10/10/22:3(WHW)
HAISLIP, Henry	FUGATE, Sarah	12 JAN 1826	AG:19/1/26:3(JR)
HALE, Benjamin	WHITE, Judith	c.18 AUG 1804	MB
HALE, Henry D.	YATES, Frances L.D.	c.29 JAN 1822	MB
HALL, Henry	BERRY, Ann Eliza	7 JUN 1827	SP; MR(WJ)
HALL, Jacob	ALLISON, Ann	1788	FB
HALL, Jacob	HALL, Delia	c.25 DEC 1813	MB
HALL, James	FISHER, Rebecca	4 OCT 1800	FPC:15(JM)
HALL, James	COAX, Ann Eliza	5 APR 1827	MR(WA); MB
	ward of Wm. B. Coax		
HALL, Lawrence	PERRY, Jane	29 MAR 1810	FPC:15(JM)
HALL, Peter	GATES, Susan	12 SEP 1830	AG:2/10/30:3
Place: Washington DC			
HALL, Richard	REYNOLDS, Ellen Melvina	c.21 JUL 1830	MB
HALL, Robert C.	NOTTINGHAM, Eleanor	13 APR 1797	FPC:15(JM)
HALL, Washington (C)	DUTCHY, Ceilla (C)	12 FEB 1812	MR(IR); MB
HALL, William	GRAHAM, Penelope	22 OCT 1818	MR(JM); MB
HALL, William J.	CRAIG, Mary Grace	25 JAN 1797	AG:28/1/97:3(PA);
Place: Res. of Capt. George Hunter, Baltimore MD			WBC:32; FPCG;
			FPC:14; TA:86;
			BMJ:27/1/97
HALL, William J.	_____, Elizabeth	-8 APR 1803	FPC:14
HALLBRIGHT, Joseph	CAMPBELL, Nancy	19 JAN 1804	MR(WM); MB
HALLEY, William	_____, Esther	-10 NOV 1805	WBC:152; 1787:72;
			1799:10;
			WB4:27; 1791:10;
			FPCC(42:71)
HALLIS, Spencer (C)	GRANT, Sarah (C)	c.28 JUL 1813	MB[46]
HALLODAY, James	_____, Mary	-2 JUL 1786	FPCG; 1787:73
HALLS, George	FURGERSON, Bitha	15 JUN 1812	MR(IR)
HALLOWOOD, Charles	BUSSELL, Rody	25 OCT 1812	FPC:15(JM); MB
HALLY, John	SUMMER, Sythe	15 JAN 1795	FB; FM(1855):6
HAMERSLEY, Lt. Thomas	NOLAND, Emily A.	21 OCT 1830	AG:28/10/30:3
Place: Middleburg			
HAMILTON, David	GOING, Ann	11 SEP 1801	FPC:15(JM); MR(JM);
			MB
HAMILTON, James	DALTON, _____	c.JUN 1798	AG:/19/6/98:3
HAMILTON, James H.	_____, Margaret	-4 JAN 1811	DBU:319; 1799:12
HAMILTON, Philip	_____, Catharine		TMCC(Q:6); WB8:175
HAMILTON, Robert	GRAY, Hester	29 OCT 1794	FPC:15(JM); 1800:57;
			1799:34
HAMILTON, Theo. James	_____, Eunice	-24 SEP 1795	HCG:157
HAMILTON, Thomas	_____, Sarah	-30 MAR 1803	DBG:113; 1800:54
HAMILTON, Wesley (C)	PAGE, Delilah (C)	25 FEB 1830	MR(LA); MB
HAMILTON, William	GILLESPIE, Martha	-5 SEP 1787	HCC:258
HAMILTON, William	EARLE, Marian	-23 AUG 1826	WB3:292
	d/o Esaias Earle		

Husband	Wife	Event or Marriage	Reference(s)
HAMMERSLEY, Francis	SLAUGHTER, Elizabeth Brent	-22 FEB 1815	AG:25/2/15:3; FDL2:204
HAM(M)ERSLEY, Francis	RODGERS, Jane	22 MAR 1816	MR(JMH); MB
HAMMETT, John B., Jr.	McINTIRE, Mary eldest d/o Capt. Charles McIntire	7 MAY 1829	NI:12/5/29; MR(EH); MB; AG:11/5/29:3(EH)
HAMMOND, James	BOWEN, Rosanna	NOV 1794	FPC:15(JM); 1799:4
HAMMOND, James	_____, Milly	-5 JUN 1815	DBC2:413
HAMMOND, James (C)	HANSON, Grace (C)	30 OCT 1822	MR(ON); MB
HAMPSON, Bryan	HATTON, Lucy	c.23 FEB 1793	DBA:388; 1791:11; AG:23/2/93:3;FDW:149
HANCOCK, John B.	HULL, Mary	4 SEP 1816	MR(JMH); MPC:E25; MB
HANCOCK, William	ELLZEY, Elizabeth d/o Lewis Ellzey	-1 OCT 1786	FWE:223
HAND, Caleb Place: Philadelphia PA	KEEN, Leah C.	23 NOV 1807	AG:30/11/07:3
HANDLESS, Moses (C)	GRANT, Nancy (C)	16 NOV 1815	MR(WHW); MB
HANES, London	MORGAN, Polly	c.20 DEC 1804	MB
HANEY, Charles	LAWS, Ann	c.20 AUG 1830	MB
HANEY, Robert	CHESHIRE, Jane	c.25 NOV 1802	MB
HANEY, William	EMERSON, Delila	11 JUL 1822	MR(EH); MB
HANLEY, Enoch	DUVAUN, Debby	26 FEB 1804	FPC:15(JM); MR(JM); MB
HANNAH, Alexander	_____, Mary		1799:36; 1800:58; FPCG
HANNAH, George Emp.	DUNLAP, Jane	-11 APR 1811	WB1:67; DBU:229
HANNAH, Nicholas Place: Anne Arundel Co. MD	LEE, Elizabeth	18 FEB 1779	IGI
HANNAH, [Nicholas]	DUNLAP, Elizabeth Isabella	-11 APR 1811	WB1:67
HANNON, Walter W.	DAILEY, Ann	19 DEC 1816	MR(ON); MB
HANNON, William H.	HODGKIN, Mary	30 DEC 1813	FPC:15(JM); MB
HANSON, Isaac K.	HARRISON, Dorothy		B:85
HANSON, Mark (C)	_____, Rachel (C)		1799:28; 1800:55
HANSON, Mark (C)	TOWNSHEND, Catharine (C)	20 MAY 1818	MR(IR); MB
HANSON, Mark	CLARKE, Elizabeth	2 MAY 1822	MR(EH); MB
HANSON, Maj. Samuel	_____, Mary	-1 NOV 1793	HCE:217; 1787:72; 1791:11
HANTZMON, Henry	_____, Elizabeth		UC:W124
HARDBOWER, G.	_____, Margaret Lena		UC:E216
HARDEN, William	ADAMS, Ann Elizabeth	c.20 DEC 1822	WB3:324; DCM
HARDGROVE, Pollard	McCRETY, July	MAR 1794	FPC:15(JM)
HARDING, _____	SINCLAIR, Mary d/o Thomas Sinclair	-2 FEB 1812	FPCG; FWL:209
HARDING, George W.	SMEDLEY, Alice d/o David Smedley	c.8 DEC 1824	MB
HARDING, Richard	CATTERTON, Lucretia	c.16 FEB 1805	MB
HARDY, Charles	GARLICK, Patience	29 OCT 1794	FPC:15(JM)
HARDY, John	ROBERTSON, Elizabeth	6 OCT 1800	FPC:15(JM)
HARDY, Patrick	WHEATON, Catharine	16 APR 1822	MR(JR)
HARDYMAN, Thomas	CARTER, Mary	1 AUG 1790	FPC:15(JM)
HARKINS, Robert	SWITZER, Ann	14 FEB 1823	MB; AG:15/2/23:3

Husband	Wife	Event or Marriage	Reference(s)
HARLEY, George	HIGS, Eleanor	c.10 MAR 1830	MB
HARLEY, John	_____, Mary	-24 SEP 1785	HCOrd:24/9/85
HARMON, Aaron D.	PASCOE, Mary	6 MAY 1823	AG:8/5/23:3; MR(WA);
	d/o Charles Pascoe		MB
HARPER, Charles	JANNEY, Sarah	28 DEC 1791	J:89
	d/o Joseph Janney		
HARPER, Edward	HIGGINSON, Rose	c.15 DEC 1785	AG:15/12/85:3;
			1787:73; 1799:26;
			1800:59; FPCG;
			BR:104
HARPER, Henson	PETTIT, Nancy	MAY 1808	PW:192
Place: Fairfax Co.			
HARPER, James	RICE, Anna	OCT 1795	FPC:15(JM)
HARPER, John	CUNNINGHAM, Mary	1790	FB; 1787:72;
			1791:11; 1799:8;
			1800:59; FPC:14
HARPER, John	GRETTER, Dorothy	-4 SEP 1800	DBI:341; CCG:A1;
			AA:4/9/00:3;
			1799:26
HARPER, Capt. John	WELLS, Sarah	20 OCT 1750	FSH:A-8
HARPER, Capt. John	CASWELL, Mary	1782	FSH:A-8
HARPER, Capt. John	DAVIS, Sarah	6 JUN 1805	DBX:259; FPC:15(JM);
	d/o Samuel Davis		FPCC(42:43); MB;
			AG:7/6/08(JM)
HARPER, John	WEST, Margaret		BR:105
s/o Capt. John Harper	d/o John West		
HARPER, John	BROADBACK, Mary Ann	c.20 JUN 1829	MB
HARPER, John W.	_____, Dorothy	-3 SEP 1800	CCG
HARPER, R.W.	LYLES, Sarah M.	2 JUL 1815	AG:8/7/15:3(Y)
	d/o Col. William Lyles, of Prince George's Co. MD		
HARPER, Robert	WASHINGTON, Sarah		BR:105; FSH:A-9;
	d/o John Washington		FWD:263
HARPER, Capt. Robert	DAVIS, Mary Ann	18 MAY 1809	DBX:259; FPC:15(JM);
	d/o Samuel Davis		AG:19/5/09:3(JM);
			MB
HARPER, Samuel	BROOKE, Sarah	23 JUL 1789	BR:142
s/o Capt. John	d/o Dr. Richard Brooke		
HARPER, Samuel D.	_____, Sarah	-27 FEB 1799	HCL:287; 1791:11;
			1799:38; 1800:55
HARPER, Samuel D.	NORTH, Sarah "Sally" K.	5 SEP 1815	AG:14/9/15:3(BN);
Place: Charlestown	d/o Capt. North		FDW2:25
HARPER, Washington T.	ELLICOTT, Ann	15 MAR 1827	AG:16/3/27:3(WA);
	d/o John Ellicott of Baltimore MD		NI:17/3/27; MB
HARPER, William	GRIMSLEY, Ann	1 FEB 1823	MR(IR); MB
	si/o Levi Grimsley		
HARPER, William, Sr.	SCULL, Mary	14 JUN 1781	R2:263; 1787:72;
s/o John Harper	d/o William Scull		1791:11; BR:105;
			1799:30; 1800:53
HARPER, Dr. William, Jr.	NEWTON, Mary Thomas	17 OCT 1810	FPCC;
Place: Loudoun Co.	d/o John and Mary T. Newton		AG:22/10/10:3(MI)
HARPER, William A.	_____, Sarah	-26 AUG 1821	WB3:24
HARRIDEN, Andrew	DATES, Ann	31 JUL 1820	MR(WHW); MB
HARRIS, Anthony (C)	WOOD, Fanny (C)	31 OCT 1816	MR(ON); MB

Husband	Wife	Event or Marriage	Reference(s)
HARRIS, Hugh	WILLIAMS, Nancy	c.13 DEC 1802	MB[47]
HARRIS(S), James	LONGDEN, Lucy A. d/o Ralph Longden	4 NOV 1813	AG:6/11/13:3(JM); TMCC(K:3);FPC:15(JM); MB
HARRIS, James	_____, Henrietta	-23 JAN 1813	DBW:406
HARRIS(S), James	SMITH, Mary	28 NOV 1830	AG:4/12/30:3
HARRIS, James	_____, Mary Elinor	-26 DEC 1837	WB4:162
HARRIS, John	LEE, Zenobia	c.2 FEB 1822	MB
HARRIS, John A.	ADDISON, Susanna	1788	FB; 1787:73
HARRIS, Joseph	DORSEY, Winnifred	17 DEC 1801	MR(JM); MB
HARRIS, Joseph	WARD, Rebecca	c.10 JAN 1824	MB
HARRIS, Loudon	MORGAN, Polly d/o Elizabeth Morgan	c.20 DEC 1804	MB
HARRIS, Matthias	MANDELL, Mary Elizabeth	11 JAN 1831	MR(WJ)
HARRIS, Nathan	CORCORN, Margaret W.	10 JUL 1823	MR(IR); MB
HARRIS, Nathan	CLAGETT, Mary d/o Horatio Clagett	3 NOV 1829	RMSD:3; MB; AG:4/11/29:3(Wal)
HARRIS, Pompey Pohra	_____, Rose	-28 MAY 1821	WB3:111
HARRIS, Pompey Pohra	_____, Lucy	-28 MAY 1821	WB3:111
HARRIS (also see "Poorer, Pompey")			
HARRIS, Theophilus	_____, Mary	-5 OCT 1797	HCI:331
HARRIS, Walter	VERNON, Julia Ann	28 APR 1829	SP; MR(WJ); MB
HARRIS, William	THOMPSON, Catharine	c.4 DEC 1817	MB
HARRIS, William	ROSS, Catharine	2 AUG 1820	MR(SC); MB
HARRIS, Wm. Alexander	SKIDMORE, Nancy d/o [Gerrard] Skidmore	c.8 MAY 1809	MB; DBW:546
HARRISON, B.E.	NORVILLE, Catherine d/o Peyton Norville	31 DEC 1820	A:2/1/21
HARRISON, Benjamin	BRANHAM, Lucy	c.24 JUN 1830	MB
HARRISON, Rev. Elias	VEITCH, Elizabeth d/o R. Veitch	15 MAY 1820	MR(JM); MB; FPCC(43:93); AG:18/5/20:3(JM)
HARRISON, George	SNYDER, Polly d/o Elizabeth Sims	13 OCT 1814	FPC:15(JM); MB
HARRISON, John	WATKINS, Mary	28 SEP 1820	MR(EH)
HARRISON, John D.	CARLIN, Elizabeth	30 DEC 1815	MR(JMH); WB6:189; MPC:E112; MB
HARRISON, Richard	CRAIK, Ann "Nancy"	24 OCT 1791	FPC:15(JM); WBB:418
HARRISON, Samuel	HESS, Barbara (Butt) wid/o Jacob Hess	-6 AUG 1793	HCE:151; 1791:12; CRA:177, 193
HARRISON, Thomas	ALEXANDER, Mary Stuart	22 FEB 1803	P:356
HARRISON, Thomas	SHEPPARD, Hannah	16 DEC 1824	AG:1/1/25:3(JR)
HARRISON, Thomas	CRANDELL, Elizabeth ward of Anthony Rhodes	15 FEB 1827	MB; AG:9/3/27:3(EH)
HARRISON, Timothy P.	MADDOCK, Ann R.	c.4 JUN 1813	MB
HARRISON, William	GOODRICK, Ann	c.25 SEP 1805	MB
HARROWER, Hyram	McDONALD, Eliza	24 OCT 1815	FPC:15(JM); MB
HARSHMAN, Henry	_____, Susaner		1800:53
HART, Edward	ZIMMERMAN, Eliza	2 APR 1825	MR(WHW); MB
HART, Hezekiah Place: Washington DC	BREST, Rosina	5 JUN 1827	SP; AG:7/6/27:3(Mc)
HARTLEY, George	PEPPER, Sarah	13 JUN 1802	MR(JM); MB

Husband	Wife	Event or Marriage	Reference(s)
HARTSHORNE, Pattison br/o William Hartshorne Place: Philadelphia PA	WALN, Susanna	10 FEB 1776	DBW:386, 410; IGI
HARTSHORNE, William Place: Philadelphia PA	SAUNDERS, Susanna d/o Joseph Saunders	8 OCT 1767	DBA:469; H:746 WB2:201; FWF:251; 1787:73; 1791:12
HARTSHORNE, William Place: Friends' Meeting House, wid/o Benjamin Shreve	SHREVE, Mrs. Susannah (Wood)	30 JUN 1803	MR(TM); DBQ:156; DBQ:230; AA:1/7/03:3
HARTSHORNE, Wm. Jr.	WILSON, Mrs. Mary wid/o Rev. Wilson	17 MAR 1803	FPC:14; NH:19/3/03
HASON, John (C)	THOMAS, Lucy (C)	c.3 JUL 1815	MB
HATHERINGTON, James	YEARLY, Mary Ann B.	24 FEB 1821	MR(IR); MB
HATHERLY, Nathan	COOKE, Rebecca	c.17 DEC 1803	MB
HATTON, Henry D. Place: Broad Creek MD	LYLES, Emily d/o Col. W. Lyles	14 JAN 1812	AG:22/1/12:3(G)
HATTON, Nathaniel Place: Prince George's Co. MD	BURCH, Ann N.	20 FEB 1816	AG:24/2/16:3(Y)
HAWKINS, Benjamin	WILLIS, Nancy	28 JAN 1801	MR(JM)
HAWKINS, John	THOMPSON, Alice Corbin d/o Dr. Adam Thompson	1781	BR:106; FDR:51
HAWL, James	COX, Ann Elizabeth	5 APR 1827	AG:7/4/27:3(WA)
HAWLEY, Rev. Wm.	POTTS, Wilhelmina Douglas	25 AUG 1818	AH:28/8/18(ON); MR(ON); MB; AG:31/8/18:2(ON)
HAYCOCK, William	MASON, Sarah	29 OCT 1794	FPC:15(JM); 1787:72
HAYES, Andrew	_____, Mary	-13 SEP 1808	DBQ:396; 1787:72; 1791:12
HAYES, Fielder	VERMILLION, Elenor	26 DEC 1799	FPC:15(JM)
HAYES, Dr. John	KNOX, Anne Somerville d/o Dr. Thomas Knox, of Stafford Co.	21SEP 1826	UT:25/9/26:3
HAYNES, John	BAYNE, Mary d/o Henry Bayne	-7 APR 1812	WB1:167
HAYNES, John	BARBER, Mary	c.13 JAN 1810	MB
HAYS, John	_____, Mary	- OCT 1812	DBW:304
HEAD, Benjamin	LIMRICK, Anna	6 JUL 1806	MR(JM); MB
HEAD, Lewis	REASON, Sarah	5 DEC 1806	MR(IR); MB
HEADLY, George	GORDON, Sarah d/o David Gordon	-27 MAY 1793	HCE:161, 292
HEALING, Edward	DUNN, Martha	15 JAN 1801	MR(JM)
HEATH, Charles	KENT, Malinda	24 DEC 1801	FPC:15(JM); MR(JM)
HEATH, John P.	DEAKINS, Elizabeth	25 MAR 1819	AG:27/3/19:2(WDA)
HEDKINS, Walter	DIXON, Margaret	28 MAY 1797	FPC:15(JM)
HEINEMAN, Jacob	_____, Mary Ann	-16 APR 1795	DBB:400; 1787:73; 1791:12
HEISER, Andrew	BRIGHT, Anna Mary d/o Wendall Bright	-1 DEC 1784	FWE:38
HEISH, Conrad	_____, Hetty	-20 DEC 1828	SP
HEISKELL, Peter Place: Winchester	WETZEL, Susannah	13 MAY 1783	DBS:449; IGI
HEITH (see "Keith")			
HELLRIGEL, Christian Lod.	_____, Barbara	-8 AUG 1807	WBC:326; SPC(64:2)

Husband	Wife	Event or Marriage	Reference(s)
HELLRIGLE, Philip Place: *Belvoir*, Fairfax Co.	HENDERSON, Ann C. d/o John Henderson	5 JAN 1820	AG:14/1/20:3(WHW); SP
HELM, Francis T.	McKINNEY, Sarah B.	16 SEP 1816	MR(JM); MB
HELM, Strother M.	VASSE, Mary Ann d/o Ambrose Vasse	17 DEC 1812	AG:19/12/12:3(M); MB
HENDERSON, Alexander	MOORE, Sarah	1773	FB; ES:95
HENDERSON, Alexander	_____, Anne	-16 SEP 1834	SPC
HENDERSON, Col. Archibald	CAZENOVE, Anna Maria second d/o Anthony Charles Cazenove	16 OCT 1823	MB; AG:18/10/23:3
HENDERSON, George	JEFFRIES, Ann	-10 JUL 1840	TMCC(F:6)
HENDERSON, James Lewis	MOORE, Julia Ann ward of Wilkerson Williams	17 DEC 1829	MR(LA); MB; AG:19/12/29:3(LA)
HENDERSON, Peter	CURREY, Elizabeth eldest d/o John Currey	27 AUG 1829	MB; AG:29/8/29:3
HENDERSON, Tarleton T.	HUGHS, Eliza Ann d/o John Hughs	29 MAR 1827	AG:31/3/27:3(WA); MB; MR(WA)
HENDERSON, William	TOWERS, Dorcas (Godfrey)	1804	R2:293
HENDERSON, Willis	SANFORD, Catharine	c.3 JUL 1823	MB
HENDRICKS, James	_____, Kitty	-25 JAN 1789	FDR:321
HENGARTY, William	KITELY, Rachel	1 MAR 1801	MR(JM)
HENNINGER, John Fredk.	SWINGSFIRE, Francisca Wilh.	-20 DEC 1770	LP#A514
HENRY, Capt. Isaac	UNDERWOOD, Martha or "Mackey"	5 AUG 1811	AG:7/8/11:3(G); SP; MB
HENRY, James	CUMMING, Margaret	-5 JUN 1816	WB2:174
HENRY, John	GATES, Emelia	c.1 MAY 1809	MB
HENRY, John	WILLIAMSON, Elizabeth	c.3 MAY 1816	MB
HENRY, John B. Place: Jefferson Co.	DOUGLASS, Nancy d/o Wm. Douglass	15 JUN 1815	AG:30/6/15:3
HENSLER, John	_____, Margaret	-21 OCT 1793	HCI:481
HENSON, James	DORSEY, Elizabeth	24 JAN 1828	AG:2/2/28:3(Sco)
HENSON, Mark	CLARKE, Elizabeth	2 MAY 1822	MR(EH); MB
HENTON, Richard	ARMSTRONG, Julia Ann	15 NOV 1830	MR(IR); MB
HEPBURN, William	_____, Agnes	-16 JAN 1773	DBB:195; 1787:72; FPCG; FDA2:311; FDK:260; HCOrd:22/4/84
HERBERT, John Carlyle	SNOWDEN, Mary d/o Thomas Snowden	7 MAR 1805	OT:42; AHM:6/1:22
HERBERT, Noblet Place: *Mount Vernon*	WASHINGTON, Mary Lee	18 NOV 1813	AG:23/11/13:3(ON)
HERBERT, Thomas	DALTON, Jane d/o John Dalton	-24 APR 1793	HCE:63; 1791:12; FDP:86
HERBERT, Thomas	_____, Fanny	-4 MAR 1803	CCG
HERBERT, Dr. Thomas S.	HAMMOND, Camillia A. d/o Denton Hammond, of Anne Arundel Co. MD	2 NOV 1830	AG:6/11/30:3
HERBERT, William	CARLYLE, Sarah Fairfax	-18 FEB 1778	OT:42; FWD:203; 1787:72; 1791:12; DBA:95
HERBERT, William, Jr.	DULANY, Maria Henrietta d/o Benjamin Dulany	22 DEC 1814	CCC(62,70); MB; DBD2:273; AG:24/12/14:3(ON)
HEREFORD, John Place: Fairfax Co.	MAUZEY, Sarah	8 APR 1804	R2:299

Husband	Wife	Event or Marriage	Reference(s)
HERNDON, Dr. Brodie	HANSBROUGH, Lucy Ellen d/o Joseph Hansbrough, of Culpeper Co.	26 NOV 1830	AG:15/12/30:3
HERYFORD, John	[BARNES], Jane	-19 FEB 1733	CC:102; IGI
HESTON, Samuel	McKAY, Susan	1 MAY 1823	MR(IR); MB
HEWES, Aaron	_____, Mary	-28 JUN 1793	HCE:231; 1791:13; 1799:4; H:748
HEWES, Abram	MILLER, Rachel d/o Mordecai Miller	-25 JAN 1827	QC; H:748; Note[48]
HEWITT, Edmund	DORSEY, Sarah Ann	c.27 SEP 1821	MB; AG:29/9/21:3(SC)
HEWITT, Richard	LAKE, Eleanor d/o Richard Lake	-23 NOV 1816	DBD2:331; FDX:31
HEWITT, Thomas W.	SMITH, Margaret Boyd d/o Dr. Augustine J. Smith	1 JUN 1819	AH:7/6/19(ON); SPC(61:2); AG:4/6/19:3(ON)
HICKEY, Daniel	GOODS, Susannah	c.26 DEC 1814	MB
HICKMAN, John	_____, Mary	-28 MAR 1795	HCF:375
HICKMAN, William	_____, Rebecca	-17 NOV 1795	HCF:528; 1787:72; 1791:13
HICKS, Nehemiah	BAYNE, Elizabeth	23 SEP 1819	AH:27/9/19(WHW); CT:25/9/19
HICKS, William	_____, Priscilla	-17 FEB 1793	HCE:70
HICKS, William (C)	PARKER, Jenny (C)	c.5 FEB 1825	MB
HICKSON, James	DAVIS, Mrs. Matilda	c.17 DEC 1829	MB; MR(LA)
HIENTZ, Mordecai	MASON, Elizabeth	c.11 JUN 1804	MB
HIGDON, John	REYNOLDS, Rebecca d/o William Reynolds	21 FEB 1816	MR(JMH); MB
HIGGINS, William	BRADSHAW, Eleanor	c.6 JUL 1807	MB
HILL, Barton	ASHFORD, Tracey	26 FEB 1791	FPC:15(JM)
HILL, Clement B. Place: Prince George's Co. MD	BERRY, Mrs. Anna Maria	23 NOV 1830	AG:26/11/30:3
HILL, George	BENTON, Elizabeth	1788	FB; 1787:73; 1791:13; 1799:32; 1800:52
HILL, Godardus	LOGAN, Rachael	12 DEC 1809	MR(IR); MB
HILL, James	TENNESON, Eleanor	11 JAN 1817	MB; AG:15/1/17:3
HILL, John	PERRY, Mary	19 MAR 1790	FPC:15(JM); 1799:32; 1800:52
HILL, John	CALENDER, Eleanor	8 AUG 1822	MR(JF); MB
HILL, John Place: Washington DC	KELL, Alesanna	3 JUL 1818	AG:10/7/28:3(WH)
HILL, John Bennett	UNDERWOOD, Mary	26 NOV 1807	FPC:15(JM); MB
HILL, Joseph	BARKER, Caroline	c.22 MAR 1827	MB
HILL, Lawrence	PERRY, Jane d/o Alexander Perry	29 MAR 1810	FPC:15(JM); MB; DBY:398; AG:31/3/10:3(JM)
HILLIARD, Joseph	LUTZ, Sophia	15 AUG 1810	MR(IR); MB
HILLIARY, Washington	JENKINS, Emeline d/o Capt. Uriah Jenkins	2 DEC 1830	AG:4/12/30:3; SP; MR(WJ); MB
HILLS, Samuel	GIRD, Mrs. Eudocia (Dorsey) d/o Maj. Richard Dorsey	6 FEB 1823	NI:14/2/23
HILTON, Samuel	STEELE, Catharine	16 FEB 1830	MR(JL); MPC:W58; MB; AG:24/2/30:3(LA)

Husband	Wife	Event or Marriage	Reference(s)
HIMINDENER, C.D.	CHURCHMAN, Ann	c.7 JAN 1829	MB
HINEMAN, George	_____, Nancy	-15 OCT 1792	HCE:101
HINES, Alfred	ODLETON, Maria	11 AUG 1830	MR(IR); MB
HINES, John	GILBERT, Isabella	4 OCT 1820	MR(WA); MB
HINES, Philip	HOWARD, Julia Ann	28 MAY 1826	UT:29/5/26:2(RD)
HINGSTON, Nicholas	BLOOMFIELD, Elizabeth	26 JAN 1806	AG:27/1/06:3(B);
Place: Georgetown DC	si/o Robert Bloomfield		NI:24/12/23
HINGSTON, Nicholas	EVANS, Jane	25 AUG 1825	MR(WHW); MB;
			AG:27/8/25:3(WHW);
			AG:22/11/30:3
HINGSTON, Nicholas	_____, Mary Jane	-18 NOV 1830	AG:22/11/30:3
HIPKINS, Lewis, Sr.	ADAMS, Susannah	17 JAN 1782	FF:229
	d/o William Adams		
HIPKINS, Capt. Lewis, Jr.	CARNE, Mary Libby	15 AUG 1809	MB; AG:16/8/09:3;
	d/o William Carne		WB1:142;
			FPCC(42:67)
HITE, Jacob	_____, Frances	-2 DEC 1773	FDL:257
HITTON, Samuel	STEEL, Catharine	16 FEB 1830	MR(LA)
HOATZ, Peter	SHULTZ, Becky	9 AUG 1789	FPC:15(JM)
HOBART, Nathaniel P.	POTTS, Johanna H.	18 APR 1813	AG:21/4/13:3(M);
			MB
HOBB, Henry	RUNNELLS, Sarah	c.18 JUN 1823	MB
HOBBS, Henry	REYNOLDS, Mrs. Louisa	19 JUN 1823	AG:21/6/23:3(RD)
HOBBY, _____	HARTSHORNE, Sarah	-4 APR 1792	FDU:92
	d/o John Hartshorne		
HODGKIN, Robert	TAYLOR, Clary	10 SEP 1817	MR(AG); MB
	d/o Rebecca Silence		
HODGKIN, Robert	FRASER, Elizabeth Beall	28 JUN 1831	MB
HODGKINS, Daniel	SCOTT, Alley	c.8 AUG 1813	MB
HODGKINS, James	ARMSTRONG, Susanna	14 JUL 1810	MR(IR); MB
HODGKINS, John	DALTON, Rachel	28 MAY 1797	FPC:15(JM); WB1:89
HODGKINSON, Anthony	_____, Phebe	-21 OCT 1816	DBD2:137
HODGSON, William	LEE, Portia	2 MAY 1799	OT:31; DBC2:429;
	d/o William Lee, of *Greenspring*		1791:13; CCC(10);
			AG:14/5/99:3
HOFF, Lewis	RAPLEY, Eliza M.	10 JUN 1821	NI:14/6/21;
Place: Norfolk	d/o Abraham Rapley		AG:13/6/21:3
HOFFMAN, Frederick	CARLIN, Anne	c.16 AUG 1815	DCM
HOFFMAN, Jacob	COCKE, Elizabeth	-8 JAN 1802	DBA:438; OT:40;
			1799:6
HOFFMAN (also see "Huffman")			
HOFFMAN, Peter	OWINS, Deborah	-5 DEC 1836	WB6:233
	d/o Samuel Owins		
HOGNER, Martin	RICH, Christiana	FEB 1794	FPC:15(JM)
HOGUE, Charles	MAGNESS, Sarah	JAN 1793	FPC:15(JM)
HOKES, George	_____, Mary	-17 NOV 1797	HCI:443; 1799:22
HOKES, George	STREET, Ann	9 JUN 1805	AG:10/6/05:3(TD);
			MB
HOKES, George	_____, Sarah	-8 MAY 1814	DBAA:230
HOLLIDAY, Henry	MOULDING, Mary	30 DEC 1821	AG:17/1/22:3(JR)
HOLLIDAY, Samuel	McDONOUGH, Ann P.	17 OCT 1815	PW:205
Place: Fairfax Co.			

Husband	Wife	Event or Marriage	Reference(s)
HOLLIDAY, William L.	McCLERAN, Ann	c.22 NOV 1802	MB
HOLLINDUFF, Henry	FELSH, Margaret	16 SEP 1798	FPC:15(JM)
HOLLINS, John	SMITH, _____	c.12 JAN 1786	AG:12/1/86:3
Place: Baltimore MD	d/o John Smith		
HOLLINSBURY, John	_____, Patsey	-2 FEB 1818	DBE2:482
HOLLOWELL, Benjamin	FARQUHAR, Margaret	13 OCT 1724	H:740
Place: Sandy Spring Meeting House MD			
HOLMES, Isaac	McGREGOR, Christian	-2 DEC 1795	FPC:14
HOLMES, Isaac	SHOEMAKER, Hannah	5 DEC 1827	QM:51
HOOD, Benjamin	LIMERICK, Mrs. Ann	6 JUL 1806	FPC:15(JM); WBB
	wid/o John Limerick		
HOOE, Alexander Seymour	MASON, Elizabeth Barnes	22 APR 1802	DBD:494;
Place: *Lexington*, Fairfax Co., eldest d/o George Mason			AG:24/4/02:3(LM)
HOOE, Bernard, Jr.	CHICHESTER, Mary Semmes	-24 APR 1815	AG:29/4/15:3;
			P:51
HOOE, Howson L.	BOYD, Eliza	6 OCT 1825	NI:11/10/25
HOOE, Howson L., Jr.	SCOTT, Ann B.	18 MAR 1824	AG:20/3/24:3
	d/o Cuthbert H. Scott		
HOOE, James Hewitt	HOOE, Eliza Thacker	20 SEP 1804	DBS:236; FC#93;
	d/o Bernard Hooe		DBS:374;
			AG:1/10/04:3
HOOE, John	FOWKE, Anne	c.1744	SWM:427
	d/o Chandler Fowke		
HOOE, Rice	MASSEY, Mrs. Mary		SD1686:244a
	wid/o Robert Massey		
HOOF, Powell	KENNER, Elizabeth	5 MAR 1816	MR(WHW)
HOOFF, John	DENEALE, Jannett	12 DEC 1805	OT:53; SPC;
Place: Fairfax Co.	d/o William Deneale		FWK:234;
			AG:14/12/05:3(K)
HOOFF, Lawrence	_____, Margaret	-22 OCT 1793	WB1:130; 1787:72;
			1791:13
HOOFF, Lawrence	GRETTER, Ann	-1 AUG 1808	DBQ:211; OT:53;
	d/o Michael Gretter		SPC(169:4)
HOOFF, Philip H.	HAMMOND, Jane B.	24 JUN 1823	AG:1/7/23:3
Place: Charlestown, Jefferson Co.			
HOOFF, William	PACKET, Mrs. Frances	5 MAR 1822	NI:15/3/22
HOOK, Jacob	TALBOTT, Sarah	-1765	FCOB1765:7
HOOKES, Jacob	_____, Mary Ann		1799:38; 1800:55;
			FPCC(42:64)
HOOKES, John	BURNES, Mary	JUL 1792	FPC:15(JM)
HOOPER, Robert	COURTNEY, Mercy	30 OCT 1800	FPC:15(JM)
HOPKINS, John	LEE, Cornelia	16 OCT 1806	AG:17/10/06:3(TD);
Place: *Bellevue*	d/o William Lee		WB2:198; LVA1:2;
			MB
HOPKINS, William	BROOKS, Mary	29 NOV 1814	MR(WHW); MB
HORNER, Inman	HENDERSON, Mary	31 DEC 1815	AG:12/1/16:3(L)
Place: Dumfries	youngest d/o Alexander Henderson		
HORNER, John	CLEVENGER, Phebe	15 FEB 1796	FPC:15(JM); 1799:8
HORNER, John	_____, Elizabeth		1799:34; 1800:54
HORNER, John	FAWCETT, Lydia	-23 DEC 1802	H:750
	d/o Thomas Fawcett		
HORTON, Cossom	RYE, Lucy	c.27 SEP 1805	MB
s/o Mary Horton	s/i Gustavus Rye		

Husband	Wife	Event or Marriage	Reference(s)
HORWELL, Charles	PHENIX, Ann	23 SEP 1801	FPC:15(JM); MR(JM); MB
HORWELL, Edward Chas. Place: Washington DC	COX, Ann Maria H.	25 MAR 1829	AG:27/3/29:3
HORWELL, Richard	SLEIGH, Susan	c.17 SEP 1817	MR(WHW); MB; AG:19/9/17:3(WHW)
HOUGH, Charles C.P. Place: Washington DC	HORWELL, Lucinda L.	20 JAN 1829	NI:22/1/29; AG:24/1/29:3
HOUGH, George S.	CARR, Susannah B. (Hamilton) d/o David Hamilton	2 JAN 1812	H:750; QC; AG:3/1/12:3
HOUGH, John	_____, Sarah	-14 JUN 1773	HCD:94; FDK:368
HOUGH, Mahlon	_____, Mary	-30 JAN 1807	DBQ:170
HOUGH, Peyton	MILLS, Harriet R.	2 JUN 1825	MR(Sco); MB
HOUNS, Henry	REYNOLDS, Mrs. Louisa	19 JUN 1823	SP
HOUSE, David	TENISON, Lucretia	DEC 1795	FPC:15(JM); 1799:22
HOVERMAN, Martin	WAPER, Elizabeth	8 OCT 1803	FPC:15(JM); MR(JM); MB
HOWARD, Beall	_____, Ann	-25 OCT 1800	HCO:179; DBZ:414; 1787:73; CCC(88)
HOWARD, Beal	HOWARD, Ann R.	c.1 JUL 1822	MB
HOWARD, Beall, Jr.	ROUNSAVELLE, Elizabeth	23 JAN 1817	AG:25/1/17:3(SC); MR(SC); MB
HOWARD, John	FULMORE, Eliza C.	1 AUG 1816	AG:3/8/16:3(ON); TMCC(J:4)
HOWARD, John	MADDOX, Ann	9 JUN 1820	MR(ON); MB
HOWARD, Samuel	ABBOTT, Mrs. Ann	26 MAY 1825	MR(JF); MB
HOWELL, _____	_____, Permelia B. mother of John Howell	-7 MAY 1817	UC:E109
HOWELL, David	JANNEY, Hannah McPherson	1 MAY 1828	H:750
HOWELL, Richard	MAY, Ann d/o Edward May	-1 AUG 1810	WBC:467
HOWELL, Samuel	HAINES, Sarah	-4 APR 1796	H:750
HOWELL, Samuel	JANNEY, Hannah	7 MAR 1810	H:750
HOY, France (C)	_____, Milley (C)		1800:58
HOYE, William	_____, Elizabeth	-20 SEP 1798	HCM:246; CRA:305
HOYT, Reuben	FLANNAGIN, Cleary	19 AUG 1810	FPC:15(JM); MB
HUBBALL, John	_____, Mary	-23 MAY 1802	WBA:293; 1800:53
HUBBARD, Jeremiah	PATTERSON, Susan Ann Maria d/o William Patterson	22 DEC 1825	SP; MR(Sco); MB; AG:24/12/25:3(Sco)
HUBBLE, William	JACKSON, Ann R. eldest d/o Spencer Jackson	22 SEP 1829	NI:26/9/29; AG:25/9/29:3(Sco)
HUCK, Thomas V.	NEILL, Mary d/o Joseph Neill	3 DEC 1818	H:751[49]; QM:47; AG:4/12/18:2
HUDGES, James	LEARY, Nancy	27 SEP 1826	MR(EH); MB
HUFF, Powell	KENNER, Elizabeth	5 MAR 1816	AG:9/3/16:3(WHW)
HUFFMAN, Peter	MASON, Arminta	13 APR 1804	MR(WM); MB
HUGHES, George G.	PILES, Elizabeth	31 MAR 1829	SP; MR(WJ); MB
HUGHES, John	_____, Sarah	-18 MAR 1774	FDL:282
HUGHES, John	HARDING, Sarah	c.26 MAR 1806	MB
HUGHES, John	SMEDLEY, Lydia I.	c.2 JUL 1823	MB
HUGHES, John	MASDEN, Ann M.	21 SEP 1824	AG:23/9/24:3(IR); MB
HUGHES, Richard	DAVIS, Betty	c.14 JAN 1817	MB

64

Husband	Wife	Event or Marriage	Reference(s)
HUGHES, Thomas	EGLING, Amelia	15 MAY 1802	MR(JM); MB
HUGLE, George F.	CARLIN, Sarah H.	4 FEB 1830	MR(LA); MB; AG:6/2/30:3(LA)
HUGUELY, George	HARRIS, Sarah d/o Benjamin Harris	-10 MAR 1810	DBS:290; FX
HUIE, Capt. James s/o James Huie	BULLITT, Helen E.C. d/o Hon. Cuthbert Bullitt	c.6 JUL 1791	GT:6/7/91
HULL, John	_____, Ann	-13 SEP 1800	WBA:185; 1799:36; 1800:57
HULL, William	COLSTON, Ann	c.24 APR 1812	MB
HULLS, George	ARMSTRONG, Fanny s/i William Armstrong	c.1 MAR 1805	MB
HULLS, George	FERGUSON, Birtha	c.16 JUN 1812	MB
HUMPHREY, Col. Thos.	MARMADUKE, Mrs. Mary	16 MAR 1814	AG:7/4/14:3(WG)
HUMPHREYS, Richard	WILSON, Mary	-23 AUG 1817	WB2:225
HUMPHREYS, Richard L.	REESE, Mary	c.19 DEC 1805	MB
HUMPHRIES, Correl	GLASSGOW, Catharine A.	17 JUN 1830	MR(LA); MB; AG:21/6/30:3(LA)
HUMPHRIES, John S.	_____, Lucy H.	-30 APR 1839	UC:E169; WB4:208
HUNT, Benjamin Whiticher	GRIFFIN, Close Ann d/o Lancelot Griffin	4 JUN 1826	UT:6/6/26:3
HUNT, Philip	YOST, Rebecca	19 DEC 1811	FPC:15(JM); MB
HUNTER, Alexander	CHAPMAN, Louisa Ann Adelaide	2 FEB 1815	AG:9/2/15:3(WHW); SP; MR(WHW); MB
HUNTER, Colin	HATTON, Henrietta Dent of Thompson's Rest MD	3 DEC 1807	FPC:14(JM); LHFC; AG:8/12/07(WDA); BR:126
HUNTER, John	CHAPMAN, Elizabeth d/o Nathaniel Chapman	1753	PC; P:376; FWB:364
HUNTER, John	HATTON, Cordelia Meeks d/o Joseph Hatton	c.1785	DBV:94; FPCG; BR:129; FPCC(42:50)
HUNTER, John	_____, Dayley		1799:34; 1800:54
HUNTER, John Chapman Place: *Abingdon*	TRIPLETT, Sarah Dade d/o Thomas Triplett	22 AUG 1799	FM(1835):59; ABC:111; 1791:14; AG:28/8/99:3(MLW)
HUNTER, Miles	GARDINER, Sally	21 MAY 1786	AG:25/5/86:2
HUNTER, Nath. Chapman	TYLER, Sarah Ann d/o Charles Tyler	-23 SEP 1794	HCF:37; 1791:14; LHFC; BR:110; PC
HUNTER, Peter	DENEALE, Julia Ann	10 JUN 1830	MB; AG:12/6/30:3
HUNTER, Richard	RICHARDSON, Mary Ann	-8 AUG 1814	DBAA:203
HUNTER, Richard A.	_____, Ann G.	-22 AUG 1810	DBU:115
HUNTER, Robert	HARLEY, Unice	18 APR 1810	AG:21/4/10:3(IR); MR(IR); MB
HUNTER, Robert	WOOD, Mary C.	3 MAR 1818	MR(AG); MB
HUNTER, Robert W., Sr.	BRYAN, Elizabeth d/o Bernard and Mary Bryan	21 AUG 1817	TMCC(R:1); MR(AG); MB; B7
HUNTER, William, Sr.	ARELL, Christiana "Kitty"	-25 AUG 1782	HCA:1; 1787:72; 1791:14; 1799:38; 1800:54; FDO:129; DBA:20, 133; LVA1:1; HCOrd:22/5/83
HUNTER, William, Jr.	_____,	-19 NOV 1792	1787:73; FPCG; AG:22/11/92

Husband	Wife	Event or Marriage	Reference(s)
HUNTER, William	SMITH, Mary Ann Harrison	c.6 MAR 1822	MB
HUNTINGTON, William	SMITHERMAN, Elizabeth	25 DEC 1806	FPC:15(JM); MB
HUNTON, Thomas L.	MOXLEY, Ann D.D.	18 NOV 1822	NI:20/11/22
HURDLE, James	REEDER, Mary Ann	c.19 NOV 1826	DCM
HURDLE, Jesse	DUTY, Rebecca	22 FEB 1816	AG:24/2/16:3(ON); MR(ON)[50]; MB
HURDLE, Lawrence Place: Georgetown MD	WHEELER, Nancy d/o Leonard Wheeler	20 OCT 1792	BR:168
HURDLE, Levi	JENKINS, Lydia Bunker eldest d/o Capt. Uriah Jenkins	8 JUN 1830	SP; MR(WJ); MB; AG:10/6/30:3(WJ)
HURLEY, Daniel	BEDINGER, Nancy	16 AUG 1791	FPC:15(JM)
HURLEY, George	SUTHERLAND, Hopey d/o Henrietta Sutherland	c.30 SEP 1815	MB(IR)
HURLIHY, Maurice	O'NEALE, Ann M.	7 JAN 1830	MB; AG:13/1/30:3(JF)
HURLIHY, Morris	CHATTHAM, Jane	22 DEC 1791	FPC:15(JM); 1799:12
HUSSEY, Andrew S.	RHODES, Maria Antoinette d/o Anthony Rhodes	29 JUN 1828	MB; AG:2/7/28:3(Wal)
HUSSEY, Henry	_____, Jane	-8 SEP 1806	WBB:506
HUSTON, William	GARRETT, Elizabeth	c.NOV 1797	WG:25/11/97
HUTCHENS, Thomas	RICHARDSON, Margaret	-8 JUL 1814	WB1:23, 289
HUTCHESON, Isaac	MAUZEY, Mary	-JAN 1804	FD1803:98
HUTCHINS, William	AUSTIN, Mary ward of John Boyer	c.15 JAN 1824	MB
HUTCHINSON, Thompson	LAWSON, Rachael	c.3 FEB 1816	MB
HUTCHISON, Alexander	JANNEY, Maria	6 JAN 1825	AG:18/1/25:3(IR); MB
HUTCHINGS, John	_____, Ann	-13 NOV 1774	CCG
HUTTON, Isaac G.	SMITH, Rebecca Emmeline d/o John [F.] Smith of *Bloomfield*	16 DEC 1823	NI:18/12/23(WA); MR(WA); MB; AG:20/12/23:3(WA)
HYDE, Charles K.	MASON, E. Cary	c.21 APR 1840	DCM
HYDE, Charles K.	FAIRFAX, Eugenia	-2 FEB 1849	WB5:223

Husband	Wife	Event or Marriage	Reference(s)
I			
IGLEHART, Thomas Place: Fairfax Co.	LUCKETT, Ann	9 SEP 1817	MR(WHW)
IMMOHR, Capt. Fredrick	JONES, Rebecca	28 NOV 1813	SPC(64:2); MB; AG:30/12/13:3(WHW)
INGLE, Joseph	SIMMON, Mary	DEC 1795	FPC:16(JM); DBX:12; CCC(49)
INGLIS, Rev. James	JOHNSTON, Jane Swan	25 NOV 1802	FPC:16(JM)

INSLEY, Capt. Abel
  Place: Westmoreland Co.
	PARKES, Mary
	  d/o Arthur Parkes
		7 JUN 1825	AG:18/6/25:3

IRWIN, James	MARSHALL, Ann Douglass	5 AUG 1828	SP; MR(WJ); MB; AG:7/8/28:3(WJ)
IRWIN, Thomas	JANNEY, Elizabeth	31 AUG 1791	DBV:381; CCC(B); H:752
ISAACKS, Samuel	POWELL, Edith	19 MAY 1810	MR(IR); MB
ISABELL, Jonah	_____, Mary	-20 APR 1803	DBW:289
ISH, Peter	KIRK, Hariet d/o Samuel Kirk, Jr.	20 NOV 1817	MR(AG); MB
ISRALEN, Jasper	TAYLOR, Elizabeth	28 OCT 1795	FPC:16(JM)

Husband	Wife	Event or Marriage	Reference(s)

J

Husband	Wife	Event or Marriage	Reference(s)
JACKSON, Annas	KIRK, Harriet d/o James Kirk	25 DEC 1803	DBR:238; DBV:128; DBX:17; AG:28/12/03:3
JACKSON, Archibald	GORDEN, Nelly	c.13 SEP 1824	MB
JACKSON, Daniel	WATERS, Ann	7 APR 1821	MR(WHW); MB
JACKSON, James	GRAY, Sarah M.	8 MAY 1825	SP; MR(WHW); MB; AG:10/5/25:3(WHW)
JACKSON, James	TURNER, Mary	c.2 MAY 1811	MB
JACKSON, John	HILL, Lucretia	c.23 JUL 1805	MB
JACKSON, John	SIMMS, Amelia Jane Watson d/o Col. Charles Simms	10 NOV 1814	AG:12/11/18:3; MB; (WHW); MR(WHW)
JACKSON, Capt. John R.	RHODES, Julia Ann Frances d/o Capt. Anthony Rhodes	8 FEB 1819	AG:10/2/19:2(SC)
JACKSON, John S.	EDELEN, Mary W.	4 MAY 1824	AG:8/5/24:3
JACKSON, Meshack (C)	_____, Easter (C)		1799:40; 1800:55
JACKSON, Styles	BONTZ, Elizabeth	7 DEC 1808	MR(IR)
JACKSON, Thomas	LOGGINS, Janney	c.27 JUN 1811	MB
JACKSON, Thomas	MOORE, Ann Caverly	20 NOV 1816	MR(ON); MB; AG:21/11/16:3(ON)
JACKSON, William	FLEMING, Kitty d/o Thomas Fleming	1 DEC 1796	FPC:18(JM); AG:3/12/97:3; HCI:466
JACKSON, William	GRAY, Nancy	c.20 NOV 1806	MB
JACKSON, William	ROBERTS, Bridget	9 JUN 1815	FPC:18(JM); MB
JACOBS, Edward H.	BOYD, Ann	22 JAN 1809	FPC:18(JM)
JACOBS, George	CHILDS, Sarah A. d/o Rev. John Childs	22 SEP 1817	MR(AG); MB; AG:1/10/17:3
JACOBS, John	SELVEY, Dorothy	23 DEC 1817	MR(WHW); MB
JACOBS, Presley	CHEW, Elizabeth d/o John Chew	6 APR 1801	FPCC(44:130)
JACOBS, Samuel	MORGAN, Hannah	3 JAN 1826	MR(RK); MB; AG:7/1/26:3
JACOB(S), Thomas	_____, Polly	-2 SEP 1810	WBC:491; 1799:12; CCC(35)
JACOBS, Thomas	HOAKS, Catharine	-8 MAY 1814	DBAA:230; TMCC(N:3)
JACOBS, Thomas	DEAGAN, Charlotte	22 DEC 1829	CCC(35); MR(EH) MB
JACOBS, Thomas, Jr.	HENRICKSON, Catharine	17 AUG 1809	MR(IR); MB
JAMES, Henry	TAYLOR, Susanna d/o Mary Taylor	4 NOV 1804	FPC:18(JM); MB
JAMES, William	SMITH, Mary	5 JAN 1790	FPC:18(JM)
JAMES, William Place: Washington DC	WASHINGTON, Mary West d/o Capt. Henry Washington	14 OCT 1828	AG:22/10/28:3
JAMESON, Samuel	BOARMAN, Jane d/o Charles Boarman	-3 OCT 1813	AG:14/10/13:3
JAMESON, Lieut. Wm.	ROSE, Catharine M. d/o Mary Rose of Norfolk	16 OCT 1819	AG:23/10/18:3(LO)
JAMIESON, Andrew	SWEET[51], Mary	FEB 1794	FPC:17-18(JM); WB3:98, 128; 1787:73; FPCC(41:28)

Husband	Wife	Event or Marriage	Reference(s)
JAMIESON, Henry	PREUSS, Celestia Jane eldest d/o A.W. Preuss	17 NOV 1829	AG:21/11/29:3(JF)
JAMIESON, John	LAIDLER, Violetta[52] of *Rose Hill*, Charles Co. MD	3 FEB 1807	DBT:7; AG:4/2/07
JAMIESON, Robert	SANFORD, Catharine Porter eldest d/o Thomas Sanford	2 NOV 1824	MB; AG:4/11/24:3(EH)
JAMIESON, Robert Brown	TRIPLETT, Penelope d/o William Triplett	c.1791	DBT:90; 1791:14; SPC; FWI:183; BR:118
JAMISON, Peter	MINCHIN, Martha S.	c.8 APR 1819	DCM
JANNEY, Abel	WILKES, Margaret d/o Samuel Wilkes	-4 OCT 1784	DBH:314; FPCG; 1799:24
JANNEY, Abijah Place: Berkley Meeting House	McPHERSON, Jane	15 AUG 1798	H:752; QM:47
JANNEY, Abijah Place: Baltimore MD	ELLICOTT, Mary J. (Mitchell) wid/o John Ellicott	16 APR 1817	H:752; WB4:325 AG:19/4/17:3; QC
JANNEY, Aquila Place: Hopewell Meeting House	McPHERSON, Ruth	12 MAY 1785	WBB:125 H:753
JANNEY, Asa Moore Place: Hopewell Meeting House	HAINES, Lydia Neill	12 OCT 1826	H:752; QM:47
JANNEY, Elisha Place: Hockassan Meeting House PA	GREGG, Albinah	19 APR 1786	H:744; QM:47
JANNEY, Elisha	GIBSON, Mary d/o John Gibson	4 MAR 1795	H:742; DBI:242; 1799:14
JANNEY, George Place: Sandy Spring Meeting House MD	BOONE, Susannah	31 OCT 1804	H:754; MGB:14/4:1
JANNEY, Henry Place: Washington DC	SCHOLFIELD, Hannah R.	26 JUN 1838	H:755
JANNEY, Israel, Jr. Place: Philadelphia PA	WARDEN, Elizabeth d/o John Warden	3 NOV 1818	AG:9/11/18:3
JANNEY, Jacob Place: Sandy Spring Meeting House MD	HUGHES, Elizabeth	23 MAY 1821	H:748
JANNEY, Jacob, Jr. Place: Indian Spring Meeting House MD, d/o Philip Hopkins	HOPKINS, Hannah	2 JUL 1807	H:749; MGB:14/4:1
JANNEY, John Place: Indian Spring Meeting House MD, d/o John Hopkins	HOPKINS, Elizabeth	26 MAR 1795	H:749; 1799:18; AG:13/2/09:3; MGB:14/4:1
JANNEY, John Place: Frankford Meeting House PA	SHOEMAKER, Ann	2 MAY 1817	H:756; WB3:93
JANNEY, Johns Hopkins Place: Baltimore MD	TYSON, Margaret T. d/o Jesse Tyson	20 NOV 1830	H:756; QC; NI:24/11/30
JANNEY, Jonathan	McPHERSON, Elizabeth	16 MAY 1810	H:756; DBV:87; WB4:187
JANNEY, Joseph Place: Indian Spring Meeting House MD	HOPKINS, Elizabeth Howell	2 JUL 1812	H:749 AG:10/7/12:3; BFG:11/7/12
JANNEY, Joseph Place: Annapolis MD	HOPKINS, Hannah Howell	14 JAN 1822	H:749; WB6:238; AG:18/1/22:3
JANNEY, Lewis J. Place: Wilmington DE	PENNOCK, Mary	1 AUG 1776	H:757
JANNEY, Moses	LAWRENCE, Mrs. Judith	21 FEB 1805	FPC:18(JM); MB; AG:22/2/05(JM)

Husband	Wife	Event or Marriage	Reference(s)
JANNEY, Phineas Place: Upper Ridge Meeting House VA	LUPTON, Ruth	13 NOV 1799	H:757
JANNEY, Phineas Place: Friends' Meeting	HARTSHORNE, Sarah "Sally" Saunders d/o William Hartshorne	28 NOV 1811	H:746; WB2:201; WB6:128; FWK:335; NI:3/12/11; QC; AG:30/11/11:3
JANNEY, Richard Mott Place: Indian Spring Meeting House MD	HOPKINS, Sarah Janney	8 MAY 1829	H:750
JANNEY, Samuel Hopkins	MARK, Elizabeth d/o Samuel Mark	c.20 JAN 1830	H:758; SPC; MB
JANNEY, Samuel McP. Place: Friends' Meeting	JANNEY, Elizabeth d/o John Janney	9 MAR 1826	H:754; AG:11/3/26:3
JANNEY, Thomas	_____, Sarah Elizabeth	-9 JUN 1801	DBC:199
JARBOE, George Place: Baltimore MD	DIXON, Ann	4 DEC 1828	AG:9/12/28:3
JARBOE, Vernon	_____, Mary	-8 JAN 1811	DBV:128
JARBOW, Andrew (C)	JOHNSON, Rachel (C)	4 NOV 1830	MR(LA); MB
JASPER, Israel	DEY, Winfred	c.9 AUG 1811	MB[53]
JAVINS, Thompson	DYER, Cassandra d/o Thomas Dyer		MPC:E93; FC#74e
JAVINS, William	COMPTON, Roda	27 SEP 1817	MR(JMH); MB
JAWIN, Thomas	_____, Elizabeth	-28 JAN 1827	QM:48
JEFFERSON, Thomas	KEADLE, Elizabeth	4 FEB 1829	AG:12/2/29:3(GM)
JEFFERY, John	HENDERSON, Nancy	14 MAR 1821	MR(SC); MB
JEFFREY, Samuel	MAHONY, Sally	17 FEB 1803	AG:19/2/03:3(E); MB
JENIFER, Walter H. Place: *Clifton Lodge*, Fairfax Co. s/o Dr. Daniel Jenifer	PATTON, Helen Seymour d/o James Patton	19 APR 1814	AG:26/4/14:3(FN)
JENKINS, Daniel	WILLIAMS, Jemimah d/o Owen Williams	-21 APR 1769	FWC:240; CCC(79)
JENKINS, Elisha	BUCKLEY, Catharine	18 APR 1822	AG:23/4/22:3(JR)
JENKINS, Elisha	CHECK, Nancy	29 APR 1825	AG:12/5/25:3(JR)
JENKINS, George	ARELL, Mary d/o Samuel Arell	-1 NOV 1794	DBK:374; LVA1:1; DBY:98; DBC2:27; FWG:130
JENKINS, John	LAY, Leannah	-12 NOV 1798	FWG:422
JENKINS, Johnston	LIGHTFOOT, Sarah	FEB 1793	FPC:18(JM); 1799:28; 1800:56
JENNERS, Abial	YOUNG, Deborah	17 MAY 1796	WG:15/6/96
JENNINGS, Thomas O. Place: Fauquier Co.	MORGAN, Lucy d/o Gen. Simon Morgan	24 OCT 1811	AG:29/10/11:3
JENNISEN, Capt. Bernard A. Place: Washington DC	LEIDBERG, Sarah	19 JAN 1829	AG:23/1/29:3
JEWELL, Elisha	HODGKIN, Mildred	20 NOV 1789	WB4:83; FMI; IGI
JEWETT, Aaron	MARK, Eliza d/o John Mark of Fredericksburg	11 JUL 1814	AG:16/7/14:3(JM) MB
JOACHIM, Henry C.	HARDING, Lettice d/o George Harding	22 NOV 1810	FPC:18(JM); MB
JOBSON, David	KEATING, Sarah	11 SEP 1808	FPC:18(JM)
JOHNS, George	RICHARDS, Mary Ann	25 DEC 1796	FPC:18(JM)
JOHNS, Peter	BOWER, Elizabeth	28 OCT 1800	FPC:18(JM)
JOHNS, Thomas	SEATON, Anna Maria V.	c.5 SEP 1821	MB

Husband	Wife	Event or Marriage	Reference(s)
(Johnson/Johnston)			
JOHNSTON, Alexious	_____, Elizabeth	-29 OCT 1842	WB3:355
JOHNSON, Aquilla	CARTER, Hetty	22 JUL 1827	SP; MR(WJ); MB
JOHNSTON, Clement	PATTON, Susannah	c.1 JAN 1812	MB
JOHNSTON, Daniel	_____, Jane		1800:54
JOHNSTON, David	STUART, Christian	1788	FB
JOHNSTON, David	MOLLIHORN, Mrs. Sarah	23 MAY 1819	AG:27/5/19:3(RE)
JOHNSTON, Dennis	SIMMS, Rebecca		FPCC; FC#98dd
	d/o William Simms		
JOHNSON, Dennis	FERGUSON, Patty	c.27 MAY 1830	MB
JOHNSON, Francis	CRANFORD, Eliza	22 JUN 1826	UT:26/6/26:3(RD)
JOHNSTON, George	McCARTY, Sarah	-21 OCT 1765	DBA:145; FWB:432; M:153; FWD:40
JOHNSTON, George	LONG, Linny	2 JAN 1818	MR(IR); MB
JOHNSTON, Hezekiah	TALBOTT, Nancy	5 NOV 1809	FPC:18(JM); MB
JOHNSTON, James	CANNON, Caroline	15 DEC 1812	MR(IR); MB
	d/o Susan Cannon		
JOHNSTON, James	BLUNT, Mary Ann B.	9 DEC 1830	AG:13/12/30:3(Sco)
Place: Washington DC	only d/o Capt. Joseph Blunt		
JOHNSTON, Rev. Jas. T.	_____, Jane		SPC(163:4)
JOHNSTON, James W.	COLEMAN, Rachel		OT:50
	d/o Joseph Coleman		
JOHNSTON, James W.	DOBBIN, Mrs. Rachael	6 FEB 1817	MB; AG:7/2/17:3
JOHNSTON, John	LeTRAIT, Mary	22 DEC 1791	FPC:18(JM); 1799:6
JOHNS(T)ON, John	HODG(S)KINS, Margaret	8 MAR 1807	FPC:18(JM); MB
JOHNS(T)ON, John	MILLS, Nancy	26 MAR 1815	AG:1/4/15:3; MR; MB
JOHNSTON, John Morgan	MOSS, Rebecca	26 FEB 1829	AG:2/3/29:3
Place: Aspen Hill, Fairfax Co., d/o William Moss			
JOHNSON, Noble H.	MORGAN, Mary Ann	27 APR 1830	MB; AG:30/4/30:3
	d/o William Morgan		
JOHNSTON, Richard	FREEMAN, Eleanor	18 MAY 1826	MB; AG:23/5/26:3(AH)
JOHNSTON, Reuben	_____, Elizabeth		FPCC(41:27)
JOHNSON, Robert	MOORE, Elizabeth	c.9 JUN 1820	MB
JOHNSON, Samuel	KING, Arminta	13 JUN 1804	MR(JM); MB
JOHNSTON, Samuel	SEXTON, Ann	c.3 OCT 1809	MB
JOHNSON, Theophilus	FOWLES, Polly	30 DEC 1820	MR(SC); MB
JOHNSON, Thomas	ASHTON, Elizabeth	-28 JUN 1749	FLC1812:68
	d/o Henry Ashton		
JOHNSTON, William	SIMPSON, Nancy	-13 FEB 1786	R2:90(SG); FDS:533
	d/o Gilbert and Rosanna Simpson		
JOHNSTON, William	REZIN, Mary	21 JUL 1798	FPC:18(JM); 1799:28; 1800:55
JOHNSTON, William	WINDSOR, Mary Ann	15 SEP 1825	AG:17/9/25:3(JJ)
Place: Orchard Grove, Fairfax Co., d/o Richard S. Windsor			
JOHNSON, William P.C.	WASHINGTON, Ann E.	15 MAR 1831	SP; MR(WJ)
JOLLIFFE, William	NEILL, Rebecca	12 SEP 1799	H:759
Place: Hopewell Meeting House			
JOLLY, John	_____, Rachel	-28 JUN 1787	HCC:118; 1787:73
JONES, Col. Augustus S.	ROBERT, Emily	2 FEB 1826	UT:22/2/26:2
JONES, Benjamin	GIESTA, Susan	c.27 OCT 1827	MB
JONES, Catesby	WELCH, Alice	17 MAY 1808	FPC:18(JM)
JONES, Charles	_____, Sarah	-10 AUG 1793	HCE:187

Husband	Wife	Event or Marriage	Reference(s)
JONES, Charles	SHUM, Mrs. Prudence	c.DEC 1795	FPC:18(JM); DBD:208; AG:2/1/96:3
JONES, Ezekiel	ALLEN, Maria	c.6 JAN 1824	MB
JONES, Francis Burdette	WRIGHT, Harriet	4 NOV 1830	AG:6/11/30:3; SP; MR(WJ); MB
JONES, George	BRYAN, Sally	c.20 JAN 1824	MB
JONES, George	LAVENDER, Martha	c.27 APR 1824	MB
JONES, George Place: Washington DC	MEYERS, Mrs. Sarah	18 MAY 1821	AG:21/5/21:3(WH)
JONES, Henry A.	SHORTELL, Eliza	c.8 DEC 1828	MB
JONES, Henry N.	BRAWNER, Mrs. Harriet R.	20 NOV 1817	AG:24/11/17:3
JONES, John	_____, Sary Ann		1799:34; 1800:54
JONES, John Courts	HARRISON, Dorothy Hanson d/o Robert Hanson Harrison	-3 NOV 1795	HCI:411; DBB:373 FDY:237
JONES, Jonathan	JONES, Sarah	19 NOV 1800	FPC:18(JM)
JONES, Joseph	WELSH, Debrah	16 NOV 1822	MB(ON); MB
JONES, Lewin	WHITMORE, Mary	23 JUL 1816	MR(JM); MB
JONES, Thomas	JONES, Ann	MAR 1795	FPC:18(JM)
JONES, Thomas	LOCKER, Amelia	JUL 1795	FPC:18(JM)
JONES, Thomas	CREASE, Grace d/o Anthony Crease	-18 SEP 1819	WB2:383
JONES, Walter	LEE, Ann Lucinda d/o Charles Lee	17 MAY 1808	AG:18/5/08:3(WM) FDL3:324
JONES, William	KITLER, Rebecca	c.18 SEP 1802	MB
JONES, William	GILL, Susanna	4 APR 1826	UT:8/4/26:3(Mc)
JORDAN, Jesse	CAVENDER, Mary	MAR 1795	FPC:18(JM)
JORDAN, Joshua	CRAMPTON, Rebecca si/o Varnall Crampton [Compton]	FEB 1792	FPC:18(JM); FDU2:136
JUDGE, Andrew	_____, Rebecca	-10 JUL 1784	DBI:341
JULIUS, Josias (C)	DOVER, Milly (C) d/o Samuel and Elizabeth Dover	c.2 JAN 1816	MR(WHW); MB
JULIUS, Thomas (C)	_____, Cloey (C)		1799:28; 1800:56
JULIUS, Thomas	DOVER, Betsy	c.7 JUN 1820	MB

Husband	Wife	Event or Marriage	Reference(s)

K

Husband	Wife	Event or Marriage	Reference(s)
KAY, Thomas	MENDENHALL, Martha	14 AUG 1800	DBD:352
KEACH, Samuel	HARMON, Mary	OCT 1792	FPC:20(JM); 1799:38; 1800:54
KEATING, Edward	DUNN, Martha	15 JAN 1801	MR(JM)
KEATING, James	_____, Mary	-22 DEC 1796	DBE:297; 1799:12; CCC(26)
KEATING, James R.	PERNEL, Thamer	9 NOV 1818	AG:16/11/18:2(ON); MR(ON); MB
KEENE, James	CLARK, Jane	30 MAY 1799	FPC:20(JM)
KEENE, Newton, Sr.	EDWARDS, Sarah		FPCC(42:69)
KEENE, Newton, Jr.[54]	DUNDAS, Nancy Moore d/o John Dundas	23 MAY 1811	FPC:20(JM); DBAA:108; MR(JM); FPCC(42:69); MB; AG:27/5/11:3(JM)
KEERL, George	MUNDELL, Susannah d/o Thomas Mundell	2 MAY 1820	AG:5/5/20:3
KEIFER, Christopher	VIOLETT, Sarah	5 SEP 1821	MR(SC); MB; AG:10/9/21:3
KEIS, William	MILLER, Elizabeth	c.7 MAY 1803	MB
KEITH, Anderson D.	KEITH, Catherine C.	c.2 NOV 1826	MR(RK); MB
KEITH, Rev. Isaac S.	SPROAT, Hannah		CBL:33
KEITH, Rev. Isaac S.	LEGARE, Catherine		CBL:33
KEITH, Rev. Isaac S.[55]	HUXNAM, Jane		CBL:33
KEITH, James	McMAHAN, Isabella	22 JUL 1802	FR(JM); 1791:15; MB
KEITH, James	VOWELL, Mary (Harper) wid/o Thomas Vowell d/o Capt. John Harper	-10 AUG 1804	DBH:257; 1799:34
KEITH, James, Sr.	_____, Elizabeth	-31 MAY 1809	DBR:305; 1800:53; CCC(1)
KEITH, John	McMAHON, Elizabeth	12 DEC 1791	FPC:20(JM)
KEITH, Rev. Reuel Place: Middlebury VT	CLEVELAND, Marietta	3 DEC 1817	NI:28/4/30; IGI
KEITH, Smith	_____, Elizabeth	-2 OCT 1812	DBW:245; 1799:12
KELL, Isaac	_____, Nancy	-11 SEP 1820	TMCC(D:2)
KELL, Isaac	HARRISON, Mary d/o John D. Harrison		FDV3:247, E4:266
KELLAM, Thomas	MANNING, Mary	c.18 OCT 1802	MB
KELLY, James	ALLEN, Rachel	-27 DEC 1794	FPC:19
KELLY, John	PUTNEY, Eleana	-29 MAR 1795	FPC:19
KELLY, Patrick	LATHAM, Elizabeth	c.7 NOV 1811	MB
KEMPFIELD, Isaac	KORNE, Mary Ann S.	5 OCT 1820	MR(ON); MB
KENNARD, Joseph	HOWARD, Mary	5 NOV 1817	MR(JMH); MB
KENNEDY, James	_____, Susannah	12 MAY 1780	FPCC(41:38)
KENNEDY, James, Jr.	_____, Letitia "Letty"	-1 NOV 1794	FPC:19; HCE:446; DBG:247; 1799:8
KENNEDY, John	_____, Eliza		FPCC(41:38)
KENNEDY, John	KENNEDY, Susanna(h) Maria d/o James Kennedy, Bookseller	1 FEB 1826	NI:7/2/26; MR(WA); MB; AG:4/2/26:3(WA)
KENNEDY, Wm. L.	HILL, Henrietta Jane	29 APR 1824	AG:4/5/24:3

Place: Prince George's Co. MD, youngest d/o Henry Hill

Husband	Wife	Event or Marriage	Reference(s)
KENNER, George	CONNER, Elizabeth	11 DEC 1806	MR(IR); MB
KENNER, Jacob	WALDERSTAFFER, Louisa	c.12 MAR 1803	MB
KENNER, James	BRICE, Mrs. Hannah wid/o John Brice	-12 MAR 1798	DBV:369; HCK:312; DBD:341
KENT, John	BALLARD, Martha	28 JAN 1802	MR(JM); MB
KENT, Dr. Thomas H.	PEYTON, Ann Maria d/o Col. Francis Peyton	c.10 MAY 1813	AG:27/11/13:3; MB
KENT, William	ROSS, Elizabeth	c.28 AUG 1805	MB
KENWORTHY, William	HOGE, Rebekah	28 APR 1791	DBBB:12; H:749 1800:58
Place: Goose Creek Meeting House, d/o Solomon Hoge			
KENYON, Nathaniel	EVANS, Emily d/o James Evans	c.19 JAN 1829	MB
KERR (also see "Carr")			
KERR, James D.	McCLEAN, Lucretia	22 SEP 1823	MB
KEY, Philip B.	SEWALL, Mary B.	2 DEC 1828	AG:6/12/28:3
Place: Poplar Hill	youngest d/o Robert Sewall		
KIBBEY, William B.	RINKER, Sarah A. d/o Joseph Rinker	7 APR 1825	AG:9/4/25:3(IR); MB
KIBBY, Alexander	McFARLANE, Binney	9 SEP 1802	MR(JM); MB
KIDWELL, Benjamin	HAMILTON, Eliza	DEC 1795	FPC:19-20(JM)
KIDWELL, James	WHEELER, Mrs. Elizabeth	6 AUG 1823	SP; AG:7/8/23:3(IR)
Place: Capt. Blasdell's, opposite Alexandria			
KIDWELL, John H.	ROBEY, Priscilla	31 DEC 1829	AG:8/1/30:3(JR)
KIDWELL, Joshua	WILLIAMS, Mrs. Ann	25 APR 1824	AG:29/4/24:3(JR)
KILTON, George	CARTER, Elizabeth	c.23 SEP 1796	WBA:180; PGM; FPCC(43:101); WG:28/9/96
KIMMERLINE, John H.	FOX, Sarah	1 FEB 1825	AG:8/2/25:3(RD)
Place: Fairfax Co.			
KINCAID, George	TYLER, Sarah	12 DEC 1819	CT:18/12/19(JR); AH:15/12/19; AG:15/12/19:3(JR)
KINCAID, John	DICKSON, Lucy d/o Archibald Dickson	-30 JAN 1811	FPCC(41:24); BR:193
KINE, Obadiah	HUNT, Elizabeth	c.12 SEP 1827	MB
KING, Benjamin	DORCEY, Elizabeth	12 JUN 1806	FPC:20(JM); MB
KING, Charles	SWORD, Anna	11 NOV 1827	AG:16/11/27:3(Sco); MR(Sco); MB
KING, Isaac Newton	SPEAR, Mrs. Hannah C.	6 JUL 1820	MR(WHW); MB; AG:10/7/20:3(WHW)
KING, James	PINDALL, Ann	15 JUN 1797	FPC:20(JM)
KING, James	GROVES, Nancy	14 JUN 1815	MR(JMH); MB
KING, James	MAHONEY, Ally	c.4 SEP 1817	MB
KING, Jedson	RUDD, Ann	6 AUG 1822	AG:10/8/22:3(WHW); SP
Place: Fairfax Co.			
KING, John W.	CHILDS, Ann W.	4 NOV 1830	AG:6/11/30:3; MR(LA); MB
KING, Patrick	BAGGETT, Susanna	29 JUN 1811	MR(IR); MB
KING, Richard	DAVIS, Mary d/o Mary Davis	5 OCT 1820	MR(ON); MB
KING, Robert Smith	McKNIGHT, Margaret Susan second d/o Capt. John McKnight	9 JUN 1829	NI:12/6/29; B9; MR(EH); MB; AG:10/6/29(EH)

Husband	Wife	Event or Marriage	Reference(s)
KING, Samuel	GATES, Elizabeth s/o Thomas Gates	25 JUN 1801	MR(JM); MB
KING, William	FORD, Elizabeth d/o Thomas Ford	-29 AUG 1774	FWC:257
KING, William	HARPER, Elizabeth d/o Capt. John Harper	APR 1794	FPC:20(JM)
KINGSBURY, Dannelin[56]	HARDY, Anne	20 MAR 1796	FPC:20(JM); AG:22/3/96:3
KINGSBURY, James	CASTILE, Rebecca	31 MAR 1796	FPC:20(JM)
KINGSTON, Nicholas Place: Georgetown DC	BLOOMFIELD, Elizabeth	c.30 JAN 1806	BA:30/1/06
KINGSTON, Thomas	HODGKINS, Susan	12 JAN 1816	MR(JM); MB
KINNY, Moses	BAKER, Elizabeth	5 JUN 1796	FPC:20(JM)
KINNY, Moses	LEWIS, Sally	1 NOV 1810	FPC:20(JM)
KINSEY, Benjamin Place: Washington DC	DRINKER, Elizabeth d/o George Drinker	29 JUL 1828	AG:6/8/28:3
KINZEY, Enos	DOXEY, Mary	4 APR 1804	MR(WM); MB
KIRBY, Edmund Place: Washington DC	BROWN, Eliza A. d/o Maj. Gen. Jacob Brown	14 FEB 1825	AG:17/2/25:3(WH)
KIRBY, John	_____, Chloe	-10 JAN 1814	DBAA:214
KIRBY, Richard	_____, Jane	-15 DEC 1830	WB4:26
KIRBY, William	HAYNE, Susanna	23 MAY 1797	FPC:20(JM)
KIRK, James	FLEMING, Bridget d/o Thomas Fleming	-7 APR 1786	HCH:49; 1787:73; 1791:15; FWE:160
KIRK, Robert William	HEYSER, Sarah d/o William Heyser	-23 APR 1804	WB1:132; DBG:530
KIRK, Samuel	BRITTON, Barbara	3 JUN 1798	FPC:20(JM); TMCC(C:3); 1799:12
KIRK, Samuel	FLETCHER, Rebecca	20 JUL 1815	AG:25/5/25; MR(IR); MB
KIRK, Samuel, Jr.	McCUE, Mary	27 JUL 1809	MR(IR); MB
KIRKLAND, Daniel	TRACY, Susannah	11 SEP 1803	MR(JM)
KITCHEN, William	BUTLER, Elizabeth L.	19 MAY 1818	AH:22/5/18
KITSON, Thomas	OGDEN, Nancy	12 DEC 1822	AG:19/12/22:3(JR)
KNIGHT, John	SHADE, Catharine	8 AUG 1807	AG:11/8/07:3(SH)
KNOWLES, John	WESTCOTT, Mary Ann	12 OCT 1815	FPC:20(JM); MB
KOON, Richard	RATCLIFF, Ann	7 DEC 1817	MR(IR); MB
KOONES, Charles	LEONARD, Rebecca W.	3 JAN 1822	SP; MB; AG:5/1/22:3(WHW)
KOONES, David	BOND, Matilda	c.22 MAY 1810	DBBB:294; PGM
KOONES, Frederick	_____, Elizabeth	-10 OCT 1821	NI:13/10/21
KOONES, Frederick	THOMPSON, Dolly	c.7 FEB 1820	DCM
KORN, John	_____, Rosannah	-20 DEC 1792	HCE:318; 1787:73; 1791:15; 1799:20; CCC(20)
KRAFFT, Jacob L.	_____, Mary Magdalene		MPC:E259
KYGER, George	_____, Mary	-23 DEC 1790	HCD:277
KYSER, George	_____, Fanny	-20 MAR 1783	HCOrd:20/3/83
KYSER, Jacob	_____, Fanny	-22 MAY 1783	HCOrd:22/5/83

Husband	Wife	Event or Marriage	Reference(s)

L

Husband	Wife	Event or Marriage	Reference(s)
LABILLE, Louis J.C.	O'NEALE, Mary T.	5 AUG 1823	MR(JF); MB; AG:7/8/23:3(JF)
LACEY, William	DAVIS, Elizabeth	22 SEP 1817	MB; AG:25/9/17:3
LADD, John Gardner[57]	EASTON, Sarah	- 1800	WB2:303; 1799:24; 1800:58; IGI
LADD, John H. Place: Beverly MA	WYER, Eliza S.	4 SEP 1819	AG:13/9/19:3
LADD, Joseph Brown	NICOLL, Mrs. Harriot V.	2 NOV 1824	NI:3/11/24(ON); MB; AG:6/11/24:3(ON)
LADD, Capt. William	GARDNER, Sarah d/o Benoni Gardner	22 DEC 1761	TA:86; FPCG; IGI
LADD, William	STIDOLPH, Sophia Ann	19 OCT 1801	FPC:22(JM); MR(JM); MB
LAKE, George	DAVIS, Mary B. d/o Samuel Davis	-23 APR 1816	DBBB:308
LAMB, George	AUBRAY, Jane E.	c.26 NOV 1818	MB
LAMBERT, Benjamin H.	WHEAT, Adeline Bond d/o Benoni Wheat	15 MAY 1828	MB; AG:19/5/29:3(RD)
LAMBERT, George	DENNISON, Catharine	30 OCT 1811	MR(IR); MB
LAMBERT, Joseph	BOGAN, Mary	1 JAN 1817	MR(IR); MB
LAMOINE, John	VASSY, Elizabeth	c.20 JUL 1809	MB
LAMMOND, Alexander	TULL, Charlotte	2 MAR 1799	FPC:22(JM); WBB:388
LAMMOND, Alexander Place: Washington DC	McINTIRE, Margaret Ann	21 OCT 1830	AG:25/10/30:3
LANDRESS, Henry W.	DAVIS, Nancy	12 APR 1801	MR(JM); MB
LANDRES, Henry White	THOMPSON, Mrs. Maria wid/o John Thompson	23 JUL 1803	MR(JM); MB
LANE, Alexander	STEELE, Nancy "Ann" d/o Thomas Steele	17 FEB 1820	MB; AG:21/2/20:3(SC)
LANE, George Wash. Place: Centerville[58]	ADAMS, Frances T.	9 MAR 1813	NI:18/3/13; FDO2:324
LANE, Hardage	GREENFIELD, Mary	c.23 NOV 1799	FD1798:365
LANE, Richard	BAYLEY, Hannah	15 NOV 1790	FPC:22(JM)
LANGFORD, Philip	SMITH, Lettice wid/o William Smith	-22 SEP 1795	FDY:196
LANGLEY, John	MURRAY, Mary	9 DEC 1819	AG:13/12/19:3
LANGSTON, Benjamin	_____, Hannah	-4 SEP 1799	DBA:107
LANHAM, Elisha	JENKINS, Mary Ann	10 JUL 1817	MR(AG); MB
LANHAM, John	LONGDEN, Olphair	22 OCT 1801	FPC:22(JM); MR(JM); MB
LANHAM, John	McFADDEN, Ann	5 SEP 1802	MR(JM); MB
LANHAM, John	SNELL, Catharine	3 FEB 1810	FPC:22(JM); MB
LANHAM, John B.	THOM, Cassa	23 NOV 1797	FPC:22(JM); 1799:34 DBC2:132
LANPHIER, Going	WILKERSON, Elizabeth	-17 APR 1801	DBB:195; IGI
LANPHIER, John	MARTIN, Ann G.	23 DEC 1830	MB; AG:28/12/30:3
LANPHIER, Robert Going	SEARS, Elizabeth	-28 AUG 1813	DBY:13; TMCC(D:3)
LANPHIER, Thomas	GOING, Elizabeth	c.1727	IGI; Note[59]
LANPHIER, Thomas	KYLE, Elizabeth		Note[60]
LANPHIER, William Place: Fredericksburg	SEXSMITH, Mary	2 FEB 1804	DBR:501; AG:8/2/04:3(JMc)

Husband	Wife	Event or Marriage	Reference(s)
LARMOUR, Samuel B.	MANDEVILLE, Susanna	29 DEC 1814	SPC(62:2); MR(WHW); AG:31/12/14:3; SP; MB
LATHAM, Edward	STEPHENSON, Rachel	19 FEB 1818	MR(WHW)
LATHAM, Rowland	HART, Elizabeth	c.19 MAR 1806	MB
LATIMER, Alexander	BURKETT, Massie	22 FEB 1797	FPC:22(JM); WBC:474
LATIMORE, Dr. John F.	BURCH, Susan R.	11 JAN 1825	AG:22/1/25:3
Place: *Pleasant Valley*, Prince George's Co. MD, d/o Capt. Joseph N. Burch			
LATRUITE, John P.	MOORE, Mrs. Barbara	9 APR 1821	AG:12/4/21:3(EH)
LATRUITE, William	MOORE, Barbara	9 APR 1821	MR(EH); MB
(Laurence and Lawrence)			
LAURENCE, George A.	CADERTON, Sarah	9 JAN 1804	MR(WM); MB
LAURENCE, James	BRIN, Betsey	6 SEP 1815	FPC:22(JM); MB
LAWRENCE, John	JANUARY, Mrs. Catharine	29 JUN 1807	AG:2/7/07:3(SH); MB
LAWRENCE, Joseph	GRINNOLDS, Mrs. Mockey	13 JAN 1814	FPC:22(JM); MB
LAURENCE, William	MARLE, Rebecca	3 FEB 1803	MR(JM); MB
LAWRENCE, William	McCOY, Mary	c.20 SEP 1811	MB
LAURIE, Rev. James	HALL, Mrs. Elizabeth B.	4 APR 1815	AG:6/4/15:3(JM); MR(JM); MB
LAW (also see "Laws")			
LAW, Edward	BERRY, Mary	c.1 APR 1818	MB
LAW, Thomas	CUSTIS, Elizabeth Parke	20 MAR 1796	FM(1802):218
LAWDEN, Isaac	LAWRASON, Hannah	7 FEB 1793	AG:9/2/93:3
LAWRASON, James	LEVERING, Alice	23 JUN 1779	OT:58; IGI; HCD:137; 1787:73; 1791:15; 1800:58; CCC(6); FDO:27
LAWRASON, Robert	SUMMERS, Elizabeth	-1 JAN 1805	DBS:73; IGI
LAWRASON, Thomas	CARSON, Elizabeth d/o Dr. Samuel Carson	18 OCT 1808	CCC(6); AG:22/10/08(SN)
LAWS (also see "Law")			
LAWS, Bolitha Place: Loudoun Co.	WILLIAMS, Elizabeth	30 JUN 1802	DBW:61; AG:6/5/24; IGI
LAWS, John P. Place: New York	CURRY, Hester	30 MAR 1826	AG:5/4/26:3(SC); UT:3/4/26:3
LAWS, Joshua Compton	LYLE, Elizabeth	c.15 MAY 1806	MB
LAWSON, John	McKAY, Elizabeth	24 MAY 1821	SPC(63:2); MR(WHW); MB; AG:28/5/21:3(ON)
LAWSON, Stephen	TRUSTLER, Elizabeth	c.9 DEC 1815	MB
LAWSON, William	FUGATE, Patsy	14 JAN 1810	FPC:22(JM)
LAWYED, John	_____, Rebeccah		1800:55
LEAP, Jacob	[NEWTON], Ann	-18 FEB 1794	WB2:405; CCG:A1; 1787:73; 1799:14; FPCC(41:42)
LEAR, Tobias	WASHINGTON, Mrs. Frances wid/o George Augustine Washington	c.6 AUG 1795	AG:6/8/95:3
LEAR, Tobias	BASSETT, Frances	1795	OT:14
LEAR, Tobias Place: Portsmouth NH	LONG, Polly		AG:6/8/1785
LeBLANCE, Allen Pike Place: Westmoreland Co.	HILLIARD, Frances	11 MAY 1821	AG:21/6/21:2
LE(E)DUM, Isaac	GOODIN, Ann	23 APR 1822	MR(ON); MB

Husband	Wife	Event or Marriage	Reference(s)
LEDDY, Hugh	SUMMERS, Charlotte	19 AUG 1822	MR(JF); MB; AG:22/8/22:3(JF)
LEE, Aaron (C)	PARKER, Polly (C)	3 MAY 1815	MR(WHW); MB
LEE, Charles	SCOTT, Mrs. Margaret C. wid/o Yelverton Peyton	19 JUL 1809	DBT:374; 1791:16; NI:28/7/09; LV:365; AG:25/7/09:3(JT)
LEE, Edmund Jennings	LEE, Sarah "Sally" d/o Richard Henry Lee of *Chantillee*	23 MAY 1796	OT:27; CCC(4); AG:26/5/96:3
LEE, Edmund J.	SHEPHERD, Eliza H. d/o Capt. Abraham Shepherd	1 OCT 1823	NI:16/10/23
LEE, Hancock Place: Fairfax Co.	NICHOLSON, Mary	22 JAN 1818	MR(WHW)
LEE, Henry	CARTER, Ann Hill	18 JUN 1793	LV:341; DBI:16
LEE, Maj. Henry Place: Westmoreland Co.	McCARTY, Ann R. d/o Daniel McCarty	1 APR 1817	AG:8/4/17:3(ON)
LEE, John	CHITTERSON, Mary	24 NOV 1825	MR(Sco); MB
LEE, Ludwell Place: Hanover Co.	ARMISTEAD, Betsey	30 MAY 1797	AG:8/6/97:3; 1791:16
LEE, Ludwell	LEE, Flora d/o Philip Lee	c.23 JAN 1788	DBG:44; LV:326; LDR:328
LEE, Richard Bland	COLLINS, Elizabeth	JUN 1794	DBQ:31; AM1:270
LEE, Richard H.	GREEN, Mary	15 APR 1817	MR(JM); MB
LEE, William	BROWN, Mary	c.4 JUN 1807	MB
LEE, Rev. William I. Place: Leesburg	CHILTON, Mary Catharine Sim d/o William Chilton	25 OCT 1827	AG:27/10/27:3
LEGG, Eli Place: Prince William Co.	PRINCE, Jane	27 FEB 1796	Legg Web Page
LEGG, Elias P.	RISENER, Catharine	26 AUG 1823	MB; AG:6/8/23:3(WHW)
LEHON, John	WILLIAMS, Sarah	26 FEB 1791	FPC:22(JM)
LEMMON, Alexander	SPEARS, Harriet E.	13 SEP 1827	NI:15/9/27
LEMOINE, John	_____, Susannah Margaret	-28 AUG 1801	FPC:21; DBB:123; 1799:16; WBA:90
LENOX, George	RILEY, Mary	c.18 MAR 1802	MB
LEONARD, Jacob	FAW, Sophia Eliza d/o Abraham Faw	3 NOV 1814	NI:7/11/14(WHW); WB3:306; MR(WHW); AG:5/11/14:3(WHW); MB
LESLIE, Benjamin	KINSEY, Rebecca	23 MAR 1814	FPC:22(JM); MB
LEVENSTON, John	TALBUTT, Elizabeth	MAR 1795	FPC:22(JM)
LEVERING, Aaron	LAWRASON, Mary Miller	c.10 APR 1801	MB
LEVERING, Aaron Righter	LAWRASON, Nancy Butcher d/o James Lawrason	3 SEP 1807	AG:4/9/07:3; WB3:133; MB
LEVERING, Septimus	WESTON, Eliza	17 JUN 1805	AG:18/6/05:3(MO); MB
LEVERING, Thomas	_____, Rachel		QM:48
LEWIS, Capt. Ansel, Jr.	CAMPBELL, Jane M.	8 FEB 1818	MR(JM); MB; AG:10/2/18:3(JM)
LEWIS, Daniel	BRUSTER, Ann d/o Thomas Bruster	-12 MAR 1803	FD1803:7
LEWIS, David	DAVIS, A.	3 JUN 1799	FPC:22(JM)
LEWIS, Edward	_____, Elizabeth	-26 NOV 1799	CRA:297
LEWIS, Enoch M.	FAW, Julian M.	14 NOV 1815	MR(WHW)

Husband	Wife	Event or Marriage	Reference(s)
LEWIS, Fielding	DADE, Betsy	c.26 MAR 1789	AG:26/3/89:2
LEWIS, Francis W.	BENNETT, Martha	c.6 SEP 1809	MB
LEWIS, George W.	LEWIS, Jane B.	25 FEB 1829	AG:6/3/29:3
Place: *Marmion*, King George Co.			
LEWIS, Henry	HUFF, Eliza	23 JAN 1798	AA:26/1/98:3
LEWIS, Henry	HAGER, Mrs. Mary	20 MAY 1802	AG:25/5/02:3(DB);
Place: Hagerstown MD	wid/o John Hager		BFG:25/5/02
LEWIS, James (C)	_____, Margaret (C)	c.17 NOV 1827	MB
LEWIS, John	_____, Catharina	-12 JUN 1802	DBC:41
LEWIS, Joseph	HOLTON, Elizabeth	16 FEB 1823	AG:18/2/23:3; MR(JF)
LEWIS, Joseph	HARRISON, Catharine	22 FEB 1827	AG:5/3/27:3(JR)
LEWIS, Laurence	CUSTIS, Eleanor Parke	22 FEB 1799	FPC:22(JM); P:295
LEWIS, Levi	TRAMMELL, Anna	1788	FB
LEWIS, Lorenzo	COXE, Esther Maria	6 JUN 1827	UT:8/6/27:3
Place: Philadelphia PA	d/o John Redman Coxe		
LEWIS, Mordecai	SAUNDERS, Hannah	-4 APR 1796	DBS:334; FWF:251;
	d/o Joseph Saunders		HCI:42
LEWIS, Richard	_____, Elizabeth	-18 APR 1799	HCL:367; DBB:466;
			1799:12
LEWIS, Robert A.	MATTOX, Eleanor A.	9 FEB 1815	MR(WHW); MB
LEWIS, Samuel	JENKINS, Sarah	7 SEP 1797	FPC:22(JM)
LEWIS, Thomas	EVANS, Nancy	29 MAY 1815	FPC:22(JM); MB
LEWIS, Vincent L.	_____, Elizabeth	-19 APR 1816	DBD2:1
LEWIS, William	WAY, Salome	18 DEC 1806	FPC:22(JM); MB[61]
LIGHTFOOT, George	SANFORD, Ann	12 NOV 1812	FPC:22(JM); MB
LIGHTFOOT, John M.	SANDFORD, Elizabeth	14 JUN 1801	MR(JM); MB
LIGHTFOOT, William	BROWN, Patty	SEP 1795	FPC:22(JM)
LIGHTFOOT, William	WALLIS, Elizabeth	24 DEC 1797	FPC:22(JM)
LIGHTFOOT, William	_____, Mary		1799:36; 1800:58
LIMERICK, John	_____, Hannah	-17 JUN 1802	CCG
LIMERICK, John	ADAMS, Susanna	12 SEP 1790	FPC:22(JM); DBA:366
LIMMERMAN, George	SIMPSON, Ann	21 AUG 1806	FPC:22(JM)
LIMRICK, John	ADAMS, Nancy	c.5 JUL 1802	MB
LINCH, Barton	WHITE, Sarah	6 MAR 1800	FPC:22(JM)
LINDO, A.	GILLINGHAM, Harriot	14 JAN 1810	AG:22/1/10:3
Place: Philadelphia PA			
LINDSAY, _____	CATON, Mary	29 DEC 1829	AG:13/1/30:3(WJ)
LINDSAY, Benjamin	ROBINSON, Amelia Rebecca	7 FEB 1798	FPC:22(JM);
			AA:9/2/98:3
LINDSAY, John	COOPER, Athy	25 JUN 1800	FPC:22(JM)
LINDSAY, John	KEATING, Mary	c.29 DEC 1829	MB
LINDSAY, John G.	BARNES, Mary	4 AUG 1818	AG:12/8/18:3(LO)
	d/o Basil Barnes[62]		
LINDSAY, Opie	_____,	- SEP 1792	AG:3/7/93:3
LINDSAY, Opie	RODES, Nancy	5 OCT 1815	Note[63]
LINDSAY, Robert	_____, Susannah	-23 JUN 1793	AG:26/6/93:3
LINDSAY, Samuel	McDOUGALL, Jane W.	17 JUN 1819	FF:352; SPC; SP;
			AG:19/6/19:2(WHW)
LINDSAY, William	KETLING, Mary	13 NOV 1817	MR(IR); MB
LINDSLEY, Abraham Brad.	JAMESON, Sarah Jane Triplett	29 SEP 1827	NI:1/10/27;
Place: Washington DC			UT:1/10/27:3
LIPSCOMB, William C.	ADGATE, Phebe	30 NOV 1815	AG:4/12/15:3(WHW);
			MB; MR(WHW)

Husband	Wife	Event or Marriage	Reference(s)
LINTER, William	HARTLEY, Latitia	17 MAY 1804	MR(JM); MB
LINTON, Edmund	_____, Hester	-21 NOV 1753	FWB:40
LINTON, George	McKINNEY, Henrietta	10 FEB 1810	FPC:22(JM); MB
LINTON, William	SAUNDERS, Mary	c.25 MAR 1806	MB
LISBY, Noble	JONES, Eleanor	c.7 MAR 1811	MB[64]
LITLE, Charles Place: Winchester	PARKINS, Lydia	24 APR 1822	H:761, 769; QM:48
LIPPITT, Rev. Edward R. Place: *Exeter*, Loudoun Co.	ALEXANDER, Mary Ann Frances d/o Charles Alexander	16 OCT 1827	AG:31/10/27:3
LITLE, John	HUMPHREYS, Hannah d/o Richard Humphreys	-23 AUG 1817	WB2:225
LITLE, Richard H. s/o John Litle Place: Washington DC	TALBOTT, Elizabeth d/o Joseph and Ann Talbott	26 DEC 1810	H:761, 785; QM:49; NI:27/12/10; AG:28/12/10:3; MGB:14/4:2
LITLE, Richard H. Place: Philadelphia PA	JAMES, Ruth d/o John James of Philadelpha PA	3 DEC 1822	NI:12/7/22; AG:10/12/22:3
LITTLEJOHN, Samuel	COFFER, Sarah d/o Thomas Withers Coffer	-1 JAN 1781	FWD:260; FDM2:98
LITTLEJOHN, Rev. John	TALBOTT, Monica d/o Daniel Talbott	-22 MAY 1777	FF:460
LIVINGSTON, John	LYLE, Mrs. Martha (Hewitt)	c.19 DEC 1793	DBA:124; PGM; DBV:512
LIZURM, William	MERICK, Sarah	21 SEP 1791	FPC:22(JM)
LLOYD, Henry	SMOTHERMOND, Eliza	26 DEC 1822	AG:2/1/23:2(JR)
LLOYD, John s/o Nicholas	JANNEY, Rebecca d/o Joseph Janney	30 NOV 1798	DBQ:1; 1799:40; CCC(93); J:89
LLOYD, John	LEE, Ann Henrietta	2 NOV 1820	MB[65]; B8
LLOYD, Nicholas	HARPER, Sarah d/o Capt. John Harper		FSH:A-9
LOCKAR, James, Jr.	SIMPSON, Mimay	6 OCT 1813	FPC:22(JM); MB
LOCKE, Thomas	_____, Catherine	-15 MAY 1797	FPC:21; 1799:2
LOCKER, James	KING, Susanna	29 JUN 1800	FPC:22(JM)
LOGAN, Hugh M.	CURRY, Elizabeth	15 OCT 1816	MR(WHW); MB
LOGAN, John (C)	FULLER, Jane (C)	23 DEC 1818	MR(WHW)
LOGAN, Peter	_____, Sarah		1799:24; 1800:58
LOGAN, Randolph	CONN, Elizabeth	20 NOV 1800	FPC:22(JM), 23; DBB:344
LOGAN, Samuel	McGAHAN, Frances "Fanny"	27 MAY 1797	FPC:22(JM), 23; FPCC(41:10)
LOGAN, William	WILLIAMS, Elizabeth	1 NOV 1821	MR(ON); MB
LOKY, Thos. McCollester	GESS, Mrs. Kitty	c.12 MAR 1796	AG:12/3/96:3
LOMAX, John	THOMAS, Rachel	-27 JUN 1785	HCC:205; 1787:73; 1791:16; FDQ:195; AG:8/12/00
LOMAX, John	McCLEA, Elizabeth	14 DEC 1803	FPC:22(JM); MR(JM); MB
LOMAX, Michael	SMITH, Sophronia A.	7 SEP 1830	AG:10/9/30:3; NI:8/9/30
LOMBARD, Benjamin H.	LANHAM, Harriet	c.29 DEC 1823	MB

Husband	Wife	Event or Marriage	Reference(s)
LONG, Capt. Seth	HARPER, Sarah "Sally" M.	9 OCT 1806	BFG:11/10/06(JM) BR:104; FPC:22(JM); AG:13/10/06:3(JM); MB
LONG, William	STEWART, Susanna	29 OCT 1807	AG:30/10/07:3(JM); FPC:22(JM); MB
LONGDEN, Elias	BADEN, Elizabeth	2 APR 1797	FPC:22(JM)
LONGDEN, George C.	SCOTT, Elizabeth Ann	7 SEP 1813	FPC:22(JM); MB: AG:11/9/13:3(JM)
LONGDEN, John	_____, Elizabeth	-18 APR 1787	HCB:415; 1787:73; 1791:16; 1799:32; WB2:403; TMCC(P:1); NI:22/7/26
LONGDEN, John A.	HOWARD, Elizabeth d/o Beale Howard	12 NOV 1816	AG:14/11/16(ON); FDZ2:329, L3:201; MR(ON); MB
LONGDEN, Thomas Place: Georgetown DC	CORVEN, Mrs. Julia	5 DEC 1815	AG:7/12/15:3(B); DCM
LONGDON, Abel	_____, Susannah		1799:34; 1800:54
LONGDON, George	SCOTT, E.A.	7 SEP 1813	FPC:22(JM)
LONGDON, Ralph	YOUNG, Mrs. Dorothy wid/o David Young		FDO:352
LORBAHAYE, Peter	WATSON, Elizabeth	c.11 MAY 1812	MB
LOTZ, J.	_____, Susanna	-6 NOV 1797	FPC:21
LOUDOUN, Frederick	JOHNSON, Nancy	c.4 APR 1827	MB
LOUDOUN, Peter	MARSH, Phebe	c.28 FEB 1824	MB
LOVE, Charles	TRIPLETT, Anne "Nancy" d/o Capt. Thomas Triplett	-9 AUG 1797	HCI:422; DBH:326; 1799:20; FM(1835):59
LOVE, John	WATSON, Elizabeth d/o Josiah Watson	c.27 MAR 1788	FB; 1787:74; AG:27/3/88
LOVE [or Lowe], John	BRAMMELL, _____	OCT 1793	FPC:22(JM)
LOVE, Richard Henry Place: Belmont, Loudoun Co., d/o Ludwell Lee	LEE, Eliza Matilda	20 FEB 1812	AG:25/2/12:3
LOVE, Samuel	JONES, Sarah	c.30 JAN 1798	NI:12/8/22; FDA2:436
LOVEJOY, John A.	HALLEY, Nancy	20 MAY 1815	MR(IR); MB
LOVEL, Ezekiel	RIGLY, Maryann	30 DEC 1830	MR(EH)
LOVELESS, Nace	DOVE, Alley	6 JAN 1814	MR(ON); MB
LOW, Rev. Samuel	SAWYER, Margaret Maria	c.2 SEP 1818	MB
LOW, Thomas, the Elder	_____, Margaret ni/o Andrew Wales	-1799	DBR:185; FPCG; 1787:73; CRA:302
LOWDEN, Jesse	THOMPSON, Mary	1788	FB
LOWE, Enoch M.	FAW, Juliana Maria	14 NOV 1815	MR(WHW); MB
LOWE, Henry	BURNETT, Mary	19 AUG 1790	FPC:22(JM)
LOWE, James M. Place: Mount Lubentia	McCARTY, Anna M.M.S.C.	16 MAY 1830	AG:18/5/30:3
LOWE, James Rector M.	ARELL, Christiana d/o David Arell grandd/o Richard Arell	c.4 APR 1803	DBG:515; PGM; DBH:497; DBK:374; DBR:107
LOWE [or Love], John	BRAMMELL, _____	OCT 1793	FPC:22(JM)
LOWE, John F.M.	LEONARD, Mrs. Sophia E. d/o Abraham Faw	30 SEP 1830	MB; AG:2/10/30:3(Sco)
LOWE, Thomas	CANNON, Mary	22 JUL 1806	FPC:22(JM); MB

Husband	Wife	Event or Marriage	Reference(s)
LOWE, Thomas	BRYAN, Mary Ann	1 MAR 1820	MR(AG); MB; AG:4/3/20:3(AG)
LOWE, William	KORN, Elizabeth W.	c.26 JUN 1817	MB(ON)
LOWNES, James	_____, Sarah	-29 DEC 1786	HCC:112; 1787:74
LOWRY, James	SWANN, Judith	6 NOV 1829	MR(IR); MB
LOWRY, Samuel	COOPER, Agnes wid/o John Cooper	-7 OCT 1843	WB4:379
LUCAS, John R.	ROBEY, Stacey	c.20 JUN 1811	MB
LUCAS, Robert	SPEAKE, Betty	-13 FEB 1786	R2:90(SG); FWL:96
LUDBERG, John G.	CRANDELL, Sarah	3 NOV 1808	FPC:22(JM)
LUDLOW, Israel L. of Cincinnati OH	SLACUM, Helen Adelia d/o Capt. George W. Slacum	24 JUN 1830	AG:12/7/30:3; NI:13/7/30
LUMPHREY, Samuel	KING, Rebecca	19 DEC 1799	FPC:22(JM)
LUMSDEN, John	OATES, Margery	19 AUG 1797	FPC:21, 23(JM); TMCC(L:2/P:2)
LUNT, Ezra, weaver	_____, Ann	-5 MAR 1804	WBB:136; 1799:8
LUNT, Ezra	_____, Elizabeth	- JAN 1817	DBD2:328; TMCC(N:3); FWU:85
LUNT, Ezra	HILL, Sarah	c.20 FEB 1830	DCM
LUPTON, Daniel S.	LAMBERT, Sarah s/o George Lambert	8 JUN 1813	MR(IR); MR
LUPTON, David, Jr. Place: Berkley Meeting House,	McPHERSON, Ann d/o John McPherson	14 FEB 1809	H:763; WB1:311; FWK:335
LUPTON, Rich. Ridgeway Place: Friends' Meeting House,	JANNEY, Anna d/o Abijah Janney	25 AUG 1825	H:753, 763; AG:30/8/25:3
LUTZ, George	LEE, Elizabeth	20 NOV 1806	MR(IR); MB
LYELLS, Thomas C.	SEATON, Rebecca	12 JAN 1814	MR(WHW)
LYLE, Robert, Sr.	HEWITT, Martha	c.24 NOV 1785	HCB:332; 1787:73; 1791:16; AG:24/11/85:3
LYLES, Dennis Magruder	SEATON, Eliza Wise	13 NOV 1817	SP; MR(WHW); MB; AG:15/11/17:3(ON)
LYLES, George Noble	_____, Elizabeth	-11 JUL 1804	DBH:302
LYLES, Henry	DAVIES, Mary d/o Benjamin Davies	31 OCT 1805	WBC:500; FPC:22(JM); FWK:115; MB
LYLES, Henry	_____, Catharine	-18 JUL 1806	DBBB:203
LYLES, James	DAVIS, Mary Ann	1 JUN 1811	MR(IR); TMCC(C:4); MB
LYLES, James	HULL, Esther	c.9 MAR 1816	TMCC(C:4); DCM
LYLES, James Place: Washington DC	GOSSUM, Mrs. Matilda	16 FEB 1826	AG:18/2/26:3
LYLES, John	TRIDLE, Betsey	8 JAN 1818	MR(IR); MB
LYLES, Robert, Jr.	_____, Elizabeth	-4 OCT 1796	HCH:428; 1787:73
LYLES, Thomas	DEETON, Isabella d/o Christopher Deeton	c.20 EEC 1825	MB
LYLES, Thomas Claggett	SEATON, Rebecca	18 JAN 1814	DBZ:212, 254; SP; AG:20/1/14:3(WHW); MB
LYLES, William	FARNESTER, Nancy	SEP 1795	FPC:22(JM)
LYLES, William	SMITH, Hannah	16 NOV 1830	MR(IR); MPC:S4; MB
LYLES, William, Sr.	_____, Sarah	-5 NOV 1785	HCB:366; 1787:73
LYLES, William H.	BRUCE, Elizabeth	26 JAN 1830	AG:30/1/30:3(GM)

Husband	Wife	Event or Marriage	Reference(s)
LYLES, William Henry	LOWRY, Ann d/o Col. William Lowry	4 NOV 1801	BFG:6/11/01 BT:14/12/04
LYLES, Zachariah	_____, Margaret	-7 APR 1793	CCG:A1
LYLE(S), Zachariah	EDWARDS, Mary "Polly"	DEC 1795	FPC:22(JM); 1799:36; 1800:55
LYMBOURN, John	HAYNES, Mrs. Mary	7 JUL 1814	AG:12/7/14:3(Mc); DCM
LYNCH, Barton	WHEELER, Dolly	c.1 JAN 1814	MB
LYNCH, James	NEALE, Catherine	29 DEC 1826	MR(Sco); MB
LYNCH, Samuel [James]	KARKEEK, Elizabeth d/o Dr. Karkeek, St. Austle, Eng.	11 JUL 1822	MB; MR(EH); AG:26/1/27:3
LYNN, Adam, Jr.	_____, Catharine	-14 DEC 1782	AG:9/1/08:3; AM1:293; SPC; FWE:144; FDO:282
LYNN, Adam	YOUNG, Elizabeth d/o John Young, Sr.	c.1830	FC#361
LYNN, Joseph C.	CARTER, Leve	13 JAN 1825	AG:18/1/25:3(JR)
LYNN, Capt. Joseph R. of *Fairview*, Prince William Co.	_____, Sarah A.	-19 MAY 1830	AG:26/5/30:3
LYON, Andrew	MASSEY, Mary	26 FEB 1805	AG:27/2/05:3(JM); FPC:22(JM); MB
LYONS, John	ANDERSON, Louisa E.	6 JAN 1824	AG:10/1/24:3; MB
LYONS, John J.	TYLER, Catharine	9 DEC 1829	MR(IR); MB
LYONS, Vincent	SIMMS, Eliza d/o Charles Simms	23 JUL 1820	MR(WHW); MB

Husband	Wife	Event or Marriage	Reference(s)

M

Husband	Wife	Event or Marriage	Reference(s)
MACHENHEIMER, Rev. George L.	PAGE, Eliza d/o Charles and Ann Page si/o W.C. Page	23 OCT 1827	SPC(146:4); SP; MR(WJ); AG:25/10/27:3(WJ)
MACKEY, Richard	LINDSAY, Salley	c.9 DEC 1809	MB
MACLEOD, David	_____, Mary Ann	-27 JUL 1810	DBT:272
MACOMB, Alexander Place: Newark NJ	M'WHORTER, Julia d/o Alexander M'Whorter	9 MAR 1826	UT:14/3/26:3
MACOMB, Gen. Alexander	WILSON, Mrs. Harriet B. d/o Rev. Dr. Walsh	27 MAY 1826	UT:29/5/26:3
MACRAE, Allan	TERRETT, Ann D. d/o William H. Terrett	1 DEC 1818	AG:8/12/18:2(ST)
MADDEN, Michael	RAMSAY, Hannah d/o William Ramsay	c.29 JUL 1784	HCB:190; FWG:431; 1787:74; 1791:17; AG:29/7/84
MADDEN, Thomas	ROBERTSON, Mary	1788	FB
MADDOX, Notley, Jr.	TUCKER, Elizabeth	14 JAN 1816	AG:15/1/16:3(Y)
MAFFITT, Rev. Wm. H.	TURBERVILLE, Mrs. Henrietta[66] d/o Richard Henry Lee	5 MAY 1803	MR(JM); LPC; LV:207; HCK:642; CWA:556; DBM:445 AG:7/5/03:3(JM); MB
MAGRUDER, _____	BEALL, Charity d/o Sophia Beall	-8 MAY 1782	FWD:326
MAGRUDER, Philip	_____, Margaret	-8 JUN 1801	WBA:34; 1799:18
MAGRUDER, Thomas	_____, Eliza	-28 DEC 1797	HCL:26
MAGUIRE, Patrick	_____, Margaret	-20 MAY 1785	AG:2/6/85:3
MAJOR, John	_____, Mary	-21 AUG 1849	TMCC(D:7)
MAHANEY, Thomas	_____, Sarah		1800:51
MAHONEY, Clement Barton	HARRISON, Mary	c.31 DEC 1813	MB
MAHONEY, John	UNDERWOOD, Ann	9 MAY 1818	MR(ON); MB
MANDELL, Daniel	NEWMAN, Nancy	23 APR 1796	FPC:24(JM)
MANDELL, Daniel	LUSTRE, Emme	3 APR 1799	FPC:24(JM)
MANDELL, John C.	ABERCROMBIE, Mary	c.10 OCT 1804	MB; TMCC(R:5); DBU:255
MANDEVILLE, Jonathan	_____, Elizabeth	-7 AUG 1798	DBU:42; CCC(72)
MANDEVILLE, Joseph	[COPE?], Lydia	-20 JAN 1813	DBX:69; SPC(51:2) WB4:143; 1799:8
MANDLEY, Joseph	WATERS, Elizabeth	c.10 JUL 1817	MB
MANERY, Samuel (C)	_____, Elisabeth	-12 FEB 1846	SPC(177:4)
MANKIN, Charles	VOWELL, Polly	21 JUN 1800	FPC:24(JM)
MANKIN, Charles	MUCLEROY, Elizabeth	20 JUL 1819	AG:2/8/19:2(IR)
MANKIN, David	_____, Ann	-13 JUL 1809	DBR:83; CCC(40)
MANKIN(S), William	COOKE, Dorcas M.	4 JUL 1822	MPC:E2; MB; AG:9/7/22:3(SC)
MANLEY, John H.	_____, Margaret B.	-12 APR 1826	AG:12/4/26
MANLEY, Matthew	TUCKER, Letty d/o Christina Tucker	c.4 FEB 1815	MB
MANLEY, Wm. Harrison	BOHANNON, Levina	12 OCT 1818	AH:16/10/18
MANN, Bernhard	_____, Johanna	-8 OCT 1794	HCF:193; 1791:18
MANNERY, _____	DIXON, Mrs. Mary	15 JUN 1819	SP; AG:18/6/19:3(WHW)
MANUEL, Anderson	HIXON, Malinda	30 NOV 1823	AG:4/12/23:3

Husband	Wife	Event or Marriage	Reference(s)
MARBLE, Henry	CLARKE, Betsey	c.26 JUL 1816	MB
MARBURY, Francis F.	BLACKLOCK, Elizabeth C.	28 NOV 1816	AG:30/11/16:3(B)
Place: Georgetown DC			
MARBURY, John H.	FENDALL, Eliza C.	7 DEC 1830	AG:10/12/30:3; SP;
	d/o Capt. Benjamin T. Fendall		MR(WJ); MB
MARBURY, Leonard	HUNTER, Mary W.	20 AUG 1816	MR(JM); MB
MARBURY, William L.	FENDALL, Susan F.	c.16 MAY 1826	MB
MARCKLEY, William	_____, Joanna	-27 JUN 1812	WB3:40
MARKELL, George C.	SHRODER, Elizabeth	1 MAY 1826	MB; MPC:E1
MARKS, William G.	EMERY, Peggy	DEC 1793	FPC:24(JM); 1791:18; 1799:18
MARKWARD, John	WARD, Sophia	c.FEB 1825	AG:1/2/25:3
Place: Piscataway, Prince George's Co. MD			
MARLE, David	SMITH, Elizabeth Harriet	30 SEP 1813	FPC:24(JM); MB
MARLE, Joseph	REED, Mrs. Elizabeth		1799:30; 1800:52; FWG:232; AG:5/10/13:3(JM)
MARLL, Henry (C)	CLARKE, Betsey (C)	26 JUL 1816	MR(WHW)
MARNER, Samuel L.	CLEMONS, Lyzyan	SEP 1792	FPC:24(JM)
MARR, Charles	_____, Esther	-21 JUN 1783	HCOrd:21/6/83
MARSHALL, Alexander J.	TAYLOR, Maria Rose	6 DEC 1827	AG:8/12/27:3(RK); MB
	d/o Robert J. Taylor		
MARSHALL, Josiah	DENEALE, Catharine	26 JAN 1815	AG:31/1/15:3(ON)
	d/o William Deneale		
MARSHALL, Thomas J.	YOUNG, Caroline M.	11 JUN 1822	AG:18/6/22:2
Place: Charles Co. MD			
MARSHALL, Dr. Wm.	BENSON, Mrs. Eleanor	11 NOV 1817	AG:18/11/17:3(JW)
MARSHALL, William	FLING, Russey	14 FEB 1826	AG:17/2/26:3(JR)
MARSHALL, William, Jr.	_____, Caroline	-13 MAY 1816	AG:15/5/16:3
MARSHALL, William Louis	LEE, Ann Kinloch	22 JUN 1826	AG:29/6/26:3(RK);
Place: Georgetown DC	d/o Maj. Gen. Henry Lee		UT:30/6/26:3
MARSTELLER, Ferdinand	HEISKELL, Margaret	30 JUN 1803	DBT:238; SPC;
	d/o Peter Heiskell		DBC2:53; AG:1/7/03:3(TD)
MARSTELLER, Col. Philip	RICE, Magdalena	c.1766	HCC:225; 1791:18;
s/o Frederich Marsteller			OT:35; Note[67]
MARSTELLER, Philip	_____, Mary	-20 DEC 1787	DBF:440; 1787:74; 1791:18
MARSTELLER, Philip G.	COPPER, Christiana[68] Davis	17 JAN 1793	DBA:269; FPCG; OT:35; 1799:14; DBB:240; LVA1:1; DBE2:298; CM:19/1/93
MARSTELLER, Philip G.	_____, Elizabeth	-10 MAR 1801	DBQ:409
MARSSTON, William	COATS, Lucinda	c.26 AUG 1824	MB
MASTER, William	JOHNSON, Elizabeth	17 AUG 1818	MR(IR)
MARTIN, David	HARPER, Sarah Wells	22 JUN 1824	SP; MB; AG:26/6/24:3(WHW)
MARTIN, Jacob L.	OLIVE, Ann	4 JUL 1826	UT:5/7/26:3
MARTIN, Jacob L.	SMITHER, Julia	8 MAY 1827	AG:10/5/27:3(IR); MB; UT:8/5/27:3[69]
MARTIN, James	GALLOWAY, Sophia	9 MAR 1791	FPC:24(JM)
MARTIN, John	COOKE, Nancy	21 MAY 1806	MR(IR); MB

Husband	Wife	Event or Marriage	Reference(s)
MARTIN, Thomas L.	LANPHIER, Harriet	c.18 OCT 1814	MB
MARTIN, William	PERRY, Joan	10 OCT 1795	LVA1:7
MARTIN, William	BAGNETT, Nancy	8 MAY 1799	FPC:24(JM)
MARTIN, William	WOODROW, Mary d/o John Woodrow	17 OCT 1805	FPC:24(JM); DBE2:45; MB
MARTIN, Hon. William D.	DORSEY, Sally Maria d/o Hon. Clement Dorsey	5 JAN 1830	AG:15/1/30:3
MARVEL, David	GRYMES, Ann	3 MAR 1803	MR(WM); MB
MASKEL, Joseph	MARSTON, Sarah	4 SEP 1830	MR(EH); MB
MASOLETTE, Vincent	HORWELL, Sarah M.	27 OCT 1818	AH:30/10/18:(WHW); MR(WHW)
MASON, Armistead	PARKER, Eliza d/o Gen. Thomas Parker	-5 MAY 1814	AG:5/5/14:3
MASON, Benjamin	STONE, Mary Ann	1 SEP 1804	FPC:24(JM); MB
MASON, Charles	_____, Ann	-7 SEP 1756	FWB:134
MASON, Edgar	FAIRFAX, Eugenia d/o Thomas Fairfax	10 JUN 1829	MB; AG:23/6/29:3(RK)
MASON, George	_____, Ann	-20 JUL 1762	FDE:102
MASON, George	_____, Elizabeth	-25 FEB 1785	CRA:180; HCOrd:25/2/85
MASON, George Place: Analostan Island	MASON, Virginia second d/o Gen. John Mason	23 OCT 1827	NI:30/10/27
MASON, George Place: Fairfax Co.	MASON, Eliza d/o Thomson Mason	c.16 FEB 1813	NI:19/2/13; DCM; AG:22/2/13:3 BPEA:20/2/13(Mc)
MASON, George Place: Clifton, Fairfax Co.	PATTON, Mary Ann d/o James Patton	8 FEB 1820	AG:11/2/20:3(JF)
MASON, George	PATTON, Elizabeth Ann eldest d/o Robert Patton of Spring Bank	2 JAN 1823	NI:14/1/23; AG:18/1/23:3[70]
MASON, James Murray	CHEW, Eliza M. d/o Benjamin Chew	25 JUL 1822	CCC(C)
MASON, John	PARSONS, Mary "Polly" d/o James Parsons	c.11 AUG 1785	DBH:176; HCM:116; AG:11/8/85:3
MASON, John	LITHCOE, Jane	13 JUN 1806	FPC:24(JM); MB
MASON, John	OLDHAM, Nancy	9 DEC 1813	AG:14/12/13:3(WHW); MR(WHW); MB[71]
MASON, John	BROWN, Jane	c.14 JAN 1822	MB
MASON, Josiah	GLADDEN, Cloe d/o Susannah Gladden	c.15 AUG 1818	MB
MASON, Maynadier Place: Friendship	FRENCH, Mary Virginia d/o Charles French	18 NOV 1830	AG:22/11/30:3
MASON, Thomson	CHICHESTER, Sarah McCarty	1784	FWG:194; OT:24; R2:90(SG); 5GM:237
MASON, Thomson	PRICE, Elizabeth C.	19 NOV 1817	AG:24/11/17:3
MASSEY, Joseph	HALL, Elizabeth d/o Jonathan Hall	-30 JUL 1794	HCE:356
MASSEY, Rev. Lee	BRONAUGH, Elizabeth d/o Jeremiah Bronaugh	c.1759	5GM:88
MASSEY, Robert	NORRIS, Mary d/o Mark Norris	20 JUL 1813	AG:24/7/13:3; MB
MASSEY, Thomas	RICHARDS, Elizabeth	NOV 1792	FPC:24(JM)

Husband	Wife	Event or Marriage	Reference(s)
MASSIE, John W.	FOOTE, Mary	3 MAR 1824	AG:4/3/24:3
Place: *Cedar Hill*	d/o William Foote, of Prince William Co.		
MASSOLETTI, Vincent	HORWELL, Sarah M.	27 OCT 1818	SP; MR(WHW); MB; AG:29/10/18:2(WHW)
MASTEN, Charles Turner	_____, Rebecca	-29 OCT 1801	DBB:501
MASTER, William	JOHNSON, Elizabeth	17 AUG 1818	MR(IR); MB
	d/o Susanna Johnson		
MASTERSON, Loughlin	SOMERS, Mary Ann	c.3 OCT 1812	MB
MATHANEY, George	SUTTON, Lucy A.	18 MAY 1826	AG:8/6/26:3
Place: Westmoreland Co.			
MATHEWS, Moses	KEYS, Lucinda	21 MAR 1827	AG:5/3/27:3(JR)
MATTENLY, Lewis	BOUTCHER, Ann	15 FEB 1821	AG:27/2/21:2(JR)
MATTHEW, Elias	FRANKLIN, Nancy	24 DEC 1827	AG:3/1/28:3(JR)
MATTHEWS, Jabez	McPHERSON, Sarah	28 NOV 1803	FPC:24(JM); MR(JM); MB
MATTHEWS, James	POWELL, Mildred	25 JAN 1827	MR(Sco); MB; AG:30/1/27:3(Sco)[72]
MATTHEWS, Thomas	_____, Sarah	-6 JAN 1801	HCMin:6/1/01
MAUKENHEIMER, Geo. L.	PAGE, Eliza	c.OCT 1827	AG:25/10/27
	d/o Charles Page		
MAURICE (also see "Morris")			
MAURICE, Capt. Theo. W.	EDELEN, Margaret Matilda	20 JUL 1819	AG:28/7/19:3
Place: *Mount Air*	d/o Joseph Edelen		
MAY, Dr. Frederick	SLACUM, Julia Matilda	17 JUN 1811	NI:20/6/11(FB); AG:19/6/11(FB)
MAY, Henry Knox	CRACROFT, Maria Rose	9 MAY 1805	AG:10/5/05:3(TD); MB
	d/o Elizabeth V. Cracroft		
MAY, John	HOWARD, Sarah "Sally"	3 JAN 1811	MR(FB); DBC2:488; MB
MAY, Joseph	_____, Dorothy "Dolly"	-23 OCT 1794	HCH:247
MAY, Richard	_____, Mary	-12 JAN 1801	DBE:85; 1799:8
MAY, Thomas	_____, Sarah	-10 NOV 1783	HCA:95
MAY, Thomas	_____, Mary	-25 FEB 1785	HCOrd:25/2/85
MAYHALL, James	COLE, Nelly	DEC 1793	FPC:24(JM)
MAYHALL, James	ELLIS, Anne	5 MAR 1801	MR(JM)
MAYHALL, Samuel	_____, Nancy	-7 SEP 1807	WB1:20
MAYHUE, Clement	_____, Mary	-10 NOV 1816	DBD2:324
MAYHUGH, Thomas	TURNBULL, Catharine	21 MAY 1829	AG:30/5/29:3
MAYNADIER, Henry G.	YELLOTT, Elizabeth	14 FEB 1828	AG:25/2/28:3
Place: *Fertility*	second d/o John Yellott, of Baltimore Co. MD		
MAYNADIER, Lt. William	EVELETH, Sarah	7 OCT 1829	AG:19/10/29:3
Place: Fortress Monroe			
MAYNADIER, Wm. M.	BROWN, Sarah S.	17 SEP 1801	DBX:270; AG:18/9/01:3(TD)
Place: *Chestnut Hill*	d/o William Brown		
MA(Y)NADIER, William M.	BROWN, Catherine S.	4 MAR 1830	AG:16/3/30:3(A)
Place: Washington DC			
MAZINGO, John	PILES, Sarah	c.24 JAN 1829	MB
McALISTER, John	_____, Elizabeth	-27 JUN 1781	FDD4:308
McALLISTER, Nathaniel	_____, Margaret	-5 JUL 1802	DBC:404; 1799:22; WB2:161
McBRIDE, Alexander	CRANDLE, Susan	21 APR 1818	MR(SC); MB; AG:24/4/18:3(SC)
	d/o Thomas Crandle		
McBRIDE, John	WATTS, Polly	13 AUG 1791	FPC:26(JM); 1787:74

Husband	Wife	Event or Marriage	Reference(s)
McCABE, Edward	WOOD, Lucy ni/o Lucy Latham	22 APR 1813	MR(IR); MB
McCABE, Henry	_____, Jane	-4 AUG 1784	FDP:51
M'CAHAN, Hugh	_____, Jennet	-22 SEP 1786	HCOrd:22/9/86
McCARTY, Daniel	MASON, Sarah d/o George Mason	c.SEP 1778	5GM:235; CWA:565
McCARTY, Daniel	CHICHESTER, Sarah d/o Richard Chichester	-10 OCT 1793	FWG:194
McCARTY, Joseph	WARE, Pender	c.27 SEP 1816	MB
McCARTY, Patrick	WEIGHTMAN, Sarah	5 FEB 1799	FPC:26(JM)
McCAUGHAN, Thomas	TAYLOR, Mary	3 JUL 1803	MR(JM); MB
McCAULEY, William	JONES, Elizabeth	12 SEP 1812	MR(IR); MB
McCAU(I)LEY, William M.	DUFFY, Eliza	15 JUN 1819	AG:19/6/19:2(ON)
McCAUSLAND, William, Jr.	GILHAM, Julia M.	15 JAN 1829	AG:27/1/29:3
Place: *Greenville*, Augusta Co., d/o William Gilham			
M'CLANACHAN, Capt. John	_____, Ann	-13 MAR 1794	AG:4/2/15:3; HCE:332

McCLEAN (also see "McLean")

Husband	Wife	Event or Marriage	Reference(s)
McCLEAN, Allen	TURNER, Jane	c.8 DEC 1826	MR(RK); MB
McCLEAN, Andrew B.	SELDEN, Ann Eliza	9 APR 1822	AG:12/4/22(HA); MB[73]
McCLEAN, Archibald	JONES, Mary d/o Rev. David Jones	22 AUG 1797	1800:51; 1799:34; AA:29/8/97:3(R)
McCLEAN, Daniel	_____, Lucretia	-25 NOV 1795	DBA:305; 1799:4; WB3:87; CCG:A1; SPC
McCLEAN, Joseph	REARDON, Elizabeth	c.18 DEC 1815	MB
McCLEAN, Richard	TUTTON, Eliza P.	10 JUN 1823	MB; AG:14/6/23:3(RD)
McCLEAN, Samuel	SMOOT, Susan Wilson d/o Hezekiah Smoot	1 JUN 1820	MR(WHW); MB; AG:5/6/20:2(WHW)
McCLEAN, William	_____, Agnes		1799:40; 1800:55
McCLEERY, William	_____, Isabella	-22 JAN 1776	FDM:192
McCLELAN, William	_____, Magdalena	-19 NOV 1802	DBF:234
McCLIESH[74], Archibald	_____, Elizabeth	-13 MAR 1797	FPC:25; 1787:74; 1799:32; 1800:51; SMC
McCLEISH, Archibald Place: Baltimore MD	GREEN, Catherine	9 MAR 1819	AH:15/3/19
McCLISH, James Place: Georgetown DC	RIGDEN, Elizabeth	9 FEB 1823	AG:11/2/23:3
McCLISH, William	OSBURN, Mrs. Elizabeth	27 MAR 1819	AH:31/3/19; DCM
McCLISH, William	WARTHRAM, Susan	7 SEP 1823	AG:11/9/23:3; MB
McCOBB, John	WESTON, Sarah "Sally"	13 MAY 1802	MR(JM); DBZ:110; TMCC(Q:4); MB
McCORMACK, Bernard	MURPHY, Lucy [Ann]	27 OCT 1801	FPC:26(JM); MR(JM); MB
M'CORMICK, Alexander	CUIRK, Hannah	c.JUL 1796	WG:20/7/96
McCONNELL, Alexander	_____, Mary	-22 JUL 1794	HCE:465
McCREA, James Mease	WISE, Catherine d/o John Wise	3 DEC 1789	FPC:26(JM); WB2:85; 1787:74; 1799:14; FPCG
McCREA, James M. Place: Georgetown DC	BEALE, Elizabeth Keibard d/o Capt. Thomas K. Beale	3 SEP 1820	AG:5/9/20:2(B)

Husband	Wife	Event or Marriage	Reference(s)
M'(C)REA, Robert	_____, Nancy "Ann"	-22 DEC 1784	HCD:393; 1787:74; 1791:16; FPCG; FDP:226; HCOrd:21/9/86
M'CREA, Robert Place: New York	FURGERSON, Jennet	15 MAR 1810	AG:23/3/10:3(HA)
McCUBBIN, Edward	DEGRAFFS, Margaret	20 AUG 1826	UT:23/8/26:3
McCUE, Henry	_____, Harriet M.	c.1787	WB1:86; 1791:17; AG:4/11/00
McCUE, Peter	REYNOLD[S], Mary	27 MAR 1803	MR(JM); MB
McCULLIN, Patrick	LANHAM, Altheir	c.17 JAN 1804	MB
McCUTCHEON, Patrick	KEATON, Lucy	26 OCT 1807	FPC:26(JM); MB
McDUNNICK, James	TALBURT, Lydia	24 APR 1803	MR(JM); MB
McDONALD, _____	HOOFF, Catherine d/o Lawrence Hooff	-22 OCT 1793	WB1:130
McDONALD, James	_____, Mary	-29 MAR 1798	DBS:145
McDONALD, John	KING, Anna	26 FEB 1807	AG:27/2/07:3(JM); FPC:26(JM); MB
McDONALD, John	PERRY, Maria	17 FEB 1825	AG:19/2/25:3(ON)
McDONALD, W.K. Place: Princeton	CARNAHAN, Hannah M. d/o Rev. James Carnahan	19 OCT 1830	AG:22/10/30:3
McDOUGALL, Daniel	TALBURT, Mary d/o Levi Talburt	17 SEP 1801	FPC:26(JM); MR(JM); MB
McEWEN, James	SMITH, Susan	14 DEC 1822	AG:19/12/22:3(JR)
McEWEN, Alexander	CARTER, Matilda	18 JAN 1823	AG:25/1/23:3(JR)
McFAD[D]EN, James	KEATING, Ann "Nancy"	28 JAN 1797	FPC:25-26(JM); 1799:20; FPCG
McFARLANE, Stephen	_____, Ann Hay	-17 DEC 1805	DBN:141
McFARLIN, George	RICHARDS, Kitty	24 JAN 1802	MR(JM); MB
McFARLIN, Ignatius	GOWEN, Mary d/o Joseph and Mary Gowen	c.17 NOV 1804	MB
McGAUGHAN, Hugh	RAWLINS, Priscilla	24 DEC 1796	FPC:26(JM); 1787:74
McGETTIGAN, William	_____, Rosanna	-4 OCT 1826	AG:10/10/26:3
McGLENNER, William	LATHAM, Rosa	22 JUL 1817	MR(WHW); MB
McGONEGAL, Capt. John Place: King George Co.	TALEE, Jane H.	25 DEC 1816	AG:15/1/17:7
McGOW, James	McLEAN, Mary	-13 SEP 1796	FPC:25
McGUIRE, Rev. Edward C.	LEWIS, Judith	17 APR 1816	MR(WHW)
McGUIRE, Dr. Hugh H.	MOSS, Ann Eliza d/o William Moss	15 DEC 1825	AG:15/12/25:3(WHW); NI:16/12/25
McGUIRE, James	_____, Lucy	-20 AUG 1798	HCL:205; DBA:285; TMCC(D:6)
McHENRY, James	_____, Ann	-10 JUN 1790	AG:10/6/90:1; 1791:17; CRA:266
McELHENNEY, William	INGRAM, Hannah	22 FEB 1814	FPC:26(JM); MR(JM); MB
McEWEN, Alexander	GAVIN, Mary d/o Margaret Gavin	c.21 JUL 1827	MB
McGEE, Peter	WOOD, Mrs. Maria Jane	14 APR 1829	MB; AG:16/4/29:3(Sco)
McINTEER, N.[75]	ALEXANDER, Mary	9 MAY 1820	AG:13/5/20:3
M'INTYRE, Capt. Charles of Portsmouth NH Place: West End, Fairfax Co.	HEINEMAN, Sinah d/o Jacob Heineman	26/27 DEC 1808	FPC:26(JM); AG:28/12/08:3(JM)

Husband	Wife	Event or Marriage	Reference(s)
M'IVER, Charles	_____, Milly	-23 SEP 1786	HCOrd:23/9/86
McIVER John	COUPAR, Margaret "Peggy"	7 NOV 1790	FPC:25-26(JM); 1787:74; 1791:17; AG:9/12/90:3
McKAY, Benjamin	SWANN, Eleanor	27 JUL 1815	MR(IR); MB
McKENNA, James L. Place: *Belmont*, Loudoun Co.	LEE, Cecilia	24 OCT 1816	AG:24/10/16:3
McKENNA, James Leslie Place: Fauquier Co.	RANDOLPH, Ann Fitzhugh d/o Col. Robert Randolph	15 OCT 1813	DBX:433; 1787:74; 1791:17; CCC(46); AG:16/10/13:3
McKENNA, Peter	LAIRD, Rebecca	1788	FB
McKENZIE, Alexander	SYMBURN, Ann	23 JUN 1798	FPC:26(JM); 1799:14; FPCG; AG:6/4/15:3
McKENZIE, Alexander	BARTON, Elizabeth "Betsey"	9 FEB 1828	AG:12/2/28:3(EH); MB
McKENZIE, Capt.	SMITH, Cassandra	29 JUN 1815	MR(WHW)
McKENZIE, James	SANFORD, Sarah Eveleth second d/o Thomas Sanford	22 SEP 1829	NI:26/9/29; MB; MR(EH); AG:25/9/29:3(EH)
McKENZIE, Capt. James	STEEL, Margaret	- NOV 1798	FPC:25; DBU:484; 1799:14; BR:134; FPCC(44:153)
McKENZIE, Kenneth	SMITH, Cassandra	c.29 OCT 1815	MB
McKEWN, James	SMITH, Susan	14 DEC 1822	SP
McKINNEY, John	_____, Sarah	-20 AUG 1803	DBW:472
McKNIGHT, Capt. John	PIERCY, Catharine "Kitty" d/o Christian Piercy	29 OCT 1799	AG:2/11/99:3; PGM; BR:109; FPCC(41:20)
McKNIGHT, William Place: Cumberland PA	BRYAN, Martha	24 FEB 1766	FPCG; 1787:74; FPCC(41:20); B9
McKNIGHT, William	EVANS, Susannah	-25 JUL 1812	OT:37; FPCC(41:20)
McKNIGHT, William H.	JACOBS, Margaret	21 JUN 1832	B9
M'LAUGHLIN, John	WAY, Juliana d/o Andrew Way, of Philadelphia PA	14 OCT 1815	AG:16/10/15:3
McLEAN, Andrew B.	SELLERS, Ann Eliza	9 APR 1822	MR(EH); AG:11/4/22:3(EH)
McLEAN, Isaac	TURNER, Mary	2 APR 1801	MR(JM); DBQ:354; MB
McLEAN, Samuel	_____, Isabella	-2 AUG 1785	LP#A499
McLEAN, Thomas	SHEPHARD, Ann	26 MAR 1808	FPC:26(JM)
McLEOD, Daniel	_____, Mary Ann	-21 MAY 1797	FPC:25; 1799:8
McLEOD, John	_____, Helen	-4 MAY 1797	FPC:25; FPCG
M'MAHAN, Michael	_____, Ann "Nancy"	-24 JUN 1786	HCOrd:24/6/86
McMASTERS, [Andrew]	CHEW, Mary	-15 APR 1807	DBO:224; 1787:74
McMECHEN, William	WILKINSON, Nancy	3 NOV 1796	DBS:44; 1799:6; AG:5/11/96:3
McMUNN, George Place: Winchester	SITTLER, Elizabeth d/o Isaac Sittler	c.23 DEC 1793	DBA:459; 1799:4; WC:354; HCG:487; VC:23/12/93
McMUNN, William	_____, Mary	-3 OCT 1815	DBC2:152
McNEIL, Patrick	NIGHT, Mariah	2 DEC 1809	FPC:26(JM); MR(JM); MB
McNEIL, Richard	OAKLEY, Margaret	c.30 AUG 1803	MB
McNISH, Horatio	DEANE, Susan O. d/o Joseph Dean	12 MAR 1821	NI:26/3/21; MR(EH); MB

Husband	Wife	Event or Marriage	Reference(s)
McQUEEN, William	GOLDSBURY, Susan	c.18 OCT 1817	MB
McPHERSON, Daniel	BEESON, Martha	-29 MAY 1790	HCD:193; 1787:74; 1791:17; CRA:30
McPHERSON, Daniel Place: Wilmington DE	GRUBB, Elizabeth	c.SEP 1803	DBC2:139 H:744; QM:49
McPHERSON, Isaac s/o Daniel McPherson Place: Elk Ridge Meeting House	ELLICOTT, Hannah d/o John and Leah Ellicott	2 JAN 1793	AG:26/1/93:3; Note[76]; MGB:14/2:2; FMI; 1787:74
McPHERSON, Isaac	_____, Tacey	-6 APR 1799	HCL:325; AG:25/3/26:3
MacPHERSON, Lt./Col. Robt. Hector	CHAPIN, Julia Ann	7 NOV 1815	AG:9/11/15:3(WHW) MR(WHW); MB
McWILLIAMS, Andrew	WISEMAN, Nancy d/o William Wiseman	10 MAY 1825	MR(WHW); MB
MEADE, William	_____,	c.28 NOV 1811[77]	DBV:287
MEADS, Samuel	McCUTCHEON, Ellenor	20 APR 1808	MR(IR)
MEASE, Robert	STEUART, Betty (Ramsay) d/o William Ramsay	MAY 1792	FPC:24(JM); HCF:179; AG:27/3/98:3; 1787:74
MEEHAN, John S.	_____, Margaret Jones	-17 JUN 1826	AG:19/7/26:3
MEEK, Joseph H.	WRIGHT, Elizabeth S.	c.31 AUG 1817	MB
MEEKS, Edward	_____, Hetty	-23 FEB 1800	CCG:A1
MELLAN, George	PILES, Mrs. Anna	c.19 DEC 1827	MB
MELLINGTON, Richard	THOMPSON, Peggy d/o Barbary Thompson	22 APR 1813	MR(IR); MB
MENDENHALL, James Place: Berkley Meeting House	JANNEY, Ruth (McPherson)	15 MAY 1811	H:764
MENDENHALL, William s/o Aaron Place: New Garden Meeting House PA	BEESON, Martha d/o John and Mary Beeson	13 SEP 1792	HCN:336; H:470
MERCER, John Francis[78]	SWANN, Mary Scott only d/o Thomas Swann	25 JUN 1818	AH:29/6/18(ON); MR(JM); AG:27/6/18:3(ON)
MERCER, John F. Place: Annapolis MD	SPRIGGS, Sophia d/o Richard Spriggs	3 FEB 1785	AG:24/2/85:2
MERCER, John Francis	SWAN, Mary	25 JUN 1818	MR(ON); MB
MERCHANT, John	KING, Margaret	c.12 SEP 1811	MB
MERCY, Robert	MERTLAND, Susannah	23 JUN 1803	MR(JM); MB
MERHY, Johna.	WHITE, Mary	c.19 SEP 1812	MB
MERRIMORE, John	BROWN, Mary	c.1 MAR 1811	MB
MEZARVEY, Thomas	STONE, Mary	DEC 1792	FPC:24(JM); 1791:18; 1799:2
MEZARVEY, Thomas	_____, Elizabeth	-16 MAY 1806	DBR:319
MEYERS, John	BOYER, Margaret	14 NOV 1799	FPC:24(JM)
MIDDLETON, David	HARRIS, Hannah	24 JUN 1830	MR(IR); MB
MIDDLETON, Electus	PARSONS, Ann d/o James Parsons	-21 MAR 1799	DBH:176; TMCC(K:1)
MIDDLETON, Henry O.	TOLLSON, Nancy	15 FEB 1814	MR(WHW)
MIDDLETON, William	MOSS, Frances	1788	FB
MIDDLETON, William	IRONMONGER, Lucy	25 NOV 1797	FPC:24(JM)
MILBURN, Benedict C.	COAD, Thirza	10 JUN 1828	SP; MR(WJ); MB; AG:16/6/28:3(WJ)

Husband	Wife	Event or Marriage	Reference(s)
MILBURN, George	MILBURN, Alice d/o Thomas Milburn	-17 APR 1822	WB3:75; TMCC(P:3)
MILBURN, Joseph	_____, Margaret	-11 OCT 1811	WB3:30; FPCC(42:62)
MILLAN, George	_____, Mary	-22 OCT 1825	AG:22/10/25
MILLAN, Henry S. Place: *Providence*	FARR, Caroline	2 MAR 1826	AG:7/3/26:3(JR)
MILLAN, James	CASH, Mrs. Susannah wid/o Joseph Cash	-9 JUL 1816	DBC2:226
MILLER, Benjamin	ROSS, Mary	26 APR 1825	MR(WA); MB
MILLER, George	PILES, Elizabeth	c.12 JAN 1803	MB
MILLER, Hezekiah	MIDDLETON, Chloe Ann	18 AUG 1818	AG:25/8/18:3
MILLER, John	EGERTON, Kathar. (Polgwen)	-19 JUL 1800	HCN:250
MILLER, John S. Place: Philadelphia PA	EARL, Susan only d/o Clayton Earl of Philadelphia PA	30 MAY 1826	NI:8/6/26; AG:3/6/26:3
MILLER, Joseph H.	JANNEY, Phebe Ann	28 JUN 1832	H:757
MILLER, Mordecai s/o Warwick Miller	HARTSHORNE, Rebecca d/o William Hartshorne	8 NOV 1792	OT:54; H:746; 1791:18; FMI; QC
MILLER, Robert	_____, Martha	-10 MAR 1797	HCK:18
MILLER, Robert	DAUGHERTY, Margaret	c.23 OCT 1802	MB
MILLER, Robert	HOWARD, Elizabeth	5 OCT 1815	FPC:24, 26(JM); MR(JM); MB
MILLER, Robt. Hartshorne Place: Fairfax Co.	JANNEY, Anna d/o Elisha Janney	14 MAY 1823	H:753; UC:W240 QM:49
MILLER, Robert H. Place: Waterford, Loudoun Co.	JANNEY, Ann(a)	23 APR 1823	NI:19/5/23; AG:3/5/23:3
MILLER, William H.	PHILIPS, Amy Ann	c.23 NOV 1820	H:766; UC:W240
MILLIAN, Abraham Place: Prince William Co.	WIGGINTEN, Elizabeth	15 JAN 1818	AG:21/1/18:3
MILLIKIN (see "Mullikin")			
MILLS, Ephraim	_____, Rebecca	-28 SEP 1808	DBQ:409; 1800:51
MILLS, James	AUBREY, Eleanor	9 SEP 1789	FPC:24(JM)
MILLS, James	TAYLOR, Fidelia	9 FEB 1815	MR(WHW); MB
MILLS, John, Sr.	_____, Susannah		ES:179
MILLS, John	_____, Nelly	-18 APR 1804	DBH:59
MILLS, John R. Place: Washington DC	McFARLAND, Mrs. Elizabeth	20 MAR 1827	NI:23/3/27; AG:26/3/27:3(RD)
MILLS, John S. Place: Washington DC	ADAM, Mary Ann d/o John Adam	14 SEP 1826	WB5:79; DCM; AG:16/9/26:3; UT:16/9/26:3
MILLS, Joseph Boneparte	SHOEMAKER, Charlotte	9 MAR 1819	AG:19/3/19:3
MILLS, Robert A.	RUSSELL, Martha	8 DEC 1814	MR(WHW); MB; DBE2:452
MILLS, William	TOLSON, Elizabeth	7 MAR 1799	FPC:24(JM)
MILLS, William	FUGITT, Lucinda	26 AUG 1818	MR(JM); MB
MILLS, William of St. Mary's Co. MD	FULTON, Mrs. Virginia	14 DEC 1828	AG:23/12/28:3(Sco); MB
MILLS, Capt. William	MONRO, Margery	-10 JAN 1796	FPC:23; TMCC(D:4)
MILLS, William Nelson	LEAP, Ann	26/27 FEB 1806	FPC:24(JM); DBQ:46; WB2:405; MR(JM); FPCC(41:42); MB; AG:28/2/06:3(JM)

92

Husband	Wife	Event or Marriage	Reference(s)
MILNER, William, Jr.	_____, Margaret	-28 MAY 1798	HCK:430; DBB:147; 1799:36
MILSTEAD, Judson	ROLINSON, Catharine Ann	2 JUL 1826	UT:8/7/26:3
MINETREE, John	HELLRIGEL, Catherine d/o Christian Hellrigel	9 APR 1807	FPC:24(JM); WBC:326; MB
MINICKS, John	_____, Jinney		1800:55
MINNIX, John	NEWTON, Catharine C. d/o William C. Newton	c.3 NOV 1814	MB
MINOR, Anthony	HARRISON, Sally	c.14 JUL 1825	MB
MINOR, Daniel	MOSS, Mary	6 APR 1815	AG:8/4/15:3(WW)
MINOR, John	_____, Mary	-30 JUN 1808	DBW:333
MINOR, Philip H.	WASHINGTON, Sally Ashton	9 MAY 1816	AG:11/5/16:3(ON); MR(ON); MB
MINOR, Smith	SOMMERS, Mary d/o S. Sommers	c.13 NOV 1817	MB
MINOR, Dr. Thos. Jeff.	HARWOOD, Matilda G.	1 MAR 1827	AG:17/3/27:3
MITCHELL, George	SPINKS, Elizabeth	c.16 MAY 1822	MB
MITCHELL, George	HOWISON, Harriet G.	c.31 MAY 1825	MB
MITCHELL, Capt. James	THOMAS, Mary d/o Robert Thomas	-12 JAN 1768	FWC:44; FPCG; SPC
MITCHELL, Capt. James Place: Georgetown DC	THOMPSON, Margaret	27 JAN 1824	AG:29/1/24:3
MITCHELL, James	SHERMANDINE, Hope d/o James Shermandine	29 APR 1813	MR(WHW); MB
MITCHELL, Mathew	_____, Elizabeth		QM:50
MITCHELL, Richard H. Place: Charles Co. MD	COMPTON, Lucinda	c.26 AUG 1821	AG:25/9/21:3
MITCHELL, T. Place: *Lawnsville*	MARSTELLER, Charlotte M.	13 NOV 1823	AG:22/11/23:3
MITCHELL, Thomas	BREAST, Lucretia	27 JUN 1824	MR(WA); MB
MITCHELL, William	LANHAM, Mary	14 JUN 1816	MR(IR); MB
MIX, Lewis	GUNNELL, Elizabeth	-15 JUL 1822	Note[79]
MIX, Thomas	_____, Ann		1800:56
MOCKLAR, Samuel	CLARK, Mary	10 MAY 1800	FPC:24(JM)
MOFFITT, John	VARDIN, Matilda Ann	21 SEP 1820	MR(EH); MB; AG:23/9/20:2(EH)
MOLEN, George	FIERNO, Margaret	c.27 NOV 1818	MB
MONCURE, Thomas G.	HOOE, Clarissa B.	6 FEB 1823	MB(ON); AT:8/2/23:3(ON)
MONEY, Alexander	STOOPS, Eliza	16 SEP 1824	AG:21/9/24:3(ON)
MONROE, Capt. Thomas	_____, Elizabeth	-29 AUG 1797	HCK:322; FPCC(43:96)
MONROE, Thomas	KELTON, Georgiana	22 APR 1826	MR(Sco); MB
MOODEY, John	BAYLEY, Sarah d/o Elizabeth Bayley	c.30 NOV 1809	MB
MOODY, Benjamin	BLUNT, Elizabeth	12 SEP 1799	FPC:23-24(JM); FPCG
MOODY, John	BAILEY, Sarah	30 NOV 1809	MR(IR)
MOONY, Neil	SMITH, Winny A.	DEC 1794	FPC:24(JM); 1787:74; 1791:18
MOONY, William	JACKSON, Nancy	2 AUG 1789	FPC:24(JM)
MOORE, Alexander	COTTRINGER, Caroline	4/6 or 7 JUN 1822	NI:13/6/22(JF); SP; MR(JF); MB; AG:11/6/22:3(JF)

Husband	Wife	Event or Marriage	Reference(s)
MOORE, Alexander s/o Cleon Moore	WEST, Ann Margaret Craik d/o Roger West	4 APR 1811	MB; DBY:461; CCC(56,83); AG:6/4/11:3(G)
MOORE, Capt. Cleon	_____, Mary	-24 JUN 1801	DBA:225; 1787:74; 1791:18; 1799:24
MOORE, Cleon Place: Anne Arundel Co. MD	TEBBS, Margaret	29 OCT 1778	DBU:58; 1791:18; 1800:59; IGI
MOORE, Henry	_____, Margaret	- 1791	ES:180
MOORE, James	SINCLAIR, Esther	c.18 SEP 1823	H:778; QM:50
MOORE, Jeremiah	RENO, Lydia	1 NOV 1765	DBU:402; IGI
MOORE, John	WILLIAMS, Sarah	1787	LVA1:1
MOORE, John	_____, Mary	-24 APR 1795	CCG
MOORE, John	HALLEY, Mary	1 FEB 1800	AA:10/2/00:3
MOORE, John Munro	CLEMSTER, Elizabeth	18 SEP 1796	FPC:24(JM); 1799:32
MOORE, Capt. Joseph C. Place: Georgetown DC	MORGAN, Mary M. d/o Wm. Morgan, of Gloucester Co.	15 SEP 1819	AG:17/9/19:3(B)
MOORE, Richard L.	CLEMENTS, Ann	c.26 AUG 1824	MB
MOORE, Stephen	SKINNER, Mary	SEP 1792	FPC:24(JM); CCG:A1; 1799:24
MOORE, Capt. Stephen	ARELL, Mrs. Phoebe wid/o David Arell	29 FEB 1796	HCG:312; AG:1/3/96:3; 1800:58
MOORE, Thomas	FISHER, Margaret	25 DEC 1818	AG:7/1/19:2
MOORE, Thomas, Jr. Place: Indian Spring Meeting House	BROOKE, Mary, d/o Roger	21 SEP 1791	H:474
MOORE, William S.	_____, Catharine	-29 JUL 1808	DBQ:363
MOPANG, John	NEILL, Betsy	c.20 MAR 1826	MB
MORELAND, Hanson	ATKINS, Sarah	7 APR 1807	FPC:24(JM); MR(JM); MB
MORELAND, Hanson B.	HOLTZMAN, Eliza	11 MAY 1826	UT:15/5/26:3
MORELAND, Levin	_____, Mary	-1 OCT 1813	DBY:108
MORGAN, Alexander	PADGETT, Catharine d/o James Padgett	14 AUG 1821	MR(ON); MB
MORGAN, Jacob	THOMPSON, Ann Harris d/o Jonas Thompson	19 FEB 1812	NI:22/2/12(M); MB; CCC(45); AG:21/2/12:3
MORGAN, Jacob	SMITH, Mary Jaqueline d/o Col. Aug. J. Smith of *West Grove*	30 MAY 1826	AG:3/6/26:3(WHW); UT:3/6/26:2
MORGAN, John	McCORMICK, Eliza	4 NOV 1812	OT:76(F); QC; H:763; AG:24/7/32:3
MORGAN, John	MYERS, Barbara	22 APR 1830	MR(WJ); MB; AG:27/4/30:3(WJ)
MORGAN, Joseph	_____, Martha	-1 MAY 1801	DBV:466
MORGAN, Thomas Place: *Lebanon*	BATES, Sarah P.	15 JUN 1818	AG:21/6/15:3(IR)
MORGAN, William (C)	RANSOM, Patty (C)	4 MAY 1815	MR(WHW); MB
MORGAN, William Place: Gunpower Meeting House MD	PRICE, Sarah	30 MAR 1791	H:768; 1791:18
MORGAN, William	MAYHALL, Eleanor	13 MAY 1799	FPC:24(JM); 1800:58; CCC(61)
MORGAN, William	JOHNSTON, Martha	4 SEP 1817	MR(AG); MB

Husband	Wife	Event or Marriage	Reference(s)
MORRIS (also see "Maurice")			
MORRIS, Henry	PAYNE, Maria	1 DEC 1816	MR(WHW); MB
MORRIS, John	_____, Margaret	-29 OCT 1802	DBD:227
MORRIS, Levin	WALKER, Sarah s/o Francis Walker	22 SEP 1812	FPC:24(JM); MR(JM); MB
MORRIS, Leven	PILES, Frances	8 MAR 1798	FPC:24(JM)
MORRIS, Thomas	SAUNDERS, Mary d/o Joseph Saunders	-5 MAY 1785	FWF:251; FMI
MORRISON, Daniel	_____, Susannah	-10 OCT 1808	DBQ:249
MORRISON, Hugh	_____, Mary		1799:38; 1800:57; CCC(41)
MORROW, Adam (C)	_____, Caran (C)		1800:59
MORROW, Robert	JENKINS, Mary H. d/o George Jenkins	-21 FEB 1831	WB3:387
MORSELL, James S. Place: Georgetown DC	FITZHUGH, Mrs. Mary Ann d/o William Marbury	21 OCT 1829	AG:29/10/29:3
MORSON, Alexander Place: Stafford Co.	ALEXANDER, Anne C.	3 JUL 1800	DBAA:180 VH:8/7/00
MORTIMER, George W.	PRICE, Julia C.K.	c.12 JUL 1823	MB
MOSEBY, John	JENKINS, Sarah	3 JUN 1807	MR(IR); MB
MOSELY, William	_____, Elizabeth	-19 JUL 1797	HCI:127
MOSS, Robert	CRUMP, Hannah d/o Adam and Hannah Crump		FDG:57
MOSS, Robert	HARPER, Margaret d/o John Harper	-29 MAR 1813	DBW:501; DBX:47; BR:105
MOSS, Stephen	McGUE, Peggy d/o Henry McGue	-3 APR 1775	DBW:189; DBAA:418
MOSS, Thomas	FULLERTON, Ann	DEC 1793	FPC:24(JM)
MOSS, William	HOLMES, Gertrude	24 SEP 1807	AG:29/9/07:3; AG:8/10/27:3
MOTHERSAID, E.J.	CHILTON, Maria	c.18 DEC 1828	MB
MOULDER, John N. Place: Baltimore MD	SOUDER, Esther d/o Charles Souder, of Philadelphia PA	22 JUN 1826	AG:28/6/26:3
MOULDING, William	DEAVERS, Elizabeth	6 AUG 1820	AG:15/8/20:2(JR)
MOUNT, Thomas	SMITH, Sarah "Sally" d/o Joseph and Mary Smith	21 SEP 1809	TMCC(J:2); MB; AG:22/9/09:3
MOXLEY, Daniel	HARE, Elizabeth	c.26 JAN 1813	MB
MOXLEY, George	JACKSON, Becky	c.15 SEP 1807	MB
MOXLEY, Thomas	BEALL, Hester d/o Sophia Beall	-8 MAY 1782	FWD:327
MOYER, John	REISCH, Maria Juliana	1 MAR 1798	FPC:24(JM)
MUDD, Aloysius	MITCHELL, Ann	c.26 APR 1825	MB
MUIR, Col. Francis	DOWNMAN, Mrs. Anne wid/o Col. Rawleigh P. Downman	30 NOV 1803	AG:22/12/03:3
MUIR, Rev. Dr. James Place: Bermuda	WELLMAN, Elizabeth	28 FEB 1783	CBL:41; 1800:56; WB2; FPC:23; Note[80]; 1799:26; FPCG
MUIR, John	LONG, Mary "Polly"	26 DEC 1800	FPC:23-24(JM); 1787:74; 1791:18; FPCC(41:17); AG:25/12/00; AA:27/12/00:3

Husband	Wife	Event or Marriage	Reference(s)
MUIR, John	ROBINSON, Lydia	16 NOV 1830	MR(LA); MB; AG:19/11/30:3(LA)
MULLIKIN, Francis	TAYLOR, Casa	5 SEP 1816	MR(WHW)
MULLON, John	DUNKIN, Cathrine	24 SEP 1789	FPC:24(JM)
MUNCASTER, John	COPPER, Elizabeth Arell	26 JUN 1798	DBA:269; 1799:30; 1800:52; CCC(68); LVA1:1
MUNDAY, William	_____, Elizabeth	-2 MAY 1782	FWD:422
MUNFORD, John P.	_____, Mary Polly	-22 OCT 1797	DBD2:177; DBE2:366
MUNRO, Robert	CRAWFORD, Catherine H. d/o Edward Crawford	24 NOV 1817	AG:6/12/17:2
MUNROE, Robert	_____, Julian	-4 OCT 1822	TMCC(C:2)
MURPHY, Edward	TOWERS, Mrs. Elizabeth	10 JAN 1822	SP; MB; AT:14/1/22:3(WHW)
MURPHY, Francis	_____, Ann	-8 NOV 1810	DBT:325; SMC
MURPHY, John	MANNING, Margaret M.	14 MAR 1811	FPC:24(JM); MR(JM); MB
MURPHY, Dr. Robert Place: *Lee Hall*	NEWTON, Eliza B.	21 MAY 1818	AG:4/6/18:2
MURRAY, Charles Place: Georgetown College	ROBINSON, Elizabeth	27 APR 1824	AG:29/4/24:3; NI:28/4/24
MURRAY, Edward	GOODWIN, Hepziba	11 MAY 1801	MR(JM); MB
MURRAY, Francis	CATTERTON, Lucretia	24 OCT 1801	FPC:24(JM); MR(JM)
MURRAY, George	NOLAND, Susan	c.1 APR 1830	MB
MURRAY, George W.	LOWRY, Olivia	c.12 JAN 1792	FPC:24(JM); AG:12/1/92:3
MURRAY, George W. Place: Residence of D. Delozier of Annapolis MD	HIGGINBOTHOM, Elizabeth	10 MAR 1796	BT:11/3/96
MURR(A)Y, Ignatius	MORRIS, Eleanor	c.24 OCT 1807	MB
MURRAY, James	PITTMAN, Nancy	2 OCT 1790	FPC:24(JM)
MURRAY, James	BUTT, Margaret	NOV 1794	FPC:24(JM)
MURRAY, James	STREET, Eliza	c.20 JAN 1813	MB
MURRAY, James	WATKINS, Eliza d/o Judy Watkins	c.4 FEB 1825	MB
MURRAY, John	M'CLENACHAN, Patty	c.11 JAN 1787	AG:11/1/87:3; 1787:74; 1791:19
MURRAY, John	WILCOCKS, Elizabeth	SEP 1792	FPC:24(JM); 1791:19
MURRAY, John	PEARSON, Milly d/o John Pearson	c. 7 APR 1806	MB
MURRAY, John B.	_____, Martha	-28 APR 1814	DBY:453
MURRAY, Lemuel N.	CARROL, Mary	7 JUL 1829	MR(LA); MB; AG:13/7/29:3(LA)
MURRAY, Oliver C.	SHERMANDINE, Lucretia	6 OCT 1817	MR(WHW); MB
MURRAY, Patrick	_____, Margaret	-7 SEP 1786	HCB:336; 1787:74; 1791:19
MURRAY, Samuel	_____, Betty	-9 FEB 1809	DBR:198
MURRAY, Thomas	PENDAL, Mary	27 OCT 1803	FPC:24(JM); MR(JM); MB
MURRAY, Thomas	McDONALD, Margaret	12 DEC 1816	MR(JM); MB
MURTLAND, John	_____, Susanna	-16 APR 1799	HCL:383
MUSCHETT, James	_____, Catharine	-26 NOV 1814	AG:3/12/14:3

Husband	Wife	Event or Marriage	Reference(s)
MUSCHETT, John Place: Dumfries	TEBBS, Mary F.	14 JUL 1803	AG:18/7/03:3(LM)
MUSE, Elliott	_____, Jane	-12 SEP 1807	DBZ:236
MUSE, Elliott	HUNTER, Hannah	10 FEB 1814	AG:12/2/14:3(WHW); DBBB:467; SP; MR(WHW)
MUSE, Elliott Place: *Pine Hill*, King George Co.	BLACKBURN, Mrs. Mary Fran.	16 FEB 1818	AG:13/3/18:3;
MUSE, William I.	EDMONDSON, Mary d/o Lucy Edmondson	31 MAR 1825	AG:2/4/25:3(Sco); MB; MR(Sco)
MUSGROVE, Israel	WODDROW, Grace	2 NOV 1797	FPC:24(JM); 1799:40
MUTTER, John	GILLIES, Lucinda	c.24 DEC 1807	MB
MYERS, Alexander Place: Washington DC	SUTER, Rebecca	4 JAN 1827	AG:6/1/27:3(RD)
MYERS, George W.	HICKLIN, Phebe	1 MAY 1828	AG:3/5/28:3(WJ); SP; MR(WJ); MB
MYERS, John	BOWYER, Mrs. Margaret wid/o Henry Bowyer	14 NOV 1799	AG:16/11/99:3
MYERS, John	STEVENSON, Margaret	c.21 APR 1817	MR(SC); MB
MYERS, Joseph	_____, Mary		CCC(24)
MYERS, Joseph[81] T.	BALLENGER, Susannah	16 OCT 1826	MR(EH); MB; AG:20/10/26:3(EH); UT:20/10/26:3
MYERS, Samuel	_____, Paulina		QM:50
MYERS, William	ROZER, Maria	-14 NOV 1812	DBW:360; DBC2:194
MYLER, James	_____, Elizabeth	-21 JUL 1786	HCB:403

Husband	Wife	Event or Marriage	Reference(s)
N			
NAINBY, Joseph	BUFFIÈRE, Eleanor	17 MAR 1791	FPC:28(JM)
NASH, George	RIPTON, Ann	7 AUG 1789	FPC:28(JM)
NASH, Robert	_____, Jane	-15 JUL 1814	FPCC(42:53)
NEAL, Daniel	_____, Susanner		1800:55
NEALE, Aloysius	BRANDT, Elizabeth L.A.	30 JUL 1818	MR(JF); MB
NEALE, Christopher	EASTON, Harriet	25 MAR 1810	DBW:21; FMI;
Place: Newport RI	d/o Nicholas Easton		DBE2:91; SPC;
			AG:9/2/10:3
NEALE, Jeremiah A.	_____, Mary Elizabeth	-20 JUL 1812	WB2:75; SMC
NEALE, Rev. John	MARTIN, Mrs. Lucy	2 NOV 1826	AG:2/12/26:3
NEBTON, John James	PETIT, Margaret	MAR 1793	FPC:28(JM); HCG:258
	d/o John B. Petit		
NEIL, John	OFFUTT, Rebecca	28 OCT 1795	FPC:27-28(JM)
NEILL, Joseph	McPHERSON, Rebekah	7 APR 1790	H:768; QM:50
Place: Bullskin Meeting House (later renamed Berkley)			
NEILL, Lewis	JANNEY, Rachel	15 JUN 1774	J:90
NEILL, Thomas	McPHERSON, Mary	4 APR 1804	H:769
Place: Berkley Meeting House			
NELSON, Hendley	_____, Delilah	-8 JUN 1815	DBC2:145
NELSON, Sampson	CARNES, Ann	c.26 JUN 1812	MB
NELSON, Thomas	McATTEE, Chloe	c.24 DEC 1802	MB
NEVIT, Thomas	MARA, Catharine	c.14 JUL 1812	MB
NEVITT, Charles L.	_____, Martha	-28 JUN 1810	DBT:81
NEVITT, Capt. Chas. L.	WAILES, Susannah G.	25 DEC 1813	AG:28/12/13:3(D)
Place: St. Mary's Co. MD	d/o the late Capt. Wailes		
NEVITT, John	BEAKLEY, Lucy	6 AUG 1808	FPC:28(JM)
NEVITT, Joseph	BAGGETT, Ann	c.11 MAY 1812	MB; SMC;
			DBE2:140
NEWLAND, John	WINDSOR, Susanna	8 SEP 1808	FPC:28(JM)
NEWMAN, _____	CAWOOD, Susanna Phillips	-11 OCT 1821	TMCC(D:4)
	si/of Moses O.B. Cawood		
NEWTON, Augustine	GADSBY, Ann Sophia	17 MAR 1808	FPC:28(JM); CCC(21);
	d/o John Gadsby		AG:18/3/08:3(JM)
NEWTON, Ignatius A.	RATCLIFF, Elizabeth	c.6 APR 1820	DCM
NEWTON, John	_____, Filey		1800:57
NEWTON, Morris	WHEELER, Eleanor	c.16 MAR 1805	MB
NEWTON, William	STEUART, Jane (Barr)	7 FEB 1792	FPC:27-28(JM);
			WB1:321;
			OT:45; 1791:19;
			1787:74; 1799:12;
			FPCC(42:95)
NEWTON, Wm. Chapman	_____, Ann	-26 OCT 1813	DBY:90; TMCC(R:3);
			AG:11/5/14:3
NEWTON, William C.	DORSETT, Sarah	c.22 FEB 1816	WB3:285; DCM
NEWTON, Lt. William S.	McCANDLESS, Mary	28 AUG 1822	AG:5/9/22:3
NICHOLAS, Jefferson	RILEY, Sarah Ann	10 MAY 1826	UT:12/5/26:3(Mc)
NICHOLAS, Zachariah	BAGGOTT, Tereca	3 FEB 1820	CT:5/2/20(JF);
			MR(JF);
			AG:4/2/20:2(JF)
NICHOLL, William	CONWAY, Harriet V.	7 MAY 1818	AG:12/5/18:2(WH)
NICHOLLS, John (C)	THOMAS, Martha (C)	25 JUL 1812	MR(WHW); MB

Husband	Wife	Event or Marriage	Reference(s)
NICHOLAS, Nathan, Sr.	HODGSON, Hannah	21 SEP 1784	
Place: Winchester	d/o Robert Hodgson		
NICHOLSON, Henry	TALBOTT, Precious	AUG 1794	FPC:28(JM); FPCC(41:32)
NICHOLSON, Henry	BALLARD, Ann	27/8 OCT 1803	FPC:28(JM); MR(JM);
	d/o William Ballard		AG:28/10/03:3(JM); MB
NICHOLSON, Henry	HEINEMAN, Margaret	14[82] JUN 1814	FPC:28(JM); MR(JM);
	d/o Jacob Heineman		DBAA:460; MB; AG:17/6/14:3(JM)
NICHOLSON, Henry W.	HIXON, Ann	7 MAR 1825	AG:15/3/25:3
Place: New York			
NICHOLSON, Joseph	FRANK, Elizabeth	15 MAY 1803	MR(SA); MB
NICHOLSON, Thomas	BAKER, Sarah	31 JAN 1803	MR(SA); MB
	s/o Elisha Baker		
NICHOLSON, Zachariah	BAGGOTT, L.	c.3 FEB 1820	MB
NICKOLLS, James Bruce	_____, Mary	17 MAR 1781	SPC; SP;
Place: Philadelphia PA			AG:16/8/27:3
NICKOLLS, Scudamore	ROBERDEAU, Selina	AUG 1793	FPC:28(JM)
NOKES, George	STREET, Ann	9 JUN 1805	AG:10/6/05(TD)
NOLAND, Philip (C)	FOOTE, Jane (C)	31 DEC 1818	MR(WHW)
NORFOLK, James	MACAYE, Delila	25 MAY 1819	AG:28/5/19:3(ON)
NORRIS(S), James	LONGDON, Lucy	4 NOV 1813	MR(JM)
NORRIS, James	PICKERELL, Susannah	10 FEB 1814	AG:12/2/14:3(WHW); SP; MR(WHW)[83]; MB
NORRIS, John	ZIMMERMAN, Emeline	27 MAR 1830	MB; AG:1/5/30:3(JF)
NORRIS, Mark	_____, Ann	-16 FEB 1819	SMC
NORRIS, Rev. Oliver	HERBERT, Sarah Fairfax.	1 JUN 1813	AG:3/6/13(WHW);
	d/o William Herbert, Sr.		CCC(62); NI:30/9/23; MR(WHW); MB
NORRIS, Seton W.	LANE, Abby M.	21 JUN 1824	AG:26/6/24:3
Place: Fairfax Co.			
NORRIS, William	EVANS, Sarah "Sally"	19 MAY 1789	FPC:28(JM); 1791:19; AG:21/5/89:2
NORTH, George	_____, Eliza	-7 JAN 1801	HCMin:7/1/01
NORTH, John	MOXLEY, Mrs. Jane	1753	FDC1:530
NORTON, Hamilton M.	WAITE, Hannah	c.10 OCT 1826	MB
NORTON, Richard C.	CRANCH, Mary	27 SEP 1819	CT:9/10/19(ON);
	second d/o Hon. William Cranch		NI:11/7/21; AG:29/9/19:3(ON)
NOWELL, James	BOOTHE, Ann	26 AUG 1824	MR(WA); MB[84]
NOWLAND, John	WINDSOR, Susanna	8 SEP 1808	FPC:28(JM)
NOWLAND, Theophilus	SKINNER, Margaret	c.23 APR 1812	MB
	d/o William Skinner		
NOYES, Robert	SKINNER, Mrs. Mary G.	7 DEC 1818	AG:12/12/18:3(SC); MR(SC); MB
NUTT, James	DEAKINS, Jemimah	c.30 SEP 1802	MB; TMCC(D:2); DBR:274
NUTT, William D.	ANDREW, Pamela		MPC:E22
NUTTER, Benjamin	BROWN, Catherine	15 MAY 1823	AG:3/6/23:3(JR)

Husband	Wife	Event or Marriage	Reference(s)
O			
O'CONNER, William	WILLIAMS, Sophia G.	25 DEC 1806	FPC:30(JM); CCC(51)
O'LOUGHLIN, Cornelius	HOOE, Catherine d/o Col. John Hooe	2 MAY 1793	AG:16/5/93:3
O'NEAL, Henry	HOWARD, Rosetta	MAR 1793	FPC:30(JM)
O'NEAL, Robert	ANDERSON, Margaret	1 JUN 1809	MR(IR); MB
OAKLEY, John	DEAKINS, Margaret	28 SEP 1798	FPC:30(JM)
ODUNEAL, James	CONYERS, Theodosia	19 OCT 1755	Note[85]
OFFUTT, Alfred D. Place: *Sycamore Hill*	WASHINGTON, Elizabeth C. d/o Edward Washington	21 APR 1829	AG:29/4/29:3
OFFUTT, Zachariah	REMINGTON, Eliza Ann d/o Wm. Remington	11 APR 1826	UT:12/4/26:3
ORR, Dr. John Dalrymple	LEE, Lucinda	-11 FEB 1795	FPC:29; HCF:265; HCN:366
OSBORN, Dennis	HOWARD, Jane	12 NOV 1818	MR(IR); MB
OSBORN, Thomas	BEEDLE, Susanna	16 MAR 1799	FPC:30(JM)
OSBORNE, Archibald	_____, Rachel	-15 NOV 1822	WB3:83
OSBURN, Lawson	THOMAS, Elizabeth	16 NOV 1815	MR(IR); MB
OSGOOD, Isaac	BEAN, Jane B.	6 FEB 1823	MR(WA); MB
OSWALD, Henry	KELLY, Martha	16 FEB 1804	FPC:30(JM); MB
OTT, Samuel Place: Winchester	HEISKELL, Sidney d/o John Heiskell	1 JUN 1825	AG:2/6/25:3
OUTTEN, John	EVANS, Phillis	SEP 1792	FPC:30(JM); 1799:38
OVERMAN, John A.	DURRINGTON, Catherine "Kitty"	31 JAN 1808	FPC:30(JM); AG:1/2/08:3:3
OWEN, James H.	HAMMOND, Jane	14 AUG 1811	MR(IR); MB
OWENS, Edward	_____, Rebecca	-30 NOV 1815	DBZ:318
OWINGS, Henry	HARTSHORNE, Amelia d/o John Hartshorne	-4 APR 1792	FDU:92

Husband	Wife	Event or Marriage	Reference(s)

P

Husband	Wife	Event or Marriage	Reference(s)
PADGETT, Joseph	JEFFERSON, Mary Ann	10 JUN 1830	AG:12/6/30:3; MR(LA); MB
PADGETT, William O.	PADGETT, Sarah Ann	20 AUG 1822	MR(EH); MPC:W23; MB
PAGE, Charles	CRAIG, Ann "Nancy"	16 MAY 1793	AG:22/5/93:3; SPC(4:1)
PAGE, Charles H.	CRAWFORD, Gabriella Sophia	5 JUL 1827	AG:19/7/27:3
Place: *Tusculum*, near New Glasgow			
PAGE, Washington C.	CLAGETT, Elizabeth Ann	21 OCT 1824	AG:23/10/24:3(ON)
	second d/o Horatio Clagett		MG
PAGE, William	RAMSAY, Mary	23 OCT 1828	AG:27/10/28:3(Wal);
	d/o John Ramsay		MB
PAGE, William Byrd	LEE, Ann "Nancy"	10 AUG 1797	AG:12/8/97:3;
	d/o Henry Lee		HCN:396
PALMER, Joseph	PAGE, Mildred P.	23 JAN 1816	AG:27/1/16:3
Place: *Cherry Grove*	d/o Thomas T. Page		
PALMER, Pennell	McPHERSON, Rebecca N.	30 APR 1828	H:763; QM:50
PANCOAST, _____	NICHOLS, Ruth	-16 SEP 1825	WB3:266
PANCOAST, David	_____, Sarah	-9 MAY 1819	AG:12/5/19
PANCOAST, John	TALBOTT, Mary	1 MAY 1799	FMI
Place: Fairfax Meeting House			
PANCOAST, Jonathan	_____, Sidney	-17 JUN 1796	DBA:249; 1799:16
PARADISE, John	SMOOT, Elizabeth	c.31 MAY 1810	MB
PARIS, Peter	_____, Mary	-16 NOV 1809	DBU:133
PARKER, George	_____, Mary	-22 NOV 1807	DBQ:123
PARKER, James	GOTIER, Dorcas	28 DEC 1800	FPC:32(JM)
PARKER, Jesse (C)	GREEN, Sarah (C)	c.30 OCT 1817	MR(WHW); MB
PARKER, John	HILL, Mary	27 OCT 1805	WBB:80; FPC:32(JM); MR(JM); MB
PARKER, Robert (C)	_____, Sarah (C)		1800:58
PARKER, Samuel	WATSON, Anna	18 SEP 1820	MR(SC); MB
PARKER, Selby	WARD, Sarah Ann	c.2 APR 1829	MB
PARKHOUSE, William	LANE, ELizabeth	15 OCT 1791	FPC:32(JM)
PARKS, George	CHURCH, Sarah	15/16 DEC 1813	FPC:32(JM); MR(JM); MB
PARRY, William H.	MADDEN, Mary F.	15 SEP 1807	AG:16/9/07:3(JM)
PARSONS, James	_____, Elizabeth	-9 DEC 1778	WB3:277; FDQ:120; 1787:75; 1791:19
PARSONS, John	PERRY, Frances	OCT 1795	FPC:32(JM)
PARSONS, John	WASHINGTON, Mary "Polly"	-14 NOV 1796	DBV:21
PARSONS, John	ASKIN, Ann M.	18 DEC 1822	MR(ON); MB
PARSONS, Solomon	COFFER, Harriot	25 JUN 1809	AG:28/6/09:2(IR)
PARSONS, Thomas	_____, Margaret	-15 JUL 1807	DBR:191
PARSONS, Thomas	BAKER, Sarah Ann	28 JAN 1829	MR(IR); MB
PARSONS, Walter	WILLIAMS, Sarah	27 AUG 1811	FPC:32(JM); MR(JM); MB
PARSONS, William	THOMAS, Margaretta B.	6 JUL 1815	MR(IR); MB
	s/o Thomas Thomas		
PARTRIDGE, James	GILPIN, Mary G.	-22 DEC 1802	DBE:56
	d/o Joseph Gilpin		

Husband	Wife	Event or Marriage	Reference(s)
PASCOE, Charles	CHAPEL, Honor(e)	15 JUL 1775	DBE2:404; IGI;
Place: Falmouth, Eng.			FPCC(41:21)
PASCOE, Frederick	DOUGLASS, Eliza	10 APR 1830	MR(EH); MB
	d/o Elizabeth Moore		
PASKELL, Abraham	SMALLWOOD, Delilah	21 APR 1825	AG:26/4/25:3(JR)
PASQUALL, Peter	LAFERTY, Elizabeth	c.21 OCT 1804	MB
PASQUALL, Peter	CHURCHMAN, Rebecca	c.5 DEC 1807	MB
PATON, John Butcher	BUTCHER, Rebecca	6 SEP 1808	AG:9/9/08:3
PATTEN, Francis	_____, Mary	-6 FEB 1797	HCH:409
PATTEN, Thomas	ROBERDEAU, Mary	NOV 1793	FPC:31-32(JM);
	d/o Daniel Roberdeau		DBA:221; 1799:36
PATTERSON, Benj. Duke	_____, Sarah	-15 FEB 1809	DBV:115;
			WB2; TMCC(H:3)
PATTERSON, James	McHENRY, Ann	1 JUL 1797	FPC:32(JM)
PAT(T)ERSON, James D.	KINCAID, Joanna	20 JAN 1818	MR(JM);
			AG:22/1/18:3(JM)
PATTERSON, John	_____, Susannah	-6 OCT 1765	FWC:35
PATTERSON, Joseph	KEENE, Elizabeth	22 MAY 1803	MR(JM); MB
PATTERSON, William	NIXON, Beulah	22 JAN 1817	H:769[86]; 1791:20
Place: Indian Spring Meeting House MD, d/o Samuel Nixon			
PATTERSON, William	SIMPSON, Sarah "Sally" B.	25 MAR 1828	MR(Sco); MPC:W62
PATTERSON, William	_____, Susannah		SPC; MB
PATTERSON, William P.	COZZENS, Mary	SEP 1794	FPC:32(JM); 1791:20;
			1799:18
PATTON, James	SEYMOUR, Mary Ann	-4 NOV 1793	HCE:251; 1799:20;
	d/o Thomas Slaughter		FDL2:204; FWC:227
PATTON, John	GREEN, Dorcas	17 JAN 1822	MR(ON); MB
PATTON, John Mercer	WILLIAMS, Margaret French	8 JAN 1824	
Place: Fredericksburg			
PATTON, Robert, Jr.	REEDER, Ann Clifton	2 SEP 1805	AG:3/9/05:3(ED);
b/o James Patton	d/o Benjamin Reeder		MB
PATTON, Robert, Sr.	MERCER, Anne "Nancy" Gordon	OCT 1782	VG:18/10/92:3
Place: *Clifton Lodge*, Fairfax Co.			
PATTON, William	_____, Mary	-30 OCT 1817	WB3:170; 1791:19;
			1799:26; 1800:57
			DBQ:460; DBS:403
PAUL, Zachariah	BOWLING, Elizabeth	21 JUL 1810	FPC:32(JM); MR(JM);
			MB
PAYNE, Edward	CONYERS, Annholand	-26 OCT 1789	FDZ:1
	d/o Henry Conyers		
PAYNE, Hezekiah	GRAY, Ann	18 NOV 1800	FPC:32(JM)
PAYNE, John	ROLLINS, Martha Ann	c.9 NOV 1811	MB
PAYNE, John, Jr.	JANNEY, Lucretia	23 OCT 1823	AG:25/10/23:3; MB
	d/o Thomas Janney		
PAYNE, Larkin	PAYNE, Nancy	12 OCT 1816	MR(JMH); MB
PAYNE, London	_____, Mary	-6 JUL 1810	DBS:437
PAYNE, London	_____, Candus	-10 NOV 1819	WB2:344
PAYNE, Loudon	BOOTH, Sarah	10 NOV 1815	MR(JMH); MB
PAYNE, Orvis S.	TERRETT, Mary Ashton	5 MAY 1831	MR(WJ)
PAYNE, William	DORRELL, Elizabeth	18 FEB 1796	AG:20/2/96:2
PAYNE, William	HUGHES, Catherine	25 FEB 1819	FF:397
PEAKE, Dr. John Hampton	PARKER, Elizabeth	12 JUN 1823	NI:19/6/23;
			AG:19/6/23:3

Husband	Wife	Event or Marriage	Reference(s)
PEAKE, William	HALLEY, Sybil d/o James Halley	-1 FEB 1792	FWF:134; FDU:101
PEAKE, William	_____, Sarah	-31 JAN 1732	CC:102
PEAKE, Dr. William	JANNEY, Sarah E. d/o Thomas Janney	16 NOV 1819	AG:22/11/19:3(WHW); AH:22/11/19; SP
PEARCE, Alexander	_____, Margaret	-10 APR 1782	FDN:355
PEARCE, Gideon	DICK, Julia	c.20 FEB 1805	MB
PEARSON, John	DUNAWAY, Alice Ann	11 JAN 1829	AG:21/1/29:3(JR)
PEARSON, Lawson B.	MEEM, Martha	c.JAN 1797	WG:7/1/97
PEARSON, Thomas	_____, Ann	-10 APR 1789	DBD:358
PEARSON, Thomas	ALEXANDER, Sarah	-8 FEB 1798	FDB2:166
PEARSON, Thomas W.	McGLENNIN, Rose	10 JAN 1822	MR(JF); MB
PEASLEY, Isthream	WEAVER, Jane Ellender	c.3 MAY 1816	MB
PEED, James	_____, Susan	-25 APR 1826	AG:25/4/26
PEERS, Valentine	_____, Margaret	-19 JAN 1784	FDO:436, 440
PEERS, Valentine	ORR, Eleanor "Nelly"	c.24 NOV 1791	DBA:178; ES:181; AG:24/11/91:3
PEIRCE, Thomas	MANDLEY, Elizabeth	3 SEP 1812	FPC:32(JM); MR(JM); MB
PELTER, James	DUFF, Sarah	19 MAY 1808	MR(IR)
PELTON, Enoch	PATTERSON, Sarah Matilda	23 DEC 1802	MR(JM); MB
PEMBROKE, Thomas (C)	WEST, Desdemona (C)	15 AUG 1816	MR(WHW); MB
PENDLETON, Nathaniel	_____, Sarah	-19 MAR 1814	DBY:364
PENNY, John	HILL, Elizabeth "Betsy"	14 OCT 1797[87]	FPC:32(JM); 1800:59; AA:18/10/97:3
PENNY, Thomas	LIGHTFOOT, Elizabeth	30 MAR 1797	FPC:32(JM)
PERIT, John Webster	_____, Margaret	-13 JAN 1809	DBU:446
PERKINS, Francis	SMITH, Ann	25 MAY 1803	MR(JM); MB
PERKINS, John	WILLING, Priscilla	15 MAR 1797	FPC:32(JM)
PERKINS, John	WILLIAMS, Henrietta	c.5 APR 1817	MB
PERLEY, James	COOK, Elizabeth	5 DEC 1828	MB; AG:11/12/28:3(Sco)[88]
PERRY, Alexander, Sr.	SOLLERS, Henrietta	4 SEP 1823	MR(WA); MB
PERRY, Alexander D.F.	_____, Jane	-26 SEP 1797	DBR:169; HCL:475; 1787:75; 1791:20; FPCC(41:15)
PERRY, Alfred	FOX, Sarah (C)	c.25 SEP 1828	MB
PERRY, James	MARVELL, Nancy	c.26 DEC 1805	MB
PERRY, John	AVERY, Sarah	c.13 FEB 1822	MB
PERRY, William H.	MADDEN, Mary F.	16 SEP 1807	FPC:32(JM); MB
PETER, Robert	_____, Elizabeth	-3 JUL 1795	FDY:292
PETER, Thomas	CUSTIS, Martha Parke	6 JAN 1795	GL:Peter[89]
Place: *Hope Park*, Fairfax Co.			
PETERS, John	NORTH, Mary	JUN 1794	FPC:32(JM)
PETIT, John Baptist	_____, Margaret	-2 NOV 1791	HCD:361
PEYTON, Craven T.	BECKETT, Elizabeth	13 MAY 1813	DBC2:410; PS:137
Place: Calvert Co. MD	d/o John Beckett		
PEYTON, Lt./Col. Francis	FOUCHEE, Sarah	-14 MAR 1796	DBA:124; SPC(68:2); WB4:124; 1787:75; 1791:20; HCI:21; PS:137

Husband	Wife	Event or Marriage	Reference(s)
PEYTON, Thomas West	DUNDAS, Sophia Matilda d/o John Dundas	26 FEB 1811	FPC:32(JM); DBV:496; AG:29/2/11:3(JM); MR(JM); MB
PEYTON, Valentine (Phillips and Philips)	BUTLER, Mary	-16 NOV 1784	FDP:345
PHILLIPS, James	AVERY, Eliza	24 JAN 1816	MR(IR)I MB
PHILIPS, John	HILLMAN, Lucy	11 OCT 1817	MR(AG); MB
PHILLIPS, John	EVANS, Catharine	c.22 DEC 1814	MB
PHILIPS, John H.	_____, Eleanor	- c.1779	DBZ:492; TMCC(M:2)
PHILIPS, Richard H. Place: Dumfries	LINTON, Mrs. Cecilia Ann d/o Dr. William Graham	5 APR 1827	AG:7/4/27:3
PHILIPS, William	BOYD, Rebecca	c.23 SEP 1812	MB
PHILIPS, William	BALL, Kitura	20 DEC 1815	MR(IR); MB
PICKERILL, Isaac	WHEAT, Charity	JUL 1794	FPC:32(JM)
PICKERILL, Richard	WELCH, Susannah	JAN 1793	FPC:32(JM)
PICKERING, Levi	NORRIS, Sarah	29 DEC 1812	MR(IR); MB
PICKETT, George B.	HERON, Courtney	2 JUL 1818	AG:7/7/18:3
PIERCE, Daniel Place: Washington DC	TAYLOR, Mary Ann	19 AUG 1819	AG:21/8/19:2
PIERCEN (see "Pearson")			
PIERCY, Capt. Henry	BURROUGHS, Mary	-20 OCT 1795	WBC:252; 1799:20; BFG:3/3/12; CCC(64); BR:108
PIERPONT, John R.	WANTON, Mary H.	26 SEP 1833	H:771; QM:53
PILES, Charles	CARROLL, Sarah Ann	c.12 DEC 1820	DCM
PILES, Christian	BROOKS, Sarah	26 MAY 1817	MR(AG); WB2:244; MB
PILES, Francis	HUTCHINSON, Valinda	c.9 JUN 1818	DCM
PILES, John	WINDSOR, Mrs. Jemima wid/o William Windsor		FWA1:230
PILES, Leonard	REED, Mary	c.28 APR 1818	DCM
PILES, Lewis	LOMAX, Elizabeth	c.8 APR 1802	MB
PILES, Lewis	HARRIS, Anne	28 APR 1803	SPC(14:1); MR(JM); MB
PILES, Lewis J. s/o Lewis Piles	BISHOP, Eliza	c.9 OCT 1827	MB
PILES, Peter	_____, Mary	-7 JUN 1804	WB2:158; 1787:70; 1791:20; 1799:12; SPC(14:1)
PILLING, William	_____, Mary	-29 SEP 1801	DBF:287
PILTER, James	DUFF, Sarah (Green)	19 MAY 1808	MR:33(IR); DBC2:3
PIPER, _____	_____, Margaret	-25 APR 1737	CC:103
PIPER, James	BONTZ, Catharine	11 AUG 1807	MR(IR); DBT:440; MB
PIPER, William (C)	_____, Sarah (C)		1799:26; 1800:56
PITMAN, Rev. Hipkins	ADAMS, Mrs. Phoebe d/o James Bates	13 MAY 1819	AG:12/6/19:2
PITTS, Thomas	_____, Marthew		1800:56
PLANT, James	BOWIE, Alice A.M.	1 SEP 1825	MR(WHW); MB
PLEAR, Peter	STIEBBY, Nancy	APR 1794	FPC:32(JM)
PLEASANTS, John H.	MASSIE, Mary L.	15 DEC 1829	AG:29/12/29:3
Place: Falling Spring, Alleghany Co., d/o Henry Massie			
PLEASANTS, John Scott	LOWNDES, Sally	c.6 MAY 1790	AG:6/5/90:3; GT:12/5/90

Husband	Wife	Event or Marriage	Reference(s)
PLUM(B), Joseph	MARLE, Elizabeth "Betsey"	2 AUG 1803	AG:4/8/03:3(JM); FPC:32(JM); MR(JM); MB
PLUM, Lewis W.	DOXRY, Susannah	7 NOV 1799	AG:9/11/99:3; PGM
PLUMMER, Benjamin	ALEXANDER, Margaret	28 JUL 1818	AG:4/8/18:3(A)
PLUMMER, Charles H.	DOUGHERTY, Eliza	c.14 OCT 1817	MR(SC); MB
PLUMMER, George	_____, Mary		QM:50
PLUMMER, Jerome	_____, Henrietta	-8 AUG 1812	DBW:283
PLUMMER, Joseph	BOLLING, Martha	1785	FC#63w
PLUMMER, Samuel	TALBOT, Lucy	22 JUL 1817	MR(WHW)
PLUNKETT, James	CARLIN, Jane	c.10 MAR 1812	MB
POCKLINGTON, John	BEACH, Mrs. Nancy	20 FEB 1825	AG:17/3/25:3(JR)
POLLOCK, George W.	SHROPSHIRE, Mrs. Elizabeth	3 SEP 1804	MR(IR); DBV:363; MB
POMELY, John	GRINNAGE, Fanny	22 MAR 1827	MR(Sco); MB
POMERY, Francis Dade	GARRETT, Nancy	24 FEB 1807	FPC:32(JM); MB
POMERY, John	_____, Nancy	-7 DEC 1797	HCL:78; FPCG
POMERY, John (C)	MARROW, Milly (C)	c.19 OCT 1807	MB
POMERY, Walter	_____, Elizabeth	-20 APR 1803	DBW:289
POMERY, William, Jr.	WRIGHT, Mrs. Elizabeth	29 NOV 1800	FPC:32(JM); HCG:399; AA:1/12/00/:3
POMERY, Wm.	BAGGETT, Jane eldest d/o Alexander Baggett	31 DEC 1829	MB; AG:13/1/30:3(JF)
POOL, Hardesty	SMITH, Hannah	21 JAN 1823	AG:25/1/23:3(JR)
POOLE, Dennis	ALLISON, Elizabeth	OCT 1792	FPC:32(JM)
POOLE, Edmund	WILEY, Susannah	9 NOV 1790	FPC:32(JM)
POOLE, Henry	STONE, Catherine	JUN 1794	FPC:32(JM)
POOR, Dudley Place: Baltimore MD	O'DONNEL, Deborah Hib. d/o John O'Donnel	c.21 MAY 1814	AG:21/5/14:3(I)
POORER (also see "Harris, Pompey Pohra")			
POORER, Pompy (C)	CLARK, Lucy (C)	c.11 DEC 1810	MB
POPE, Abner	PARKINS, Maria d/o Joseph Parkins	30 APR 1818	H:769; QM:21, 50
POPHAM, John	THOMPSON, Mary Ann d/o Jonah Thompson	14 APR 1818	MR(ON); MB; AG:16/4/18:3(ON)
POPLAR, James	WHEELER, Sarah	c.14 NOV 1804	MB
PORTER, John	SPEAKS, Rosanna	1 AUG 1801	MR(WM); MB
PORTER, Morris	ALLEN, Maria	27 DEC 1827	AG:3/1/28:3(JR)
PORTER, Reuben	CHADWELL, Franny	12 FEB 1801	FPC:32(JM)
PORTER, Thomas	RAMSAY, Sarah d/o William Ramsay	-20 AUG 1794	HCE:401; H:36; 1787:75; CRA:325; 1791:20; FPCG
POSEY, Henry	KING, Elizabeth	20 MAY 1812	FPC:32(JM); MR(JM); MB
POSEY, James	_____, Mary	-1 DEC 1837	WB4:140
POSEY, James (C)	LEE, Cecelia (C)	23 APR 1822	MR(ON); MB
POSEY, John	HARRISON, Mrs. Martha wid/o George Harrison	-19 MAY 1756	FDD:260
POSEY, John	FORD, Ann d/o Thomas Ford	-29 AUG 1774	FWC:257
POSTON, Francis E.	DAY, Amelia	7 OCT 1817	MR(JM); MB
POSTON, John of Loudoun Co.	MAJOR, Ann James d/o John Major	18 FEB 1830	MR(LA); MB; AG:26/2/30:3(LA)

Husband	Wife	Event or Marriage	Reference(s)
POTTEN, John	_____, Sarah	-7 SEP 1829	TMCC(C:2/A:5)
POTTER, John Place: Washington DC	CAMPBELL, Ann	7 SEP 1815	AH:11/9/15
POTTER, Rheuben	CHADWELL, Fanny	12 FEB 1801	MR(JM)
POTTS, John	COOKE, Margaret	8 APR 1797	FPC:32(JM); 1791:21; 1799:18
POTTS, John, Jr.	RAMSAY, Eliza(beth) d/o Patrick Ramsay	c.29 JUN 1786	AG:29/6/86:3; 1787:75; DBC:394; CCC(65)
POTTS, Samuel J.	ROSS, Mary Ann d/o Andrew Ross	28 JAN 1817	AG:1/2/17:3(B)
POTTSULL, Michael	HOOFF, Barbara d/o Lawrence Hooff	-22 OCT 1793	WB1:130
POULTNEY, Francis	RIMER, Catherine d/o Mark Rimer		PWDE:443
POULTNEY, Thomas, Jr. Place: Sandy Spring MD	THOMAS, Nancy d/o Evan Thomas	21 APR 1790	AG:29/4/90:3; 1791:20; MGB:14/4:3
POWELL, Alfred	FAR, Ann	29 APR 1820	MR(IR); MB
POWELL, Alfred H. Place: Brandon, Prince George's Co. MD	HARRISON, Elizabeth	29 MAR 1829	AG:25/5/29:3
POWELL, Burdett Place: Georgetown DC	LEWIS, Sara	17 JUL 1819	AG:20/7/19:3(B)
POWELL, Charles L.	LLOYD, Selina d/o John Lloyd	28 OCT 1830	AG:30/10/30:3; MB; NI:9/11/30; B8
POWELL, Cuthbert s/o Col. Levin	SIMMS, Catherine d/o Charles Simms	-14 JUL 1786	WB2:358; CCC(28)
POWELL, Cuthbert, Jr. Place: Llangollen, Loudoun Co.[90]	POWELL, Mary Emily	10 MAY 1825	B2
POWELL, Edward	SISSION, Mary	21 JAN 1800	FPC:32(JM)
POWELL, Leven	HARRISON, Sarah "Sally" d/o Burr Harrison	2 FEB 1763	FSH:6
POWELL, Leven, Jr. Place: Waterside, Loudoun Co., d/o John Orr	ORR, Susanna Elizabeth	20 SEP 1797	DBA:448; HCK:585 FX(TD); PF:327; B2; AG:3/10/97:3
POWELL, William	CORNWELL, Cornelia	c.15 APR 1822	MB
POWELL, William Alex. Place: Winchester, Frederick Co.	LEE, Lucy Peachy	20 DEC 1820	B2(AB)
POWELL, Wm. Harrison	GREEN, Sarah	c.17 MAR 1785	PF:322; 1787:74; PGM
POWER, John	CRUSE, Ann H. d/o Thomas Cruse	12 DEC 1812	BA:17/12/12(M); AG:15/12/12:3(M); MB
POWERS, John	HEISKELL, Mary Louck	c.23 DEC 1802	MB
PRATT, Leven	WEIGHTMAN, Betsy d/o Richard Weightman	-13 DEC 1806	FPC:31; WB1:157
PRATT, Shuball	ZWILLE, Mrs. Margaret wid/o Robert Zwille		FWD:80
PRATT, William A.	_____, Elizabeth	-22 JUN 1843	WB4:397; WPC(178:4)
PRESTON, Thomas	JACKSON, Jane	7 JUN 1798	FPC:32(JM)
PRESTON, Thomas	PHILIPS, Eleanor	30 DEC 1804	MB; AG:1/1/05; DBQ:214; TMCC(N:2)
PRETTYMAN, David G. Place: Washington DC	FORTNEY, Mrs. Priscilla (Hicky) wid/o Jacob Fortney	31 DEC 1818	FPCC(43:102); DCM; AG:5/1/19:2(Mc)

Husband	Wife	Event or Marriage	Reference(s)
PRETTYMAN, Thomas G.	PELTON, Mary d/o E. Pelton	10 OCT 1825	AG:15/10/25:3(OB)
PRICE, David	CROOK, Margaret	1 AUG 1810	MR(IR); DBV:404; MB
PRICE, Ellis/Elias	FLEMING, Sarah "Sally" d/o Thomas Fleming	-31 MAR 1797	HCI:466; 1799:6; 1800:57
PRICE, Oliver	_____, Jane	-21 OCT 1784	HCD:107; 1787:75; 1791:20; FDP:131; HCOrd:22/12/86
PRICE, Thomas	_____, Mary	-31 OCT 1794	HCF:16
PRICE, Thomas	TRAMMELL, Susannah d/o John Trammell	-12 OCT 1789	FDD4:386; 1799:14
PRICE, Willam	MAY, Sarah Jane	10 MAR 1825	SP; MB; AG:12/3/25:3(RD)
PRINCE, John	DENNISTON, Sarah	c.2 FEB 1805	MB
PRING, Henry	GRIMES, Mary Ann	7 JUN 1820	MR(ON); MB
PRITCHARD, Stephen	BALLENGER, Sarah	3 APR 1818	MR(JM); MB
PUMPHREY, Samuel	KING, Rebecca	19 DEC 1799	FPC:32(JM)
PUPPO, Daniel C., of SC	STROMAN, Elizabeth	6 SEP 1803	FPC:32(JM); MR(JM); AG:7/9/03(JM); MB
PURCIEL, James Place: Prince William Co.	CLARKE, Catharine A.	7 FEB 1828	AG:12/2/28:3(JW)
PURCELL, Peirce	HARDING, Elizabeth	c.APR 1797	WG:29/4/97
PURSELL, Thomas	FLOOD, Elizabeth	c.10 DEC 1827	MB

Q

Husband	Wife	Event or Marriage	Reference(s)
QUEST, John W.	HESCOTT, Jane	25 APR 1828	SP; MR(WJ); MB
QUIGLEY, Michael	O'MEARA, Anastasia	-3 SEP 1811	WB1:326; FWU:433; FDL2:275
QUINN, William	WHITTINGTON, Louisa	19 APR 1823	MR(IR); MB
QUIRK, Richard	_____, Mary		1800:57

Husband	Wife	Event or Marriage	Reference(s)
R			
RAGAN, Basil	WATSON, Mary	22 MAR 1799	FPC:34(JM)
RAILEY, Bennett	FRAZIER, Frances	c.28 DEC 1803	MB
RAMSAY, Andrew	GRAHAM, Catharine	c.1795	DBB:273; DBM:79; IGI
RAMSAY, Col. Dennis	TAYLOR, Jane Allen d/o Capt. Jesse Taylor	17 NOV 1785	HCF:259; OT:39; AG:24/11/85:3; 1787:75; 1791:21; FPCC(42:73)
RAMSAY, Edward Mitchell	_____, Mary	-11 JUN 1793	HCE:165; 1787:75; 1791:21
RAMSAY, John Place: Loudoun Co.	COUTSMAN, Clarissa	10 JAN 1794	HCN:361; DBC:275; 1787:75; 1799:20; FPCC(41:8); IGI
RAMSAY, Robert T. Place: Washington DC	MARBURY, Mrs. Eliza	12 OCT 1830	AG:16/10/30:3
RAMSAY, Thomas	_____, Susannah	-10 SEP 1788	FDR:242
RAMSAY, William	McCARTY, Ann	-21 JUL 1757	AG:7/4/85:3; SV:55; 1787:75; 1791:21; FDD:450; HCOrd:21/5/84
RAMSAY, William	TUCKER, Sarah "Sally"	-21 JUL 1787	CRA:169
RANDALL, Theophilus	BOZWELL, Rachel	1788	FB; 1799:32; 1800:51
RANDALL, Theophilus	CLIFFORD, Ann	22 FEB 1816	MR(IR); MB
RANKIN, Samuel	_____, Elizabeth	-23 DEC 1786	HCOrd:23/12/86
RATCLIFFE, Joseph	JACOBS, Julia Ann d/o Thomas Jacobs	17 MAR 1825	MB; AG:22/3/25:3(RD)
RATCLIFFE, Richard	BOLLING, Locian d/o Gerrard Bolling	-16 MAR 1800	DBQ:39; FWD:221; FC#63; 1791:21; HCO:129
RATCLIFFE, Richard	DEMAIN, Ann	31 MAR 1825	MR(WA); MB; AG:2/4/25:3(WA)
RATCLIFFE, Samuel s/o Richard Ratcliffe	WILKINSON, Matilda d/o John Wilkinson	c.7 DEC 1805	MB
RATLIEF, Ignatious	_____, Viletter		1800:55
RATTLE, James	_____, Ann	-10 APR 1788	HCH:270; 1787:75
RAWLINGS, John	_____, Mary		QM:50
RAWLINS, John	_____, Susannah	-13 FEB 1796	HCG:473
RAWLINS, John	PEARSON, Jane	c.6 NOV 1804	MB
RAWLINS, John F.	BROOKS, Jane	19 JAN 1811	FPC:34(JM); MR(JM); AG:30/1/11:3(JM); MB
REAGAN, Nicholas	SPENCE, Mrs. Elizabeth	-23 OCT 1765	FPWB:407
REARDON, John	BROOKS, Rachael	JUL 1792	FPC:34(JM); 1800:51; SMC
REARDON, John T.	JACKSON, Elizabeth P.	c.13 APR 1830	MB
REARDON, M.D.	_____, Mildred D.	-6 AUG 1828	AG:6/8/28
REARDON, Michael	McNAMER, Margaret	JAN 1792	FPC:34(JM)
RECTOR, Ludwell, Jr.	SATTERWHITE, Rachel	c.8 JUL 1829	MB; MR(LA)
REDMAN, Henry	KELLY, Mary	NOV 1793	FPC:34(JM)
REDMAN, Henry	HILL, Ann	c.13 AUG 1804	MB

Husband	Wife	Event or Marriage	Reference(s)
REDMAN, Thomas	_____, Sarah "Sally"	-20 JAN 1800	DBA:362; 1791:21; 1799:18; CRA:319
REDWOOD, William	SAUNDERS, Sarah d/o Joseph Saunders	-5 MAY 1785	FWF:251

REED (also see "Reid")

Husband	Wife	Event or Marriage	Reference(s)
REED, Alexander	DALTON, Ann	MAR 1795	FPC:34(JM)
REED, Ellis	CREEDY, Betsy	10 DEC 1817	MR(JMH); MB
REED, Frank	JOHNS(T)ON, Polly	7 JUN 1827	MR(Sco); MB
REED, James	FRANCE, Charlotte	FEB 1794	FPC:34(JM)
REED, Joab	WEST, Nancy	-13 FEB 1786	R2:90(SG)
REED, John	DAY, Catherine	24 OCT 1791	FPC:34(JM)
REED, John	_____, Mary	-23 FEB 1802	DBD:485
REED, Nelson	_____, Rebeckah	-27 FEB 1798	WBB:519
REED, Silas	_____, Betsey	-24 OCT 1844	WB6:108
REED, Thomas	_____, Elizabeth	-18 AUG 1786	HCB:389; 1787:75; 1791:21
REED, Thomas	SEXTON, Mary	1 JUN 1809	MR(IR); WB2:216; DBU:201; MB
REED, William	HUTCHESON, Catharine	24 OCT 1805	MR(IR); WB1:335; MB
REEDER, Alexander	_____, Rebecca	-30 JAN 1797	FPC:33
REEDER, Benjamin	SLAUGHTER, Eleanor Clifton	-1 MAR 1791	FWG:412; FD L2:204
REELER, Samuel	HARRIS, Mary	c.10 FEB 1820	MB(ON)
REESE, Samuel	McCUIN, Harriet	9 7 JAN 1823	MB[91]; AG:11/1/23:3
REESE, Thomas L.	McCORMICK, Mary	26 NOV 1840	H:763
REESE, William L.	DORSEY, Ann	c.19 JUL 1827	MB
REEVES, Charles	BROOKS, Sarah Ann	c.25 DEC 1828	MB
REEVES, Courtney	COLTER, Delilah	7 DEC 1826	AG:15/12/26(JR)
REEVES, Hermes	HALLEY, Sarah C.	19 JAN 1826	AG:25/1/26:2(JR)
REEVES, Leonard	CREED, Mary	1788	MB; 1787:75; 1791:21
REEVES, Nicholas	SCRIVENER, Mary	c.10 JUN 1824	MB
REEVES, Randolph B.	ELLIOT, Ellen	c.NOV 1829	NI:20/11/29

REID (also see "Reed")

Husband	Wife	Event or Marriage	Reference(s)
REID, James	GRIFFIN, Polly	7 MAR 1796	FPC:34(JM)
REID, John	DAY, Catherine	OCT 1791	FPC:34(JM)
REID, Noah	BECKHAM, Lucinda	1 JAN 1822	AH:11/1/22; AG:10/1/22:3(JR)
REID (Reed), Sanford	PATTEN, Ann Fielder	20 JUN 1816	AG:24/6/16:3(IR); MR(IR); MB
REID, William	CALVERT, Lydia	15 JUN 1820	AG:20/6/20:2(JR)
REILEY, William	KENT, Sabina	28 DEC 1803	FPC:34(JM); MR(JM); MB
REILY, William	_____, Barbara	-10 JUL 1811	DBT:434; DBY:302
REINS, Anthony	TYLER, Elizabeth	2 SEP 1806	FPC:34(JM)
REINTZELL, Andrew	_____, Catharine	-26 OCT 1812	DBV:487; 1799:22
REISINGER, George	DEVAUGHN, Sarah	c.12 JUN 1804	MB
RESLER, Jacob	_____, Mary	-14 DEC 1798	HCM:272; DBB:179; WBB:35; 1791:21; 1799:6; AG:30/4/27:3
REYNOLDS, John	_____, Sarah	-15 OCT 1791	HCD:350; 1787:75; 1791:21; FPCG; CRA:231

Husband	Wife	Event or Marriage	Reference(s)
REYNOLDS, John	SIMPSON, Elizabeth	24 SEP 1803	FPC:34(JM); MR(JM); MB
REYNOLDS, John	LEE, Mary	28 SEP 1808	FPC:34(JM); MR(JM); MB
REYNOLDS, William	_____, Elizabeth	-10 NOV 1797	DBB:501; FPCC(41:26)
REYNOLDS, William	_____, Sarah	-15 NOV 1811	1799:30; 1800:56; FPCC(41:26)
REYNOLDS, William	McALISTER, Margaret	15 FEB 1821	MR(EH); MB; AG:19/2/21:2(EH)
RHIVES, Randolph B.	ELIOTT, Eleanor	c.NOV 1829	AG:25/11/29:3
RHODES, Peter	STROUD, Drusilla	c.31 MAR 1812	DBZ:420; DCM
RHODES, William	_____, Rosanna(h)	-27 MAY 1800	HCN:246; DBR:156; 1791:21; AG:21/10/23
RICE, George	O'CONNOR, Hannah	2 JAN 1812	MR(IR); MB
RICHARDS, Dr. John	_____, Jane		FPCC(43:109)
RICHARDS, John	CARLIN, Rebecca	20 SEP 1815	MR(JMH); MB
RICHARDS, Thomas	_____, Anne "Nancy"	-30 JUL 1794	HCE:404; DBE:38; 1787:75; 1791:21
RICHARDS, William	LAY, Lida d/o Sarah Lay	-12 NOV 1798	FWG:421; 1799:14
RICHARDS, Wm. Burton	CROOK, Celia d/o Bernard Crook	26 DEC 1820	A:28/12/20(WE); MB
RICHARDSON, Achilles	_____, Priscilla	-2 NOV 1810	DBT:315
RICHARDSON, Forrest	_____, Elizabeth	-8 AUG 1814	DBAA:203; 1799:38; 1800:54
RICHARDSON, George	_____, Lucy	-28 DEC 1802	DBD:304
RICHARDSON, Judson	RICHARDS, Milley	18 JUL 1811	FPC:34(JM); MR(JM); MB
RICHARDSON, William	McCARTY, Margaret	29 JUL 1830	SP; MR(WJ); MB
RICHEY (see "Ritchie")			
RICHTER, Charles	RUSSELL, Margaret	21 NOV 1796	FPC:34(JM)
RICHTER, John	ETSER, Mary	23 MAY 1803	MR(JM); MB
RICK, William	_____, Christiana	-10 DEC 1792	CRA:117
RICKETTS, Benjamin	STEWART, Mary M.	12 DEC 1805	AG:13/12/05:3(TD); MB
RICKETTS, David	BARR, Elizabeth	6 DEC 1804	FPC:34(JM); FPCC(41:6)
RICKETTS, John Place: Cecil Co. MD	PENNINGTON, Sarah	2 JUN 1760	FPCG; BM:151
RICKETTS, John Thomas Place: Cecil Co. MD	BARR, Mary	20 JAN 1783	OT:46; CMG:10; HCI:164; 1799:10; FPCC(41:6); AG:30/9/29:3
RICKS, George	JOHNSTON, Eleanor	22 JUN 1816	MR(JMH); MB
RIDDLE, James	STEUART, Arianna	8 MAY 1800	FPC:34(JM); PGM
RIDDLE, James R. Place: Staunton	HEISKELL, Amelia d/o Peter Heiskell	21 JUL 1807	DBZ:438; SPC(48:1); AG:29/7/07:3
RIDDLE, Joseph	KERSLEY, Sarah Morrow	-17 JAN 1796	DBB:42; OT:46; DBV:466; FPC:33; 1799:4; FPCG
RIDDLE, Joshua	HARPER, Frances Rush d/o Capt. John Harper	FEB 1795	FPC:33-34(JM); FPCG; HCH:203; 1799:4

Husband	Wife	Event or Marriage	Reference(s)
RIDG(E)WAY, David Place: Frederick Co.	McPHERSON, Martha (Beeson) wid/o Daniel McPherson	3 OCT 1793	HCH:481; IGI
RIDGEWAY, Mordecai	SOPER, Margaret	14 FEB 1826	UT:17/2/26:2
RIGG, John	_____, Charlotte	-12 MAR 1778	DBC:232; 1787:75; 1791:21; 1799:6
RIGG, John	_____, Ann "Nancy"	-24 JUN 1786	DBP:525; 1791:21; HCOrd:24/6/86
RIGGS, Elisha	LAWRASON, Alice d/o James Lawrason	17 SEP 1812	AG:21/9/12:3(WHW); MR(WHW); MB
RIGGS, Romulus s/o Samuel Riggs	LAWRASON, Mercy Ann	29 MAY 1810	AG:1/6/10:3(FB); MR(FB)
RILEY, Joshua	LUKENS, Elizabeth	c.24 AUG 1826	H:773
RILEY, Mark M.	WISEMAN, Mary	c.16 FEB 1826	MB
RILEY, William	HARPER, Celia d/o John Harper	c.13 NOV 1823	MB
RINGGOLD, Tench	LEE, Polly d/o Thomas Simm Lee	16 APR 1799	CL:19/4/99:3(FN)
RIN[C]KER, Joseph	GOOD, Susanna	2 JUN 1796	FPC:34(JM); 1799:36; 1800:55
RIORDAN, John T.	JACKSON, Elizabeth P.	14 APR 1830	AG:16/4/30:3(Sco)
RISTON, Benjamin	_____, Elizabeth		MPC:W84
RITCHIE, William	MAY, Ann Maria	19 FEB 1828	AG:21/2/28:3(WJ); SP; MR(WJ); MB
ROACH, James	CARSON, Elizabeth d/o Dr. James Carson	29 JUN 1837	B4
ROACH, John	DRURY, Monica	14 JUN 1801	MR(JM); MB
ROBBINS, Rev. Isaac	HOWELL, Mary D.	3 SEP 1803	MR(HJ); DBT:21; TMCC(L:2); MB
ROBERDEAU, Daniel	_____, Jane	-7 MAY 1785	HCG:297; 1787:75; 1791:22
ROBERDEAU, Isaac Place: Germantown PA	BLAIR, Susan Shippen	7 NOV 1792	AG:22/11/92:3 1787:75; DBW:504
ROBERTS, John	[GREEN], Ann	-8 SEP 1808	DBQ:328; 1799:36; 1800:53; CCC(14); FX
ROBERTS, Richard	SPEARS, _____	c.5 MAY 1812	MB
ROBERTS, Robert B.	CASEY, Bridget "Biddy"	14 MAR 1799	FPC:34(JM); DBS:291; CCG:A1; 1800:52; TMCC(K:4)
ROBERTS, Robert R.	_____,	c.13 JUL 1811[92]	DBU:268
ROBERTSON, Edward	KENNER, Jane H.	c.28 JAN 1817	MB
ROBERTSON, James	_____, Mary	-18 JUL 1788	DBS:263
ROBERTSON, Capt. John	MOXLEY, Betsey	c.7 APR 1785	AG:7/4/85:3
ROBERTSON, John	SNALUM, Elizabeth	JUN 1794	FPC:34(JM)
ROBERTSON, Robert	_____, Ann	-25 JUL 1811	DBU:332
ROBERTSON, Samuel	MURDOCH, Eliza d/o Col. Murdoch of Georgetown DC	12 NOV 1811	AG:21/11/11:3
ROBEY, Charles	MORELAND, Hannah	6 JAN 1825	AG:11/1/25:3(JR)
ROBEY, Joseph	SIMPSON, Margaret	c.15 AUG 1822	MB
ROBEY, L.S.	THOMAS, Delia	30 DEC 1824	AG:6/1/25:3
ROBEY, Levi	KIDWELL, Mary Ann	1793	FM(1855):6
ROBINSON, _____	ROWLAND, Susanna	-1 JUN 1815	DBBB:85
ROBINSON, Edward	KENNER, Jane H.	28 JAN 1817	MR(WHW); AG:30/1/17:3(WHW)

Husband	Wife	Event or Marriage	Reference(s)
ROBINSON, George	ALLEN, Barbara	18 JUL 1798	FPC:34(JM)
ROBINSON, James	YOUNGSTON, Mary	1788	FB
ROBINSON, Capt. James	ROWLAND, Mrs. Susannah	15 MAY 1814	AG:17/5/14:3(WDA);
Place: Georgetown DC			FPCC(42:68)
ROBINSON, Matthew	BOA, Mrs. Margaret	16 APR 1799	AG:18/4/99:3;
	relict of Cavan Boa		1799:6; SMC
ROBINSON, Matthew	BACON, Elizabeth	16 JUN 1810	AG:19/6/10(F); MB
ROBINSON, William	_____, Ann C.	-3 OCT 1823	AG:7/10/23
ROBINSON, William	ZIMMERMAN, Eliza	11 MAR 1829	AG:16/3/29:3
Place: Washington DC			
ROBY, Joseph	SIMPSON, Margaret	15 AUG 1822	MR(EH)
ROCK, Richard	SPUNAUGLE, Margaret	10 DEC 1812	FPC:34(JM); MR(JM);
			MB
RODDY, John Mc.	SHIELDS, Mary	c.4 SEP 1828	MB
RODES, Charles (C)	_____, Cloey (C)		1800:57
RO(D)GERS, William	ALLISON, Elizabeth	15 OCT 1818	MB; MR(IR)
	d/o Harrison Allison		
RODMAN, Alexander	CRUMP, Sally	20 SEP 1798	FPC:34(JM)
ROE (also see "Wroe")			
ROE, Absalom	CLARK, Ann	-13 DEC 1784	FWE:180; WBC:381
ROE, Gerard	MEHAUL, Margaret	25 JUN 1796	FPC:34(JM)
ROGERS, Beverly	COOK, Sarah Ann	9 FEB 1826	UT:15/2/26:2
ROGERS, John	BARRINGER, Mary	4 APR 1826	UT:8/4/26:3(Mc)
ROGERS, Lloyd N.	HAY, Hortensia Monroe	5 JUL 1829	AG:11/7/29
Place: Oak Hill, Loudoun Co., d/o George Hay			
ROGERSON, Francis L.	DENT, Martha Ann	24 FEB 1829	AG:3/3/29:3(GM)
ROGERSON, Thomas	OLNEY, Anstis	-17 APR 1796	HCH:44; FPC:33;
			1799:16
ROLLINS, William	DONALDSON, Mary Catharine	c.12 DEC 1809	MB
ROPER, George	SHARPE, Anna	23 JUL 1811	AG:30/7/11:3(JL)
	d/o Peter Sharpe		
ROSE, Alexander M.	SMITH, Ann Augusta	28 FEB 1826	SP;
	d/o Col. Aug. J. Smith of West Grove		AG:2/3/26:3(WHW)
ROSE, Henry	_____, Ann	- MAR 1807	DBAA:464
ROSE, Henry B.	DUNBAR, Ann R.	3 NOV 1825	MR(EH); MB
ROSE, Henry S.	SHAW, Jane	26 DEC 1826	MR(EH); MB
	ward of Horatio Day		
ROSS, David	JANNEY, Mary	14 DEC 1808	H:757; J:89;
			AG:20/12/08:3
ROSS, Edward	_____, Isabella	-25 NOV 1779	CCG:A1
ROSS, John	_____, Margaret	-6 MAY 1816	DBD2:104
ROSS, John	HANDY, Louisa	c.14 AUG 1815	MB
ROSS, Samuel	HAMILTON, Sarah	9 MAR 1816	MR(IR); MB
ROSS, William Sterrett	DADE, Eleanor	29 APR 1823	P:117
ROTCH, George	McBRIDE, Mrs. Susan	9 FEB 1825	MR(Sco); MB;
			AG:12/2/25:3(Sco)
ROTCH, John	ROTCH, Melinda	c.19 MAY 1820	MB; MR(JF)
ROTCHFORD, Bartholomew	CARNE, Jane	c.4 FEB 1815	MB
ROUGER, Charles	_____, Eve		1800:58
ROUNSEVAL, Andrew	WEST, Elizabeth	19 JAN 1808	FPC:34(JM); WB3:258;
			FPCC(44:127)
ROUSEE, James	SHEID, Sarah E.	10 MAR 1829	AG:1/4/29:3(JR)
ROUZIE, Reuben	POWED, Mrs. Eleanor	31 DEC 1829	AG:8/1/30:3(JR)

Husband	Wife	Event or Marriage	Reference(s)
ROWEN, Rev. Joseph	RHODES, Nancy	22 APR 1804	AG:23/4/04:3(WW);
	d/o William Rhodes		MB
ROZELL, William	SETTLES, Julia Ann F.	8 SEP 1825	NI:13/9/25(Mc)
ROZER, Francis E.	WHEELER, Mary	16 APR 1822	AG:18/4/22:3(JF)
Place: Hayfield			
ROZER, Henry	_____, Eleanor	-1 NOV 1784	HCB:382
ROZIER, Francis E.	BROOKE, Harriet E.	30 MAY 1826	AG:2/6/26:3
Place: Baltimore MD	d/o Richard Brooke, of Fredericktown MD		
ROZIER, Francis Hall	ROZER, Maria Helena Hall	12 DEC 1792	DBA:61; X:70; IGI;
Place: Prince George's Co. MD			DBQ:168; PGM
RUDD, John	PADGETT, Sarah	17 DEC 1822	AG:19/12/22:3(EH)
RUDD, Richard A.	WARD, Elizabeth	26 JUL 1821	MR(IR); MB
	d/o Walter Ward		
RUMNEY, John	HAMMATT, Lydia	-6 APR 1816	DBBB:281
RUMNEY, John	McKNIGHT, Martha B.	8 FEB 1824	AG:12/2/24:3(B); B9
Place: Georgetown DC	d/o Capt. John McKnight		
RUNKLES, David	GOULD, Mrs. Eliza	24 MAR 1824	AG:25/3/24:3(WA);
of Madison Co. KY	wid/o John Gould		MB; MR(WA); Note[93]
RUNNELS, John H.	_____, Abigail G.	-23 DEC 1818	TMCC(K:4);
			AG:24/12/18:3
RUSSELL, Isaac K.	PERRY, Matilda	24 MAR 1818	AG:2/4/18:3
	d/o Alexander Perry		
RUSSELL, John	DENNISON, Sarah	c.21 SEP 1829	MB
RUSSELL, John B.F.	PEYTON, Cornelia	28 FEB 1828	NI:1/3/28; MR(WJ);
	d/o Col. Francis Peyton		MB; AG:29/2/28:3;
			SP
RUSSELL, James	_____, Nancy "Ann"	-7 SEP 1798	FPC:33; 1799:6;
			FPCG; AG:26/3/07:3
RUSSELL, James	JANNEY, Susannah	20 NOV 1804	H:758
Place: Fairfax Co.			
RUSTICK, Thomas	PIERCE, Elizabeth	4 JUN 1803	MR(JM); MB
RUTHERFORD, Francis	TOLER, Frances	30 SEP 1830	MB; AG:2/10/30:3(Wal)
RUTHERFORD, Robert	_____, Mary	-7 APR 1774	FDL:277
RUTTER, George	_____, Mary	-3 JUN 1801	DBA:158; 1791:22
RUTTER, Robert	_____, Ann		1799:2; 1800:57
RYAN, Col. Michael	DUDLEY, Frances	c.9 JUN 1785	AG:9/6/85:3
Place: Richmond			
RYE, Jesse	ASKIN, Jane V.	30 JUL 1828	MR(IR); MB

S

Husband	Wife	Event or Marriage	Reference(s)
SAFFORD, Dr. Eliel T. Place: *Summer Hill*	HUNTER, Ann H. d/o Nathaniel Chapman Hunter si/o Alexander Hunter	2 AUG 1825	NI:6/8/25; SP; MB; AG:11/8/25:3(ON)
SALES, William	TATE, Rockey	c.27 DEC 1805	MB
SALKELD, Henry	_____,	-13 SEP 1755	FWB:93
SALMAN, Isaac	_____, Sarrah		1799:28; 1800:54
SAMBOY, Sampson	COLE, Letty (C)	c.5 MAY 1813	MB
SAMPSON, Alexander	_____, Elizabeth	-16 AUG 1789	DBD:256
SANDERS, Henry White	THOMPSON, Maria	23 JUL 1803	MR(JM)
SANDFORD, John	_____, Betty	-24 JUL 1783	FDO:58
SANDS, Robert	REMSEY, Catharine S.	c.1 SEP 1824	MB
SANFORD, Lawrence	_____, Catharine	-1 JAN 1802	DBB:105; 1791:22; FPCG
SANFORD, Manly Whiting	MITCHELL, Deborah	c.FEB 1823	MR(WA)
SANFORD, Richard	PRICE, Elizabeth d/o John Price	-7 JAN 1786	FWE:127
SANFORD, Thomas Place: Marietta OH	LEAVENS, Esther	27 NOV 1803	DBT:251; BR:157
SANGER, Stephen	_____, Ann	-20 APR 1809	DBS:76
SANGSTER, Alexander Place: Harford Co. MD	GIBSON, Mary Ann d/o I.L. Gibson	15 DEC 1815	AH:22/12/15; AG:21/12/15:3
SANGSTER, Capt. Thomas	LEE, Elizabeth Eustace d/o Hancock Lee, of *Greenview*	20 OCT 1825	AG:29/10/25:3
SARRATT, Dickerson	HARDEN, Susannah d/o Thomas G. Harden	c.21 AUG 1813	MB
SARTIN, James	FLATFORD, Mary d/o Thomas Flatford	31 DEC 1818	AG:17/1/19:2(SP)
SATTERWHITE, Jeremiah W.	DROUN, Mary	c.2 OCT 1828	MB
SAUL, Joseph	_____, Mary	-13 JUN 1796	1799:10; 1800:54; HCG:402
SAUNDERS, John	PANCOAST, Mary	9 APR 1783	DBE:85; 1787:76; 1791:22; CRA:24; DBQ:451; H:769
SAUNDERS, Joseph	_____, Hannah	-4 FEB 1775	HCD:330
SAUNDERS, Nicholas	STANHOPE, Elizabeth	26 DEC 1822	AG:7/1/23:3(JR)
SAUNDERS, Peter Place: Jefferson Co.	M'PHERSON, Hannah d/o John M'Pherson	7 FEB 1810	DBBB:412; QM:51; H:763(25); AG:14/2/10:3
SAVAGE, George	COLLINS, Frances	2 SEP 1797	FPC:36(JM)
SAX, Joseph	YOST, Lucy	28 MAY 1820	MR(ON); MB
SAYRE, John C.	WOOD, Harriot	c.2 JAN 1823	MB
SAYRE, John J.	SPEAKE, Sophia d/o Capt. Francis Speake	28 JUL 1801	P:115
SAYRES, John J.	ROBERTS, Matilda E. d/o John Roberts	17 DEC 1829	SP; MR(WJ); MB; AG:19/12/29:3(WJ)
SCHOLFIELD, Andrew	_____, Elizabeth	-23 DEC 1803	DBG:458; QC
SCHOLFIELD, Isachar Place: Delaware Co. PA	MARSHALL, Edith	6 MAY 1802	H:764
SCHOLFIELD, Jonathan Place: Fairfax Co.	BROWN, Eleanor d/o David Brown	29 OCT 1806	H:733; DBQ:194; AG:4/11/06:3

Husband	Wife	Event or Marriage	Reference(s)
SCHOLFIELD, Joseph L.	_____, Mary		QM:51
SCHOLFIELD, Mahlon	NEILL, Ann	5 MAR 1807	H:768; DBQ:194
Place: Hopewell Meeting House			
SCHULTS, Frederick	AUSTIN, Emily	11 JUL 1822	AG:18/7/22:3
SCISSON, Lewis	POWELL, Frances	6 MAR 1798	FPC:36(JM)
SCOTT, Allen	DARNE, Mary	c.13 DEC 1809	MB
SCOTT, Scott	DOUGHERTY, Mrs. Jane	22 DEC 1825	AG:24/12/25:3(OB)
Place: Washington DC			
SCOTT, Charles R.	STANTON, Lucinda	8 NOV 1798	AG:15/11/98:3;
Place: Fauquier Court House, d/o Col. Stanton			1799:36
SCOTT, Charles W.	BEADLE, Mrs. Elizabeth	23 SEP 1806	AG:24/9/06:3(JM)
			FPC:36(JM); MR(JM);
			MB
SCOTT, David Wilson	_____, Elizabeth	-3 FEB 1801	DBB:287
SCOTT, George	MORRIS, Violet	31 AUG 1797	FPC:36(JM)
SCOTT, Gustavus Hall	MARSHALL, Elizabeth D.	1 JUL 1806	RMSD:1
SCOTT, Henry	BONTZ, Amelia	c.2 JUL 1824	MB
SCOTT, Horatio C.	KOONES, Caroline	1 JUN 1815	AG:3/6/15:3(WHW);
	d/o Frederick Koones		MR(WHW); MB
SCOTT, Horatio C.	HODGES, Ellen O.	5 OCT 1826	AG:12/10/26:3
Place: *Bellefield*			
SCOTT, James S.	ADGATE, Mrs. Mary	26 NOV 1801	DBQ:476; MR(JM);
			AG:27/11/01:3;
			FPC:36(JM); MB
SCOTT, Jesse	_____, Clarinda	c.DEC 1830	AG:1/12/30
SCOTT, Jesse G.	DENT, Rebecca T.	6 OCT 1816	AG:15/10/116:3
Place: Fauquier Co.			
SCOTT, John	_____, Mary	-26 OCT 1797	FPC:35
SCOTT, John Dennis	_____, Elizabeth	-10 MAR 1795	DBE:295;
			AG:10/3/95:4
SCOTT, Lt. R.I.	LEWIS, Mary Ann	22 SEP 1818	AG:24/9/18:2
	d/o Henry Lewis		
SCOTT, Richard	_____, Elizabeth	-27 APR 1825	TMCC(L:5)
SCOTT, Richard Marshall	LOVE, Mary	c.1788	HCF:349; FMI;
			RMSD:1
SCOTT, Richard Marshall	MARSHALL, Eleanor Douglass	25 NOV 1828	RMSD:3; CCR;
Place: *Bush Hill*	d/o James Marshall		NI:28/11/28;
			AG:27/11/28:3
SCOTT, Richard Marshall	FITZHUGH, Lucinda	-15 MAR 1832	WB4:199l FDK3:296
SCOTT, Richard Marshall	GUNNELL, Virginia	15 SEP 1846	RMSD
SCOTT, Robert	LEWIS, Mary Ann	23 SEP 1818	MR(WHW); MB
SCOTT, Sabret E.	MANDEVILLE, Maria	17 JUL 1817	WB4:143; MR(WHW)
	ni/o Joseph Mandeville		
SCOTT, Thomas	CHAFLINE, Mary	10 JUL 1810	FPC:36(JM); MR(JM);
			MB
SEAHORN, John	GOLDSMITH, Catharine	c.22 DEC 1804	MB[94]
SEAMAN, John L.	COOKE, Martha	7 NOV 1818	MR(JM); MB
SEARS, Hector	KING, Sally	c.2 APR 1818	MB
	d/o Charles and Susannah King		
SEARS, William Bernard	_____, Elizabeth	-25 OCT 1825	AG:25/10/23
SEARS, William B.	BUCKLEY, Sophia	23 AUG 1825	AG:1/9/25:3(JR)
SEATON, George	SMITH, Lucinda	c.23 SEP 1815	TMCC(H:7); DCM
SEATON, John Curson	_____, Ann	-28 OCT 1809	AG:31/10/09:3

Husband	Wife	Event or Marriage	Reference(s)
SEDWICK, Dr. Benjamin	ALEXANDER, Anne Pearson d/o Thomas Pearson Alexander	7 NOV 1806	KGM1:25; CCC(84) P:248
SEDWICK, Benjamin	KIBBY, Penny	c.2 JAN 1819	DCM
SEDWICK, Thomas	WELLS, Matilda M.	19 JAN 1817	AG:23/1/17:3
SEITLER, Abraham Place: Fredericksburg	CLARK, Mrs. Bathsheba	25 OCT 1819	AG:22/11/19:3
SELBY, Isaac	KILLUM, Sally	c.21 APR 1805	MB
SELECMAN, William D.	SELECMAN, Margaret d/o Thomas Selecman	3 DEC 1829	AG:13/1/30:3(Sco)
SELECTMAN, Henry	FISHER, Mary	22 AUG 1798	FPC:36(JM); 1799:38
SELECTMAN, Henry	SIMPSON, Mary	23 DEC 1823	AG:23/12/23:3
SEMMES, Dr. Thomas Place: *Mt. Eagle*, Fairfax Co.	POTTS, Sophia W. d/o John Potts	28 JUN 1808	CCC(65); AG:30/6/08:3(G)
SEMPLE, William	ST. GEORGE, Elizabeth	FEB 1793	FPC:36(JM)
SERGEANT, John	MOODY, Peggy	16 DEC 1810	MR(FB); MB
SERVOICE, William (C)	RAMSAY, Mary (C)	19 APR 1822	MR(ON); MB
SETON, John Curson Place: Georgetown MD	WISE, Ann, of *Summer Hill*	5 JAN 1800	AA:7/1/00:3(B) BFG:9/1/00
SEWALL, W.	ADAMS, Eliza W.	9 AUG 1821	AG:13/8/21:3(Mc)
SEWELL, Clement	_____, Eleanor	- AUG 1811	WB1:191
SEWELL, Joseph	PAYNE, Catherine (Hughes)		FWR:373
SEWELL, William	_____, Elizabeth	-4 MAY 1796	HCH:6
SEXSMITH, Matthew	LANPHIER, Elizabeth	OCT 1792	FPC:36(JM); CWA:485
SHAKES, John	LaTREAT, Sarah "Sally"	15 MAR 1803	SPC; AG:16/3/03:3(B); UC:W108
SHAKESPEARE, William	PRICE, Susannah	27 JUL 1801	MR(WM); MB
SHANNON, Samuel	DARBY, Elizabeth	1788	FB
SHARPE, Joseph	HOWARD, Sarah "Sally"	12 SEP 1811	AG:14/9/11:3; MB
SHAW, Alexander	TOUPLEY, Kitty	23 MAR 1798	FPC:36(JM); 1799:2
SHAW, George Place: Annapolis MD	ROBINSON, Eliza	4 APR 1819	AG:9/4/19:3
SHAW, John	HITT, Mrs. Mary	3 NOV 1791	DBT:457; VG:17/11/91
SHAW, John Place: Leesburg	CORWIN, Cynthia	2 MAY 1826	AG:11/5/26:3
SHAW, John	McPHERSON, Henrietta	c.17 APR 1827	UT:18/4/27:3
SHAW, John R.	RIKER, Mrs. Margaret E. d/o Dr. Thomas W. Montgomery	12 OCT 1815	AH:13/10/15
SHAW, Washington	MATTINGLY, Catharine	2 MAY 1826	UT:10/5/26:3
SHAW, William	_____, Eleanor	-24 JUL 1772	HCE:431
SHEAFFER, Henry	_____, Mary	-15 JUN 1778	DBI:196
SHEARFELD, John	PAYNE, Merkey	c.10 JAN 1818	MB
SHEARS, Peter	PARKER, Nancy	28 FEB 1799	FPC:36(JM)
SHEEHY, Edward	McLAUGHLIN, Ann	c.22 JUN 1816	MB
SHEID, George	DULIN, Serena G.	8 MAR 1829	AG:4/1/29:3(JR)
SHERIFF, Joshua	LOCKER, Mary	19 FEB 1811	FPC:36(JM); MR(JM); MB[95]
SHERIFF, Samuel	LOCKER, Susanna	8 JAN 1812	FPC:38(JM); MR(JM); MB
SHERMANDINE, Levius	SIMMS, Susannah G.	4 APR 1822	AG:6/4/22:3(WHW); MB
SHERRON, Peter	_____, Eleanor	-23 APR 1803	DBF:8; 1799:6; SMC

Husband	Wife	Event or Marriage	Reference(s)
SHERWOOD, Job	DAY, Elizabeth	29 JUL 1800	FPC:36(JM)
SHERWOOD, Lewyllen	ROBINSON, Polly	4 JUN 1815	FPC:38(JM); MR(JM); MB
SHEURMAN, Abraham	KITELEY, Mary	c.17 NOV 1802	MB
SHIELDS, John	DAVIS, Sally	c.18 MAY 1811	MB
SHIELDS, John	WARD, Nancy	12 AUG 1811	MR(IR); MB
SHIELDS, Luke	_____, Elizabeth	-13 JAN 1816	DBBB:455
SHIELDS, Thomas	GEE, Mary Ann	2 APR 1807	AG:3/4/07:3(IR); DBZ:426; MR(IR); MB
SHIELDS, Thomas	STEVENS, Elizabeth	28 APR 1810	MR(IR); MB
SHIELDS, William	WALDRON, Mrs. Kitty	1 DEC 1808	BFG:14/12/08
SHINN, Adam	FOWLER, Kitty	18 FEB 1790	FPC:36(JM)
SHINN, Adam	DAVIS, Elizabeth	APR 1792	FPC:36(JM)
SHINN, Robert	MYERS, Elizabeth ward of Benjamin Greenwood	c.9 AUG 1827	MB
SHINN, Stephen	MUIR, Mary d/o Mary Muir	16 MAY 1826	MB; AG:18/5/26:3(AH)
SHIPLEY, Robert	TOUCH, Pernica	24 JUL 1800	FPC:36(JM)
SHOALS, Manassa	_____, Polly	-8 JAN 1817	WB2:203
SHOEMAKER, Arnold	_____, Hannah		QM:51
SHOEMAKER, David	PEIRCE, Abigal Davidson	c.29 DEC 1815	DCM; AG:19/12/26:3
SHOEMAKER, George	LUKENS, Elizabeth	c.AUG 1821	H:778; QM:51
SHOLL, Philip	REARDON, Rachael	c.29 JUL 1806	MB
SHORT, John	_____, Ann(e)	-3 MAY 1787	HCC:154; 1787:76; FDR:83
SHORTER, Capt. Roger	HUNT, Sarah Ann Birch ward of John McFarlane	11 JAN 1827	MB; AG:13/1/27:3(AH)
SHREVE, Benjamin	_____, Hannah	-30 DEC 1784	AG:30/12/84:3; 1787:75; 1791:22
SHREVE, Benjamin Place: Upper Springfield	WOOD, Susannah	6 APR 1786	H:778; WBA:48; 1791:22; 1799:26; 1800:58
SHREVE, Benjamin	KITELY, Sarah	14 JAN 1802	MR(JM); MB
SHREVE, Benjamin	SWINK, Barbara d/o William Swink	-27 APR 1821	WB3:270; FWM:335
SHREVE, Benjamin, Jr.	GOODHUE, Mary	c.30 JUN 1804	MB; DBU:36
SHREVE, Isaac s/o Benjamin Shreve	VERY, Hannah	c.8 APR 1802	MB DBQ:111, 360
SHREVE, Jehu	BALL, Anna d/o John Ball	7 SEP 1797	GA:61
SHREVE, Samuel	BOWLING, Margaret "Peggy"	7 MAY 1791	FPC:36(JM); WB1:110; AG:27/2/11:3
SHREVE, Samuel	THOMAS, Elizabeth	c.19 JAN 1812	WB2:57; DCM
SHREVE, Samuel B.	SMEDLEY, Rachel J.	2 DEC 1813	DBBB:270; H:778; QM:51
SHREVE, Thomas Place: Indian Spring Meeting House MD s/o Caleb Shreve	HOPKINS, Ann d/o John Hopkins	5 NOV 1801	DBW:369; AG:11/11/01:3; MGB:14/4:4
SHROPSHIRE, William	_____, Elizabeth	-9 JUN 1800	DBV:363; 1799:20; 1800:55; CRA:338

Husband	Wife	Event or Marriage	Reference(s)
SHUCK, Frederick	BOGAN, Elizabeth	14 MAR 1805	FPC:36(JM); DBQ:343; MR(JM); MB
SHUCK, Jacob	_____, Barbara	-13 MAY 1802	DBE:8; 1791:23; 1799:30; 1800:52
SHUGHART, Eli Place: Wilmington DE	WILSON, Mrs. Elizabeth	8 AUG 1811	AG:15/8/11:3
SHULER, George	KING, Jemima	3 NOV 1790	FPC:36(JM)
SIEVERMAN, John Christ.	DEVEREUX, Elizabeth	15 AUG 1801	MR(JM); MB
SILKMAN, Henry	_____, Mary		1800:54
SILLICK, Thomas	MASON, Sarah G.	c.29 OCT 1807	MB
SILLICK, Thomas	MASON, Chloe	c.7 JAN 1825	MB
SIMMONDS, Jeremiah	GOODRICK, Eleanor	1788	FB
SIMMON(D)S, Samuel	_____, Jane	-18 JUL 1793	HCE:107; 1787:75; 1791:23; 1799:36; 1800:57
SIMMONS, Samuel	HUNTER, Mrs. Enua	25 JAN 1827	MB; AG:27/1/27:3(AH)
SIMMS, Charles	DOUGLAS, Nancy d/o William Douglas	DEC 1778	WB2:358; 1787:76; 1791:23; BR:117; FPC:35; TMCC(R:1); FSH:A-5
SIMMS, James	LIGHTFOOT, Betsey	9 JAN 1803	MR(JM); MB
SIMMS, John	McGEE, Elizabeth	c.15 JUN 1830	MB
SIMMS, John Douglas Place: Residence of Dr. James Craik, eldest d/o Roger West	WEST, Mary	7 SEP 1809	AG:8/9/09:3(G); BFR:23/9/09; MB
SIMMS, John Douglas Place: Richland, Stafford Co., d/o Daniel Carroll Brent	BRENT, Eleanor Carroll	6 FEB 1816	AG:9/2/16:3(ON)
SIMM(S), Robert	KING, Elizabeth	c.19 JAN 1786	AG:19/1/86:3; 1787:76; 1791:23
SIMMS, Thomas	FRISTOE, Margaret "Peggy"	18[96] NOV 1797	FPC:36(JM); 1799:2; AA:29/12/97:3
SIMMS, William	_____, Ann	-MAY 1823	AG:29/5/23
SIMPSON, Aaron	WISHEART, Charlotte	1783	FB
SIMPSON, Alfred	CASH, Susana	3 DEC 1817	MR(AG); MB
SIMPSON, Caleb	WEBSTER, Matilda	5 APR 1827	AG:23/4/27:3(JR)
SIMPSON, Gerrard	BENSON, Ann	c.26 JUN 1817	MB
SIMPSON, Gilbert	ZIMMERMAN, Susannah	3 FEB 1803	MR(JM); MB
SIMPSON, Hanson	RANDELL, Sarah	23 MAY 1816	MB; MR(IR)
SIMPSON, Henry L.	MILSTEAD, Elizabeth	25 DEC 1825	AG:3/1/26:3(JR)
SIMPSON, John	FORD, Caty d/o Thomas Ford	-29 AUG 1774	FWC:257
SIMPSON, John	BARKER, Decie	8 OCT 1791	FPC:36(JM)
SIMPSON, Joseph	STONE, Elizabeth	31 AUG 1799	FPC:36(JM)
SIMPSON, Lewis	UHLER, Catherine (Young) wid/o Valentine Uhler d/o David Young	7 DEC 1797	FPC:36(JM); DBA:137; DBC:131; HCL:391
SIMPSON, Moses	GARRETT, Mrs. Mary d/o Thomas Lucas and wid/o William Garrett	-13 FEB 1786	R2:90(SG); FMI
SIMPSON, Peter W.	TRIDEL [TRYDEL], Mary Ann	12 OCT 1826	AG:16/10/26:3(WHW); MB; UT:16/10/26:3
SIMPSON, Presley	RIFFETTS, Mary H.	c.23 MAR 1824	MB
SIMPSON, Thomas	MOORE, Jane	c.29 JUL 1820	MB

Husband	Wife	Event or Marriage	Reference(s)
SIMPSON, Thompson	KEENE, Frances d/o Francis Keene	19 OCT 1815	AG:20/10/15:3(ON)
SIMPSON, William	GRETTER, Elizabeth	-13 FEB 1775	HCD:311; FDM:136
SIMPSON, William	LIGHTFOOT, Ann	14 JAN 1798	FPC:36(JM)
SIMPSON, William	DAVIS, Elizabeth	8 JAN 1816	MR(IR); MB
SINCOX, Aron	WINDSOR, Rebecca	8 JAN 1828	AG:18/1/28:3(JR)
SINGLETON, John	BAYLEY, Nancy d/o William Bayley	-25 JUN 1780	FWD:439
SIPPLE, Samuel	HO(O)KES, Mary Ann	24 APR 1822	MR(EH); MB; AG:27/4/22:3(EH)
SKIDMORE, Gerrard	RICHARDS, Mariah	c.27 APR 1810	MB
SKIDMORE, Jesse	BOYD, Sarah	18 OCT 1815	MR(JMH); FPCC; MB
SKIDMORE, William	ROBINSON, Catharine	c.15 APR 1814	MB
SKILMAN, Christopher	PAYNE, Henrietta d/o Joseph Payne	-13 NOV 1799	DBA:323; HCM:408
SKINNER, Burditt	CHESHIRE, Margaret	20 MAR 1816	MR(IR); MB
SKINNER, George	MILLS, Mary	c.6 MAY 1812	MB; WB2:118
SKINNER, Price	ROLLINS, Julia d/o John Rollins	c.15 MAR 1828	MB
SKINNER, Thomas L.	SMITH, Elizabeth d/o Joseph Smith	-1 MAR 1843	TMCC(P:5); FC#78; FDH3:159
SKINNER, William	SAYRE, Valinda	5 JUL 1789	FPC:36(JM)
SKINNER, William A.	MOAN, Aletha	3 MAR 1816	MR(ON); MB
SLACUM, George W.	HOWARD, Jane Harriet	-17 JAN 1793	S:xiv; DBA:356; OT:51; 1791:23; 1799:38; 1800:54; CCC(36)
SLADE, Charles	_____, Mary	-19 MAR 1804	DBG:452; CCG:A1; 1800:54
SLADE, Richard	_____, Susan	-25 OCT 1821	AG:25/10/21
SLATER, Capt. F.	DORSHTIMER, Mrs. Elizabeth	15 MAY 1808	AG:20/5/08:3(MI)
SLATER, John	THOMPSON, Delila	c.19 JUL 1824	MB
SLATER, Thomas (C)	_____, Florrer (C)		1799:38; 1800:52
SLATER, William	TAYLOR, Mary Ann	4 DEC 1800	FPC:36(JM)
SLAUGHTER, Thomas	CLIFTON, Ann d/o William and Elizabeth Clifton	-26 NOV 1772	FWC:225; FWG:412; FD D1:769
SLEIGH, Isaac	NEWMAN, Ann M.	7 JUL 1825	AG:12/7/25:3(JR)
SLEIGH, Isaac	BOWIE, Maria	29 APR 1829	MR(JM); AG:3/5/19:3(JM)
SLIMMER, Christian	_____, Mary	-22 JAN 1784	HCOrd:22/1/84
SLIMMER, Christian	TROUGANTT, Ann	1 FEB 1798	FPC:36(JM); 1791:23
SLIMMER, Christian [Daniel]	WILLIAMS, Ellenor	10 MAR 1810	MR(IR); MB
SLOAN, James	THROOP, Hariott	9 SEP 1809	MR(IR); MB
SLOAN, John	_____, Ann Rebecca	-23 FEB 1815	WB2:10; 1799:18; TMCC(F:2)
SLY, John S.	CURTAIN, Susannah	22 JUN 1801	MR(JM); MB
SLY, Thomas	BEECH, Rebecca	c.26 MAY 1827	MB
SMACK, William	_____, Ann		1800:53
SMALL, Noah	JACKSON, Lucretia	c.26 OCT 1818	MR(SC); MB
SMART, John P. Place: Leesburg	HILLIEARD, Emily d/o Joseph HIllieard	26 NOV 1829	AG:1/12/29:3
SMETHERS, Dr. Robert	BAGGS, Elizabeth	28 FEB 1826	UT:1/3/26:3

Husband	Wife	Event or Marriage	Reference(s)
SMITH (also see SMYTH)			
SMITH, _____	DRINKER, Susannah	-24 SPR 1828	H:779
SMITH, Maj. _____	BRODIE, Charlotte B.	c.JUL 1811	AG:26/7/11:3
Place: Williamsborough NC			
SMITH, Alexander	_____, Rachel	-23 MAY 1796	HCH:55; 1787:75; 1791:23; 1799:8; 1800:52
SMITH, Alexander	SAID, Mrs. Susannah	JUL 1810	AG:18/8/10:3
SMITH, Amos	DAVY, Sophia	26 FEB 1814	AG:3/3/14:3
Place: near Germantown PA, d/o Wm. Davy			
SMITH, Augustine Jacq.	TAYLOR, Susanna d/o Jesse Taylor	23 MAR 1796	FPC:36(JM);SPC(61:2); AG:26/3/96:3
SMITH, Benjamin P.	PRICE, Matilda R.	6 APR 1830	MB; AG:10/4/30:3
SMITH, Charles	LLOYD, Elizabeth	25 DEC 1814	FPC:38(JM); MR(JM); MB
SMITH, Charles	BOWIE, Mary H.	c. 7 DEC 1818	MR(SC); MB
SMITH, Daniel	DUVALL, Nelly	FEB 1792	FPC:36(JM); 1791:23
SMITH, Daniel	STITLEY, Betsey	29 OCT 1801	FPC:36(JM); MR(JM); MB
SMITH, Edward	ROACH, Susan(na)	26 OCT 1817	MB; AG:30/10/17:3
SMITH, Fleet	HOLLIDAY, Jane	27 APR 1809	AG:13/5/09:3
Place: Winchester	d/o William Holliday		
SMITH, Hugh	_____, Mary	-1 FEB 1797	FPCG
SMITH, Hugh	[WATSON], Elizabeth	-10 OCT 1804	DBH:249; FPCC(41:30)
SMITH, Hugh	_____, Jane	-5 FEB 1807	OMP:35, 37
SMITH, Hugh Charles	KEIGHTLY, Isabella	29 JUL 1830	AG:7/9/30:3
Place: Liverpool	d/o Archibald Keightly		
SMITH, Isaac	WELCH, Mary	26/27 FEB 1806	AG:28/2/06:3(JM); MB; FPC:36(JM); MR(JM)
SMITH, Jacob	_____, Elizabeth	-8 FEB 1794	DBB:501
SMITH, James	MOORE, Margaret F.	10 AUG 1803	DBR:68; AG:15/8/03:3
SMITH, John	TRAMMELL, Lucinda	1788	FB; 1787:76; 1791:23
SMITH, John	YOST, Catherine	- JUL 1796	FPC:35
SMITH, John	DAVIS, Nancy	12 MAY 1796	FPC:36(JM)
SMITH, John	WILLIAMS, Dolly	13 NOV 1800	FPC:36(JM)
SMITH, John	_____, Agnes	-20 OCT 1803	WBA:177
SMITH, John	MANLY, Barbara d/o Elizabeth Manly	c.3 NOV 1807	MB
SMITH, John	WAY, Catherine	1 JUN 1809	NI:2/6/09; AG:5/6/09:3(Mc)
Place: Washington DC			
SMITH, John	JENKINS, Louisa	15 JUN 1825	MR(EH); MB
SMITH, John	LEWIS, Ann Elizabeth	5 JUN 1827	AG:7/6/27:3(Mc)
SMITH, John A.W.	McPHERSON, Julia Anna d/o Gurden Chapin wid/o Robert H. McPherson	18 OCT 1827	MR(WJ); CCC(81); AG:22/10/27:3; SP; AG:6/10/28; MB
SMITH, Rev. John C.	LOWREY, Jane d/o Samuel Lowrey	-7 OCT 1843	WB4:379
SMITH, John F.	KENT, Martha	20 JUN 1811	FPC:38(JM); MR(JM); AG:22/6/11:3(JM); MB

Husband	Wife	Event or Marriage	Reference(s)
SMITH, John F.	YOST, Rebecca	17 NOV 1808	AG:18/11/08:3(G)
SMITH, John K.	WHALING, Mary	c.19 FEB 1814	MB
SMITH, John R.	BYRNE, Sally	22 SEP 1825	AG:29/9/25:3(JR)
SMITH, John Thomas	GRIMES, Sarah Ann	26 DEC 1826	MR(RK); MB; AG:2/1/27:3(RK)
SMITH, John W.	HOUSE, Louisa d/o David House	28 JAN 1813	AG:29/1/13:2(RO); SP; MB
SMITH, John W.	CAMPBELL, Rebecca W. eldest d/o William Campbell	23 NOV 1829	AG:28/11/29:3(OB)
SMITH, John Y.	DORSEY, Ann "Nancy"	3 SEP 1818	AG:7/9/18(SC); MB
SMITH, Joseph	CRADOCK, Elizabeth	JUL 1794	FPC:36(JM)
SMITH, Joseph	SKIDMORE, Eliza	c.25 NOV 1817	MB
SMITH, Joseph T. Place: Hopewell Meeting House	ROSS, Hannah	11 OCT 1827	H:774
SMITH, Joseph W.	FINDLEY, Mary	28 OCT 1795	FPC:36(JM); TMCC(P:2)
SMITH, Julius	TENNISON, Mary Ann	11 SEP 1816	MR(JM); MB
SMITH, Madison	DELPHY, Matilda	10 NOV 1817	MR(JMH); MB; AG:15/11/17:3
SMITH, Robert	_____, Mary	-12 NOV 1800	DBS:341; 1799:12
SMITH, Robert	WATSON, Ann	19 FEB 1801	FPC:36(JM); MR(JM); FPCC(41:12)
SMITH, Samuel	_____, Mary	-15 NOV 1787	DBA:165; 1799:32; FDR:303
SMITH, Samuel P.	WOOD, Maria	1 DEC 1825	MR(WHW); MB
SMITH, Dr. Sidney W. Place: Washington DC	HESSELIUS, Rachael B. youngest d/o John Hesselius	1 JUL 1830	AG:3/7/30:3
SMITH, Thomas	WINGATE, Susanna	1788	FB
SMITH, Thomas	LEWIS, Thesea	DEC 1793	FPC:36(JM)
SMITH, Thomas	_____, Rebecca	-14 SEP 1803	AG:14/9/03:3
SMITH, Thomas	DEANE, Mary C.	26 NOV 1818	MR(JM); MB; AG:28/11/18:3(JM)
SMITH, Thomas Place: Georgetown DC	LUCAS, Miranda B.	26 FEB 1829	AG:2/3/29:3
SMITH, Thomas A. Place: Fredericksburg	SHORT, Priscilla T.	7 MAR 1810	AG:12/3/10:3
SMITH, William	DRINKER, Hannah	28 FEB 1822	AG:2/3/22:3(WHW)
SMITH, William	WALTERS, Rebecca	7 MAR 1799	FPC:36(JM); FPCG
SMITH, William	MORGAN, Sarah	19 JUL 1802	MR(JM)[97]
SMITH, William	GLOVER, Nancy	c.25 NOV 1802	MB
SMITH, William	CARR, Mrs. Margaret	c.18 JUL 1803	DBD2:25(HA); AG:18/7/03:3(EH)
SMITH, William d/o Leonard Smith	_____, Mary "Dolly"	-20 DEC 1813	WB2:125
SMITH, William	McKEE, Sarah	19 JUL 1822	MR(EH); MB
SMITH, William (C)	SOMBY, Nancy (C)	14 MAR 1826	MR(Sco); MB
SMITH, William C.R.	MORGAN, Mary	27 JUL 1805	FPC:36(JM); MR(JM); MB
SMITHER, Catesby C.	WEBB, Mary	c.27 JUL 1812	MB
SMOOT, Alexander	_____, Elizabeth	-3 JUN 1827	NI:8/6/27
SMOOT, Barton	BARTON, Polly	APR 1795	FPC:36(JM)
SMOOT, Charles Calvert	BRYAN, Sarah Walters	c.21 JAN 1824	MB; P:152
SMOOT, George A.	BLAND, Elizabeth	22 AUG 1817	MR(AG); MB

Husband	Wife	Event or Marriage	Reference(s)
SMOOT, George C.	EDELIN, Mary	15 JAN 1828	NI:16/1/28
SMOOT, George Hendley	WESTON, Mary	3 NOV 1825	AG:8/11/25(WH); SP;
Place: Washington DC	d/o Capt. William Weston		P:155
SMOOT, George H.	COOK, Mrs. Catharine	13 OCT 1829	AG:16/10/29:3
Place: Philadelphia PA			
SMOOT, Hezekiah	_____, Elizabeth	-2 JUL 1804	DBH:193; 1799:26;
			1800:58
SMOOT, Hezekiah Briscoe	McNEALE, Harriet E.	-26 MAY 1827	P:157
SMOOT, James Edgerton	LOWE, Phoebe Caverlly	13 MAR 1828	SP; MR(WJ); MB;
	d/o Rector M. Lowe		AG:17/3/28:3(WJ);
			P:156
SMOOT, James H.	BRISCOE, Barbara Mackall	29 AUG 1819	CT:4/9/19(WHW); SP;
Place: Prospect Hill, Charles Co. MD			AG:1/9/19:3
	second d/o Dr. Briscoe		
SMOOT, Matthew H.	SULLIVAN, Catherine	28 NOV 1822	SP;
			AAG:17/12/22:3(JR)
SMOOT, Wilson	HARGRAVES, Ann	7 APR 1807	AG:10/4/07:3(MLW)
SMYTH (also see SMITH)			
SMYTH, _____	HEWES, Mary M.	-24 SEP 1835	H:779
SMYTH, William	DRINKER, Hannah	c.28 FEB 1822	H:779; MB
	d/o George Drinker		
SNOWDEN, Samuel	LONGDON, Nancy "Ann"	7 JAN 1802	MR(WM); WB3:366;
	d/o John Longdon		AG:8/1/02:3(WM);
			MB
SNYDER, Mathias, Jr.	MARTIN, Jane	5 FEB 1828	NI:7/2/28;
Place: Washington DC	d/o James Martin		AG:11/2/28:3(A)
SNYDER, Mathias	_____, Elizabeth	-19 FEB 1850	TMCC(Q:2)
SNYDER, Richard	JOHNSON, Ann	29 DEC 1818	AG:31/12/18:2(Mc)
Place: Washington DC			
SOLEY, William	LIGHTNEM, Lenny	7 MAY 1791	FPC:36(JM)
SOLOMON, Samuel	PADGETT, Ann	c.25 DEC 1827	TMCC(M:5); MB
SOMBEY, Samson (C)	_____, Lettey (C)		1800:56
SOMMERS (also see "Summers")			
SOM(M)ERS, Capt. John	_____, Hannah	-10 JUN 1815	SPC(13:1)
SOMMERS, John A.	YOUNG, Susannah	18 JAN 1816	CWA:486; AG:27/1/16;
			SP
SOMMERS, Simon	_____, Elizabeth		CWA:486
SOMMERS, William	CASH, Mary	6 MAY 1819	AH:12/5/19;
Place: Washington DC			AG:11/5/19:2(Mc)
SOUTHARD, William	BEATLY, Sarah	26 DEC 1820	MR(SC); MB
SPACEY, John	TAYLOR, Astley	FEB 1794	FPC:36(JM)
SPADDEN, Robert	HENNINGER, Mrs. Ann	-6 JUN 1797	HCI:146
	wid/o Frederick Henninger		
SPANGLER, Daniel	_____, Margaret	-12 JAN 1803	DBF:234
SPANGLER, Samuel	_____, Mary	-19 NOV 1802	DBF:234
SPARROW, Henry	JAMES, Nancy	c.2 FEB 1791	GT:2/2/91
SPEAK, George	LOVE, Elizabeth	28 JAN 1819	AG:3/2/19:2(IR)
SPEAKE, Josias Milb.	_____, Sarah	-17 MAR 1807	DBQ:230
SPENCER, Capt. Benj. F.	HILLS, Prudence	7 OCT 1829	AG:9/10/29:3
Place: Washington DC	d/o Samuel Hills, of Baltimore MD		
SPENCER, James	BLADEN, Dorothy	10 AUG 1817	MR(WHW); MB
SPENCER, Jesse	SPENCER, Nancy	c.15 NOV 1817	MB
SPENCER, John	BOGGESS, Elizabeth	DEC 1793	FPC:36(JM)

Husband	Wife	Event or Marriage	Reference(s)
SPENCER, Thomas	_____, Alice		QM:52
SPENCER, William	HAISLOP, Margaret	1788	MB
SPENCER, William	EDWARDS, Elizabeth	21 SEP 1797	FPC:36(JM)
SPENCER, William (C)	LOUDON, Nancy (C)	c.10 DEC 1823	MB
SPIDEN, John A.	MARTIN, Ann	c.29 MAR 1823	MB
SPIDEN, Robert	WILLIAMS, Nancy	c.APR 1797	WG:12/4/97
SPIERS, John	CAMPBELL, Jean	-24 DEC 1782	HCA:26
	d/o John Campbell		
SPILLMAN, James	_____, Martha	-10 OCT 1814	DBAA:245
SPILMAN, William C.	OGDON, Ann	c.23 OCT 1824	MB
SPOONER, Holden [Walter]	BALLARD, Mary	10 JUN 1802	MR(JM); MB
SPRAGUE, Joshua	LEE, Susannah	2 SEP 1804	FPC:36(JM); MR(JM); MB
SPUNAUGLE, George	_____, Barbara	-23 NOV 1820	CCC(80); AG:13/11/24
SPURLING, William	CHALTREN, Ann	-10 SEP 1800	DBQ:149; FWH:172
STABLER, Caleb Bentley	MOORE, Ann	17 AUG 1825	H:783
STABLER, Edward, Sr.	ROBINSON, Mary	3 NOV 1757	H:774, 780
Place: Providence Meeting House PA			
STABLER, Edward, Jr.	PLEASANTS, Mary	27 FEB 1794	HV:92; OT:81; H:771, 781; QC; 1799:34; 1800:55
Place: Goochland Co.			
STABLER, Edward, Jr.	HARTSHORNE, Mary	28 JUL 1808	H:746; WB2:201; AG:29/7/09:3
	d/o William Hartshorne		
STABLER, Edward H.	JEFFRIES, Mary C.	21 NOV 1833	H:781
STABLER, James P.	GILPIN, Elizabeth	30 DEC 1816	H:783[98];
Place: Sandy Spring Meeting House			
s/o William Stabler	d/o Bernard Gilpin		
STABLER, Robinson	DAVIS, Mary Annie	16 OCT 1828	H:782
Place: South River Meeting House			
STABLER, Thomas P.	BROOKE, Eliza P.	2 JUN 1813	H:783; MGB:15/2:98
Place: Sandy Spring Meeting House			
s/o William Stabler			
STABLER, William	PLEASANTS, Deborah	4 JUN 1789	H:771
Place: Goochland Co.			
STABLER, William	HEWES, Deborah	22 OCT 1818	H:748; AG:31/10/18:3
Place: Chesterfield NJ	d/o Abram Hewes		
STABLER, Wm. Henry	THOMAS, Elizabeth	16 FEB 1825	H:783
STANDLEY, George	CHURCH, Mary	19 APR 1804	FPC:36(JM); MR(JM); MB
STANHOPE, John	GUNNELL, Ann "Nancy"		FDG2:428
STANHOPE, William H.	GARDNER, Jemima	27 DEC 1827	AG:3/1/28:3(JR)
STANTON, Richard	PERRY, Harriet	26 SEP 1811	FPC:38(JM); X:137; AG:28/9/11:3(JM); MR(JM); MB
	d/o Alexander Perry		
STAPLES, Samuel J.	BYRD, Mrs. Mary	c.3 OCT 1829	MB; AG:6/10/29:3(Sco)
STAUGHTON, William, D.D.	PEALE, Anna C.	27 AUG 1829	AG:3/9/29:3
	d/o James Peale, of Philadelphia PA		
STEED, Robert E.	LOWE, Mrs. Julianna M.	31 MAY 1829	SP; MR(WJ); MB; AG:3/6/29:3(WJ)
STEDLEY, Robert	ZOUCH, Permia	24 JUL 1800	FPC:36(JM)
STEEL, Horatio N.	RAY, Mary	31 MAY 1827	AG:4/6/27:3
Place: Georgetown DC			

Husband	Wife	Event or Marriage	Reference(s)
STEEL, Jonathan H.	ADAMS, Julia Ann d/o L. Adams	27 FEB 1823	MR(WA); MB; AG:6/3/23:3(WA)
STEER, Joseph H. Place: Fairfax Co.	MOORE, Sarah	29 FEB 1805	H:767; QM:52
STEIBER, Michael	_____, Margaret	-10 SEP 1800	HCN:284; DBD:22; 1787:75; 1799:8
STEPHEN, Peter	_____, Sarah	-23 JAN 1797	FPC:35
STEPHENS (also see "Stevens")			
STEPHENS, Charles	HAMILTON, Polly	4 NOV 1800	FPC:36(JM)
STEPHENS, Robert	BOWLING, Helena Eliza. Moxley d/o Ann Bowling	c.16 DEC 1824	MB
STEPHENS, Russell	SHUTZ, Catherine	9 SEP 1800	FPC:36(JM); CCC(31)
STEPHENS, Stephen	_____, Mary		1800:54
STEPHENSON, William	HOGAN, Margaret G.	19 JUL 1810	AG:21/7/10:3(F); MB
STEPHESON, George G.	PILES, Elizabeth	31 MAR 1828	MR(WJ)
STEPPER, George W.	PFISTER, Maria Magdalena	c.MAR 1827	NI:6/3/27
STERRET, James	MILLS, Polly	9 OCT 1803	FPC:36(JM); MR(JM); MB
STETHAM, William	DOVE, Alley	2 FEB 1797	FPC:36(JM)
STETSON, John	CLARK, Mary	4 MAR 1824	MB; AG:6/3/24:3(WHW)
STETWELL, John	BOSWELL, Sally	17 DEC 1807	FPC:36(JM)
STEUART, Thomas	KEY, Eleanor	27 JAN 1790	FPC:36(JM)
STEUTERS, Morris	MAYHALL, Betsey	c.8 JUL 1822	MB
STEVENS (also see "Stephens")			
STEVENS, Rev. Henry	BARKER, Sabilla d/o Leonard Barker	26 JUL 1825	AG:30/7/25:3(JR)
STEVENSON, John	SILENCE, Rebecca	23 DEC 1828	MR(IR); MB
STEVENSON, Robert	_____, Elizabeth		1799:38; 1800:57
STEVENSON, Robert	YOUNG, Mary	c.19 APR 1817	MR(SC); MB
STEWART (also see "Stuart")			
STEWART, Hugh	_____, Rebecca	-8 JUN 1818	SPC
STEWART, Hugh	ORR, Ann d/o John Orr	-1805	FX
STEWART, James M.	RAMSAY, Elizabeth "Betty" d/o William Ramsay	-9 MAY 1792	HCD:423; 1791:24; FPCC(42:64)
STEWART, James M.	TRETCHER, Elizabeth d/o Thomas Tretcher	23 APR 1812	FPC:38(JM); DBZ:201; MR(JM); MB
STEWART, John	_____, Cicily	-21 SEP 1795	HCF:325; 1791:24
STEWART, John	DOUGHERTY, Mary "Polly"	2 OCT 1797	FPC:36(JM); FPCG
STEWART, John A.	DUNLAP, Eliza d/o William Dunlap	9 NOV 1824	MR(WA); MB; AG:11/11/24:3(WA)
STEWART, Robert	WARD, Elizabeth d/o William Ward	17 SEP 1801	FPC:36(JM); MR(JM); AG:18/9/01:3; FPCC(42:64)
STEWART, William	_____, Helena	-18 AUG 1798	FPC:35
STEWART, William	HOOKES, Sarah Ann	c.10 JAN 1811	MB
STEWART, William	DOWNES, Mrs. Delia	30 JUL 1821	MR(SC); MB
STEWART, William B.	REED, Mrs. Catharine	2 MAY 1815	DBZ:464; FPC:38(JM); AG:4/5/15:3(JM); MB
STEWART, William F.	HODGKIN(S), Ann Maria	26 NOV 1829	SP; MR(WJ); MB; AG:28/11/28:3(WJ)
STIER, Charles Jean	_____, Marie Josephine A.	-22 SEP 1802	DBC:295

Husband	Wife	Event or Marriage	Reference(s)
STILLWELL, John	BO(S)WELL, Sally	17 DEC 1807	FPC:36(JM); MB
STITH, Everard	GRYMES, Eliz. Mary A.	19 JUL 1829	AG:27/7/29:3
Place: *Mount Chene*, King George Co., d/o George Grymes			
STOKES, John	_____, Margaret	-17 JUN 1790	AG:17/6/90:3
STONE, Capt. Charles	MARLE, Hannah	20 DEC 1808	FPC:36(JM); AG:24/12/08:3(JM)
STONE, Frederick	PATTON, Eliza(beth)	28 JAN 1819	AH:3/2/19(JF); AG:2/2/19:2(JF)
Place: *Clifton*, Fairfax Co., d/o James Patton			
STOOPS, William	_____, Elizabeth	-12 DEC 1799	HCN:45; CCG:A1
STOOPS, William	SMITH, Elizabeth	c.5 FEB 1802	MB
STRICKLAND, Daniel	TRACY, Susannah	11 SEP 1803	FPC:36(JM); MR(JM); MB
STROMAN, Henry	_____, Elizabeth	-24 JAN 1792	HCD:386; 1791:24
STRONG, John	SHEAF, Sally	c.16 FEB 1805	AG:16/2/05
STROTHER, James W.	FOLLIN, Letitia	18 FEB 1836	CWA:380
STROTHER, John	SOMMERS, Maryan	3 SEP 1816	CWA:380
STUART (also see "Stewart")			
STUART, Dr. Chas. Banes	THORNTON, Maria	29 FEB 1820	AG:2/3/20:3
Place: Fredericksburg			
STUART, Charles Calvert	TURBEVILLE, Cornelia Lee	20 FEB 1817	SPC(117:3); MB; AG:27/2/17:3(ON)
STUART, Chas. Townshend	DENEALE, Ann Lucretia d/o George Deneale	27 APR 1820	WB4:290; MR(ON); BR:116; MB; AG:2/5/20:3(ON)
STUART, Dr. David	CUSTIS, Eleanor (Calvert) wid/o John Parke Custis	c.1787	DBE:127 LV:95
STUART, Peter M.	RUDD, Elizabeth	c.27 MAY 1830	MB
STUART, William	_____, Mary	-14 JUL 1802	DBE:77
STUART, William	FORREST, Sarah	18 MAY 1831	MR(WJ)
STUBLE, William	COOPER, Margaret	-11 FEB 1796	FPC:35
STUDDS, Abram	_____, Elizabeth		MPC:W20
STUERTEN, Morris	MAYHALL, Betsy	11 JUL 1822	MR(EH)
SUDDATH, James G.	LYLES, Elizabeth	29 SEP 1825	AG:6/10/25:3(JR)
SUIT, Nathaniel	MAGRUDER, Mary	11 JUL 1826	UT:14/7/26:6(Mc)
SULLIVAN, John	_____, Honora	-27 OCT 1796	HCH:333; 1787:76; 1791:24; 1799:18
SULLIVAN, John C.	GUNNELL, Catherine		FWU:220
SULLIVAN, Owen	DARRINGTON, Elizabeth	c.3 SEP 1803	MB
SULLIVAN, Timothy	_____, Elizabeth	-2 JAN 1798	CRA:253
SULLIVAN, William	CONNERS, Honoria	26 JAN 1790	FPC:36(JM)
SUMMERS (also see "Sommers")			
SUMMERS, Francis	CHALTREN, Mrs. Jane wid/o Andrew Chaltren	-10 SEP 1800	SS:12; FWH:171; SC
SUMMERS, George	MOORE, Susanna d/o Henry Moore	-17 MAY 1772	FWC:149; FDM:271
SUMMERS, George	_____, Nancy S.	-19 JAN 1810	DBT:166; 1787:76
SUMMERS, John	DULIN, Elizabeth d/o Edward Dulin	-12 FEB 1778	FWD:298; FWD:299
SUMMERS, John	ZIMMERMAN, Maria d/o John Zimmerman	1 DEC 1825	AG:6/12/25:3(WHW)
SUMMERS, Samuel	BLACKBURN, Willianner d/o Lewis Blackburn	14 JUL 1825	AG:19/7/25:3
SUMMERS, Thomas	HOOPER, Rachel	2 SEP 1802	DBT:94; MR(JM); MB

125

Husband	Wife	Event or Marriage	Reference(s)
SUMMERS, William	ELTON, Isabella (Shaw) wid/o John Elton d/o William Shaw	c.1 NOV 1787	HCD:166; 1791:24; AG:1/11/87:2; 1787:76; HCG:477; CRA:242
SUNDAY, Jacob	_____, Sarah		1800:55
SUTER, Alexander	FLETCHER, Maria	2 MAY 1811	AG:4/5/11:3(G); SP; MB
SUTER, John	DORSEY, Sarah d/o Richard Dorsey	-16 AUG 1822	WB3:65; SPC
SUTER, Nicholas Place: Washington DC	COHEN, Margaret	1 JUL 1827	AG:10/7/27:3
SUTHERLAND, David	WEBB, Mary	c.15 APR 1816	MB
SUTTON, John	_____, Ann	-12 OCT 1789	FDS:146
SUTTON, John	PURDIE, Patience	20 MAY 1817	MR(JM); MB
SUTTON, John	SHRODER, Sophia	c.9 FEB 1824	MB
SUTTON, John D.	_____, Sally	-16 MAR 1816	DBBB:463; 1787:75; 1791:24
SWALLOW, William	MOORE, Elizabeth	5 MAR 1801	MR(JM)
SWAN, Lawrence	_____, Agnes	-28 NOV 1797	HCK:1
SWANN, John	BELLFORD, Ann	21 APR 1803	MR(JM); MB
SWANN, John Blak(e)	UNDERWOOD, Ann	15 FEB 1811	AG:19/2/11:3(G); MB
SWANN, Laurence	WALT, Ann	-12 FEB 1796	FPC:35; 1799:20
SWANN, Thomas	PAGE, Jane Byrd d/o Mann Page	c.1790	CCC(13); Page:101; 1787:76
SWANN, Thomas Place: Rich Hill, Charles Co. MD	COX, Sarah	5 JUN 1817	AH:11/6/17(MLW)
SWANN, Thomas	DREWRY, Mary	28 DEC 1819	MR(JF)
SWANN, Thomas Place: Lynn ME	MARTIN, Mary	12 DEC 1820	A:21/12/20
SWANN, Wm. Thomas	ALEXANDER, Frances Brown d/o Charles Alexander	12 JUL 1810	AG:16/7/10:3(FB); DBE2:316; MR(FB); MB
SWAYNE, Charles W.	SCHOLFIELD, Sarah Ann	18 OCT 1832	H:776
SWAYNE, George	VIOLETT, Mary	4 OCT 1817	MR(AG); MB
SWAYNE, John	_____, Sarah H.	-9 MAY 1816	DBD2:128; QM:52
SWAYNE, Joshua Place: Crooked Run Meeting House	SMITH, Rebecca	11 NOV 1786	H:785
SWEENEY, John H. Place: Fairfax Co.	WILCOXEN, Jennette Hooff d/o Capt. Rezin Wilcoxen	13 MAY 1824	AG:18/5/24:3
SWIFT, Alexander	_____, Rachel	-4 OCT 1796	DBZ:331
SWIFT, Jonathan	ROBERDEAU, Ann "Nancy" d/o Gen. Roberdeau	c.29 SEP 1785	DBA:239; 1791:24; 1787:76; 1799:38; AG:29/9/85:2; 1800:57; FPC:35
SWIFT, Jonathan	FOSTER, Ann		BR:127
SWIFT, Joseph G. Place: Wilmington NC	WALKER, Margaret Louisa	c.17 JUL 1805	AG:17/7/05
SWIFT, Wm. Roberdeau s/o Jonathan Swift	HARPER, Mary D. d/o Edward Harper	1 AUG 1815	AG:4/8/15:3(JM); BR:104; FPCC(44:142); FPC:38(JM); MR(JM); MB
SWILER, Joseph	McFADDEN, Elizabeth	8 JAN 1806	FPC:36(JM); MB
SWOOPE, Jacob	_____, Mary	-29 JUN 1809	DBX:330

Husband	Wife	Event or Marriage	Reference(s)
SWOPE, George	PATTERSON, Sarah "Sally"	-30 MAY 1807	DBX:326; FWL:55
SWOPE, Michael	_____, Eve	-23 MAR 1787	DBC:138
SYDEBOTHAM, Wilfred	GRADY, Ardry	10 DEC 1816	MR(IR); MB
SYKE, Peter	McFADDEN, Isabella	2 NOV 1809	FPC:36(JM); MB

Husband	Wife	Event or Marriage	Reference(s)

T

Husband	Wife	Event or Marriage	Reference(s)
TAFFE, James	DOWNS, Elizabeth ni/o Daniel Downs	c.3 JAN 1811	MB
TAITE (also see "Tate")			
TAITE, Nicholas (Similar Spellings)	NEALE, Betsy	5 JUN 1817	MR(AG); MB
TALBUT, Daniel	WEST, Ann d/o John West	-27 MAR 1776	FWD:25
TALBOTT, Elisha	SAUNDERS, Sarah d/o John Saunders	2 OCT 1806	DBR:269; QM:52; DBU:126; H:775; AG:3/10/06:3
TALBOTT, George Place: *Fox Hall*, Prince George's Co. MD	NEALE, Mrs. Elizabeth	4 JAN 1820	AG:7/1/20:3(Mc) SP
TALBERT, Henry	WOOD, Sarah	c.24 DEC 1803	MB
TALBOTT, Jesse Place: Washington DC s/o Joseph Talbott	LITLE, Hannah d/o John Litle	1 JUN 1808	H:761; WB2:225; NI:3/6/08; MGB:15/2:99
TALBOTT, Joseph III	PLUMMER, Ann	3 MAR 1772	H:785; MGB:15/2:99
TALBOTT, Levi	_____, Elizabeth	-12 JUL 1802	DBC:516; 1791:24; 1799:8
TALBOT, McKenzie	_____, Constantia	-20 JUL 1787	HCC:93; DBQ:468; AG:9/3/15:3
TALBURT, Mackinsey	DAVIDSON, Ann	7 SEP 1826	UT:13/9/26:3(WHW)
TALBUT, Sampson	JARBER, Cassandra	2 JAN 1791	FPC:40(JM)
TALBUT, Thomas	MOLONY, Mary	31 JUL 1798	FPC:40(JM)
TALBOT, Thomas	ROTCH, Winiferd Ann	10 NOV 1829	MB; AG:14/11/29:3(JF)
TALBOTT, William	LINDSAY, Mary	c.5 JUN 1817	MB
TANNER, Paul	WALKER, Mary Ann	DEC 1784	RWP
TANNER, Pierce Lacy	_____, Pamela	-3 JUN 1802	DBC:70
TARBRER, James	HARPER, Mary	7 NOV 1799	FPC:40(JM)
TARLTON, Henry Place: Washington DC	SMITH, Susanna B.	11 OCT 1829	AG:14/10/29:3(Sco)
TATE (also see "Tait")			
TATE, Benjamin	SMALLWOOD, Nelly	11 AUG 1803	FPC:40(JM); MR(JM)
TATE, Isaiah (C)	SIMMS, Patsy (C)	1 MAR 1815	MR(WHW); MB
TATE, Jesse	MITCHELL, Peggy	c.27 DEC 1803	MB[99]
TATE, Simeon	SMITH, Martha	c.23 JUL 1817	MB
TATE, Simeon	CLARKE, Cassandra	c.15 MAY 1822	MB
TATSAPAUGH, Henry	GATES, Margaret	7 JAN 1819	AG:9/1/19:3(JF); MR(JF)
TATSAPAUGH, John	O'NEALE, Elizabeth	c.31 OCT 1815	MB
TATSAPAUGH, Peter	_____, Susannah	-10 AUG 1830	AG:14/8/30:3
TATSAPAW, Adam	_____, Elizabeth		1799:36; 1800:57
TATSEBAUGH, Peter	_____, Susannah	-7 SEP 1792	HCD:459; 1787:76
TATTERSHALL, Thomas	BOYD, Nancy	4 DEC 1803	FPC:40(JM); MR(JM); MB
TATTERSON, Richard	HOOPER, Polly	1788	FB
TATZEBAUGH, Henry	HOOFF, Margaret d/o Lawrence Hooff	-22 OCT 1793	WB1:130; T0:300
TAYLOR, Bazil	LYNN, Mary	c.12 APR 1828	MB
TAYLOR, Calby	HUMPHREYS, Rebecca	31 AUG 1797	FPC:40(JM)

Husband	Wife	Event or Marriage	Reference(s)
TAYLOR, Charles	TATSAPAUGH, Rosetta	23 DEC 1830	MR(WJ); MB
TAYLOR, Daniel	WATKINS, Eliza	c.20 NOV 1821	MB
TAYLOR, Duke	JOHNSTON, Henny	24 AUG 1790	FPC:40(JM)
TAYLOR, Elijah	_____, Arina		TMCC(Q:1)
TAYLOR, Evan P.	LAWRENCE, Mrs. Rebecca	16 FEB 1813	FPC:40(JM); AG:18/2/13:3(JM); MR(JM); MB
TAYLOR, George	HOOKER, Love	17 MAR 1796	DBS:81; 1791:25; 1799:8; CCC(8); AG:19/3/96:3
TAYLOR, George	EATON, Mary	25 JUN 1801	MR(JM); MB
TAYLOR, Harrison	DENNISON, Mary	c.16 NOV 1829	MB
TAYLOR, Henry	GATES, Sarah	3 NOV 1799	FPC:40(JM)
TAYLOR, Henry	SKINNER, Mrs. Catharine	14 DEC 1826	AG:20/12/26:3(JR)
TAYLOR, Henry R.	PLUNKITT, Mrs. Jane wid/o Capt. James Plunkitt	17 NOV 1829	AG:21/11/29:3(WH)
TAYLOR, James	COMBS, Susanna	MAR 1794	FPC:40(JM); 1787:76
TAYLOR, Jesse, Jr. Place: near Winchester[100]	SMITH, Mary J. d/o Austin Smith	31 JAN 1793	HCM:267; 1799:10; AG:9/2/93:3(AB); FRM:224; FPCG
TAYLOR, Jesse, Sr.	_____, Elizabeth	-16 DEC 1796	HCH:303; 1787:76; 1791:25; FPCG; CCGB:24/12/87
TAYLOR, John	KIRK, Ann	18 OCT 1798	FPC:40(JM)
TAYLOR, John	CROOK, Mrs. Mary	c.30 OCT 1826	MB
TAYLOR, Joseph	JACOBS, Elizabeth second d/o Presley Jacobs	15 SEP 1825	AG:17/9/25:3(EH); MB; MR(EH)
TAYLOR, Joshua	HARRIS, Cornelia	18 MAY 1827	MR(WA); MB
TAYLOR, Robert Johnson	ROSE, Maria M. d/o Alexander Rose	6 MAR 1806	AG:7/3/06:3(TD); FPCC(41:22); MB
TAYLOR, Robert I.	BERRY, Molly Eliza d/o Lawrence Berry of King George Co.	3 MAY 1810	FPC:39(JM); DBV:492; AG:8/5/10:3; FPCC(41:22)
TAYLOR, Thomas	SHUCK, Sarah "Sally"	28 OCT 1802	AG:29/10/02:3(JM); MR(JM); MB
TAYLOR, Vincent	REYNOLDS, Margaret	1 DEC 1799	FPC:40(JM)
TAYLOR, William	McDOWELL, Susan		BR:95
TAYLOR, William	SIMPSON, Sally	3 MAR 1802	MR(JM); MB[101]
TAYLOR, William	POSTON, Ann Lucinda	5 MAR 1818	MR(AG); MB
TEBBS, Foushee	CHAPIN, Nancy Reeder d/o Gurden Chapin	6 MAY 1819	AH:10/5/19:3(WHW); CCC(12)
TEBBS, Dr. Thomas F. Place: Leesburg	BINNS, Margaret d/o Charles Binns	6/13 OCT 1818	AH:19/10/18(JD); AG:20/10/18:2; P:231
TEBBS, Willoughby Place: Dumfries	CARR, Betsy d/o William Carr	c.14 SEP 1786	AG:14/9/86:3
TELIFRO, Andrew	SULLIVAN, Polly	AUG 1794	FPC:40(JM); 1799:10
TENLEY, William H. Place: Old Point Comfort	TUTTON, Margaret W.	4 SEP 1825	AG:13/9/25:3
TENNISON, Samuel	MANKINS, Catherine	14 JAN 1802	MR(WM); MB
TENNESSON, Samuel	MARTS, Lucinda d/o John and Rachel Marts	c.7 FEB 1820	MB
TERRETT, John	DADE, Julia Alzira	6 MAY 1813	AG:12/5/13:3(WW)

Husband	Wife	Event or Marriage	Reference(s)
TERRETT, William Henry	PEARSON, Margaret	c.27 JAN 1735	P:377; DBR:138; FWB:181
TERRETT, William Henry	_____, Amelia	-16 APR 1793	FDW:190
THOM, David	_____, Mary	-5 AUG 1773	FPCG
THOMAS, _____	CROSBY, Rebecca	-4 NOV 1804	WBB:102
THOMAS, Bazil	LUCAS, Molly	c.24 MAR 1806	MB
THOMAS, Benson	TUCKER, Ann	c.5 JAN 1824	MB
THOMAS, Israel of Fairfax Co. Place: Sandy Spring Meeting House MD	RICHARDSON, Ann	2 APR 1754	MGB:15/2:98
THOMAS, James	BALL, Jemima d/o James Ball	-21 JUL 1833	MPC:W3; FM1835:69
THOMAS, James	SUDDICK, Penelope	6 FEB 1821	AG:15/2/21:3(JR)
THOMAS, John Hanson	COLSTON, Mary I. d/o Rawleigh Colston	5 OCT 1809	AG:13/10/09:2(AB)
THOMAS, John Valentine	_____, Deborah	-30 JUN 1798	HCK:607; DBA:498
THOMAS, Joseph	LOMAX, Mrs. Rachel wid/o John Lomax and wid/o Robert Jones	- 1770	FM/1770:96; FMI; 1791:25; HCM:2; AA:8/12/00:3;FDA2:311
THOMAS, Joseph	FARRELL, Mrs. Ann	1 APR 1809	CCC(37); DBY:419; AG:3/4/09:3(G); MB
THOMAS, Richard	_____, Mary		CCG
THOMAS, Simon	_____, Elizabeth	-14 MAY 1810	DBS:326
THOMAS, Simon W.	MONEY, _____ d/o Nicholas Money	25 DEC 1820	AG:12/1/21:3
THOMAS, William	HILTON, Mary d/o William Hilton	25 APR 1815	FPC:40(JM); MR(JM) MB
THOMAS, William	CROSS, Mrs. Malinda	15 FEB 1820	AG:23/2/20:3(JR)
THOMAS, Wilson L.	TUCKER, Sarah si/o James O. Tucker	c.27 MAY 1822	MB
THOMPSON, Amos	EVANS, Jane	-11 SEP 1775	CBL:23
THOMPSON, Andrew	_____, Nancy	- OCT 1812	DBW:304
THOMPSON, Andrew	SIMPSON, Elizabeth	20 APR 1826	UT:24/4/26:3
THOMPSON, Charles	BLADEN, Henrietta A.	6 JUL 1791	FPC:40(JM)
THOMPSON, Craven Peyton	TUCKER, Sarah Eliza d/o Capt. John Tucker	12 NOV 1807	MB; DBZ:27; CCC(45); AG:13/11/07(G)
THOMPSON, Douglas	CRANSTON, Eliza	30 JAN 1821	MR(ON); MB; AG:2/2/21:3(ON)
THOMPSON, Edward K.	_____, Sarah	-31 DEC 1816	DBC2:507; 1787:76; 1791:25
THOMPSON, F.	DAVIS, Mary	8 JAN 1829	AG:20/1/29:3(JR)
THOMPSON, George	GARDNER, Rebecca	12 SEP 1803	FPC:40(JM); MR(JM); MB
THOMPSON, Israel Peyton	ROBINSON, Angelica d/o Andrew Robinson	27 MAR 1817	AG:1/4/17:3(I)
THOMPSON, James	_____, Ann	-24 APR 1788	HCC:182; 1787:76
THOMPSON, James	BROONER, Barbary	c.14 FEB 1805	MB
THOMPSON, John	McCARTY, Polly	DEC 1795	FPC:40(JM)
THOMPSON, John	AVERY, Frances	22 AUG 1799	FPC:40(JM); 1799:20
THOMPSON, John	DAVIES, Mattey	25 AUG 1802	MR(JM); MB
THOMPSON, John	MANLY, Jenny	2 NOV 1803	FPC:40(JM); MR(JM); MB
THOMPSON, John	JACKSON, Anna	c.29 NOV 1806	MB

Husband	Wife	Event or Marriage	Reference(s)
THOMPSON, John	ROGERS, Sabina	27 DEC 1814	AG:29/12/14:3(B)
THOMPSON, Jonah	PEYTON, Margaret	-8 FEB 1793	HCE:79; OT:58; 1787:76; 1791:25; 1799:4; CCC(45)
THOMPSON, Joseph	_____, Ann	-18 DEC 1769	FDH:313(x)
THOMPSON, Richard	DONALDSON, Elizabeth	c.12 DEC 1809	MB
THOMPSON, Richard	WILLIAMS, Sophia	5 JAN 1811	MR(IR); MB
THOMPSON, Richard	HORNER, Lydia	c.27 MAR 1815	MB
THOMPSON, Robert L.	KITCHEN, Leah W.	9 MAY 1822	AG:16/5/22:3(JR)
THOMPSON, Samuel	SLACUM, Emeline	30 OCT 1821	NI:31/10/21(ON); MR(ON); MB
Place: St. John's, Washington DC			
THOMPSON, Woodward	BAGGETT, Frances	23 JUL 1811	MR(IR); MB
THORN, Rev. David	_____, Mary	-5 AUG 1773	TA:84
THORN, John	CLEMENTS, Winney	c.28 DEC 1809	MB
THORN, Thomas E.M.	SHERIFF, Elizabeth	24 FEB 1829	AG:3/3/29:3(GM)
THORNBERRY, James	ANDERSON, Catharine	19 DEC 1822	AG:11/1/23:3
	d/o John Anderson		
THORNTON, Benjamin	NORTH, Mary K.	21 JAN 1813	AG:25/1/13:3(M)
	d/o George North		
THORNTON, George A.	_____, Frances J.	-30 NOV 1818	WB2:266
THORNTON, George W.S.	BUCKNER, Margaret E.	21 AUG 1823	AG:4/9/23:3
Place: Auburn, Loudoun Co., d/o Ariss Buckner			
THORNTON, Joseph	_____, Jane	-22 NOV 1811	DBU:474; 1791:25; 1799:10; CCC(42)
THORNTON, Nicholas	CARNE, Susanna L.	29 FEB 1816	AG:2/3/16:3(ON); MR(ON); MB
THORNTON, William	_____, Mary Ann		CCG:A1
THRIFT, _____	TRAMMELL, Ann	-16 NOV 1775	FWE:148
	d/o Gerrard Trammell		
THRIFT, George	HURST, Elizabeth	-10 MAR 1787	FWE:350; FWG:310
THROOP, John	_____, Rebecca	-1 JUL 1800	HCN:193; DBR:349
THROOP, Phares	BONNER, Elizabeth	c.22 MAY 1804	MB
	b. 28 OCT 1779		
THROOP, Thomas S.	MANKIN, Mary Ann Elizabeth	2 FEB 1826	MR(Sco); MB; AG:9/2/26:3(Sco)
THUBER, Jacob	BOYD, Elizabeth	28 NOV 1808	MR(IR)
THUMBLER, George	_____, Margaret	-10 OCT 1785	FDQ:77
TIBBET, Walter	HUNTER, Ann Margaret	22 FEB 1827	MR(Sco); MB
TIGNELL, Major	WOOD, Louisa	12 JUN 1806	FPC:40(JM); MR(JM); MB[102]
TIL(L)SON, Martin Luther	GRAY, Frances B.	4 MAR 1830	MB; AG:6/3/30:3
of Plymouth MA	d/o John G. Gray		
TIMMONS, John	FIGG, Matilda	24 JUN 1816	MR(WHW)
TINGEY, Capt. Thomas	DULANY, Elizabeth Ann	c.16 DEC 1812	DBY:33; AG:16/12/12:3
	d/o Benjamin Dulany		
TINNARD, Joseph	HOWARD, Mary	5 NOV 1817	MR(JMH)
TODD, Charles	PEPPER, Elizabeth	JAN 1794	FPC:40(JM)
TOFFLER, Peter	SHUCK, Catherine	OCT 1792	FPC:40(JM); 1799:2
TOLBERT, Thomas	BURGESS, Penny	4 OCT 1798	FPC:40(JM)
TOLLSON, Francis	MIDDLETON, Sarah	18 SEP 1817	MR(WHW)
Place: Maryland			
TOLSON, Alfred	GANTT, Mary E.	15 FEB 1826	UT:23/2/26:2
Place: Prince George's Co. MD			

Husband	Wife	Event or Marriage	Reference(s)
TOLSON, Edward	MIDDLETON, Susan H. d/o Theodore Middleton	25 JAN 1825	MB; AG:3/2/25:3(ON)
TOOMEY, Martin	MURPHY, Mary	30 MAR 1790	FPC:40(JM)
TOTTEN, Mark	JENKINS, Violett	c.29 MAR 1824	MB
TOWERS, John	_____, Susanna	-8 APR 1800	DBA:417
TOWERS, Thomas	CHATHAM, Eliza(beth)	30 JAN 1806	CCC(54); FPC:40(JM); AG:31/1/06:2(JM); MR(JM); MB
TOWNSEND, Henry Place: *Hayes*, Montgomery Co. MD, d/o John Chesley	CHESLEY, Rebecca	11 DEC 1785	AG:29/12/85:3
TOWNSHEND, Samuel H.	LUMSDON, Catharine	28 JAN 1823	MR(IR); MB
TRACEY, John	MOONY, Mary Ann	1 JAN 1797	FPC:40(JM)
TRACY, Thomas D.	MAY, Sarah	14 AUG 1817	MR(IR); MB
TRAVERS, Capt. Thomas	COOK, Henrietta Ann ward of George Coryell d/o Thomas Cook	16 OCT 1828	UC:E61; MR:157; MB; AG:23/10/28:3(Gu)
TRAVERSE, John, Jr. Place: Baltimore MD	MOALE, Susan R.H. d/o Samuel Moale	3 APR 1816	AG:9/4/16:3
TRAVIS, Robert	WILLIAMS, Nancy d/o Elijah Williams	23 AUG 1820	MR(IR); MB
TREACKLE, John	ALLEN, Barbara	12 JUN 1797	FPC:40(JM)
TRESIZE, Thomas	MORRIS, Sarah "Sally" d/o Zachariah Morris	c.23 JUN 1802	DBE:85; MB
TRETCHER, Capt. Thomas	_____, Eleanor	-2 FEB 1811	WB1:258; FPCC(42:60); AG:25/9/13:3
TRIPLETT, Francis	_____, Elizabeth	-4 OCT 1757	FWB:195
TRIPLETT, Thomas	[DADE], Sarah ni/o Daniel French	-20 MAY 1771	FWC:134
TRIPLETT, Dr. Thomas Place: Dumfries	TEBBS, Margaret C.	11 APR 1810	AG:13/4/10:3
TRIPLETT, Thomas	PATTON, Jane	3 SEP 1819	AG:4/9/19:3
TRIPLETT, Dr. Thomas Place: *Springfield*	MASSEY, Nancy d/o Rev. Lee Massey	3 NOV 1825	AG:10/11/25:3
TRIPE, Thomas	_____, Carthrin		1800:56
TRISLER, Peter	_____, Priscilla	-12 MAR 1848	UC:W103; FWZ1:435
TROOP, George	CARTER, Ann d/o George Carter	8 NOV 1809	AG:11/11/09:3
TROTTER, Mark	JENKINS, Violet	29 MAR 1824	MR(WA)
TULEY, Thomas C.	COHEN, Mary Ann	22 AUG 1822	MR(EH); MB
TRUNNELL, Isaac	JANSEN, Caroline	19 OCT 1815	AG:21/10/15:3(WHW); MR(WHW)
TRUNNELL, Isaac	MARTINDALL, Eleanor	c.23 APR 1822	MB
TUCKER, Charles	BAGNELL, Catherine	5 AUG 1790	FPC:40(JM)
TUCKER, John[103]	MURRILL, Frances	-19 DEC 1803	DBH:71
TUCKER, John	_____, Susannah M.	-12 NOV 1808	DBR:447
TULEY, Thomas C.	COHEN, Mary Ann	22 AUG 1822	AG:29/8/22:3(EH)
TURBEVILLE, George R.	LEE, Harriot	-13 FEB 1797	DBB:190; HCI:245; DBV:153
TURLEY, Henson	_____, Cathrine		UC:SW47
TURNBAUGH, [Henry]	LONGDEN, Ann	-23 MAR 1803	DBD:513; 1787:76

Husband	Wife	Event or Marriage	Reference(s)
TURNER, Charles	WEST, Francina d/o John West	11 SEP 1791	WBB:506; FWX:328
TURNER, Charles	_____, Rebeckah		1799:26; 1800:57
TURNER, Charles G.	SHAW, Mary A.M.	20 FEB 1827	AG:3/3/27:3(JR)
TURNER, Henry S.	BLACKBURN, Kitty d/o Christian Blackburn	-5 JAN 1815	WB1:337
TURNER, Henry Smith	HOPKINS, Lucy Lyons d/o John Hopkins	-10 OCT 1871	CCC(27)
TURNER, James	COLSTON, Susan	c.5 OCT 1805	MB
TURNER, John	RIELY, Mary	26 JUL 1811	FPC:40(JM); MR(JM); MB
TURNER, John Place: Piscataway MD	WARD, Mary Ann only d/o Rev. Benjamin Ward	13 APR 1829	AG:19/5/29:3
TURNER, John W.	_____, Hannah	-23 MAY 1808	DBQ:35
TURNER, Joseph	_____, Elizabeth	-5 DEC 1798	DBB:304; 1787:76
TURNER, Walker	_____, Elizabeth		1800:56
TURNER, William	ELLZEY, Sarah d/o Lewis Ellzey	-1 OCT 1786	FWF:70; FWE:223
TURNER, William	WEST, Kitty d/o Thomas West	29 JUL 1804	AG:1/8/04:3(TD); MB
TURPIN, Capt. William S.	FORTNEY, Ann	30 JUL 1822	MB; AG:6/8/22:2(SC)
TUTTON, John	WILLIAMS, Ann	4 SEP 1803	FPC:40(JM); MR(JM); MB
TYLER, Charles	_____, Catharine	-24 APR 1816	DBC2:126
TYLER, Daniel	BINDER, Rebecca	2 JAN 1820	MB; AG:5/1/20:2(ON)
TYLER, Gustavus Brown	ALEXANDER, Ann H. d/o Richard B. Alexander	29 AUG 1816	AG:3/9/16:3(ST) P:228
TYLER, Henry	WILLIS, Mary Ann	5 DEC 1817	MR(IR); MB
TYLER, James	_____, Sylvia	-6 AUG 1808	WB2:295
TYLER, John Place: Prince William Co.	BROWN, Seignora	27 MAR 1816	AG:5/4/16:3(L)
TYLER, Joseph	JACKSON, Amelia	20 FEB 1817	AG:3/3/17:3(SP)
TYLER, Thompson G.	GRUVER, Mary Ann d/o John Gruver	21 JUN 1827	AG:25/6/27:3(RK); MB

U

Husband	Wife	Event or Marriage	Reference(s)
UHLER, Valentine	YOUNG, Catherine d/o David Young	-30 JUN 1784	HCB:406; 1787:76; 1791:25; DBA:137; FDO:354
UNDERHILL, Levi	MATTINGLY, Elizabeth	1 JUL 1818	H:765; QM:53
UPHAM, Giles	JENKINS, Ann	c.23 OCT 1823	MB
URIE, Arthur T.	HOWARD, Elizabeth	c.2 APR 1823	MB

Husband	Wife	Event or Marriage	Reference(s)

V

Husband	Wife	Event or Marriage	Reference(s)
VACCHARI, Frederick	PEARSON, Rosa	18 SEP 1823	MR(JF); MB(JF)
VAIZ, Anthony	STEWART, Sarah	26 MAR 1816	MR(ON); MB
VALDINEAR, Francis	PARKER, Margaret	16 FEB 1796	FPC:42-43(JM)
VALENTINE, John	_____, Mary		1800:53
VALENTINE, John	THOMAS, Deborah	-1 MAY 1799	HCM:21
VALENTINE, John	EVANS, Fanny	21 NOV 1826	AG:2/12/26:3(JR)
VALETTE, Eli	FLEMING, Betty d/o Thomas Fleming	-9 APR 1794	HCH:49; FDX:125; FDZ:486
Van DEVANTER, Dr. John Place: Georgetown DC	THOMPSON, Pleasant	4 JUN 1805	AG:5/6/05(B)
Van HAVRE, J.M.A.	_____, Isabella Maria	-22 NOV 1802	DBC:341
Van NESS, Lt. David	YEATON, Julia Ann Eliza youngest d/o William Yeaton	18 MAY 1824	AG:22/5/24:3; NI:22/5/24; MB
VANSANT, James	ABERCROMBIE, Elizabeth S.	31 OCT 1816	MR(JMH); MB; AG:2/11/16:3
Van SOLINGEN, Henry	HILL, Siloam d/o Laurence Hill	2 SEP 1828	MB; AG:4/9/28:3(EH)
VARNELL, George W. Place: Georgetown DC	GIBSON, Mary Ann Catharine	25 NOV 1830	AG:26/11/30:3
VASSE, Ambrose	_____, Sarah	-25 JAN 1815	DBBB:1
VAUGHN, David	FRAZIER, Sally	19 APR 1814	MR(ON); MB
VEALE, William	TURLEY, Lydia d/o Paul Turley	-23 MAR 1772	FWD:39; LWD
VEITCH, Alexander Place: Prince George's Co. MD, d/o Christian L. Hellrigel	HELLRIGEL, Barbara	11 JUL 1798	WBC:326; PGM; DBU:250; 1799:38; 1800:59; IGI; FPCC(42:48)
VEITCH, Richard	CREASE, Elizabeth Black d/o Anthony Crease	-27 NOV 1795	FPC:42; DBA:518; WB2:383; FPCC; 1799:4; FWM:283
VEITCH, William	PAGE, Rachel d/o A. & H. Page	-3 NOV 1808	DBZ:525; TMCC(M:3); WB7:63
VEITCH, William Conn	CHILDS, Sarah d/o Carroll Baker	c.15 NOV 1827	MB
VENABLE, George W.	PIERCY, Catherine M.K.	9 MAR 1826	UT:11/3/26:3
VERNELL, George	PURKIS, Sally d/o Thomas Purkis	23 JUL 1807	FPC:43(JM); MB
VERNON, William T.	JEFFERSON, Sarah E.	c.30 DEC 1824	MB
VERONA, Joseph	KELLY, Mary	-29 MAR 1795	FPC:42; 1787:76
VINTON, Rev. Robert Sp. Place: Baltimore MD	BERRY, Juliet Matilda d/o Benjamin Berry	21 FEB 1826	UT:28/2/26:3
VIOLETT, John	_____, Jane	-17 JUN 1800	DBA:492; 1799:20
VIOLETT, John	GRAY, Catharine	2 JAN 1809	DBW:529; MR(IR)
VIOLETT, Robert G. Place: Georgetown DC	ENGLISH, Louisa d/o James English	12 FEB 1826	AG:15/2/26:3; AG:12/3/30
VIOLETT, Thomas	GROVES, Ann	31 JAN 1796	FPC:43(JM); FPCC(41:27)
VOSS, Dr. Alexander	CHICHESTER, Milicent d/o Richard Chichester	15 OCT 1789	FX
VOSS, Nicholas	RICHARDS, Catharine deL. d/o Capt. Wm. Richards	14 DEC 1809	DBZ:271; VH:16/12/09

Husband	Wife	Event or Marriage	Reference(s)
VOSSON, John	_____, Ellen		1800:56
VOWELL, Ebenezer	ORME, Eliza d/o Col. Edward Archibald Orme	12 OCT 1813	FPC:43(JM); FPCC; AG:14/10/13:3(JM); DBW:195; MR(JM); MB
VOWELL, John Cripps	HARPER, Margaret "Peggy" d/o Capt. John Harper	28 OCT 1795	FPC:43(JM); DBC:269; FPCG; 1799:34; 1800:54
VOWELL, John Cripps	TAYLOR, Mary Jacq. (Smith) wid/o Jesse Taylor and d/o Austin Smith	6 DEC 1810	FPC:43(JM); DVW:1; NI:8/12/10; MR(JM); AG:7/12/10:3(JM); FPCC(42:44); MB
VOWELL, John D. Place: Baltimore MD	BROWN, Margaretta d/o Stewart Brown	8 JUN 1815	BA:10/6/15; AG:17/6/15:3(I)
VOWELL, Thomas	DOUGLAS, Charlotte (Orme)	3 APR 1806	FPC:43(JM); FPCC(42:61)
VOWELL, Thomas, Jr.	HARPER, Mary d/o Capt. John Harper	SEP 1794	FPC:43(JM); HCH:186; 1800:54
VOWELL, Thomas, Sr.	_____, Sarah	-16 FEB 1801	DBA:73; 1791:25; 1799:34; FPCG

Husband	Wife	Event or Marriage	Reference(s)

W

WADE, George	WILLIAMS, Sarah	13 JAN 1801	FPC:45(JM); MR(JM)
WADE, Robert	SMALLWOOD, Elizabeth	17 JAN 1811	MR(BN); MB
WADDEY, Thomas	COX, Elizabeth	23 JUL 1829	MB; AG:27/7/29:3(Sco)
WADSWORTH, Charles	FERRISS, Elizabeth	15 APR 1806	AG:16/4/06:3(TD); MB
WAGGENER, Andrew	_____, Mary	-22 SEP 1797	HCL:89
WAIGLY, George	MURRAY, Ann	c.22 APR 1830	MB
WAIR, George	_____, Joyce	-2 OCT 1816	WB2:164
WAITE, William	_____, Jane	-3 JUN 1767	FDG:263
WALCOM, John	_____, Mary	-17 MAY 1803	DBE:297; 1799:2
WALDEN, Thomas	STENTSMAN, Kitty	27 OCT 1803	FPC:45(JM); MR(JM); MB
WALES, Andrew	_____, Margaret	-10 DEC 1771	HCB:136; 1791:25; DBA:395; FPCG; FDK:302
WALKER, Edward	LEGG, Frances Ann d/o Eli Legg	c.31 JUL 1823[104]	MB
WALKER, George W.	SAVAGE, Penelope	15 AUG 1822	AG:17/8/22:3(JR)
WALKER, Henry	_____, Hannah	-1 OCT 1798	HCL:133
WALKER, James	WILSON, Elizabeth	31 JUL 1810	FPC:45(JM); MR(JM); MB
WALKER, James	WISE, Kitty	11 NOV 1813	FPC:45(JM); MR(JM); MB
WALKER, John	SMITH, Sarah	25 APR 1822	MR(ON); MB
WALKER, Levin	WILLIAMS, Margaret	30 JAN 1806	FPC:45(JM); MR(JM); DBE2:484; MPC:W54
WALKER, Robert	_____, Mary		1799:32; 1800:52; MB
WALKER, Robert	ADAMS, Sally	c.23 MAR 1805	MB
WALKER, Robert D. Place: Baltimore MD	STEVENSON, Mary E.	29 MAR 1821	AG:12/4/21:3
WALKER, Samuel P.	LEE, Caroline H. d/o Theodoric Lee	5 NOV 1812	AG:11/11/12:3
WALKER, William	PIPER, Jean	-21 NOV 1774	DBD:151; FWD:162
WALKOM, Jonathan P.	ROWE, Elizabeth	18 NOV 1820	MR(ON); MB
WALLACE, Benjamin L.	HOOFF, Julia Maria	27 MAY 1823	AG:3/6/23:3
WALLACE, James	DOUGLASS, Susanna Mary Ann d/o Dr. Charles Douglass	3 DEC 1805	AG:5/12/05:3(TD); MB
WALLACE, Jonathan	DODDS, Hepsabah Martha	28 MAY 1818	AH:1/6/18(RE); MB; AG:30/5/18:2(RE)
WALLACE, Nathaniel	FERGUSSON, Nanny	10 MAR 1798	FPC:45(JM); 1799:14
WALLACE, Richard	BALLINGER, Peggy	15 JAN 1801	FPC:45(JM); MR(JM)
WALLACE, Richard	GRIFFITH, Sarah	26 JUN 1816	MR(JM); MB
WALLACE, Thomas	GLANDERS, Tobitha	19 JAN 1804	MR(WM); MB
WALLACE, William	HENNING, Elizabeth	c.15 SEP 1827	MB
WALLACH, Richard	SIMMS, Ann "Nancy" D. d/o Charles Simms	2 MAR 1813	AG:4/3/13:3(JM); BPE:5/3/13;FPC:45(JM); MR(JM); MB
WALSH, Patrick	WHITE, Mary (Gird) wid/o John White	-4 JAN 1813	DBW:490
WALTERS, William Place: Washington DC	LANPHIER, Ann L.	26 JUN 1828	AG:30/6/28:3(RD)

Husband	Wife	Event or Marriage	Reference(s)
WANNALL, Thomas	ROBERTS, Mary	24 JUN 1816	MR(JMH); MB
WANSCHER, Martin	KELLY, Elizabeth	21 MAY 1801	MR(JM); MB
WANSHEAR, Martin	CHARLES, Margaret	20 JUN 1807	MB; DBS:36
WANTON, Philip	SAUNDERS, Mrs. Mary	31 MAY 1792	DBB:233; 1799:18;
	d/o David Pancoast and		DBU:152; H:775(F);
	wid/o John Saunders		QC; AG:28/11/46:3
WARD, B.	FITZHUGH, Harriet	4 MAR 1823	AG:11/3/23:3(WHW)
	d/o R. Fitzhugh		
WARD, George W.	FISHBACK, Susan M.	18 APR 1820	AG:27/4/20:3
Place: *Fleetwood*, Culpeper Co., d/o Martin Fishback			
WARD, James	MYERS, Prudence	20 MAY 1809	AG:22/5/09:3(JC); MB
WARD, James	SWALLOW, Hepsey	3 AUG 1815	MR(IR); MB
WARD, James	COATES, Lucy	21 MAR 1821	MR(SC); MB
	d/o Lucy Coates		
WARD, John	_____, Mary	-17 AUG 1793	DBR:451
WARD, John	GLOVER, Charlotte	12 MAR 1819	AH:16/3/19(IR)
WARD, Jonathan	_____, Catharine		MPC:E28
WARD, Jonathan	BEALLE, Sarah	15 JAN 1818	MR(AG); MB
WARD, Lewis	LAMBKIN, Eleanor	21 JAN 1830	MR(EH); MB
WARD, Thomas	YOUNG, Ann	23 DEC 1809	MR(IR); MB
WARD, William	_____, Celia	-8 JUL 1793	DBD:306
WARD, William	_____, Alice	-11 DEC 1811	FPCC
WARD, William	DODDS, Ann	11 JUN 1818	AG:13/6/18(HA); MB
WARE, John McKenzie	_____, Caroline	-4 JAN 1848	MPC:S31
WARNER, Samuel	REEDY, Polly	c.18 JUL 1805	MB
WARNER, Samuel L.	CLEMONS, Lyzyan	SEP 1792	FPC:45(JM)
WARREN, William	BRUNTON, Anne	-28 JUN 1808	TA:83; CCG
	d/o John Brunton		
WARRENBURGH, Andrew	_____, Sarah	-21 MAY 1785	HCOrd:21/5/85
WASHINGTON, Bushrod	BLACKBURN, Julia Anne	OCT 1785	JW; Y:316;
	d/o Christian Blackburn		WB1:337; 1791:26
WASHINGTON, Corbin	LEE, Hannah	10 MAY 1787	JW; DBC:281
WASHINGTON, Edward S.	ELLZEY, Ann E.	14 APR 1829	AG:29/4/29:3
Place: *Ithica*, Loudoun Co.			
WASHINGTON, Fayette	FRAME, Mariah	30 NOV 1813	AG:2/12/13:3
Place: Charlestown, Jefferson Co., d/o Matthew Frame			
WASHINGTON, Fran. Allen	MARKS, Nancy	9 SEP 1819	SP;
			AG:13/9/19:3(WHW)
WASHINGTON, George	HARTLEY, Elizabeth	c.25 JUL 1811	MB
	gd/o Elizabeth Semple		
WASHINGTON, George A.	BASSETT, Frances	15 OCT 1785	JW; R2:90(SG)
WASHINGTON, H.S.	GRYMES, Virginia	1 APR 1829	AG:7/4/29:3
Place: *Eagle's Nest*, King George Co., d/o Wm. F. Grymes			
WASHINGTON, John	SAUNDERS, Ann G.	3 DEC 1818	AG:5/12/18:3
Place: Leesburg			
WASHINGTON, John	CRACROFT, Harriet	11 MAR 1819	AG:13/3/19:2(ON)
WASHINGTON, John A.	BLACKBURN, Jane Charlotte	14 NOV 1811	AG:20/11/11:3
Place: *Rippon Lodge*	d/o Maj. Richard S. Blackburn		
WASHINGTON, John H.	ASHTON, Mary Ann	18 FEB 1825	AG:26/2/25:3
	d/o Richard W. Ashton of King George Co.		
WASHINGTON, Nathaniel	HAWKINS, Peggy	c.2 DEC 1790	AG:2/12/90:3
WASHINGTON, Richard C.	SMITH, Mary	13 OCT 1825	AG:22/10/25:3
Place: Baltimore MD			

Husband	Wife	Event or Marriage	Reference(s)
WASHINGTON, Richard C.	ROBERTS, Sophia May d/o John Roberts	8 JAN 1829	NI:9/1/29; MB; AG:10/1/29:3
WASHINGTON, Wm. A. Place: Princeton NJ	BAYARD, Juliet Elizabeth d/o Samuel Bayard	7 OCT 1823	AG:14/10/23:3
WASHINGTON, Wm. H.	ALEXANDER, Mrs. Elizabeth wid/o Philip G. Alexander d/o John Alexander	-17 MAY 1790	DBE2:301 FWE:373; BT:22/6/03
WASHINGTON, William H.	CRACROFT, Rebecca W.	21 JUL 1814	MR(ON); MB[105]
WATERHOUSE, Elias B.	CARTWRIGHT, Alice d/o Seth Cartwright	5 FEB 1818	MR(SC); MB; AG:7/2/18:2(SC)
WATERS, Jonathan M.	BECKLEY, Maria d/o William Beckley	c.30 MAR 1825	MB
WATKINS, Robert (C)	TATE, Eliza (C)	14 SEP 1809	MR(JM); MB
WATKINS, Thomas	ROBERTSON, Nancy	c.JUL 1796	WG:20/7/96
WATKINS, Thomas	WILLIAMS, Mary	12 DEC 1812	FPC:45(JM); MR(JM); MB
WATSON, Dr. George	RIDDLE, Nancy		OT:47
WATSON, James	LOVE, Elizabeth d/o Samuel Love	-27 NOV 1797	DBL:175; FX
WATSON, John	KEFFER, Mrs. Caroline E.	9 JAN 1830	MR(IR); MB; AG:13/1/30:3(IR)
WATSON, Dr. John	HOWE, Ann	8 JUL 1804	AG:17/7/04:3
WATSON, Josiah	TAYLOR, Jane	-4 JAN 1786	DBT:541; 1787:77; 1791:26; 1799:8; IGI
WATSON, Leven	ROBERTS, Kitty	2 APR 1800	FPC:45(JM)
WATSON, Thomas	WATTLES, Chloe	24 DEC 1803	MR(WW)
WATSON, Thomas	McDANIEL, Anna	c.14 JAN 1818	MB
WATSON, William	UHLER, Elizabeth	20 NOV 1806	FPC:45(JM); MR(JM); MB
WATT, Rev. John Gill	BINNS, Mrs. Dewanner	12 NOV 1816	AG:15/11/16:3
WATTERS, Rev. William	ADAMS, Sarah d/o William Adams	-20 DEC 1806	DBS:263; FF:224; DBAA:391
WATTLES, Capt. Nathaniel	TAYLOR, Betsy	26 MAY 1796	AG:28/5/06:3
WATTLES, Capt. Nathaniel Place: Newburyport	SMITH, Sarah "Sally"	22 OCT 1811	AG:15/11/11:3; MB
WAUGH, Albert P.	ATWELL, Rachael d/o John Atwell	19 SEP 1821	MR(IR); MB; AG:22/9/21:2(IR)
WAUGH, James, Jr.	HOOE, Ann "Nancy" d/o Robert Hooe of Prince William Co.	12 MAY 1814	AG:14/5/14:3(RO); MB
WAUGH, Laurence L.	_____, Sidney	-3 AUG 1827	AG:3/8/27
WAUGH, Townshend	JUDGE, Rachel	c.15 JUN 1813	MB
WAY, Frederick	SHORTELL, Elizabeth	27 NOV 1806	MR(IR); DBS:398; MB
WAYLEY, George	MURRAY, Ann	22 APR 1830	MR(LA)
WEAVER, Emanuel	WILSON, Eliza	c.18 NOV 1823	MB(ON)
WEAVER, John	_____, Rebecca	-17 NOV 1797	DBB:501
WEAVER, Samuel	HUNTER, Christiana	-13 MAY 1813	DBX:60
WEAVER, William	LEE, Juliann	c.15 APR 1823	MB
WEBB, James	PRICHARD, Mary	c.11 APR 1805	MB
WEBB, John	CONWAY, Hannah d/o Thomas Conway	-14 DEC 1784	HCA:133; FDQ:226
WEBSTER, Adam L.	HAND, Sarah H.	3 NOV 1810	FPC:45(JM); MR(JM); MB

Husband	Wife	Event or Marriage	Reference(s)
WEBSTER, Armstead (C)	MURRAY, Liddy (C)	2 JAN 1822	MR(ON); MB
WEBSTER, John	PEARSON, Elizabeth	4 OCT 1798	FPC:45(JM)
WEBSTER, John B.	LATHAM, Sarah	22 JUN 1817	MR(WHW); MB
WEBSTER, John Stone	LYNN, Mary	12 OCT 1786	HCE:26; HCK:114;
Place: St. John's Parish, Prince George's Co. MD, d/o Adam Lynn			IGI
WEBSTER, Philip	LYNN, Elizabeth	-24 JUN 1786	DBA:205; 1787:76;
	d/o Adam Lynn		1791:26;
			DBD:62; FWE:144
WEDGE, James	BROOKES, Ann	c.13 JUN 1820	MB
WEED, E.J.	M'LEAN, Arabella	27 MAR 1827	AG:30/3/27:3(RD);
Place: Washington DC	d/o Hon. John M'Lean, Postmaster		UT:29/3/27:3
WEEKS, Robert (C)	GASPER, Sarah (C)	c.23 MAR 1824	MB
WEEMS, Jesse E.	RICKARD, Nancy O.	23 JUN 1818	MB; AG:1/7/18:3(RE)
WEEMS, Dr. John	FRENCH, Eliza	7 MAR 1797	CL:10/3/97:3(B)
	d/o George French		
WEEMS, Dr. Mason Locke	SLADE, Ascenath O.	6 JUL 1829	AG:11/7/29:3(JeW)
Place: Bellair, Prince William Co., d/o Charles Slade			
WEEVER, John	ROBERTS, Eleanor	c.20 FEB 1806	MB
WEIGHTMAN, Henry T.	SIMMS, Phoebe	7 MAY 1822	AH:10/5/22
Place: Washington DC	d/o Col. Charles Simms		
WEIGHTMAN, John	LYLES, Sidney	2 JUN 1816	DBE2:430;
Place: Broad Creek MD	d/o Col. William Lyles		AH:3/6/16;
			AG:4/6/16:3(Y)
WEIGHTMAN, Richard	CHEW, Elizabeth	c.14 APR 1785	WB1:157; 1787:77;
			1791:26; CCC(38);
			AG:14/4/85:3
WEIGHTMAN, Roger Chew	HANSON, Louisa Serena	5 MAY 1814	DBD2:491; DCM;
	youngest d/o Col. Samuel Hanson		AG:12/5/14:3(G)
WELLFORD, John Spots.	NELSON, Frances Page	5 FEB 1807	DBS:179;
Place: King Wm. Co.	d/o Col. William Nelson		VH:10/2/07
WELLS, David	BOSWELL, Hannah	6 MAR 1828	AG:5/4/28:3(JR)
WELLS, John	FRIZEL, Catharine	4 JAN 1827	AG:13/1/27:3(JR)
WELLS, William	SAWKINS, Sarah	21 MAY 1811	MR(IR); MB
WELLS, William	VALENTINE, Elizabeth	28 JUL 1825	AG:2/8/25:3(JR)
WELTZ, Peter	GOWAN, Caty	14 AUG 1797	FPC:45(JM)
WENSHA [see "Winshear" or "Wanscher"]			
WEST, Francis (C)	JACKSON, Clara (C)	23 DEC 1815	MR(WHW); MB
WEST, George	GARDNER, Mrs. Mary	20 NOV 1815	AG:2/4/16:3
WEST, Hugh	HARRISON, Sybil	29 DEC 1725	HCC:186; FF:455;
	d/o Capt. William Harrison		FMI; FWB:74
WEST, Hugh	____, Ann	-20 SEP 1800	HCO:1
WEST, James	DUDLEY, Sarah	27 DEC 1827	MR(Sco); MB
WEST, James Craik	PAYNE, Eliza	22 AUG 1809	FPC:45(JM);
	d/o Col. William Payne		AG:25/8/09:3(JM);
			FO(1813):182
WEST, John	____, Mary	-19 NOV 1759	FDD:718
WEST, John	BAGGETT, Sally	19 NOV 1812	AG:23/11/12:2(IR)
Place: Fairfax Co.			
WEST, John, Jr.	COLVILLE, Catherine	-6 MAY 1755	FWB:97
	d/o John and Mary Colville		
WEST, Roger	CRAIK, Mariamne		BR:104
	d/o Dr. James Craik		

Husband	Wife	Event or Marriage	Reference(s)
WEST, Thomas	_____, Ann	-12 DEC 1783	HCB:420; 1791:26; FDO:316; FDQ:115
WEST, Thomas	GRAY, Elizabeth	24 DEC 1818	AG:7/1/19:2(SP)
WEST, Thomas Wade	_____, Margaretta	-8 JUL 1797	HCN:337; 1791:26
WEST, William	ELLZEY, Mary	-1 OCT 1786	FWE:224
WESTCOTT, James D.	_____, Anne	-5 AUG 1799	FPCC(42:58)
WESTCOTT, John	_____, Mary Ann	-1 JUL 1815	DBC2:32; FPCG; FPCC(42:58)
WESTERHOUSE, Rubin	_____, Margaret	-23 JUN 1787	HCOrd:23/6/87
WESTON, Clement B. Place: Baltimore Co. MD	DAY, Julia	4 APR 1816	BFG:6/4/16; AG:9/4/16:3
WESTON, Lewis	_____, Mary	-26 MAR 1795	DBP:177; 1787:77; 1791:26; CRA:151
WESTON, William	_____, Rebecca	- JUL 1812	DBW:189; TMCC(P:5)
WEYBORN, Horace Place: Washington DC	DARLEY, Susan	2 MAY 1830	AG:5/5/30:3
WEYMOUTH, John	FORREST, Sarah	c.18 MAY 1825	MB
WHALEY, James	GOODING, Harriet	16 FEB 1812	FPC:45(JM); MR(JM); MB
WHEAT, Benoni	NAPHLER, Mary	-13 SEP 1834	TMCC(R:4)
WHEAT, John Thomas	PATTON, Selena Blair d/o Thomas Patton	10 MAR 1825	MB; AG:12/3/25:3(ON)
WHEAT, William	FAGINS, Molly	7 JUN 1804	FPC:45(JM); MR(JM); MB
WHEATON, John Robert	_____, Elizabeth	-14 JUL 1794	HCF:118
WHEATING, Henry	_____, Sarah		1800:58
WHEELER, Richard	HAMMANTREE, Elizabeth	c.20 NOV 1810	MB[106]
WHEELER, Samuel	PARSONS, Sarah	19 DEC 1803	MR(WM); DBW:95; TMCC(J:1); MB
WHEELER, Samuel	WINKFIELD, Winefred	16 AUG 1805	FPC:45(JM); MR(JM); MB
WHEELER, Samuel	SUMMERS, Jane	24 JUL 1817	MR(IR); MB
WHEELER, Thomas	LUCAS, Catharine	16 SEP 1816	MR(JMH); MB
WHEELWRIGHT, John	PAYSON, Caroline Eliza	c.7 SEP 1815	MB
WHERRY, Benjamin C. Place: Richmond	HIX, Emily	3 MAR 1829	AG:14/3/29:3
WHERRY, Jesse	CHAPIN, Anna Howard d/o Benjamin Chapin si/o Gurden Chapin	7 FEB 1793	FPC:45(JM); B:234; AG:9/2/93:3; AG:16/4/14:3
WHITACRE, Caleb Place: Goose Creek Meeting, Fairfax Co.	GORE, Phebe	30 OCT 1776	DBH:334; IGI
WHITE, _____	BEALL, Cassia d/o Sophia Beall	-8 MAY 1782	FWD:326
WHITE, Hon. Alexander Place: Berkeley Co.	HITE, Mrs. Sarah	c.8 JUN 1784	AG:10/6/84:3
WHITE, Enos R. Place: Fairfax Co.	PEARSON, Lynna Ann R.	8 JAN 1825	AG:18/1/25:3; NI:14/1/25
WHITE, Horatio	DANLEY, Tracey Ann	20 FEB 1798	FPC:45(JM)
WHITE, J.M.	BAKER, _____	c.NOV 1797	WG:4/11/97
WHITE, James C.	BLUFFIELD, Elizabeth	8 FEB 1816	FPC:45(JM); MB
WHITE, John	_____, Elizabeth Anne	-23 JUL 1795	FPCG; 1787:76
WHITE, John	GIRD, Mary	DEC 1795	FPC:45(JM); 1799:14
WHITE, John	KENNA, Catherine	28 MAR 1798	FPC:45(JM)

Husband	Wife	Event or Marriage	Reference(s)
WHITE, John	HILL, Mary d/o George Hill	c.2 JUN 1804	MB
WHITE, Joseph	MANLEY, Ann N.T.	6 JUN 1816	AG:12/6/16:3(P)
WHITE, Joseph H.	MANDELL, Martha d/o John C. Mandell	3 JAN 1827	MB; AG:8/1/27:3(AH)
WHITE, Patrick	_____, Mary	-10 JUL 1809	DBS:279
WHITE, Raisin (C)	COLE, Faith (C)	30 NOV 1815	MR(WHW); MB
WHITE, Robert	_____, Sarah		1800:53
WHITE, Robert L.	NICHOLSON, Maria	18 APR 1822	AG:23/4/22:3
Place: Col. W. Hunter's in New York			
WHITE, Samuel B.	HUTCHESON, Ann	11 NOV 1815	MR(JMH); MB
WHITE, Thomas	HAWKES, Elizabeth	25 APR 1790	FPC:45(JM); 1791:26; MPC:E31
WHITE, Thomas	MARSHALL, Mary	17 OCT 1796	FPC:45(JM)
WHITE, Thomas	HAILY, Ann d/o Mary Healy	c.10 FEB 1803	MB
WHITE, Thomas M.	WOOD, Marian d/o William Wood	24 AUG 1828	MB; AG:26/8/28:3(Wal)
WHITE, Vachel	CALLENDER, Mary Ann ward of Gabriel Bradley	12 JAN 1826	MB; AG:16/1/26:3(JF)
WHITING, Carlyle Fairfax	LITTLE, Sarah Manly only d/o Charles Little	14 DEC 1797	OT:22; FDM2:348; IGI
WHITING, Fabius	YEATON, Louisa Toscan eldest d/o William Yeaton	3 DEC 1821	NI:7/12/21; MR(ON); MB; AG:4/12/21:3(ON)
WHITING, Thomas	_____, Mary	-12 DEC 1794	DBF:235
WHITTINGTON, John	LOCKE, Louisa R.	1 JUN 1820	AG:7/6/20:2
Place: Georgetown DC			
WHITTINGTON, Thomas	DEARBORN, Margaret C.	29 DEC 1825	MR(WA); MB
WHITTLE, Thomas	BUCKLAND, Mary	5 DEC 1816	MR(WHW); MB; AG:9/12/16:3(WHW)
WIGART, Andrew	DAVIS, Sally	29 OCT 1807	FPC:45(JM); MB
WIGGINS, William	OWENS, Mary	24 NOV 1799	FPC:45(JM)
WIGGS, John	LEARY, Sarah "Sally"	19 FEB 1829	MB; AG:23/2/29(Sco)
WILBAR, John T.O.	PERRY, Sarah d/o Alexander Perry	9 JUL 1816	AG:12/7/16:3(JM); MR(JM); MB
WILCOX, Anthony	LACOCK, Phebe	23 APR 1811	MR(IR); MB
WILEY, Ephraim	HISSEN, Phillis	22 JUL 1802	MR(JM); MB
WILEY, Hugh	BLADES, Ann	15 JAN 1807	FPC:45(JM)
WILEY, Hugh G.	WRIGHT, Mary	6 FEB 1816	MR(JMH); MB
WILEY, Jesse	HICKS, Anne d/o William Hicks	c.12 FEB 1814	MB
WILEY, Littleton s/o George Wiley	DEAKINS, Margaret d/o Ambrose Deakins	30 JUN 1803	MR(JM); MB
WILKINSON, Henry	HARPER, Mira	24 DEC 1806	DBS:44; AG:29/12/06:3
WILKINSON, Thomas	_____, Jane	-15 SEP 1783	DBS:44; 1791:26; DBO:33
WILLIAMS, Alexander	GRIGSBY, Eliza	25 DEC 1806	FPC:45(JM)
WILLIAMS, Charles (C)	TENLEY, Mary	c.8 DEC 1828	MB
WILLIAMS, Edward	DULANY, H.C.	5 FEB 1822	AG:7/2/22:3
Place: *Hayfield*	d/o Benjamin Dulany of Charles Co. MD		
WILLIAMS, Elijah	DUFFEY, Elizabeth	SEP 1794	FPC:45(JM)
WILLIAMS, Elijah	BEDINGER, Dolly	24 DEC 1797	FPC:45(JM)

Husband	Wife	Event or Marriage	Reference(s)
WILLIAMS, Evan	SELDON, Ann	c.16 MAY 1816	MB
WILLIAMS, George	BECKLEY, Betsy d/o William Beckley	c.25 FEB 1824	MB(ON); MB
WILLIAMS, Hampton C.	CHAPMAN, Frances Alexander	17 NOV 1835	FDS3:400; B6(PS)
WILLIAMS, Harry	WILLIAMS, Eleanor	c.10 SEP 1805	MB[107]
WILLIAMS, Henry (C)	_____, Elner (C)		1799:30; 1800:53
WILLIAMS, Henry	BOYER, Elizabeth	30 OCT 1806	FPC:45(JM); MR(JM); MB
WILLIAMS, Hiram O.	SIMMS, Matilda W.	21 DEC 1820	MR(ON); MB
WILLIAMS, John	BAGGOTT, Elizabeth	21 JAN 1804	MR(WM); MB[108]
WILLIAMS, John	GOLDSMITH, Catherine	23 DEC 1804	FPC:45(JM); MR(JM)
WILLIAMS, Joseph	KNIGHT, Elizabeth	3 JUN 1822	MR(ON); MB; AG:11/6/22:3(ON)
WILLIAMS, Joseph (C)	DARNELL, Priscilla (C)	26 JAN 1830	MR(LA); MB
WILLIAMS, Presley	ROBINSON, Nelly	14 DEC 1803	MR(WW); MB
WILLIAMS, Richard	EATON, Nancy	3 JAN 1822	AG:10/1/22:3(JR)
WILLIAMS, Samuel Place: Prince William Co.	PAGE, Eliza d/o Thomas Page	13 MAR 1821	AG:16/3/21:3(WHW)
WILLIAMS, Thomas	BOND, Mrs. Jane	1 MAY 1795	WBB:190; 1787:76; 1791:26; 1799:4; AG:7/5/95:2
WILLIAMS, Thomas, Jr.	THOMAS, Eliza d/o James Thomas	21 FEB 1802	MG:25/2/02; MB
WILLIAMS, Thomas	WILKINS, Lucy "Ann"	23 AUG 1818	AH:52/8/18:(JF); MR(JF)
WILLIAMS, Lt. W.G. Place: Tudor Place	PETER, America Pinkney d/o Thomas Peter	27 JUN 1826	UT:6/7/27:3
WILLIAMS, William	DAVIS, Sarah	c.19 JAN 1810	MB
WILLIAMS, William A.	WARD, Catharine	25 JUL 1820	AG:3/8/20:2(ON)
WILLIAMS, William C. Place: Fairfax Co.	MINOR, Ann d/o Col. George Minor	30 NOV 1815	AH:4/12/15
WILLIAMSON, John	_____, Lucretia	-1 NOV 1814	DBZ:55
WILLIAMSON, Dr. Philip D.	VOWELL, Mary M. d/o John C. Vowell	9 JAN 1823	MR(WA); MB; AG:11/1/23:3(WA)
WILLIAMSON, William	HALL, Jane	-17 JUN 1760	FWB:233
WILLIS, Abel	_____, Ann	-2 DEC 1808	DBQ:317; 1799:2
WILLIS, Abel	CHISHOLM, Mary Ann	15 DEC 1813	SP; MR(WHW); MB
WILLIS, William	McMANIN, Nancy	JUN 1794	FPC:45(JM)
WILLS, John	THOMAS, Ailsey	12 MAR 1816	MR(IR); MB
WILMER, Rev. William H.	COX, Marion Hannah	-15 SEP 1821	SPC; NI:20/9/21; IGI
WILMER, Rev. William H.	FITZHUGH, Ann Brice	5 FEB 1823	AG:11/2/23:3; SP; MB(ON)
WILSON, David	IRWIN, Hannah d/o Thomas Irwin	4 MAR 1813	H:752; CCC(B); AG:9/3/13:3
WILSON, Isaac	BROCKETT, Margaret d/o Robert Brockett, Sr.	5 DEC 1811	FPCC(41:9); BR:195
WILSON, James	TAYLOR, Elizabeth Johnston	21 JAN 1790	FPC:45(JM); OT:45; 1791:27
WILSON, Rev. James	CLARK, Mary	-12 OCT 1796	FPC:44; 1799:4; FPCG; FPCC(42:37)
WILSON, James	FLETCHER, Alice	29 MAY 1811	MR(IR); MB
WILSON, James C. Place: Georgetown DC	BALCH, Ann E.B. d/o Rev. S.B. Balch	18 JAN 1816	FPC:45(JM); BA:20/1/16(JM)

Husband	Wife	Event or Marriage	Reference(s)
WILSON, Dr. John Place: Leesburg	HARRISON, Juliet	2 FEB 1813	AG:3/2/13:3(MI)
WILSON, Joseph	_____, Chloe	-11 SEP 1786	FDQ:279
WILSON, Nathaniel K.	MOULDZ, Elizabeth	24 JUL 1801	MR(WM); MB
WILSON, Oliver	HEINEMAN, Mary d/o Jacob Heineman of West End	29 MAR 1810	AG:31/3/10:3(JM) FPC:45(JM); MR(JM); MB
WILSON, Richard	COFFER, Fanny B.B. d/o Mary Coffer	18 APR 1812	MR(IR); MB
WILSON, Robert	OTWAY, Margarita	-17 JAN 1803	WBA:161
WILSON, Robert Place: Washington DC	SYLVESTER, Caroline	14 FEB 1822	NI:15/2/22; AG:16/2/22:3
WILSON, Robert J.T.	RICKETTS, Mary Elizabeth d/o David Ricketts	25 DEC 1828	MB; AG:27/12/28:3(EH)
WILSON, Stephen	POPE, Hannah d/o Folger Pope	27 MAY 1819	H:771; QM:22
WILSON, Thomas	CRUSE, Mary H. d/o Thomas Cruse	6 MAY 1815	BA:11/5/15(ON); MR(ON); MB(ON)
WILSON, William	SMITH, Sarah	24 DEC 1789	FPC:45(JM); 1787:76; 1791:27; 1799:34
WILSON, William, Jr.	CARSON, Ann d/o Dr. Carson	19 AUG 1806	BFG:26/8/06; MB; FPC:45(JM); MR(JM)
WILSON, William	CHISSELL, Deborah	c.7 MAY 1811	MB
WILSON, Capt. William	MILLS, Mary Ann eldest d/o William Mills	20 APR 1819	AG:22/4/19:2
WILSON, William	GLOVER, Catharine d/o Thomas P. Glover	16 APR 1820	MR(ON); MB; AG:18/4/20:3(ON)
WILSON, William	_____, Ellender		1800:54
WILSON, William B. Place: *Mount Pleasant*	JAMIESON, Sarah Queen d/o Walter Jamieson	9 OCT 1822	AG:15/10/22:2
WILSON, Capt. William L.	WINTERBURY, Mary d/o John Winterbury	25 AUG 1810	OT:44; MB; AG:28/8/10:3(G)
WINCHESTER, Stephen	_____, Sarah	-14 OCT 1806	DBS:95
WINDSOR, Olney	WATERMAN, Freelove		AHy
WINDSOR, Olney	THURBER, Hope	-21 MAY 1811	DBW:18; 1787:77; 1791:27; AHy
WINDSOR, Richard	LOWE, Ann Magruder	c.18 OCT 1821	MB
WINDSOR, Richard W.	JENKINS, Behethelon		FPCC(43:103); FWV:350; FC#97k
WINDSOR, Robert N.	SHEPPARD, Sarah Ann H.	18 DEC 1809	MR(IR); MB
WINDSOR, William	SNELL, Susanna	11 MAR 1802	MR(JM); MB
WINN, Timothy	DULANY, Rebecca d/o Benjamin Dulany	7 MAR 1811	DBY:33; MB; AG:8/3/11:3(G)
WINDSHEAR (see "Wanscher")			
WINTER, Gabriel	PEYTON, Sarah Ann d/o Col. Francis Peyton	17 MAR 1818	MR(WHW); MB; AG:19/3/18:3(WHW)
WINTER, John	MOONEY, Mary d/o Neal Mooney	-28 AUG 1799	HCM:258
WINTERBURY, John	_____,		1787:77
WISE, George	MASON, Anna	OCT 1792	FPC:45(JM); FPCG
WISE, George	NEWTON, Martha	c.16 APR 1801	MB; DBT:148
WISE, George	MILLER, Elizabeth d/o Elizabeth Keys	13 JAN 1814	AG:15/1/14:3(WHW); SP; MR(WHW); MB

Husband	Wife	Event or Marriage	Reference(s)
WISE, George	GREER, Margaret	10 APR 1817	AH:14/4/17; MB; FPCC(44:132); MR(JM)
WISE, George	KIRBY, Ann	c.1 JUL 1824	MB
WISE, George Carr	FULTON, Mary Ann	c.23 JUL 1801	FPC:45(JM); FPCG; DBAA:16; MR(JM); FPCC(41:2); MB
WISE, George P.	NEWTON, Sinah Ann youngest d/o William Newton	12 MAR 1829	MR(EH); MB; AG:14/3/29:3(EH)
WISE, John	_____, Elizabeth	-16 SEP 1796	DBQ:98; 1787:76; 1791:27; FPCG
WISE, Joseph	FRY, Elizabeth	23 JUL 1804	FPC:45(JM); MB
WISE, Michael	WILLIAMS, Elizabeth	16 AUG 1791	FPC:45(JM); 1799:16
WISE, Nathaniel Seaton	McKINNEY, Jane Caroline	13 OCT 1808	FPC:45(JM); OT:48
WITHERS, Addison L.	BUCKEY, Frances T.	19 MAY 1829	MR(KA); MR
WITHERS, Reuben Place: New York	DUNHAM, Matilda A. d/o David Dunham	24 SEP 1818	AG:29/9/18:2
WIZER, Thomas	RIORDAN, Nancy	c.3 APR 1806	MB
WOLF, John	BERRY, Mrs. Elizabeth H.	25 JAN 1829	AG:12/2/29:3(GM)
WOLFE, Dr. Thomas	PATTEN, Mary Ann d/o Thomas Patten	14 MAY 1816	AH:17/5/16(ON); AG:16/6/16:3(ON); MR(ON); MB
WOOD, _____	SAUNDERS, Hester	-18 FEB 1821	WB2:424
WOOD, Benjamin	HARTLEY, Elizabeth	c.16 APR 1812	MB; DBW:208
WOOD, Benjamin Place: Albemarle Co.	ANDERSON, Jane Lewis	6 OCT 1819	AG:19/10/19:3
WOOD, Elijah	WESTERN, Sarah	c.16 APR 1812	MB
WOOD, James	MONCURE, Jane d/o John Moncure	-18 JUL 1795	FDY:141
WOOD, James	TURNER, Margaret d/o Margaret Turner	25 JUN 1823	MB(ON)
WOOD, John	FIG, Elizabeth	5 DEC 1801	FPC:45(JM); MR(JM); CCC(47); MB
WOOD, John	MYERS, Elizabeth	21 MAR 1810	MR(IR); MB
WOOD, John	HALL, Jemima	31 DEC 1811	FPC:45(JM); MR(JM); MB
WOOD, John	BAGGETT, Mary	5 JAN 1819	AG:7/1/19:2(ON)
WOOD, John	BURK, Maria d/o Mary Coats	11 MAR 1824	MR(WA); MB
WOOD, Richard	BAGGETT, Catharine	3 MAY 1810	AG:8/5/10:3(JM); MR(JM); MB
WOOD, William	PARSONS, Elizabeth d/o James Parsons	c.3 SEP 1801	MB; DBH:176
WOOD, William Place: Frederick Co.	RIDGEWAY, Margaret	27 FEB 1816	AG:5/3/16:3
WOOD, William	BOND, Susan Key	22 OCT 1818	MR(WHW); MB; AG:24/10/18:2(WHW)
WOOD, William	M'FEE, Maria	21 DEC 1819	AG:24/12/19:3(WHW)
WOOD, Wm. Wallbridge	DIXON, Mrs. Eleanor	19 FEB 1801	AG:20/2/01:3; WBA; FPC:45; MR(JM)
WOODARD, Joseph	OLIVER, Catharine	10 NOV 1816	MR(JMH); MB
WOODCOCK, William	HOOPER, Elizabeth	19 DEC 1798	FPC:45(JM); 1799:30
WOODFORD, William	_____, Elizabeth[109]	-13 SEP 1811	DBU:386

Husband	Wife	Event or Marriage	Reference(s)
WOODROW, John	_____, Mary	-20 APR 1796	HCH:337; 1799:12
WOODSIDE, Capt. Jas. D.	PRESTON, Julia A.	13 JUL 1819	AH:16/7/19(B);
Place: Georgetown DC			AG:15/7/19:3(B)
WOOLLS, Stephen	_____, Maria		MPC:E85
WOOLLS, William	_____, Ann	-9 DEC 1821	SMC; 1787:77
WORDON, Marmix	CURRY, Sarah	c.5 SEP 1825	MB
WORMELEY, Ralph	_____, Jane	-19 MAY 1786	HCOrd:19/5/86
WORMELY, Ralph	_____, Charlotte Fitzhugh	-18 DEC 1812	AG:8/1/13:3
WORRELL, Morris	SEWELL, Mrs. Elizabeth	-19 OCT 1786	HCH:6; 1787:77;
	wid/o William Sewell		1791:27; 1799:8;
			HCOrd:19/10/86
WORTHINGTON, Isaac	REASE, Catharine	27 JAN 1821	MR(ON); MB
WORTHINGTON, Joseph	YOUNG, Sarah "Sally"	c.10 NOV 1825	MB
	d/o Berthy Young		
WREN, David	_____, Eleanor	-1 APR 1798	CCG:A1
WREN, Hugh	WREN, Harriet	8 APR 1819	AG:12/4/19:3(WW)
	d/o John Wren		
WREN, James	BRENT, Catharine	27 MAR 1753	ANSC; IGI
Place: Overwharton Parish, Stafford Co.			
WREN, James	JONES, Sarah	c.4 MAR 1804	MB
WREN, John	HITE, Sarah	-13 AUG 1792	CCG:A1;
			FGRC(1977)1:71
WREN(N), Richard	HIPKINS, Susannah (Adams)	c.1799	DBI:196; FF:229;
	wid/o Lewis Hipkins, Sr.		FWV:321; 1787:76
	d/o William Adams		
WRIGHT, Daniel	MARR, Harriet Lee	17 DEC 1798	FPC:45(JM); 1799:36;
			FPCC
WRIGHT, George	COPPER, Charlotte	12 NOV 1815	MR(WHW); MB
WRIGHT, James	BLACK, Mrs. Sarah	-15 DEC 1783	DBX:102; 1791:27;
	wid/o Alexander Black		FDO:153
WRIGHT, James	PIPER, Margaret	c.27 NOV 1817	MB
WRIGHT, John	SOPHY, Jenny	29 DEC 1796	FPC:45(JM)
WRIGHT, Richard	HORWELL, Emily Malvinia	1 MAR 1828	NI:12/3/28; MB;
	fourth d/o Richard Horwell		AG:4/3/28:3(Gu)
WRIGHT, William	SHARP, Mary	1788	FB
WRIGHT, William	_____, Ann	-13 DEC 1792	HCD:474; 1787:77;
			1791:27; 1799:40;
			1800:52
WRIGHT, William	CONNER, Elizabeth	9 APR 1803	MR(JM); MB
WROE, Thomas	PILES, Linney	c.3 JUL 1804	MB
WYLEY, George	WHALING, Mary	24 NOV 1796	FPC:45(JM)

Husband	Wife	Event or Marriage	Reference(s)

Y

Husband	Wife	Event or Marriage	Reference(s)
YEAMAN, _____	EVANS, Mary	15 MAR 1797	BWM:19/3/97(LR)
YEARLY, Nathaniel	SMITH, Elizabeth	c.30 MAR 1807	MB
YEARLY, Nathaniel	BOOTHE, Nancy	3 AUG 1820	MR(WHW); MB
YEATES, William Place: Fairfax Meeting House	CAVIN, Sarah	6 MAR 1814	H:736; FMI
YEATES, William	MONEY, Sarah d/o Nicholas Money	-14 MAR 1799	FWG:433
YEATES, William, Jr.	_____, Hannah		QM:53
YEATON, Joshua Place: Bermuda	PRUDDEN, R.	25 OCT 1817	AG:27/11/17:3
YEATON, William	_____, Sally	-23 SEP 1802	DBC:368; FPCG; AG:29/7/03:3
YEATON, William Place: Portsmouth NH	CHAUNCEY, Lucia[110] d/o Hon. Charles Chauncey	c.14 DEC 1805	DBQ:127; PM:7; CCC(116); AG:14/12/05:3
YOST, John	_____, Rebecca	-26 JUN 1798	DBR:433; 1787:77; 1791:27; FPCG
YOUNG, _____	FRIZZELL, Comfort d/o William Frizzell	-29 JUL 1767	FWC:48
YOUNG, Charles Place: Georgetown DC	DABNEY, Polly	8 SEP 1796	AG:10/9/96:3
YOUNG, David	_____, Nancy	-21 JUL 1787	HCOrd:21/7/87
YOUNG, Henry	HUNTER, Amelia T. d/o Gen. John C. Hunter	3 JUN 1823	NI:6/6/23
YOUNG, James	_____, Mary	-7 NOV 1796	FPC:46; FPCG; 1787:77; AG:22/12/15:3
YOUNG, John	_____, Rebecca	-15 JUL 1806	FPCG; CCG:T2
YOUNG, John	DAVIS, Mary	18 JUN 1807	AG:19/6/07:3; MB
YOUNG, Manduit	BELL, Eliza T.	9 DEC 1813	AG:11/12/13:3(MB)
YOUNG, Nicholas	_____, Nancy	-30 MAR 1810	DBS:352
YOUNG, Notley	_____, Mary	-19 OCT 1798	HCK:599
YOUNG, Gen. Robert	CONRAD, Elizabeth	c.SEP 1800	DBP:496; FPC:46; FPCC(42:53)
YOUNG, William	_____, Eleanor	-16 JUN 1767	FDG:239
YOUNG, William	FARRELL, Ann	AUG 1794	FPC:47(JM); 1791:28
YOUNG, William	SULLIVAN, Ellen	9 JUN 1815	MR(JMH); MB
YOUST, Hiram	BRENT, Nancy d/o Sarah Brent	c.19 SEP 1825	MB

Husband	Wife	Event or Marriage	Reference(s)
ZEPPERNICK, _____	_____, Mariana	-20 MAY 1810	FPCG; AG:21/5/10:3
ZIMMERMAN, Adam	SIMPSON, Sinah E.	18 DEC 1817	MR(JMH); MB
ZIMMERMAN, George	SIMPSON, Ann	24 AUG 1806	MR(JM); MB
ZIMMERMAN, Jacob	SMITH, Nelly	10 JAN 1808	FPC:49(JM)
ZIMMERMAN, Jacob	SMITH, Jane	22 MAR 1810	FPC:49(JM); MR(JM); MB
ZIMMERMAN, Jacob	FREDERICK, Emily	8 JUL 1829	SP; MR(WJ); MB
ZIMMERMAN, Lodowick	_____, Mary	-28 JUL 1784	FDP:5
ZIMMERMAN, Tobias	_____, Elizabeth	-22 MAY 1794	HCH:115; 1787:77

Z

END NOTES

1. West River Meeting was located near West River in southern Anne Arundel Co. MD, and was also located near the Calvert Clifts, a range of bluffs fronting on the bay.

2. There were two known reverends named Balch. Rev. Stephen Bloomer Balch of the Presbyterian Church of Georgetown and Washington, D.C., d. 22 SEP 1833; and Reverend Thomas B. Balch of Maryland.

3. Piscataway Parish, Accokeek, Prince George's Co. MD; IGI also gives St. John's Parish.

4. Newspaper notice gives name of the bride as Mary Hyees.

5. Amos Alexander was owner of lot 7, section 41 of the First Presbyterian Church Cemetery on Hamilton Lane off Wilkes Street. Since there are no tombstones visible in this lot, it is uncertain whether he was actually buried there. His obituary in the Phenix Alexandria Gazette (Alexandria, 11 SEP 1826), p. 3, indicates he was buried in the cemetery next to the grand lodge of the District of Columbia of which he was a member. The location of this burial place has not been identified.

6. Library of Virginia, Legislative Petitions, Alexandria City, #A482, Phebe Caverley [sic] divorced from Joseph Caverley. She remarried 29 FEB 1796 to Capt. Stephen Moore.

7. Consent slip attached to marriage bond is signed by Alisabeth [her mark] Chisam, and states that *Alisabeth Chisam was bornd in the year of 1781 march the 4th & daughter of wiliam chisam and alisabeth chisam.*

8. The Alexandria Advertiser & Commercial Intelligencer, of 8 APR 1803, indicates Miss Birch was a daughter of Mr. William Birch of *Spring Lands*, near Philadelphia PA.

9. Minister return by Seely Bunn is filed with the marriage bonds.

10. Marriage bond gives name of prospective groom as James Barry.

11. Newspaper in error gives marriage date as 5 FEB 1822.

12. Minister return appears to give bride's surname as "Emery."

13. Hinshaw, gives 28 APR 1791, yet the West River Register gives "the 4th month the 20th day in 1791."

14. Arlington Co. chancery file, Mills v. McKnight.

15. Newspaper announcement gives name of the groom as Ignatius Carusi.

16. Marriage record appears to give her surname as Robertson.

17. Date is engraved on a silver snuff box owned by Charles Williams, acquired from an auction in Philadelphia PA.

18. Alexandria Gazette, Commercial & Political, 26 SEP 1816. Died in England in December last [1815], Mr. Horatio Clagett, a native of Maryland, who was a meritorious officer in the American army during the entire revolutionary war, and for nearly the whole time since the peace of 1783, a respectable merchant and underwriter in London.

19. Attached to the bond is a slip of paper, thus: "I have given my man Joseph Colston leave to Marry again as he has been seperated from his former Wife for four Years, this is from under my hand this 3 day of May 1806. [signed] Reba. Flannery.

20. Bond shows that prospective groom signs as "Antonio Correia."

21. Arlington Historical Society Magazine, Volume 6 Number 1 (1977), page 25; Ancestral Records and Portraits (Baltimore: Genealogical Publishing Co., 1969), Volume II, p. 656.

22. Minister return appears to give the bride's surname as Fullerton.

23. Consent for the marriage given in writing by Peter Tertzbaugh, guardian of Mary Coons [sic].

24. It is interesting to note that the bondsman Frederick Churchman signs his name Fredrick Kerchner.

25. Minister return gives name of bride as Eve Frederickson.

26. A slip attached to the bond shows that Alexander Moore makes oath that Maria Rooe is free and was liberated by Leonard Marbury. Another slip notes that Philip Dogan makes oath that Anthony Dogan, his son, was born since the liberation of his mother and is now free.

27. Newspaper notice gives name of groom as James Doughterty, and marriage date 15 DEC 1818.

28. Henry C. Peden, Jr., Methodist Records of Baltimore City, Maryland, Volume 1, 1799-1829 (Westminster MD: Family Line Publications, 1994), p. 29. For marriages performed by ministers of the Methodist Episcopal Church. Editor notes that the marriage notice in the Baltimore American, of November 6, 1810, gives groom's name as Gilson Dove, and bride's name as Mary Drugan.

29. License was issued in Prince William Co., and notes that the celebration occurred the same day by Rev. O. Norris.

30. Will of John C. Ehlers indicates he is a gardener at Mount Vernon. See Alexandria Will Book 2, page 415.

31. Although the face of the bond gives year 1819, it is marked 1820 on the outside.

32. Bond is dated 23 JUN 1823.

33. Also see Brockett's Lodge of Washington, p. 147. Mary W. Butts is daughter of Mark Butts; burials in Oak Hill Cemetery of Georgetown, D.C., Lot 743.

34. The 1799 city census of the 2nd ward, shows Philip Fernow and wife (not named), carpenter, with two children.

35. Attached to the bond is a slip of paper, thus: "I have given my man Joseph Colston leave to Marry again as he has been seperated from his former Wife for four Years, this is from under my hand this 3 day of May 1806. [signed] Reba. Flannery.

36. Graveyards of Arlington County, Virginia, by the Arlington Genealogy Club (1985), p. 79; evidence of a Reintzel family Bible can be found on the Internet.

37. Jesus Christ Church of Latter Day Saints, Family Search, Pedigree Resource File #21/207282.

38. St. Paul's Episcopal Church, Baltimore MD, transcript of record, page 504, at the Maryland Historical Society.

39. Mary G. Powell, George Washington's Last Guard of Honor, no page, sketch of Col. George Gilpin.

40. Prince George's Co. MD Land Records, Liber BB#2, folio 42-4.

41. The First Presbyterian Church record gives the groom name Francis Gonsalves; yet a marriage announcement in the Alexandria Daily Gazette, Commercial & Political, of 22 FEB 1811, indicates Capt. Samuel Gonsoloe was married to Miss Mary Byrne, daughter of Patrick Byrne, toll-keeper.

42. Although on the face of the bond the year is 1817, it is marked 1818 on the outside.

43. Bond in error gives name of the bride as William Patterson.

44. Virginia Genealogist, Volume 25 Number 4 (1981), page 296.

45. Martha Gunnell witnessed the will of Richard Lee, written March 3, 1714; Westmoreland Co. Deeds & Wills No. 5, 1712-1716, pp. 445-50. Gunnell members mentioned in the estate inventory of Richard Lee are William Gunnell, Mary Gunnell, Martha Gunnell, and William Gunnell, Jr. Also see Westmoreland Co. Court Order Bk. 1705-1721, p. 346a.

46. Slips filed with the marriage bond show: (1) "The Bearer Known to me by the name of Spencer was entitled to his Freedom on arriving at the age of Twenty one, being one of a family of negroes formerly belonging to Mr. John Ward. [signed] Thomas Moore, [witnessed] Sarah Grant. Dated 27 JUL 1813; (2) I certify that I have known Sarah Grant Ever since she was a small girl allways under stood and believe her to be a Free girl. [signed] Thos. Jacob. Dated July 29th, 1813.

47. As part of the bond, a letter describes Mr. Harris' character. The letter is signed by Saml. Bayly, Sinah Wagener and Cornelius Wells. It describes that Hugh Harris, a bright Mulatto about twenty-one years old, was born in the Town of Colchester; his father was a free Mulatto who served William Bayly twenty one years; his mother was a Scotch woman Indented and consigned to this town to Hector Ross, Esq. That Harris is about 5 feet two inches high and tolerably well set, short-black curley hair. The said Hugh Harris' mother is Catherine Monroe who has served her full time and married to William Harris of Colchester. Hugh was born free.

48. Fairfax County Superior Court Wills, page 62.

49. Hinshaw, gives month as March, yet this date from the newspaper notice.

50. Minister return by Rev. Oliver Norris, gives bride's name as Rebecca Duty, and may also seen as Dougherty.

51. Mary Steele in the baptism record of the same register.

52. Violetta also went by the surname of Barnes.

53. Included with the marriage bond is a slip that states: The bearer Israel Jasper is a free man, he belonged to the Geo. Washington estate and was left free by the Gen. He served several years with me. S. Snowden, Alexa., Aug. 8th, 1811. Another slip gives a similar statement about the bride (spelling preserved): "The bearer Winny Dey, to my knoledge is a free Women: born in Charels [sic] County, Maryland. She lived in the Family of Mr. Theodore Dent till within this two years, in that County. [signed] C. Hunter.

54. First Presbyterian Church Cemetery, section 42, lot 69, tombstone indicates "Newton Keene, youngest son of Newton / and Sarah Edwards Keene, born at Cherry Point / Northumberland Co., Va., died Sept. 21, 1841."

55. Alexandria Gazette, Commercial and Political, 1 JAN 1814. Died at Charleston, South Carolina, on Tuesday the 14th inst. [i.e. 14 DEC 1813], the Reverend Dr. Isaac Stockton Keith ...The deceased was well known in Alexandria. He officiated as their pastor in the Presbyterian Church from the year 1780 for eight years.

56. Columbian Mirror and Alexandria Advertiser, 22 MAR 1796, gives names of parties as Damilian Kinsbury and Ann Harding.

57. John Gardner Ladd and Capt. William Ladd were natives of Rhode Island.

58. Marriage performed by Jeremiah Moore.

59. Prince George's Co. MD Land Records, Liber BB#2, folio 42-4.

60. Prince George's Co. MD Land Records, Liber BB#2, folio 42-4.

61. Attached to the bond is a slip, "Miss Salome Way Was Born the 29th of May 1784 in York, Pennsylvania. [signed] Fredk. Way.

62. Basil Barnes of Swan Creek Neck, Prince George's Co. MD.

63. Also found in published Fluvanna Co., Va. Marriages, 1777-1858.

64. Signature of prospective groom appears like "John Obelusby."

65. License issued in Loudoun Co., shows John Lloyd is of Shelburne Parish.

66. Her name is often found spelled Harriot.

67. Mary G. Powell, George Washington's Last Guard of Honor, no page, sketch on Philip Marsteller; Linda Crocker Simmons, Jacob Frymire, an American Limner (An Exhibition Organized by the Corcoran Gallery of Art, Washington, D.C.) (1975), page 26.

68. Columbian Mirror and Alexandria Advertiser, of 19 JAN 1793, gives the name of the bride as Miss Catharine Copper.

69. The United States' Telegraph newspaper gives name of the bride as Julia Smethers.

70. The Alexandria Gazette & Advertiser gives the name the bride as Eleanor Ann Patton, daughter of Robt. Patton, of Spring Bank, Fairfax Co., Va.

71. Bond gives name of bride as Nancy Oldery.

72. Newspaper announcement in the Phenix Alexandria Gazette, of 30 JAN 1827, gives name of groom as James Matthias.

73. Marriage bond gives surname of the bride as "Sellers."

74. Spelling used on his grave marker in Trinity Methodist Church Cemetery, Wilkes Street.

75. Mr. N. McInteer, merchant of Warrenton, married to Miss Mary Alexander of Dumfries.

76. Minutes of West River Meeting MD, as in Maryland Genealogical Society Magazine, Volume 14, page 4.

77. Edmund J. Lee and Thomas Swann, sureties.

78. John Mercer, Esq., of West River MD. Newspaper gives date of 22 JUN 1818.

79. Fairfax Co. Minute Bk., 1829, p. 194; Fairfax Co. Chancery File #42j, Hunter v. Powell (1840).

80. Rev. James Muir, born Cumnock, Scotland on April 12, 1757, was son of Rev. George Muir, educated at Glasgow University in 1776, minister in Bermuda 1782-1787, minister in Virginia 1789 until death in 1820. See David Dobson's Emigrants and Adventurers From Glasgow and the West of Scotland, page 19.

81. Marriage notice in the Phenix Alexandria Gazette, of 22 OCT 1826, gives groom's name as Josiah T. Myers.

82. Marriage date from the First Presbyterian Church record is 14 JUN 1814, but disagrees with Alexandria Gazette, Commercial & Political, of 17 JUN 1814, which indicates the marriage took place 15 JUN 1814.

83. Minister return by Rev. Wm. H. Wilmer, Rector of St. Paul's Church, gives bride's name as Rebecca Pickering.

84. Groom signs as James Nowell, however, record is marked Knowel.

85. Marriage from register of Overwharton Parish, Stafford Co.

86. Hinshaw, gives date of 20 JAN 1817, this date from West River Register.

87. The Times and Alexandria Advertiser, for Wednesday, 18 OCT 1797, gives that the marriage took place on Saturday evening, inst., thus making date of marriage 14 OCT 1797. The First Presbyterian Church record transcript provides date of 18 DEC 1797.

88. Newspaper announcement gives name of groom as Joseph Perley.

89. Curator staff at Tudor Place, Georgetown DC, confirm date, and add that the original marriage record has been lost.

90. Marriage performed by Rev. Wm. Williamson.

91. Although on the face of the bond is given year 1822, it is marked 1823 on the outside.

92. Jacob Hoffman and Joseph Smith, sureties.

93. Also see original wills at Arlington Co. Courthouse, File #222A, will of John Gould.

94. Written consent given by Forest Richardson, guardian of Catherine Goldsmith.

95. Included with the marriage bond is a slip that shows: "Joshua Sheriff was born November the 19, 1785; Mary Locker in November 22, 1785.

96. The Times and Alexandria Advertiser, on 20 NOV 1798, page 3, gives "on Sunday eve. last, Mr. Thomas Sims to Miss Fritter ...,"making the date of marriage 16 NOV 1798.

97. Bond for this date is between William Smith and John Dunn. No bride's name is given.

98. Hinshaw, gives date 30 OCT 1816, this date from the West River Register.

99. Attached to the marriage bond is a note by Cuthbert Powell, dated 26 DEC 1803, that Negro Jesse was emancipated by Powell's father and is entitled to his freedom.

100. Married at *Hackwood*, seat of Col. John Smith near Winchester.

101. Bond in error places William Thompson where name of groom is normally found.

102. At the time of marriage, Louisa Wood was a ward of Dixon Brittingham. On 10 JUN 1806, D. Brittingham gave his written consent for the proposed marriage.

103. Alexandria County, Report of Aliens, dated 24 JUN 1801, John Tucker, b. Bermuda, age 38 yrs., wife Francis [sic], with children Maria D. and Sally E. Tucker.

104. Bond in error gives name of Rice C. Ballard as bride. Ballard is a bondsman.

105. A copy of the marriage license for William H. Washington and Rebecca W. Cracroft is found amongst the marriage bonds for 1824.

106. Marriage bond gives name of the bride as Alexander Bickerton, in error. However, becuase Richard Wheeler and Elizabeth Hammantree are names inserted where bondsmen are normally found, these pare presumed to be the prospective groom and bride.

107. Two pieces of paper attached to bond infer that Harry and Eleanor were servants. N.C. Hunter states that Harry belonged to his family, and Elinor belonged to that of Capt. John Pope of Prince William Co.

108. Alexander Williams, guardian of Elizabeth Baggott, gives his consent for the marriage.

109. She may be Elizabeth D. Goodwin, daughter of Lyttleton Goodwin, who was married to a William Woodford, Jr. on Thursday, 14 OCT 1819, by Rev. McGuire, all of Caroline Co. See <u>Virginia Herald</u>, 16 OCT 1819.

110. Lucia Chauncy was married as the second wife of William Yeaton.

INDEX (NO GROOMS)

155

AUBREY
Eleanor 92
Auburn 131
Augusta Co. 88
AULDRIDGE
Jean (Williams) x
AUSTIN
Emily 115
Mary 66
AVEREY
Anne 28
AVERY
Carrie W. x
Eliza 104
Frances 130
Sarah 103
AVORY
Elizabeth 10

B

BACON
Elizabeth 112
BADEN
Elizabeth 81
BAGGETT
Alexander 105
Ann 98
Catharine 144
Elizabeth 6
Frances 131
Jane 105
Julia 6
Mary 51, 144
Sally 139
Susanna 74
BAGGOTT
Alexander 6
Anna 26
Elizabeth 142
L. 99
Tereca 98
BAGGS
Elizabeth 119
BAGNELL
Catherine 132
BAGNETT
Nancy 86
BAILESS
Nancy 35
BAILEY
Sarah 93
BAKER
(Bride) 140
Carroll 134
Elisha 99
Elizabeth 75
Sarah 99
Sarah Ann 101
BALCH
Ann E.B. 142
Rev. 13

S.B. 142
BALL
Ann Catharine 41
Anna 117
James 130
Jemima 130
John 41, 117
Kitura 104
Martha 16
Mary Ann 6
Sarah 8
BALLARD
Ann 99
Liven 7
Martha 74
Mary 123
William 99
BALLENGER
Sarah 107
Susannah 97
BALLINGER
Peggy 136
BALMAIN
Alexander xv
Baltimore Co. MD 87, 140
Baltimore MD 2, 11, 14, 19, 20,
31, 37, 38, 48, 49, 51, 53,
55, 57, 63, 69, 70, 88, 95,
122, 132, 134, 136, 137
BANKS
Ann 7
BARBER
Mary 59
BARCLAY
Francis xv
BARKER
Caroline 61
Decie 118
Eliza 25
Leonard 124
Matilda Ann 46
Sabilla 124
BARNES
Basil 79
Catharine "Kitty" 23
Jane 61
Margaret () 53
Mary 79
Robert W. ix
BARNETT
Mary Ann () 30
Nancy 34
BARR
Elizabeth 23, 110
Jane 98
Mary 110
Mary Ann 3
BARRET
Peggy 3
BARRINGER
Mary 112
BARTLEMAN
Margaret Douglass 52

William 52
BARTLETT
Margaret 3
BARTON
Elizabeth "Betsey" 90
Polly 121
BARWELL
Mary 39
BASSETT
Frances 77, 137
BASSFORD
Sarah 29
BATES
Ann 17
Jane 21
Matilda 51
Sarah P. 94
BAXTER
Polly 3
BAYARD
Juliet Elizabeth 138
Samuel 138
BAYLEY
Betsy 13
Elizabeth 26, 93
Hannah 76
Lydia 26
Nancy 119
Sarah 93
William 119
BAYNE
Catharine B. 16
Elizabeth 61
Henry 59
Mary 59
Susan 52
BEACH
Catharine 51
Nancy () 105
BEADLE
Elizabeth () 115
BEAKLEY
Lucy 98
BEALE
Elizabeth Keibard 88
Thomas K. 88
BEALL
Ann 43
Cassia 140
Charity 84
Eleanor 16
Hester 95
Sophia () 84, 95, 140
BEALLE
Sarah 137
BEAN
Jane B. 100
BEANE
Ann Elizabeth 31
BEATLY
Sarah 122
BEATTY
Betsey 6

James 6
BECKETT
  Elizabeth 103
  John 103
BECKHAM
  Lucinda 109
BECKLEY
  Betsy 142
  Maria 138
  Susanna 29
  William 138, 142
BECKWITH
  Marmaduke 15
  Peggy 15
BEDINGER
  Hannah 53
  Nancy 66
  Polly 141
BEECH
  Rebecca 119
BEEDLE
  Eliza Ann 8
  Susanna 100
BEESON
  John 91
  Martha 91, 111
  Mary () 91
BELCHER
  Elizabeth 28
BELL
  Eliza T. 146
  Harriet 27
  Priscilla 46
Bellair 139
Bellefield 115
Bellevoir 55
Bellevue 63
BELLFORD
  Ann 126
Bellmont 19
BELLONA
  Anne 38
Belmont 81, 90
BELTZ
  Elizabeth 52
Belvoir 36, 60
BENHAM
  Mary L. xiii
BENNETT
  Dozier 23
  Elizabeth 25
  Hannah 38
  Martha 79
  Mary 23
BENSON
  Ann 118
  Eleanor () 85
BENTER
  Mary 12
BENTLEY
  Joseph 10
BENTON
  Elizabeth 61

Berkeley Co. 140
BERKLEY
  Stacy (Ellzey) 52
Berkley Meeting House 69, 82,
  91, 98
Bermuda 95, 146
BERRY
  Ann Eliza 55
  Anna Maria () 61
  Bayne S. 9
  Benjamin 134
  Catharine S. 31
  Elizabeth 9
  Elizabeth H. () 144
  Julianna 31
  Juliet Matilda 134
  Mary 77
  Molly Eliza 129
  Thomas 31
BEST
  Susan 29
Beverly MA 76
BIDDLE
  Margaret 33
BIGGS
  Sophia 50
  Sophia Ann 27
BINDER
  Rebecca 133
BINNS
  Charles 129
  Dewanner () 138
  Margaret 129
BIRCH
  Albina 5
  Elizabeth 36
  Joseph 5
BISHOP
  Eliza 104
BLACK
  Alexander 145
  Sarah () 145
BLACKBURN
  Christian 133, 137
  Elizabeth 29
  Jane Charlotte 137
  Julia Anne 137
  Kitty 133
  Lewis 125
  Mary F. () 97
  Richard S. 137
  Sarah Brown 28
  Willianner 125
BLACKLOCK
  Elizabeth C. 85
  Maria 37
BLADEN
  Dorothy 122
  Henrietta A. 130
BLADES
  Ann 141
BLAIR
  Susan Shippen 111

BLAKELEY
  Liddia 41
BLAKENEY
  Liddia 41
BLAND
  Elizabeth 121
BLASDELL
  Capt. 74
Bloomfield 66
BLOOMFIELD
  Elizabeth 62, 75
  Robert 62
BLUE
  Elizabeth 14
  Jane Selina 37
  John J. 37
BLUFFIELD
  Elizabeth 140
BLUNT
  Elizabeth 93
  Joseph 71
  Mary Ann B. 71
  Sarah 52
BOA
  Cavan 112
  Margaret () 112
BOARMAN
  Charles 68
  Jane 68
BOGAN
  Elizabeth 118
  Mary 76
BOGGESS
  Elizabeth 122
  Verlinda 5
BOHANNON
  Levina 84
BOLLING
  Gerrard 108
  Martha 105
  Polly 32
BOND
  Jane () 142
  Matilda 75
  Sarah 40
  Susan Key 144
  Thomas 40
BONNER
  Elizabeth 131
BONTZ
  Amelia 115
  Ann 10
  Catharine 104
  Elizabeth 68
BOONE
  Ignatius 39
  Jane Maria 39
  Susannah 69
BOOTH
  Sarah 24, 102
BOOTHE
  Ann 99
  Nancy 146

BORROWDALE
  Bridget 42
Boston MA 22
BOSWELL
  Hannah 139
  Sally 124, 125
  Sarah 16
BOTTS
  Kitty 36
BOUTCHER
  Ann 87
BOWEN
  Rosanna 56
BOWER
  Elizabeth 70
BOWERS
  Dr. xv
BOWIE
  Alice A.M. 104
  Allen 16
  Ann Blizard 16
  Elizabeth 25
  July Ann 24
  Lucinda 41
  Maria 119
  Mary H. 120
BOWLES
  Susan 51
BOWLIN
  Martha 16
BOWLING
  Ann 28
  Ann () 124
  Elizabeth 102
  Elizabeth "Betsy" 32
  Helena Eliza. Moxley 124
  Locian 108
  Margaret "Peggy" 117
  Marian (Plummer) 7
  Mary 11
  Sarah 37
BOWYER
  Henry 97
  Margaret () 97
BOWZER
  Elizabeth 47
BOYD
  Ann 68
  Catherine 4
  Eliza 63
  Elizabeth 12, 131
  Nancy 128
  Rebecca 104
  Sarah 119
BOYER
  Elizabeth 44, 142
  John 66
  Margaret 91
  Margaret E. 18
BOYLE
  Lucy 25
BOZWELL
  Rachel 108

BRADDOCK
  Nancy 20
  Robert 20
BRADEN
  Mary 38
  Robert 38
BRADLEY
  Ann 40
  Gabriel 141
BRADSHAW
  Eleanor 61
BRAMMELL
  (bride) 81
BRANCH
  John 36
  Margaret 36
  Brandon 106
BRANDT
  Elizabeth L.A. 98
BRANHAM
  Lucy 58
BRAWNER
  Catharine 41
  Harriet R. () 72
  John 14
BREAST
  Lucretia 93
BRECKENRIDGE
  M. xv
BRENT
  Catharine 145
  Daniel C. 118
  Eleanor Carroll 118
  Lucretia 49
  Nancy 146
  Sarah () 146
  Brentsville 44
BREST
  Rosina 58
BREWER
  Ellen 17
  William 17
BRICE
  Hannah () 74
  John 74
BRIGHT
  Ann Elizabeth 51
  Anna Mary 59
  Wendall 51, 59
BRIN
  Betsey 77
BRISCOE
  Barbara Mackall 122
  Courtney A. 40
  Dr. 122
  Lucinda M. 45
  Richard S. 45
  Sarah M. 45
BRITTINGHAM
  Elizabeth 32
BRITTON
  Barbara 75
  Broad Creek MD 59, 139

BROADBACK
  Mary Ann 57
BROCKETT
  Anabella 46
  Elizabeth 29
  F.L. ix
  Margaret 142
  Robert, Sr. 29, 46, 142
BRODIE
  Charlotte B. 120
BRONAUGH
  Ann 24
  Elizabeth 86
  Jeremiah 24, 86
BROOK
  Sarah Ann 16
BROOKE
  Deborah 22
  Eliza P. 123
  Harriet E. 113
  James 22
  Mary 94
  Rachel 32
  Richard 57, 113
  Roger 10, 94
  Sarah 10, 43, 57
BROOKES
  Ann 139
  Benjamin x
  John S. x
  Mary 13
BROOKS
  Ann 51
  Jane 108
  Mary 63
  Rachael 108
  Sarah 104
  Sarah Ann 109
BROONER
  Barbary 130
BROWN
  Amie 19
  Catherine 99
  Catherine S. 87
  David 7, 114
  Eleanor 114
  Eliza A. 75
  Elizabeth 6
  Frances 2
  Helen Bailey Clarke 7
  Jacob 75
  Jane 86
  Margaretta 135
  Margie G. ix
  Martha 3
  Martha L. 4
  Mary 27, 32, 78, 91
  Mary Worth 17
  O.B. xv
  Patty 79
  Polly 15
  Sarah 4
  Sarah () 7

159

162

Culpeper Co. 61, 137
Cumberland PA 90
CUMMING
  Margaret 60
CUNNINGHAM
  Mary 57
CURREY
  Elizabeth 60
  John 60
CURRY
  Elizabeth 14, 80
  Hester 77
  Sarah 145
CURTAIN
  Elizabeth 15
  Susannah 119
CURTIS
  Charlotte 49
  Jane W. 47
  Mary 28
CUSTIS
  Eleanor (Calvert) 125
  Eleanor Parke 79
  Elizabeth Parke 77
  John P. 125
  Martha Parke 103

D

DABNEY
  Polly 146
DADE
  Ann M.S. 37
  Baldwin 2, 33
  Betsy 79
  Catharine F. 2
  Eleanor 112
  Elizabeth 43
  Julia Alzira 129
  Sarah 33, 132
  Sarah Ann 33
  Townshend 43
DAILEY
  Ann 56
DAINGERFIELD
  Bathurst 16
  Sarah T. 16
DALL
  Eleanor Addison 26
DALTON
  (bride) 55
  Ann 109
  Catharine 11
  Jane 60
  John 11, 60
  Rachel 62
DANEAL
  Catherine 20
DANIEL
  Catharine 12
  Julia Ann 45

DANLEY
  Tracey Ann 140
DARBY
  Elizabeth 116
DARLEY
  Susan 140
DARLY
  Mary 51
DARNE
  Margaret 15
  Mary 115
  Penelope "Penny" 33
DARNELL
  Priscilla 142
DARNES
  Nancy 3
DARRELL
  Rachel () 25
  William 25
DARRINGTON
  Elizabeth 125
DATES
  Ann 57
DAUGHERTY
  Margaret 92
DAVIDSON
  Ann 128
DAVIES
  Ann 8, 11, 12
  Benjamin 82
  Eliza 3
  Jane 24
  Mary 82
  Mattey 130
DAVIS
  A. 78
  Ann "Nancy" 1
  Betty 64
  Catherine 16
  Delila 8
  Eliza 14
  Elizabeth 76, 117, 119
  Evelina W. 21
  Frances 32
  Jane 35
  Jemima 4
  John xv
  Mary 43, 74, 130, 146
  Mary Ann 57, 82
  Mary Annie 123
  Mary B. 76
  Matilda () 61
  Nancy 5, 33, 53, 76, 120
  Nancy (Hughes) 32
  Rebecca 20
  Sally 117, 141
  Samuel 57, 76
  Sarah 47, 57, 142
  Sarah () 8
  Sarah Ann (Dade) 33
  Susanna 48
  Thomas xvi, 30

DAVY
  Elizabeth (Cockrell) 3
  Sophia 120
  William 120
DAW
  Mary Ann 24
DAY
  Amelia 105
  Ann 19, 21
  Catherine 109
  Elizabeth 117
  Horatio 112
  Julia 140
De POINCY
  Zephorine 49
DEAGAN
  Charlotte 68
DEAGEN
  Catharine 24
  Fanny 24
  George 24
DEAKINS
  Ambrose 141
  Elizabeth 59
  Jemimah 99
  Margaret 100, 141
DEANE
  Joseph 90
  Mary C. 121
  Susan O. 90
DEARBORN
  Margaret C. 141
DEARY
  Bridget () 2
DEATH
  Mariah T. 19
DEAVERS
  Elizabeth 95
DEBUTTS
  Mary Ann 38
  Samuel 34
Dedham MA 31
DEEBLE
  Mary 37
DEETON
  Christopher 82
  Frances "Fanny" 14
  Isabella 82
DEGRAFFS
  Margaret 89
Delaware Co. PA 114
DELAWHAN
  Martha 28
DELOZIER
  D. 96
DELPHY
  Matilda 121
DEMAIN
  Ann 108
DENEALE
  Ann Lucretia 125
  Catharine 85
  George 19, 125

Jannett 63
Julia Ann 65
Mary Catharine 19
William 63, 85
DENICK
Martha 37
DENNISON
Catharine 76
Maria 10
Mary 129
Sarah 113
DENNISTON
Sarah 107
DENT
Martha Ann 112
Rebecca T. 115
DEREA
Catherine 44
DEROSSI
Lenora x
DEVAUGHN
Polly 40
Ruth 44
Sarah 109
DEVEREUX
Elizabeth 118
DeWARREN
Mary 20
DEY
Winfred 70
DICK
Julia 103
DICKSON
Archibald 74
Lucy 74
DIGGES
Jane 44
DIMENT
Elizabeth 41
DIXON
Ann 70
Eleanor () 144
Grace 29
Jane 6, 44
Margaret 59
Mary () 84
DOBBIN
Rachael () 71
DODDS
Ann 137
Hepsabah Martha 136
DOGAN
Harriet W. 9
Philip 36
DONALDSON
Anna 3
Catharine 25
Elizabeth 131
Hannah 36
Mary Catharine 112
Mildred 26
Sybil (Reagan) 26
William 26

DORCEY
Elizabeth 27, 74
DORRELL
Elizabeth 102
DORSETT
Sarah 98
DORSEY
Ann 109
Ann "Nancy" 121
Clement 86
Elizabeth 10, 60
Elizabeth O. 2
Eudocia 50, 61
Julia Ann 5
Owen 2
Richard 50, 61, 126
Sally Maria 86
Sarah 126
Sarah Ann 61
Winnifred 58
DORSHTIMER
Elizabeth () 119
DOUGHERTY
Eliza 105
Mary "Polly" 124
DOUGLAS
Charlotte (Orme) 135
Nancy 118
William 118
DOUGLASS
Charles 136
Eliza 102
Margaret 8
Martha 20
Nancy 60
Susanna Mary Ann 136
William 60
DOVE
Alley 81, 124
Sally 27
Sarah 10
Zachariah 10
DOVER
Betsy 72
Elizabeth 72
Milly 72
Samuel 72
DOWELL
Ellen 41
DOWNES
Delia () 124
DOWNMAN
Anne () 95
Rawleigh P. 95
DOWNS
Daniel 128
Elizabeth 128
Sarah 27
DOXEY
Mary 75
DOXRY
Susannah 105

DOYNE
Eliza 51
Mary () 17
DREWRY
Mary 126
DRINKER
Elizabeth 75
George 75, 122
Hannah 121, 122
Susannah 120
DROUN
Mary 114
DRURY
Monica 111
DUDLEY
Cloanna 42
Frances 113
Sarah 139
DUFF
James 50
Jane 50
Sarah 103
Sarah (Green) 104
Susan 50
DUFFEY
Elizabeth 141
DUFFY
Eliza 88
DUGAN
Mary 37
DUKE
Rev. xv
DULANY
Benjamin 23, 34, 46, 48, 60,
131, 141, 143
Daniel F. 7
Elizabeth 46
Elizabeth A. 131
H.C. 141
Julia 23
Louisa F. 34
Maria Henrietta 60
Mary 7
Mary G. 18
Rebecca 48, 143
DULIN
Edward 21, 125
Elizabeth 125
Maria 21
Serena G. 116
Dumfries 24, 97, 129, 132
DUNAWAY
Alice Ann 103
DUNBAR
Ann R. 112
DUNDAS
John 73, 104
Nancy Moore 73
Sophia Matilda 104
DUNHAM
David 144
Matilda A. 144

165

70, 71, 74, 78, 86, 89, 92, 99, 102, 103, 113, 114, 116, 124, 125, 130, 140, 142
Fairfax Meeting House 12, 15, 16, 22, 101, 146
Fairview 83
Falling Spring 104
Falmouth, Eng. 102
FAR
 Ann 106
FARNESTER
 Nancy 82
FARQUHAR
 Margaret 63
FARR
 Caroline 92
 Frances 7
FARRELL
 Ann 146
 Ann () 130
 Anne 38
 Sarah 17
Fauquier Co. 25, 33, 90, 115
Fauquier Court House 115
FAW
 Abraham 78, 81
 Julian M. 78
 Juliana Maria 81
 Sophia E. 81
 Sophia Eliza 78
FAWCETT
 Lydia 63
 Thomas 63
FELSH
 Margaret 63
FENDALL
 Benjamin T. 85
 Eliza C. 85
 Susan F. 85
FENWICK
 Rev. xv
FERGUSON
 Anna 21
 Birtha 65
 Patty 71
FERGUSSON
 Jenny 24
 Nanny 136
FERRISS
 Elizabeth 136
Fertility 87
FIELD
 Simpha Rosa Ann 15
FIERNO
 Margaret 93
FIG
 Elizabeth 144
FIGG
 Matilda 49, 131
FINDLEY
 Mary 121
 Sarah 25

FINNIX
 Linney 21
FISHBACK
 Martin 137
 Susan M. 137
FISHER
 Mary 116
 Rebecca 55
FITZGERALD
 Ann 29
FITZHUGH
 Ann Brice 142
 Ann Randolph 28
 Harriet 137
 Henrietta S. 44
 Lucinda 115
 Mary Ann (Marbury) 95
 Mary Lee 30
 Nicholas 44
 R. 137
 William 28, 30
FLANNAGIN
 Cleary 64
FLATFORD
 Mary 114
 Thomas 114
FLEMING
 Betty 134
 Bridget 75
 Catharine 13
 Kitty 68
 Margaret 37
 Nancy 34
 Sarah "Sally" 107
 Thomas 34, 68, 75, 107, 134
FLEMMING
 Ann 49
FLETCHER
 Alice 142
 Maria 126
 Rebecca 75
FLING
 Russey 85
FLOOD
 Elizabeth 107
 Margaret 14
FLUDD
 Eleanor 17
Fluvanna Co. 43
FOLLIN
 Jane 47
 Letitia 125
FOOTE
 Jane 99
 Mary 87
 William 87
FORD
 Ann 105
 Caty 118
 Elizabeth 75
 Jane 24
 Priscilla 44
 Thomas 44, 75, 105, 118

FORREST
 Joseph F. 34
 Sarah 125, 140
 Sophia 34
FORRESTER
 Lucy 18
FORTNEY
 Ann 133
 Jacob 106
 Priscilla (Hicky) 106
 Rosina () 38
FOSTER
 Ann 126
 Sarah 27
FOUCHEE
 Sarah 103
Four Mile Run 8
FOUSHEE
 Susanna Garner 49
FOWKE
 Anne 63
 Chandler 63
FOWLE
 Rebecca H. 53
FOWLER
 Kitty 117
 Mary 22
 Samuel G. 22
FOWLES
 Polly 71
FOX
 Lucinda 11
 Sarah 74, 103
Fox Hall 128
FRAME
 Mariah 137
 Matthew 137
FRANCE
 Charlotte 109
FRANCES
 Mary 44
FRANCIS
 Mary 46
FRANK
 Elizabeth 99
Frankford Meeting House PA 69
Frankham 41
FRANKLIN
 Nancy 87
FRANKS
 Lucinda 48
 Mary 48
FRASER
 Elizabeth Beall 62
FRAZIER
 Frances 108
 Sally 134
FREDERICK
 Emily 147
Frederick Co. 12, 44, 49, 106, 144
Frederick MD 6

166

Fredericksburg 19, 38, 52, 70, 76, 102, 116, 121, 125
FREDERICKSON
  Eve C. 35
Fredericktown MD 113
FREEMAN
  Ann 22, 23
  Cecilia 51
  Eleanor 71
  Nancy 53
  Sarah 7
FRENCH
  Charles 86
  Daniel 38, 132
  Eliza 139
  Elizabeth 38
  George 139
  Mary Virginia 86
Friends' Meeting House 59, 70, 82
Friendship 86
FRISTOE
  Margaret "Peggy" 118
FRIZEL
  Catharine 139
FRIZZELL
  Comfort 146
  William 146
FRY
  Elizabeth 144
FUGATE
  Patsy 77
  Sarah 55
FUGETT
  Catharine 27
FUGGIT
  Peggy 16
FUGITT
  Lucinda 92
  Mary Ann 4
FULFORD
  Mary 51
FULLER
  Jane 36, 80
FULLERTON
  Ann 95
FULMORE
  Eliza C. 64
FULTON
  Mary Ann 144
  Virginia () 92
FURGERSON
  Bitha 55
  Jennet 89
FURGUSSON
  Mary 10

G

GADSBY
  Ann Sophia 98
  John 98

Margaret Sarah 22
GALLAHAN
  Eleanor 20
GALLOWAY
  Sophia 85
Galway, Ire. 51
GANTT
  Mary E. 131
GARAT
  Jeanie 49
GARDINER
  Sally 65
GARDNER
  Benoni 76
  Jemima 123
  Mary () 139
  Rebecca 130
  Sarah 76
GARLIC
  Mary Ann 47
GARLICK
  Patience 56
GARNER
  Theodotia 9
GARRETT
  Eleanor 24
  Elizabeth 66
  Mary () 118
  Nancy 105
  William 118
GASPER
  Sarah 139
GATES
  Elizabeth 75
  Emelia 60
  Margaret 128
  Sarah 129
  Susan 55
  Thomas 75
GAVIN
  Margaret () 89
  Mary 89
GEE
  Mary Ann 117
GEIGER
  Ann 3
Georgetown College 96
Georgetown DC 8, 9, 21, 23, 27, 29, 34, 40, 41, 46, 48, 51, 52, 62, 75, 81, 85, 88, 93-95, 106, 111-113, 121, 123, 134, 141, 142, 145, 146
Georgetown MD 66, 116
Germantown PA 111, 120
GESS
  Kitty () 80
GIBBONS
  Emeline Jane 29
GIBSON
  Amelia Thame 26
  I.L. 114
  John 69
  Mary 69

Mary Ann 32, 114
Mary Ann Catharine 134
Mr. 9
Sybill 26
Sybill () 26
William 32
William L. xv
GIESTA
  Susan 71
GILBERT
  Isabella 62
GILBRETH
  Jane 26
GILHAM
  Julia M. 88
  William 88
GILL
  Susanna 72
GILLBREATH
  Mary 17
GILLESPIE
  Martha 55
GILLIES
  Lucinda 97
GILLINGHAM
  Harriot 79
GILLWITH
  Joanna 49
GILMORE
  William xvi
GILPIN
  Ann 46
  Bernard 123
  Elizabeth 2, 123
  Joseph 2, 101
  Mary G. 101
GIRD
  Eudocia (Dorsey) 61
  Mary 136, 140
GLADDEN
  Cloe 86
  Diana 51
  Susan 6
  Susannah 86
GLANDERS
  Tobitha 136
GLANVILLE
  Mary 32, 33
GLASGOW
  Anna 35
  Mary 9
GLASSGOW
  Catharine A. 65
GLENDY
  John xv
Gloucester Co. 94
GLOVER
  Catharine 143
  Charlotte 137
  Nancy 121
  Thomas P. 143
GODFREY
  Dorcas 60

GOING
  Ann 55
GOLDSBOROUGH
  Anna Maria 45
GOLDSBURY
  Susan 91
GOLDSMITH
  Catharine 115
  Catherine 142
  Elizabeth 7
  Mary 13
Goochland Co. 123
GOOD
  Susanna 111
GOODHUE
  Mary 117
GOODIN
  Ann 77
GOODING
  Eleanor 22
  Harriet 140
GOODRICK
  Ann 58
  Benjamin 6
  Eleanor 118
  Sarah 6
GOODS
  Abey "Ebby" 37
  Susannah 61
GOODWIN
  Elizabeth 37
  Elizabeth D. 144
  Hepziba 96
  Lyttleton 144
Goose Creek Meeting 74, 140
GORDEN
  Nelly 68
GORDON
  David 59
  Sarah 59
GORE
  Phebe 140
GOSSUM
  Matilda () 82
GOTARE
  Dorcus 50
GOTIER
  Dorcas 101
GOULD
  Eliza () 113
  John 113
  Julia 17, 92
GOULDING
  Margaret 52
GOVER
  Samuel 51
GOWAN
  Caty 139
GOWEN
  Joseph 89
  Mary 89
  Mary () 89

GRADY
  Ardry 127
GRAHAM
  Catharine 108
  Cecilia Ann 104
  Fanny 15
  John 12
  Penelope 55
  Polly 12
  Robert 15
  William 104
GRANT
  Nancy 37, 56
  Sarah 55
GRAY
  Ann 102
  Catharine 134
  Elizabeth 140
  Frances B. 131
  Hester 55
  Jane 28
  John G. 131
  Nancy 68
  Nelly 35
  Precilla 53
  Sarah M. 68
GRAYSON
  Letty 32
  Spence xvi
GREEN
  Ann 111
  Catherine 88
  Dorcas 102
  Elizabeth 6, 27, 48
  Elizabeth H. 24
  Hannah () 44
  Mary 78
  Priscilla 11
  Sarah 3, 37, 43, 101, 104, 106
  Susannah 8
GREENE
  Elizabeth 14
GREENFIELD
  Mary 76
GREENLEAF
  Anna "Nancy" 28
  Samuel 22
  Sarah E. 22
  Susan () 6
Greenspring 62
Greenview 114
Greenville 88
GREENWOOD
  Benjamin 117
  Rebecca 37
GREER
  Ann (Crawford) 38
  Margaret 144
GREGG
  Albinah 69
GREGORY
  Matilda 36

GRETTER
  Ann 7, 63
  Dorothy 57
  Elizabeth 50, 119
  Mary 52
  Mary Goulding 16
  Michael 50, 63
GRIFFIN
  Ann 51
  Close Ann 65
  Elizabeth 38
  Frankey 13
  Lancelot 65
  Mary () 40
  Polly 109
  Walter 40
GRIFFITH
  Alfred xv
  Sarah 136
GRIGSBY
  Eliza 21, 141
  Enoch 21
  Mary Ann 23
GRIMES
  Ann 33
  Mary Ann 107
  Nancy 32
  Sarah Ann 121
GRIMSLEY
  Ann 57
  Levi 57
GRINNAGE
  Fanny 105
GRINNOLDS
  Mockey () 77
Grove 33
GROVES
  Ann 134
  Nancy 74
GRUBB
  Beulah 55
  Elizabeth 91
GRUVER
  John 133
  Mary Ann 133
GRYMES
  Ann 86
  Eliz. Mary A. 125
  George 125
  Virginia 137
  William F. 137
GUEST
  Job xv
  Robert 25
  Sarah E. 25
GULATT
  Mary 24
GULLATT
  Catharine 28
  Mary 28
  William 28
GUNNELL
  Ann "Nancy" 123

Catherine 15, 125
Elizabeth 93
Virginia 115
Gunpower Meeting House MD
  94
GUTHRIE
  John 34
  Lucretia 34
  Mary Ann 36
GUZMAN
  Peggy 47

H

Hackwood 129
HAGER
  John 79
  Mary () 79
HAILS
  Margaret 49
HAILY
  Ann 141
HAINES
  Lydia Neill 69
  Sarah 64
HAISLIP
  Elizabeth Jane 52
HAISLOP
  Margaret 123
HALE
  Lucinda 37
HALKERSON
  Elizabeth () 16
HALL
  Delia 55
  Elizabeth 19, 86
  Elizabeth B. () 77
  Hannah 28
  Jane 142
  Jemima 144
  Jonathan 43, 86
  Letty 54
  Mary G. 14
  Sarah 43
  William I. 14
HALLAM
  Rebecca 48
HALLEY
  James 103
  Jane 45
  Mary 94
  Nancy 81
  Sarah C. 109
  Sybil 103
HAMBLETON
  Elizabeth xii
HAMILTON
  David 64
  Eliza 74
  Jane 20
  Lucy 19
  Mary 40

Polly 124
Sally C. 40
Sarah 112
Susannah B. 64
HAMMANTREE
  Elizabeth 140
HAMMATT
  Lydia 113
HAMMERSLAY
  Sarah S. 35
HAMMOND
  Camillia A. 60
  Denton 60
  Jane 100
  Jane B. 63
Hampton 43
HAND
  John 25
  Sarah H. 138
  Tryphosa N. 25
HANDY
  Louisa 112
HANEY
  Elizabeth 47
HANNA
  Elizabeth 38
HANNAH
  Jane 53
Hanover Co. 78
HANSBROUGH
  Joseph 61
  Lucy Ellen 61
HANSON
  Grace 56
  John M. xv
  Louisa Serena 139
  Samuel 139
HARCUM
  Priscilla 28
HARDEN
  Elizabeth 55
  Susannah 114
  Thomas G. 114
HARDING
  Elizabeth 107
  George 70
  Lettice 70
  Sarah 64
HARDY
  Anne 75
HARE
  Elizabeth 95
Harford Co. MD 114
HARGRAVES
  Ann 122
HARLE
  Brittania 10
HARLEY
  Unice 65
HARMON
  Hannah 35
  Jacob 35
  Mary 73

HARPER
  Celia 111
  Edward 33, 126
  Elizabeth 9, 75
  Frances Rush 110
  John 9, 47, 52, 57, 73, 75, 80,
    95, 110, 111, 135
  Margaret 47, 95
  Margaret "Peggy" 135
  Mary 128, 135
  Mary D. 126
  Mira 141
  Nancy 4, 35
  Rachel Wells 11
  Rebecca 52
  Sally 52
  Samuel 11
  Sarah 80
  Sarah M. 33
  Sarah Wells 85
  Sarah "Sally" M. 81
HARRIS
  Anne 104
  Benjamin 65
  Cornelia 129
  Elizabeth 20
  Hannah 91
  Joseph 22
  Mary 22, 51, 109
  Nancy "Ann" 27
  Sarah 65
  Selia 18
HARRISON
  Anne 9
  Burr 106
  Catharine 79
  Dorothy 56
  Dorothy Hanson 72
  Elias xv
  Elizabeth 106
  George 105
  John D. 10, 73
  Juliet 143
  Margaret A. 10
  Martha () 105
  Mary 73, 84
  Matilda 26
  Robert 40
  Robert Hanson 28, 72
  Sally 9, 93
  Sarah 28, 40
  Sarah "Sally" 106
  Sybil 139
  Theodocia 9
  William 139
HART
  Elizabeth 77
HARTLEY
  Elizabeth 137, 144
  Latitia 80
HARTSHORNE
  Amelia 100
  John 62, 100

Mary 123
Rebecca 92
Sarah 62
Sarah "Sally" Saunders 70
William 59, 70, 92, 123
HARWOOD
  Benjamin 16
  Eleanor 16
  Matilda G. 93
HATTERSLEY
  Sarah 51
HATTON
  Cordelia Meeks 65
  Henrietta Dent 65
  Joseph 65
  Lucy 56
HAWKES
  Elizabeth 141
HAWKINS
  Adelaide Eleanor 54
  John 54
  Peggy 137
HAWLEY
  Mary 33
  William xvi
HAY
  George 112
  Hortensia Monroe 112
Hayes 132
HAYES
  Jane 7
  Mary 1
  Sarah 23
Hayfield 141
HAYNE
  Susanna 75
HAYNES
  Mary () 83
HAYS
  Jane 46
HEALY
  Mary () 141
HEATH
  Adeline 19
  Margaret 21
HEBB
  Sarah T. 49
HEINEMAN
  Jacob 89, 99, 143
  Margaret 99
  Mary 143
  Sinah 89
HEISKELL
  Amelia 110
  John 100
  Margaret 85
  Mary Louck 106
  Peter 85, 110
  Sidney 100
HELLRIGEL
  Barbara 134
  Catherine 93
  Christian 93

Christian L. 134
  Elizabeth 36
HELMBOLD
  Ann Maria 51
HEMPHILL
  Andrew xv
HENDERSON
  Alexander 63
  Amey E. 36
  Ann C. 60
  Frances 55
  John 60
  Mary 63
  Nancy 70
  Sarah 19
HENNIKEN
  Ann 14
HENNING
  Elizabeth 136
HENNINGER
  Ann () 122
  Frederick 122
HENRICKSON
  Catharine 68
  Henrico Co. 53
HENRY
  Ann 13
  Sarah S.B. 44
HENSON
  Elizabeth 33
HEPBURN
  Agnes "Nancy" 38
  Latitia 53
  William 38
HERBERT
  Ann Caroline 43
  John C. 43
  Sarah Fairfax 99
  William 99
HERON
  Courtney 104
HESCOTT
  Jane 107
HESS
  (bride) 18
  Barbara (Butt) 58
  Jacob 18, 58
  Miss 18
HESSELIUS
  John 121
  Mary 38
  Rachael B. 121
HEWES
  Abram 123
  Deborah 123
  Mary M. 122
HEWITT
  Johanna 53
  Martha 80, 82
HEYSER
  Sarah 75
  William 75

HICKEY
  Ann D. 13
  Priscilla 46
  Rebecca 52
  Sarah E. 32
HICKLIN
  Phebe 97
HICKMAN
  Mary 28
HICKS
  Anne 141
  William 141
HICKY
  Priscilla 106
HIGDON
  Elizabeth 28
  Sally 37
HIGGINBOTHAM
  Ralph xv
HIGGINBOTHOM
  Elizabeth 96
HIGGINSON
  Rose 57
HIGS
  Eleanor 57
HILL
  Ann 108
  Elizabeth "Betsy" 103
  George 141
  Henrietta Jane 73
  Henry 73
  Laurence 134
  Lucretia 68
  Mary 101, 141
  Sarah 46, 82
  Siloam 134
  William xv
HILLIARD
  Frances 77
HILLIEARD
  Emily 119
  Joseph 119
HILLMAN
  Lucy 104
HILLS
  Prudence 122
  Samuel 122
Hillsborough 51
HILLYARD
  Mary 29
HILTON
  Mary 130
  William 130
HINSHAW
  William W. viii, xi
HIPKINS
  Lewis 145
  Susannah (Adams) 145
HISSEN
  Phillis 141
HITCHMANN
  Mary 41

HITE
  Courtney Ann (Briscoe) 40
  Jacob 18
  Mary 18
  Sarah 145
  Sarah () 140
HITT
  Mary () 116
HIX
  Emily 140
HIXON
  Ann 99
  Malinda 84
HOAKS
  Ann 15
  Catharine 68
  George 15
  Mary 15
Hockassan Meeting House PA
  69
HODGES
  Ellen O. 115
HODGKIN
  Mary 56
  Mildred 70
HODGKINS
  Ann Maria 124
  Margaret 71
  Susan 75
HODGSON
  Hannah 99
  Robert 99
HOFFMAN
  Mary Eliza 11
HOGAN
  Anne 21
  Margaret G. 124
HOGE
  Rebekah 74
  Solomon 74
HOKES
  Elizabeth 46
  Mary Ann 119
HOLLEYWOOD
  Mary Jane 21
HOLLIDAY
  Jane 120
  William 120
HOLLOWOOD
  Rhoda 7
HOLMES
  Gertrude 95
  Sythia C. 14
HOLTON
  Elizabeth 50, 79
HOLTZMAN
  Eliza 94
HOOE
  Ann "Nancy" 138
  Bernard 63
  Catherine 100
  Clarissa B. 93
  Eliza Thacker 63

John 100
Robert 138
Sarah 2
HOOFF
  Barbara 106
  Catherine 89
  Elizabeth 32
  Julia Maria 136
  Lawrence 32, 37, 89, 106, 128
  Margaret 128
  Mary 37
  Mary Amelia 10
HOOKER
  Love 129
HOOKES
  Sarah Ann 124
HOOPER
  Elizabeth 144
  Polly 128
  Rachel 125
Hope Park 103
HOPEWELL
  Julia 27
Hopewell Meeting House 16, 69,
  71, 115, 121
HOPKINS
  Ann 117
  Elizabeth 69
  Elizabeth Howell 69
  Frank S. xi
  Hannah 69
  Hannah Howell 69
  John 69, 117, 133
  Lucy Lyons 133
  Philip 69
  Sarah Janney 70
HORNER
  Lydia 131
HORWELL
  Amanda Maria 11
  Emily Malvinia 145
  Lucinda L. 64
  Nancy E. 46
  Richard 11, 145
  Sarah M. 86, 87
HOSKINS
  Sarah 4
HOUGH
  Amelia 24, 25
  Elizabeth 19
  Mahlon 24
HOUSE
  David 121
  Elizabeth 13
  Louisa 121
HOWARD
  (bride) 1
  Ann R. 64
  Beale 81
  Catharine L. 44
  Elizabeth 20, 81, 92, 133
  Jane 100
  Jane Harriet 119

Julia Ann 62
Mary 73, 131
Nancy 21
Rosetta 100
Sarah "Sally" 87
Sarah "Sally" 116
HOWE
  Ann 138
HOWELL
  John 64
  Mary D. 111
  Permelia B. () 64
HOWISON
  Harriet G. 93
HOYE
  Francis 18
  Nelly 18
HUBBALL
  Eletia 13
  John 37
  Mary "Polly" () 37
HUCORN
  Esther H. 52
HUDSON
  Julia Ann 14
  Sarah 7
HUFF
  Eliza 79
HUGHES
  Catherine 102, 116
  Elizabeth 1, 69
  Nancy 32
HUGHS
  Eliza Ann 60
  John 60
HUGHUELY
  Matilda Lee 9
HUGUELY
  Elishaba Harris 14
HUIE
  James 65
HULL
  Esther 82
  Mary 56
HUMPHREY
  Mary 42
HUMPHREYS
  Hannah 80
  Rebecca 128
  Richard 80
HUNT
  Elizabeth 74
  Sarah Ann Birch 117
  Sophia 14
HUNTER
  Alexander 114
  Amelia T. 146
  Ann 54
  Ann H. 114
  Ann Margaret 131
  Catharine A. 6
  Christiana 138
  Eliza 32

171

L

LACOCK
  Phebe 141
LAFERTY
  Elizabeth 102
LAIDLER
  Violetta 69
LAIRD
  Rebecca 90
LAKE
  Cassina 26
  Eleanor 61
  Richard 26, 61
LAMBERT
  George 82
  Isabell 34
  Mary 27
  Sarah 82
LAMBKIN
  Eleanor 137
LAMMING
  Eleanor 31
LANE
  Abby M. 99
  Andrew 44
  Ann Carr 44
  Elizabeth 101
  Jane 3
  Richard 3
  William, Sr. 44
LANGWORTHY
  Provy 48
LANHAM
  Altheir 89
  Elizabeth 54
  Harriet 80
  Letty 53
  Mary 93
  Sarah 41
  Susannah 14, 52
LANNUM
  John 53
  Letitia 53
LANPHIER
  Ann L. 136
  Eliza S. 6
  Elizabeth 116
  Harriet 86
LARKIN
  Jacob xv
LATHAM
  Elizabeth 73
  Ellender 20
  Ellinder 19
  Lucy 88
  Rosa 89
  Sarah 139
  William 20
LATIMER
  Mercy Hawkins 20
  Rebecca A. 8

LaTREAT
  Sarah "Sally" 116
LAVAZON
  Elizabeth 10
LAVENDER
  Martha 72
Lawnsville 93
LAWRASON
  Alice 111
  Hannah 77
  James 78, 111
  Mary Miller 78
  Mercy Ann 111
  Nancy Butcher 78
LAWRENCE
  Judith () 69
  Rebecca () 129
LAWS
  Ann 56
  Ann E. 25
  Elizabeth 25
LAWSON
  Rachael 66
LAY
  Leannah 70
  Lida 110
  Sarah () 110
LAYFIELD
  Mary 53
LEAP
  Ann 92
LEARY
  Andrew 13
  Frances 13
  Nancy 64
  Sarah "Sally" 141
LEATHRUM
  Maria 16
LEAVENS
  Esther 114
Lebanon 94
LEDDY
  Owen 10
  Virginia C. 10
LEE
  Ann "Nancy" 101
  Ann Henrietta 80
  Ann Kinloch 85
  Ann Lucinda 72
  Caroline H. 136
  Cecelia 105
  Cecilia 90
  Charles 72
  Cornelia 63
  Daniel 47
  Edmund J. xii
  Eliza Matilda 81
  Elizabeth 56, 82
  Elizabeth Eustace 114
  Flora 78
  Hancock 114
  Hannah 137
  Harriot 132

  Henry 20, 44, 85, 101
  Juliann 138
  Lucinda 31, 100
  Lucy Grymes 20
  Lucy Peachy 106
  Ludwell 19, 81
  Mary 110
  Mary "Molly" 44
  Mary Ann 19
  Philip L. 78
  Polly 111
  Portia 62
  Presha 47
  Richard Henry 78, 84
  Sarah "Sally" 78
  Sarah Lettice 44
  Susannah 123
  Theodoric 136
  Thomas Simm 111
  William 62, 63
  Zenobia 58
Lee Hall 96
Leesburg 78, 116, 129, 137, 143
LEGARE
  Catherine 73
LEGG
  Eli 17, 21, 136
  Elizabeth Hughes 21
  Frances Ann 136
  Margaret 17
LEGGE
  Sarah M. () 4
LEIDBERG
  Sarah 70
LEMMON
  George xv
LENNOX
  Margaret 4
LEONARD
  Rebecca W. 75
  Sophia E. (Faw) 81
LESTER
  Mary 43
LETRAIT
  Mary 71
LEVERING
  Alice 77
  Mary 21
LEWIS
  Ann Elizabeth 120
  Catharine 12
  Elizabeth 10
  Frances Parke 18
  Henry 115
  Jane B. 79
  Judith 89
  Lawrence 18
  Mary Ann 115
  Roxa 31
  Sally 75
  Sara 106
  Thesea 121

175

MAFFITT
  Ann B. () 20
  William xvi
MAGEE
  Mary Ann 21
MAGNESS
  Sarah 62
MAGRUDER
  Maria H. 19
  Mary 125
MAHANNY
  Maria 16
MAHONEY
  Ally 74
MAHONY
  Nancy 29
  Sally 70
MAJOR
  Ann James 105
  John 105
MANDELL
  John C. 141
  Martha 141
  Mary Elizabeth 58
MANDEVILLE
  Ann 20
  Joseph 115
  Maria 115
  Susanna 77
MANDLEY
  Elizabeth 103
MANKIN
  Mary Ann Elizabeth 131
MANKINS
  Catherine 129
MANLEY
  Ann N.T. 141
  Penelope 47
  Sarah 4
MANLY
  Barbara 120
  Elizabeth () 120
  Jenny 130
MANN
  Elizabeth Brown 10
MANNING
  Margaret M. 96
  Mary 73
  Mary H. 19
MARA
  Catharine 98
MARBURY
  Eliza () 108
  Mary Ann 95
  William 95
MARCEY
  Catherine 7
Marietta OH 114
MARK
  Eliza 35, 70
  Elizabeth 70
  John 70
  Samuel 70

MARKELL
  Sarah Ann C. 33
MARKLEY
  Capt. 34
  Elizabeth 34
MARKS
  Nancy 137
MARLE
  Elizabeth "Betsey" 105
  Hannah 125
  Rebecca 77
MARMADUKE
  Mary () 65
  Marmion 79
MARR
  Harriet Lee 145
MARROW
  Milly 105
MARSH
  Phebe 81
MARSHALL
  Ann Douglass 67
  Edith 114
  Eleanor Douglass 115
  Elizabeth D. 115
  James 115
  Mary 141
  Mary S. 47
MARSTELLER
  Charlotte M. 93
  Elizabeth 25
MARSTON
  Sarah 86
MARTIN
  Ann 49, 123
  Ann G. 76
  Edward, Jr. 15
  Elizabeth 29
  James 122
  Jane 15, 122
  Lucy () 98
  Mary 126
  Nancy 50
MARTINDALL
  Eleanor 132
MARTS
  John 129
  Lucinda 129
  Rachel () 129
MARVEL
  Betsey 38
MARVELL
  Nancy 103
  Maryland 24, 131
MASDEN
  Ann M. 64
MASON
  Ann E. 33
  Anna 143
  Arminta 64
  Chloe 118
  E. Cary 66
  Eleanor 40

Eliza 86
Elizabeth 61
Elizabeth Barnes 63
George 63, 88
John 86
Leeanah 8
Mary Ann 41
Sarah 59, 88
Sarah G. 118
Sarah Maria 27
Thomas 33
Thomson 86
Virginia 86
MASSEY
  Lee xv, 132
  Mary 83
  Mary () 63
  Nancy 132
  Robert 63
  Sigismunda Mary 2
MASSIE
  Henry 104
  Mary L. 104
MASTIN
  Susan 16
MATTHEWS
  Mary 15
  Thomas xvi
MATTINGLY
  Catharine 116
  Elizabeth 133
MATTOX
  Eleanor A. 79
MAUSSEE
  Millie 12
MAUZEY
  Mary 66
  Sarah 60
MAY
  Ann 64
  Ann Maria 111
  Edward 64
  Mary 15
  Sarah 132
  Sarah Jane 107
MAYHALL
  Betsey 124
  Betsy 125
  Eleanor 94
MEADE
  Jane F.M.B.A. 51
  William xv
MEADS
  Elizabeth 5
MEARSHEIMER
  Mary 19
MEDLEY
  Delila 7
MEEKS
  Susannah 21
MEEM
  Martha 103

180

183

185

Mary S. 91
Thomas 91
SWEET
Margaret 26
Mary 68
SWIFT
Mary S. 3
SWINGSFIRE
Francisca W. 60
SWINK
Barbara 117
William 117
SWITZER
Ann 56
SWORD
Anna 74
Sycamore Hill 100
SYLVESTER
Caroline 143
SYMBURN
Ann 90

T
TALBOT
Elizabeth M. 25
Helen 11
Joseph 128
Lucy 105
Talbot Co. MD 6
TALBOTT
Ann 80
Daniel 80
Eliza 14
Elizabeth 80
Jane 28
Joseph 80, 128
Julia Grenville 27
Mary 101
McKenzie 28
Monica 80
Nancy 71
Precious 99
Sarah 63
TALBURT
Levi 89
Lydia 89
Mary 89
TALBUTT
Elizabeth 78
Nancy 11
Rebecca 11
TALEE
Jane H. 89
TALIAFERRO
Lucy 2
TALLICHET
Marjorie E. xiv
TARLETON
Peggy 34
TARLTON
Hopewell Ginther 52

TATE
Eliza 138
Rockey 114
TATSAPAUGH
Mary 24
Mary Ann 49
Rosetta 129
TATTERSON
Catharine 18
TAYLOR
Amanda Wentworth 50
Ann 53
Astley 122
Betsy 138
Casa 96
Catharine 18
Clary 62
Eliza 14
Elizabeth 9, 67
Elizabeth "Betsey" 54
Elizabeth Johnston 142
Erasmus 7
Fidelia 92
George 9, 50
Hetty D. 46
Jane 138
Jane Allen 108
Jesse 108, 120, 135
Kemer T. 8
Lucy 7
Maria Rose 85
Marie 45
Mary 37, 68, 88
Mary (Smith) 135
Mary Ann 104, 119
Nancy 12
Rhodey 32
Robert J. 85
Sarah L. 20
Sarah "Sally" 33
Susan 27
Susanna 68, 120
TEBBS
Ann F. 39
Margaret 94
Margaret C. 132
Mary F. 97
TENISON
Lucretia 64
TENLEY
Mary 141
TENNESON
Eleanor 61
TENNISON
Catherine 4
Mary Ann 25, 121
Samuel 4
TERRETT
Ann D. 84
Mary Ashton 102
William H. 84
THOM
Cassa 76

THOMAS
Ailsey 142
Ann 24
Deborah 134
Delia 111
Eliza 142
Elizabeth 100, 117, 123
Evan 106
James 142
Jemima 48
Lucy 59
Margaretta B. 101
Martha 98
Mary 47, 93
Mary Ann 29
Nancy 106
Rachel 80
Robert 93
Thomas 101
THOMPSON
Adam 59
Alice Corbin 59
Ann Harris 94
Ann Louisa 23
Barbary () 91
Betsey 42
Delila 119
Dolly 75
James xv
John 76
Jonah 23, 105
Jonas 94
Margaret 93
Maria 114
Maria () 76
Mary 81
Mary Ann 105
Peggy 91
Pleasant 134
Thompson's Rest 65
THOMSON
Nelly 17
THORNTON
Charlotte 45
Maria 125
Presley 45
THRELKELD
John 52
Mary 52
THRIFT
Ann 7, 13
Mary Ann 7
Pricilla 13
THROOP
Elizabeth 33
Hariott 119
THURBER
Hope 143
TILLETT
Levina 9
Winny 24
TINGEY
Hannah 28

Sarah Ann 38
Thomas 28, 38
TINSELL
Mary 38
TOLER
Frances 113
TOLLSON
Nancy 91
TOLSON
Elizabeth 92
TOMLINSON
Sarah 53
TOUCH
Pernica 117
TOUPLEY
Kitty 116
TOWERS
Dorcas (Godfrey) 60
Elizabeth () 96
Mary G. 38
TOWNLEY
Elizabeth 16
TOWNSHEND
Catharine 56
TRACY
Susannah 75, 125
TRAMMELL
Ann 131
Anna 79
Elizabeth 54
Gerrard 131
John 107
Lucinda 120
Susannah 107
Trenton NJ 5
TRESCOTT
Catharine 4
TRETCHER
Elizabeth 124
Thomas 124
TRIDEL
Mary Ann 118
TRIDLE
Betsey 82
TRIPLETT
Anne "Nancy" 81
Elizabeth 2
Lucy 15
Penelope 69
Sarah Dade 65
Thomas 2, 65, 81
William 15, 69
TROTTER
Jane 13
TROUGANTT
Ann 119
TROUT
Margaret 15
TRUSTLER
Elizabeth 77
TUCKER
Ann 130
Christina 84

Elizabeth 84
James O. 130
John 28, 42, 130
Letty 84
Maria Dorcas 28
Sarah 130
Sarah Eliza 130
Sarah "Sally" 108
Tudor Place 142
TULL
Charlotte 76
TURBERVILLE
Henrietta () 84
TURBEVILLE
Cornelia Lee 125
TURLEY
Jane 23
Lydia 134
Paul 23, 134
Susan 18
TURNBULL
Catharine 87
TURNER
Elizabeth 39
Elizabeth Jane 29
Jane 88
Margaret 144
Margaret () 144
Mary 32, 68, 90
Molly 29
Rebecca () 45
Thomas 38
Walker 39
TUTTON
Eliza P. 88
Margaret W. 129
TYLER
Catharine 83
Charles 65
Elizabeth 109
Elizabeth Maria 53
Sarah 74
Sarah Ann 65
TYSON
Jesse 69
Margaret T. 69

U

UHLER
Catherine (Young) 118
Elizabeth 138
Valentine 118
UNDERWOOD
Ann 84, 126
Martha 60
Mary 61
Upper Ridge Meeting House 70
Upper Springfield 117

V

VALANCE
Mary 48
VALENTINE
Elizabeth 139
VALIENT
Mary 6
Van HORNE
Alethia 2
Archibald 2
VAN LANDINGHAM
Marian xii
VARDIN
Matilda Ann 93
VARNELL
Sarah () 28
VASSE
Ambrose 60
Mary Ann 60
VASSY
Elizabeth 76
VAUGHAN
Jane 36
Nancy 49
VEITCH
Eliza 48
Elizabeth 13
R. 58
VENABLE
Ann 16
VERMILLION
Elenor 59
Margaret 54
Vermont 4
VERNON
Ann 23
Julia Ann 58
VERY
Hannah 117
VIETCH
Elizabeth 58
VIOLET
Jane E. 32
John 32
VIOLETT
Ann 37
Eleanor 50
Ellen 37
Jane E. 33
John 41
Juliet G. 41
Mary 126
Sarah 73
VOGT
John xi
VOWELL
Eliza C. Keith 37
Elizabeth 10
John C. 37, 142
Margaret B. 31
Mary (Harper) 73
Mary Ann 45

190